The Race War

Ronald Segal

The Race War

The Viking Press
New York

Published in 1967 by The Viking Press, Inc.
625 Madison Avenue, New York, N.Y. 10022

Library of Congress catalog card number: 67–11266
Printed in U.S.A.

Acknowledgments

The author is grateful to the following for permission to use excerpts from the works
named:
Time, issue of December 4, 1964; © Time Inc., 1964
Gilberto Freyre, The Masters and the Slaves (New York, Knopf, 1963)
Aimé Césaire, "Cahier d'un retour au pays natal," translated by M. Greene. Quoted
in Muntu, by Janheinz Jahn (London, Faber & Faber, 1958; New York, Grove
Press)
Frantz Fanon, The Wretched of the Earth, translated by Constance Farrington; Copy-
right © 1963 by Présence Africaine (New York, Grove Press)
Nathan Glazer's Introduction to Slavery, by Stanley M. Elkins (New York, Grosset
& Dunlap, 1963, by arrangement with the University of Chicago Press)
C. Vann Woodward, The Burden of Southern History (New York, Random House,
1960, by arrangement with the Louisiana State University Press); and The Strange
Career of Jim Crow (New York, Oxford University Press, 1955)
George Padmore, Pan Africanism or Communism? (London, Dennis Dobson, 1956)
Jan Carew, Green Winter (New York, Stein & Day Publishers, 1965)
The Editor, The China Quarterly, Nos. 1, 9, 11, 17, 21, and 24
John Gittings, China and the Cold War (London, Eyre & Spottiswoode, 1965)
C. P. Fitzgerald, Flood-Tide in China (London, The Cresset Press, 1958)

Contents

Bibliographical Note

The sources for this study are given in footnotes throughout the text. Among the titles cited a number are also available in American editions:

Sherman Adams, *First Hand Report*, New York, Harper & Row, 1961

Edward Behr, *The Algerian Problem*, New York, Norton, 1962

Mary Benson, *The African Patriots*, Chicago, Encyclopaedia Britannica, 1964

James Burnham, *Suicide of the West*, New York, John Day, 1964

James Duffy, *Portugal in Africa*, Cambridge, Harvard University Press, 1962

Frantz Fanon, *The Wretched of the Earth*, translated from the French by Constance Farrington, New York, Grove Press, 1965

C. P. Fitzgerald, *Revolution in China*, New York, Praeger, 1952

Felix Greene, *Awakened China: The Country Americans Don't Know*, New York, Doubleday, 1962. Published in London under the title *The Wall Has Two Sides*

John Gunther, *Inside Latin America*, New York, Harper & Row, 1941

Hubert Herring, *A History of Latin America*, New York, Knopf, 1955

E. R. Hughes, *The Invasion of China by the Western World*, New York, Macmillan, 1938

Harold R. Isaacs, *The New World of Negro Americans*, New York, John Day, 1963

Janheinz Jahn, *Muntu*, New York, Grove Press, 1961

C. L. R. James, *The Black Jacobins*, New York, Dial Press, 1938

John Killens, *And Then We Heard the Thunder*, New York, Knopf, 1963

Owen and Eleanor Lattimore, *The Making of Modern China*, New York, Norton, 1944

Tibor Mende, *China and Her Shadow*, New York, Coward-McCann, 1962

C. Wright Mills, *Listen, Yankee: The Revolution in Cuba*, New York, McGraw-Hill, 1960. Published in London under the title *Castro's Cuba*

George Padmore, *Pan-Africanism or Communism?*, New York, Roy, 1956

Sheila Patterson, *Dark Strangers*, Bloomington, Indiana University Press, 1964

Elliott M. Rudwick, *W.E.B. Du Bois—A Study in Minority Leadership*, Philadelphia, University of Pennsylvania Press, 1961

Edgar Snow, *Red Star Over China*, New York, Random House, 1938

Kenneth M. Stampp, *The Peculiar Institution*, New York, Knopf, 1956

Barbara Ward, *The Rich Nations and the Poor Nations*, New York, Norton, 1962

Denis Ashton Warner, *The Last Confucian*, New York, Macmillan, 1963

Sir Roy Welensky, *4,000 Days*, New York, Roy, 1965

Alexander Werth, *The Strange History of Pierre Mendès-France and the Great Conflict over French North Africa*, New York, Abelard-Schuman, 1958

Keith Wheelock, *Nasser's New Egypt*, New York, Praeger, 1960

Theodore H. White, *The Making of the President, 1960*, New York, Atheneum, 1961

David Wise and Thomas B. Ross, *The Invisible Government*, New York, Random House, 1964

Richard Wright, *The Color Curtain*, New York, World, 1956

The Race War

The Race War

I have called this book *The Race War*, though the word 'race' is of disputed definition and the conflict with which I deal is more readily one of colour. I have used the word 'race' none the less because it has commonly come to mean a division of mankind by colour, just as 'racism' has increasingly come to mean the hostility that one man feels for another because of his colour alone. The phrase 'race war' is a strong one, but no stronger, I believe, than the steadily increasing hostility between white and non-white fully warrants. The two colours or races are physically clashing in a dozen parts of the world already, whether through riots in the slums of American cities or the engagement of guns in South Vietnam and Angola. It is the contention of this book that the occasions for clash must multiply, and the war grow ever more intense, unless the circumstances which provoke the antagonisms of race are themselves removed.

I do not attempt to deny that whites may, for greed or fear or a difference of belief, fight each other, as they have done so often before; I am well aware that non-whites, similarly excited, have recently been fighting with each other, from the Himalayas to the Sudan. But it is my belief that the whites and the non-whites are, for the most powerful of reasons, each drawing closer together, and that the struggle between them is the major preoccupation of mankind.

I have dealt at length with the past. And this is not only because the circumstances provoking the race war today are rooted in the past, but because race war is itself nothing new. Indeed, it is as old as human greed, the fears and hatreds of inequality, the distrust of difference, the arrogance of strength. But its dimensions have terribly changed, and a world which wishes to escape the consequences must learn in time adequately to control the human stupidities behind it.

*   *   *

At no other period in history have there been such enormous differences in power as exist at present between the few and the many of mankind. A mere handful of men possess a capacity beyond the imaginings of the greatest warlords in the past – to destroy not just an enemy but human society itself. But comparisons do not need to be apocalyptic. The middle classes of the white industrial states enjoy a comfort and – barring war – a security, a command over their environment, that in the past the most magnificent of the princes lacked, while hundreds of millions of peasants in the rest of the world live as they have always done, menaced constantly by hunger, disease, and unseasonable death. Pharaoh or Caesar would have coveted air-conditioning, the modern lavatory, the aeroplane and motor car; their subjects would have found little to covet in the way that multitudes of Asians, Africans and Latin Americans still scratch a precarious survival from the obstinate earth.

If in Egypt and Rome there were slaves to men, there are in Nicaragua and Malawi and India many more slaves to nature, as little able to control the direction and diminish the cruelty of their lives as if they had been captured in war, chained to a market post, and sold. Classic slavery at least involved negotiable assets, and if only because the slaves themselves were private property, with a price, their owners fed and clothed and sheltered them. Why should landlords in much of the world today concern themselves with the survival of tenants when there are always peasants without any land at all ready to replace the dead? And whose profit and responsibility are the peasants with their own scraps of land, working fitfully for enough to live a while? And of what use at all are the slum flotsam of Rio de Janeiro and the Calcutta streets? Society seems to have discarded them altogether, denying them even the use of their hands. On the land, however poor and neglected, they still had a meaning. But what meaning lies on the pavements, where nothing is theirs to plant and harvest and eat? If any human life has value and it is a crime to destroy it, then the world is vastly more criminal today than it was at any other stage of history. There are millions more dying needlessly now in peace than ever died under the onslaught of the Huns or in the trenches of Belgium and France.

It is not, moreover, merely the middle-class standard of living in the industrial states that differs so enormously from the condition of most men elsewhere. There is poverty and squalor, even hunger, still in the rich world of machines, but it is the poverty and squalor and hunger of a shrinking minority. Most workers and their families live lives that would seem – and are – reaches of prosperity far beyond the purpose of striving for the mass of mankind. Above all, the rich societies, through their tech-nological sophistication and accumulated resources, have the manifest

means to enrich themselves immeasurably further, while the poor societies, far from enjoying the confidence of one day catching up or even
lagging a constant distance behind, face the threat of sinking into ever yet
deeper impoverishment. It is a prospect that the rich themselves regard in
general with complacency or mere indifference. No orthodox Brahmin
in a remote Indian village could display less concern for the suffering of
an untouchable than the average citizen of the industrial world displays
for the suffering of the extraneous poor. It is the common response of an
aristocracy. And the industrial nations with their workers no less than
their managers and professional classes, company directors and legislators,
constitute an aristocracy within mankind.

There may well have been occasions in the past when a rich and powerful minority surrendered some or all of its privileges spontaneously; but
these are not suitably recorded. In the overwhelming main, men have
tended to take what they could and hold what they had, shaping the law
and not seldom religion to their purposes, till violence or the threat of
violence defeated their desire. All this is commonplace enough. The
second man was doubtless the first cynic. But it is a commonplace that
most men conspire to deny. The first man was probably the first hypocrite.

The rich states today are generous only in their cant about the necessity
for rescuing the poor from their predicament, and no competent politician
fails to allure public regard by devout determinations to help the 'developing countries'. But public and politicians are alike contentedly aware that
no sacrifice will be made; that such money as is given can easily be spared
and will effectively be repaid, if not in the purchase of machinery and
arms, then by some strategic consideration; that their own immediate
interests will always take precedence over the needs of others. The pretence, however, remains essential. For it is not enough that an aristocracy
should retain its privileges; it must feel itself secure in its possession. And
so the rich states of the world give and withhold simultaneously, attempting to persuade the poor that assistance will change their condition, and
meanwhile persuading themselves of the stability that their liberal intentions will produce.

It will not work. Poverty is safe when it is unaware and alone. But
poverty in today's world is increasingly aware. And it no longer needs a
still uncommon literacy to inform it. The air is full of pictures and sounds,
from advertising posters, television and cinema screens, radio sets. The
most ragged of the workless in the cities of Brazil can catch sight of television, and the cinema glares in a thousand small Indian towns, within
reach of the otherwise forsaken villages around. The cheap radio set,

pouring unsuspected desires and denials in a cataract of local languages, finds an audience in stretches of Africa or Andean America which have never seen a book. And disaffection is just the other side of discovery.

Nor is poverty alone. The villagers who crouch round their radio sets in Kenya hear of the world in Swahili from Moscow or Peking, as well as – if rather more sedately – from Nairobi and London, and they find soon enough how numerous and similar are the poor. And they find, if they do not know it already, a new division too – that, by and large, the rich of this world are white and the poor are coloured. It is a powerful discovery.

In the rich world, of course, they know how easily racial prejudice may be acquired, and what strenuous and careful application is necessary then to remove it. The whites of English or American cities have to be gradually soothed and cajoled away from prejudice, their natural fears placated, and their frustrations relieved, lest impatience and compulsion incite their suspicions to fury. Yet why should black or brown or yellow men be any less susceptible to racial prejudice, or any less difficult to dissuade from their unreason, than white ones? And who will gradually soothe and cajole them, placating their fears and relieving their frustrations?

If poverty is not unaware or alone any longer, it is not resourceless either. Nationalism excited mass action, sometimes violent, for the eviction of alien rule, and its success is both a pride and a prod. Why should techniques that have succeeded in displacing one formidable enemy, not succeed in displacing another? Of course, many of the nationalist leaders themselves are satisfied to enjoy the first success and evade the need for a second, but they are increasingly seen as the ones with the most to lose by any further struggle. The masses with neither office nor a flush of personal wealth to satisfy them, were promised much by nationalist endeavour, and the more they were promised, the greater in the main has been their disappointment. Theirs is the fury of the discovered deceit, and their turbulent discontent will force a way through the most recalcitrant efforts to contain it.

It is not, however, merely that the coloured nations are poor and feel themselves to be getting poorer. It is also that they are weak, and feel themselves to be getting weaker. And here the sense of outrage rouses all regions of the population, driving even many of those cajoled by privilege into revolt. The very technological triumphs of the white states serve not to intimidate the coloured ones, but to stir them with resistance to their own vulnerability. Each satellite orbiting the earth bleeps not only the success of the white world but the failure of the coloured one. Britain alone, a white power of the second rank, has more real control over the immediate course of developments in Southern Africa than have the independent states of Africa themselves acting in concert. Poverty, of course, is related to powerlessness. The coloured nations are getting poorer in part because they are unable, despite their numerical dominance of the international community, to employ power as an instrument to redress the economic imbalance by extracting substantial loans or grants from the rich, higher or even assured prices for their own commodities, a larger share of world trade. Even the opportunities of playing off West and East against each other – always risky since a challenge to the interests of great powers may invite intervention instead of bribery – have diminished with the improvement in relations between the United States and the Soviet Union. Equally the coloured nations are getting weaker because their poverty makes them ever more vulnerable to foreign pressure. The rich do not regard giving as its own reward; they require a return – in the lease of bases or of votes at the United Nations, in the adjustment of policies, domestic and foreign, to suit the creditor's interests.

In their poverty and their weakness, the coloured nations cannot but be impressed by the one amongst their number which has acquired power and, if not yet a white standard for all its citizens, at least the capacity for independent economic advance. The West – and perhaps in the present phase of her policy, the Soviet Union for reasons of political manageability – would prefer to hold up Japan as an example. But Japan set out to become a dynamic industrial state a century ago, when the price of achieving effective competitiveness was much lower than it is today; and the quantity of investment and skills that she has since accumulated puts her now alongside the white states, in the ranks of prohibitive precedent. Besides, her era of crucial early expansion, when the ruthless exploitation of her labour resources produced the necessary investment for the purchase of industrial equipment, was commanded by a despotism of privilege that modern poor societies would find it explosive to sustain. And, in any event, if Japan is rich, she is also effectively dominated, her alliance with the United States involving a degree of open dependence that the heady nationalism of other coloured countries, whatever the immediate wish of their rulers, would scarcely long allow, even in the very improbable event that a Japanese dependence would soon produce a Japanese prosperity. For the coloured peoples, by and large, Japan is part of the very status quo against which they are rebelling, and Japan herself, though of course in theory recognized as coloured, is viewed in practice as no more than a satrap of the white world.

China is much the more impressive example. She is, still, an over-whelmingly agricultural society, like all the poor coloured states, with her principal resources in her own labour supply. Her industrial sector, rela-tively very small, was all but devastated by war, and her massive pro-gramme of industrialization since the communist victory in 1949, undertaken overwhelmingly with investment of her own making, has achieved alluring results. Moreover, she has done so without producing a provocatively rich business community, and the simple living standard of her political leaders, whether artificial or not, is in marked contrast with the corruption and extravagance of the leadership in much less successful Western-aligned coloured societies with an allegiance to free enterprise. She has become the third power of the world – if power is measurable by the ability to influence the course of international events – and she has done so in the face not only of Western hostility, but also of increasingly bitter relations with the Soviet Union. Of course she is the most populous state in the world; her natural resources are substantial; and she has a long tradition of effort and enterprise. But other peoples, impressed by her example, do not have to suppose that they can ever equal it. What they may well suppose, in considering her progress, is that a poor country, denied adequate help from outside and forced to rely on its own exer-tions, can change a subsistence economy into a dynamic one, making agriculture more productive and squeezing from it a surplus for invest-ment in industry. They may well suppose that by such a process they can, individually or in collaboration, secure a proper independence from the white world – or as much independence, at least, as the modern world permits – and that in doing so they can wipe away the humiliation of their past.

The white peoples see the imperial era as a source of pride, its excesses perhaps to be regretted but its achievements far surpassing them. It brought peace, if necessarily by the gun, and with peace the benefits of commerce, religion and culture. For the white world, the past has been victory, a record of power. The coloured peoples, however, see the im-perial era as a source of shame. It distorted their commerce, assailed their religions, and devastated their cultures. It seized in some places men, in others land and possessions, and always it humiliated, reducing all to a common servitude. For the coloured world the past has been defeat, a record of weakness.

Pride is a universal preoccupation. It has promoted war after war in Europe, to the most recent. It is a positive obsession of American policy today in the Far East. And the conduct of modern China cannot seriously be considered without taking it into account. China herself was for more than a century humiliated by the whites – her territory seized, her revenues expropriated, her traditions disparaged, her very ability to govern herself decried. The Kuomintang regime of Chiang Kai-shek lost the allegiance of the Chinese people not only because it was corrupt, arbitrary and voracious, but also, perhaps principally, because it was ineffectual in ridding the country of foreign control. The communist revolution was only in part a movement of social and economic change; it was, too, a fury of affronted nationalism. Is it not likely that other coloured peoples as well should seek to expunge the embarrassment of the past by a new assertion? The Egyptian revolution – from the first stirrings of the army officer plot, through the nationalization of the Suez Canal, to the policies of Nasser today – has in considerable measure been a response to the series of mortifying intrusions by European powers. From the doctrine of 'negritude' espoused by Senghor and other French colonial intellectuals in the 'forties to the extravagant portrayals of African intellectual discovery in the murals of some Ghanaian public buildings, Africans have sought to assert their pride, with a passion that shows how deep has been the hurt. The Rastafarian movement in Jamaica, the secret cults in Brazil, the Black Muslim organization in the United States are attempts by Negroes to assuage the pain not only of their present condition but of their past.

The new China speaks to such peoples – directly over the radio in dozens of different languages and dialects, or through their leaders, actual and potential, by books and magazine articles, conferences and covert exchanges – in eloquent accents. She reaches American Indians, in the most remote districts of the Andes, with whom their own government long ago lost, if it ever had, communication. She seeks out protégés in every part of Africa, nourishing their aspirations with advice and sometimes with more material help, learning assiduously all the while she teaches. She has, of course, made mistakes; but she has frequently chosen with astuteness, adopting those whose popular strength was apparently suspected by no one else in the outside world. And despite the doctrinal rigidity she has displayed in her quarrel with the Soviet Union, she has been generally flexible in her dealings with the coloured world. She has given aid to movements and regimes of widely differing political complexion, pursuing the cause not of a narrow Leninism but ubiquitous revolution.

The import of her message is harsh, but no harsher, after all, than the circumstances of those whom she addresses demand. The world is dominated by the white states (including, of course, the Soviet Union) which profit from contemporary conditions and consequently resist any serious attempt at change. But contemporary conditions are, for the mass of humanity, unbearable, and it is precisely change, of the most fundamental kind, that the mass of humanity needs. To suppose that the white states will surrender their dominance without compulsion is denied alike by history and common sense. And the only compulsion that coloured people can employ lies in their own efforts. But the costs must be fearlessly faced. (Not the least persuasive feature of the Chinese argument is the deliberate realism in which it is dressed. And China underlines her contention by directing her aid to the rapid achievement of self-reliance. Zanzibaris and Guineans have been impressed by the determination of Chinese technicians to teach themselves out of their jobs as soon as possible.) The Chinese revolution was not easy, and the progress achieved since then has not been easy either. Yet what, after all, was – and is – the alternative? Will the white West, or the white Soviet Union indeed, provide the means of escaping from want? Loans are available, but at rates of interest that the future must be mortgaged to pay. Grants are occasionally made, but they are small, and seldom reach beyond the extravagance of officials and the further enrichment of the already far too rich. Is this the earth that the peasantry must inherit? Is life as a coloured to be, for all but a few, a losing struggle for no more than survival? Does revolution, by long and accumulating violence, none the less carry at least the prospect of eventual betterment?

There can be little doubt now that China is recruiting racial as well as economic discontent to the cause of revolution. And she does not have to make the racial element explicit. There is no need to emphasize that the old imperial powers of the West and the new two 'super powers' of the world are white; the knowledge lies in the experience of the coloureds themselves. The mere effect of her example and her propaganda against the West and the Soviet Union serve to stir the coloured masses of the world to insurrection, not only against their poverty, but, with increasing self-awareness, against a racial dominance that stretches beyond memory. Of course racism is dangerous – may prove, indeed, ultimately calamitous for all mankind – in its abandonment of the rational and in the enormous popular energy that it can destructively as well as creatively provoke. But is nationalism not similarly irrational? And has the sensible recognition of its dangers stopped peoples from repeatedly waging war on its account? The truth is that everyone else's racism, like everyone else's nationalism, or – in its current equivalent – strategic interest, is irresponsible and aggressive; but never one's own. Americans justify their intervention in Formosa, South Vietnam, Guatemala and the Dominican Republic, but condemn Soviet intervention in Hungary or East Germany; the Russians justify their intervention anywhere, and condemn American intervention wherever it takes place; the British condemn the Russians for ignoring the express will of the United Nations while cheerfully flouting United Nations' resolutions on Rhodesia, South Africa, Aden (Suez alone seriously split British opinion). China's claim to areas on her border with India is denounced in New Delhi, while India's claim to Kashmir is denounced in Peking.

It may be thought, indeed, that nationalism presents a far greater danger to the survival of humanity than does racism; that countries will be far too occupied in pressing their own interests against one another to engage themselves in a general confrontation of colour. It may even be claimed, with reason, that where racial conflict is taking place today outside of nationalist engagements, it is at least as much in evidence between non-whites themselves as between whites and non-whites. The struggle between Negro and Arab African in the Sudan; between Negro and Indian in Guyana; between Chinese and Malay in Singapore and Malaysia, seems to suggest an indiscriminate rise in racial distemper. But the rapids of circumstance rush mankind in a single direction. While riches remain a final white monopoly, the nationalism and communal racism of coloured peoples must appear increasingly irrelevant to them in their passion to escape their poverty. And the dynamics of modern power make all but the largest entities or coalitions increasingly vulnerable. Both Britain and France, the major forces of the imperialist era, have been reduced, by the rapidly accelerating costs of any significant military posture and of economic competitiveness, to an ultimate dependence – on the United States and on new relationships with other European countries. Nationalist aggrandisement in the contemporary world cannot – as the Suez adventure of 1956 signally showed – be successful without the acquiescence of the 'super powers', while the manœuvrability of either 'super power' itself is restricted by the vital interests of its rival. And if the United States and the Soviet Union are the 'super powers' at present, China alone among the nation states offers the slightest prospect of achieving a similar status in the foreseeable future. For the other countries of the world, ultimate security, in the sense that the world now allows, must lie in the protective shadow of an existing 'super power', or in a close association aimed at producing a new 'super power' of their own.

The highly industrialized rich states of Western Europe may well, if they unite, produce a force, economic and military, able to rival that of the United States or the Soviet Union. And it is no accident that so many disciples of a united Europe today come from the ranks of yesterday's fervent nationalists. For this is internationalism of a very selective kind. It does not envisage an association to which African and Asian peoples may belong as equal members in consideration of their one-time political and commonly still strong economic ties. The imperial mystique, so passionately propagated to excuse colonial control, has been (by all but Portugal) relegated to the reference shelves of history. The French, who spoke once as if a separation from any part of their empire was a draining of their blood, see now a closer community of interest with Holland than with Senegal. The British, so much of whose past was invested in colonial expansionism, search now for their future in Germany rather than in India or Nigeria.

The rich industrial states are enabled, by the huge and mounting surplus of natural products in the world, to pick and choose among the available suppliers, while the steadily rising cost of manufactures makes the poor agricultural states little more than marginal markets. There is a steadily growing demand for consumer goods – of widening variety and increasing sophistication – across the world, and the price of competitive production requires not only an enormous investment of capital, but a rich and ready mass purchasing public as a base. For the nations of Western Europe, the various projects for closer association involve a clubbing together of the industrially advanced, to produce a domestic capacity for investment and a consumer market large enough effectively to contend with the massive economies of the United States and the Soviet Union.

The Europeans may well see in such an endeavour an imaginative surrender of narrow traditional allegiances, so costly of men and money in the past, for a new internationalism that acknowledges ever widening responsibilities and brings nearer the prospect of a permanent peace in the world. General de Gaulle himself, one of the most pragmatic of the European leaders, has spoken of an association from the Atlantic to the Urals, while others have explored the possibility of an ultimate Atlantic Community, encompassing Europe and North America. And the slogan of the cause is European culture, which has spread itself across the world, to cradle capitalism and communism alike. Is not the Soviet Union part of Europe? And is not the United States, in de Gaulle's favourite phrase, Europe's daughter?

The poor agricultural states, of course, see it all differently. For the over-supply of their principal products in the world and the rising costs of industrialization have placed them in a seemingly inescapable squeeze. The greater the bulk of commodities they produce, the lower does the price for such commodities fall. Yet how, but by increasing the income from their commodity exports, can they meet the cost of importing constantly more expensive industrial equipment, to manufacture their own consumer goods? The rich states have in general low birth rates, and their well-nourished citizens have a high productive capacity; they therefore have little difficulty in achieving a surplus for investment capital to modernize their equipment and diversify their manufactures. The poor states, on the other hand, have in general high birth rates, and their undernourished citizens have a low productive capacity; they urgently need to achieve a surplus for investment in mechanization and industry, but see their most strenuous efforts at saving swallowed by multiplying mouths and inefficient labour. The rich states collaborate with one another, in shoring up the weaker of their currencies and in costly development projects like the supersonic aircraft. Huge cartels operate a common market in practice by promoting different industrial activities in different countries, so as to reduce competition and concentrate investment. The poor states, able with their small resources to diversify their economies principally by producing new commodities for export, compete with each other; while traditional producers of cotton, sugar, coffee, cocoa, tea, find it difficult to dispose of their crops, other countries start cultivation of the same commodities, adding to the general over-supply and driving down prices still further. Moreover, where the first faltering steps in industrialization are taken, they are often those which – because they are the cheapest or carry the most easily realizable prestige – several poor countries, even neighbours, take simultaneously. Instead of collaborating, therefore, to specialize in different industrial activities and ensure a sizeable market for each, the agricultural societies waste their resources in duplication and restrict themselves to their tiny individual consumer publics. To the rich it will be given and from the poor it will be withheld, appears the proper gospel of the contemporary world.

The poor themselves inevitably see the collaboration of the rich as a 'ganging up' against them, an alliance to preserve and indeed increase the privileges of the past. Their mounting despair at ever being able to alter their condition by present endeavour must drive them, sooner or later, to the classic recourse of the desperate throughout history, revolution, and the division of rich and poor along broad colour lines must add immeasurably to the passion of the conflict. The cultural cohesion of a Europe stretching from the United States to the Soviet Union may be the pride and the promise of the rich and the white; it is the reminder and the menace of the poor and the coloured. Ghana and Mali, Aztec and Inca, Aśoka and Akbar, are not the less rousing for their presence behind the centuries than Athens and Rome, Renaissance and Reformation, Elizabeth and Peter the Great. As the Chinese revolution has shown, an awareness of what was achieved and lost in the past is worth an abundance of artillery. Such poles, of course, fly separate flags, but together they may well produce a display of coloured self-assurance and solidarity against white dominion.

Certainly a recognition must grow that in their separate poverty, the coloured peoples possess only a common vulnerability. When China therefore calls for an alliance of the poor, she may expect her call to be heard, if not by indigenous rulers who have risen above the condition of the mass, and who can sublimate their humiliation at national or racial weakness in personal power and wealth, then by the masses themselves, who have no such substitutes. This is not to say that the coloured poor of the world will rally round China's personal standard, uncritical recruits to a new power domination. There is a difference, and a vital one, between China and the 'Chinese line', though Western comment does not seem to recognize it. The Indian Communists of the 'Chinese line' have scored their popular successes against colleagues still loyal to the leadership of the Soviet Union not because they have appeared to offer Indians the promise of Chinese suzerainty, but because the 'Chinese line' of militancy and revolution has corresponded more to Indian reality than has the 'Soviet line' of compromise and collaboration with the Congress government. The war in South Vietnam is not about an expansion of Chinese power, though the Americans talk and behave as though it was; it is a national rising under communist leadership against the concentration of land and power in the grasp of a few and against the foreign – first French and then American – presence that has dominated and divided the country for so long.

What the 'Chinese line' promises and promotes, therefore, is not an imperial China, with colonies all over Africa and Latin America as well as Asia, but a coloured world rising in revolutionary alliance to establish the millennium of the poor. The Chinese leaders have publicly proclaimed the strategy of the struggle. Their own revolution was conducted by the peasantry, recruited and trained in the countryside for the encirclement and eventual capture of the cities. In the world of the present, Western Europe and North America (even perhaps, if the 'Khrushchevite revisionists' continue to hold sway there, Eastern Europe and the Soviet

Union as well) are the cities, rich in industry and weapons but cut off
from the only real ultimate source of power, the people. Asia, Africa and
Latin America are the world's countryside, their peasantry desperate and
ready for recruitment. Why should the Chinese revolution not be repeated then on a world scale, with the slow encirclement of the cities and
their eventual capture?[1]

The racial aspect is not incidental; it can provide the same cement of
popular ardour and awareness that racism and nationalism together
provided in China, for the struggle to expel the 'foreign devils' and make
the Chinese once more respected in the world. (It can also, as the Chinese
are no less aware than the Americans, provide insurrection in the streets of
the cities themselves, sapping their capacity to resist.) Indeed, the stirrings
of race may precede, and themselves produce, the stirrings of poverty,
may even widen the base of struggle to include the economically contented. The involvement of white Americans in Vietnam, fighting
coloured Asians in the field and bombing them from the air, is arousing
resentment even in Japan, the one coloured country in the world that
belongs to the ranks of the rich. In Angola and Moçambique, white
Portuguese are suppressing a classic colonial revolt of black Africans,
while in South Africa a government openly committed to perpetual white
supremacy survives against the mounting clamour of the coloured world
by the refusal of the white West to countenance international intervention. For Africans all over the continent, whatever their economic status
and political alignment, the South African policy of apartheid is a personal affront, and its survival a personal humiliation. The Chinese are not
unaware that precisely such affronts, such humiliation, draw into revolutionary struggle many dissidents of comfortable background.

The power of the dominant industrial societies is, of course, literally
annihilating. The nuclear bomb provides the possibility not just of defeat,
but of extermination for a people waging war against a state that possesses
it. Yet the very power of the bomb, with its proliferating possession,
makes its use increasingly improbable. China herself already has it, and
will surely not long lack the means to deliver destruction sufficiently far
to discourage yet further its use. Certainly the prospect of employing
nuclear bombs to crush or contain revolution is so insane as to deflect no
serious revolutionary from his purpose. Men live on the assumption that
the world will continue on its way, though there are doubtless several
possibilities of accident in space from which life cannot hope to escape.

[1] 'Long Live the Victory of People's War!', by Lin Piao, in *Peking Review*, No. 36, 1965,
pp. 9–30.

Nuclear war may well be a more probable threat, but one still so apocalyptic as to seem finally incredible. And on the assumption that wars will continue to be fought without nuclear bombs, the Chinese have some evidence – no less in Vietnam today than in their own long war against Japan – that people are more important than weapons. The strategy of guerilla struggle, as developed in China and Cuba, and developing yet in Vietnam, makes it difficult to believe that the power of the rich industrial states, even if combined, could permanently prevent the success of concerted revolution in much of the remaining world.

The likelihood that revolution itself will spread through the regions of the poor seems increasingly evident. This does not, of course, mean that the process is likely to be a speedy one, as the newspaper measures speed. The despair and confusion of the poor are likely first to produce over large areas of the world – have begun to do so already, indeed – a semblance of endemic chaos, with military repression contending against not one but several movements of popular disaffection, themselves struggling against each other for supremacy. But in the end, because such chaos is insupportable and because no other escape seems possible, a cohesive revolutionary force will emerge, to absorb differences and attract general allegiance.

Revolution itself need not be dogmatically communist. In Cuba, although several of the guerilla leaders closest to Castro were Communists, the revolution was, in its early stages, itself undogmatic, and propelled to proclamation as communist in substantial measure under the pressures of American hostility and of Soviet protection. It is all too probable of course that similar hostility to similar attempts at radical reform, regarded as damaging to Western economic or security interests, will propel similar national revolutions to the protection of communist power and proclamation as formally communist. And this must restrict the excited experimentation, the search for new social forms and new patterns of individual liberty within a communal endeavour, that revolution produces. Not the least cruel aspect of Western hostility to revolution is precisely that it turns the successful struggle from independent striving to the safely beaten paths of dogma. Yet revolutions will continue to be undertaken as discoveries, not made as mere imitations of experience, for every new attempt seeks to evade the mistakes of the past. Moreover, the dogma of formal communism itself is stretching, to find room for revolutions that produce new patterns of strategy, leadership and endeavour. The Chinese revolution, in its achievement and employment of power, was different from the Russian, and the Cuban different from either. It will soon be as meaningless for a revolution to proclaim itself communist as for a religious sect to proclaim itself Christian.

This very elasticity of communism, of course, promotes revolution, since it diminishes the hostility of communist power to new probes and to new areas of popular assertion. The Cuban Communist Party, whose role under the Batista regime was scarcely edifying, speedily attached itself to Castro's July 26th movement after the revolution had accomplished power, and while naturally trying to influence the leadership, did not attempt to set up its own leadership and programme – such as it was – in conflict. *Fidelismo* today, for all Cuba's dependence on Soviet aid, remains a largely home-grown product, and Latin American pressures are likely to sharpen its individuality. The Sino-Soviet dispute has allowed far more room for idiosyncratic expression within the formal communist family than would have been generally thought possible for decades a few years ago. Poland is as different from Albania as, within the West, is Sweden from Portugal. And the principal communist powers are themselves increasingly pragmatic in their attitude to others. China especially, for all her pronounced devotion to Leninist purity, is concerned less with doctrine than with struggle in the rest of the poor coloured world. She will adopt and assist revolutionaries who know nothing of Leninism at all or have even shown themselves hostile to organized communism.

This enables revolutionaries who have no commitment beyond the ending of a minority despotism and foreign supervision, with the achievement of power and control over national wealth by the masses, to work alongside communist parties and take help from communist governments, in the belief that revolution will itself produce the necessary popular institutions, and promote a unique development suitable to the circumstances and aspirations of the whole society. The South African revolutionary movement is catholic in just this way, harnessing together African nationalists, liberals, socialists, and Communists for the eradication of white supremacy and the establishment of institutions which will promote the independence of the society and submit its resources to popular control. Of course there are wide differences of view within the leadership itself; there are nationalists whose objective is a liberal democracy (though one with a Pan-Africanist commitment) and Communists whose objective is a tightly disciplined endeavour on the Soviet (or Chinese) pattern. Yet, to the consternation of many Western – and some Eastern – observers, the disruptions of the Cold War conflict have not taken place. In 1959 former members of the African National Congress, who had resigned in protest at its alliance with revolutionary movements

of other racial groups and the influence of Communists within its leadership, established the Pan-Africanist Congress; by 1965 leaders of the new
movement were not only wooing the collaboration of other racial groups,
but seeking material help from Peking as well as from American trade
unions. The African National Congress itself takes help wherever it
can and continues to maintain an alliance of revolutionaries from distant
areas of ideological commitment.

The South African situation is crucial precisely because it is concerned
so overwhelmingly with race. Indeed, though the white supremacy
doctrines and practices of the South African government are gratuitously
crude, they correspond closely enough to the racial realities of power and
wealth in the world as a whole for the coloured poor everywhere to see in
them a sort of magnifying mirror of their own domination by whites. And
the correspondence is not solely assumed. Asians and Latin Americans
no less than Africans are aware of the economic relationship between
South African industry and Western – especially British – capital, and of
the influence that this relationship has wielded on Western policies.
Certainly if they remained in any doubt, the persistent protection given to
South Africa by the main Western powers against calls for international
intervention, both openly at the United Nations and in covert diplomatic pressures, has confirmed their deepest suspicions. The result is not
only that the racial clash in South Africa may exacerbate racial antagonism
in the rest of the world but also that it may easily provide the specific
occasion for spreading racial interventions and warfare to the ends of the
earth.

In the very catholic character of its composition, the revolutionary
struggle in South Africa, encompassing African, Asian and Coloured
(with a scattering but calamitously insignificant number of whites),
nationalists, liberals, socialists and Communists, may well mirror, too,
the broad base of racial upheaval in the rest of the world. And that is why
the Western – and especially, of course, American – obsession with
communism is so dangerously irrelevant. It provokes hostility to revolution in itself, as an extension of communist power. But Western
attempts to contain revolution must promote it, as a natural response to
foreign domination, just as the blind seeing of communism in every
revolution must spread communist influence by provoking calls for the
aid and protection of communist governments.

In the end this refusal to countenance revolution simply advances the
prospects of racial struggle, for it perpetuates the economic inequalities,
the national poverty and the resentment at white domination in the

present and the past that produce the coloured consensus of rebellion. And should the West and the Soviet Union really reach an agreement to police the world together, as an alliance of white communism and white capitalism to control unrest, it will increase, not diminish, the possibilities of race war.

The need for international peace is, of course, far more apparent to those who have much to keep than to those who have little to lose. Peasants in vast areas of the earth feel themselves somewhat closer to death from hunger or disease than from nuclear conflagration. And, doubtless unreasonably, some of their leaders see in the very proclaimed anxiety of the dominant peoples for peace an argument against it. If peace serves the interests of the rich and strong, how then can it benefit at the same time the poor and weak? Peace is a good thing, yes, but not at the price of preserving the world as it is. (And, after all, the rich are also devoted to peace only at a price – their own price. Or why is peace in any danger from the poor?)

What the world, therefore, has to face is a despair so deep among the poor, a resentment against established conditions so passionate, that normal fears are ceasing to exercise their expected restraint. That is why the war in South Vietnam goes on, however many new intimidating weapons the United States employs, and however high the casualty figures among the peasantry mount. And the violence must, surely, spread – till the rich and the poor, the dominant and the dominated, are alike, in the final accommodation of an equal humanity or an equal annihilation.

The waste of it all is stupefying. For poverty and ignorance and disease – as the leaders of the rich world themselves proclaim, when thinking of their own societies – are infinitely wasteful of the world's greatest asset, people, and their unused, indeed, undiscovered potential. Does it not seem probable that a world without rich and poor striving against each other to preserve or escape their unequal circumstances – a world instead of people striving together still further to dominate their environment – would be sheerly more efficient and creative, and clearly more free? For it is nonsense to talk of freedom for those who are captive to their circumstances, whether they are poor and so imprisoned by want, or rich and so imprisoned by fear. Would not the energies and resources of separate nations, now separately invested in degrading rivalries and a squandering on stockpiles of destruction, be better invested in a co-ordinated international endeavour? What does democracy mean if it exists only within the nation state and requires for its survival the perpetuation of privilege? How rancid humanity has become that such sentiments sound somehow absurdly unrealistic, the daydreams of a political Pollyanna. Yet they must be real, or the only reality left is the havoc of race.

It is the overwhelming reality now. And there is escape neither in the deceit of cumulative intimidation nor in the distracting probes of doctrine or space. Indeed, such distractions are the ultimate deceit, a distortion of the whole human purpose, since they attempt to conceal the terrors of life as it is. For it is only when the human condition is stripped down to its bones, when the basic gratuitousness of so much suffering and the inevitable extent of the violence that such suffering must excite are properly measured, that perhaps men will at last rebel against their past and themselves, and provide somehow an excuse, a resolve, and a method for their decent survival.

2

The Black World of Africa

The American magazine *Time* devoted its cover and main story on December 4th, 1964, to the murder of Dr Paul Carlson, an American missionary, and other whites, by Congolese in arms against the American-backed government of Moise Tshombe. The story lingered over the ferocity of the killers and the agonies of the killed; explored the extent of atrocities and mutilations; but leapt across the long turbulence stretching behind the event. It did not mention the many thousands of murders – and atrocities – committed by Tshombe's troops under the command of white mercenaries, with the victims no less among the innocent, suddenly waylaid by circumstance. It did not answer the African contention – that the Belgian paratroop drop from American transport planes had killed numberless blacks for each white whose life it had been mounted to save. It could not, of course, deal with the whole cruel history of white and black in Africa, from which the crisis in the Congo drew not only its peculiar character but the quality of the Western response. It did, none the less, provide room for general conclusions.

Carlson symbolized all the white men – and there are many – who want nothing from Africa but a chance to help. He was no saint and no deliberate martyr. He was a highly skilled physician who, out of a strong Christian faith and a sense of common humanity, had gone to the Congo to treat the sick. His death did more than prove that Black African civilization – with its elaborate trappings of half a hundred sovereignties, governments and United Nations delegations – is largely a pretence. The rebels were, after all, for the most part, only a rabble of dazed, ignorant savages, used and abused by semi-sophisticated leaders.

But virtually all other black African nations, including all the more advanced and moderate ones, supported the rebels without even a hint of condemnation for their bestialities. Virtually all these nations echoed the cynical communist line in denouncing the parachute rescue as 'imperialist aggression'. When this happened, the sane part

of the world could only wonder whether Black Africa can be taken
seriously at all, or whether, for the foreseeable future, it is beyond the
reach of reason.

This passage deserves attention not because of any special authority
attaching to its source but precisely because it reflects so common a
reaction in the West to African standards, aspirations and attitudes. And
this reaction was engendered not by the Congo crisis (which none the less,
of course, substantially fortified it), but by the clashes of appetite and
power and culture around the fires of the past. Today belongs equally to
yesterday and tomorrow. The passion that submerged the life and death of
an American missionary is part of yet unrecorded international dissen-
sions, no less than of the march by imperial Rome through North Africa
and the sighing of the slave ships through the middle passage.

The racial arrogance of the West is old only as the power of the West is
old, which has been for a mere moment of human time and a few centuries of registered history. Civilization is composite, an accretion of
experiences and ideas beyond race or region, and the term 'Western civilization' is ultimately meaningless. Europe reads with letters and counts in
numbers that come from the crossroads of Africa and Asia. If in an area of
the world commonly called the West, man first discovered how to split
the atom, it was in the South that he probably first discovered how to
make tools, and in the East that he probably first made fire. Newton's
apple-tree was planted a great deal closer to the Congo than to London or
New York.

If it is the ability to make and use tools that basically differentiates man
from the animal, it was in what is now northern Tanzania, nearly two
million years ago, that this differentiation first, present evidence suggests,
took place.[1] The earliest tools were no more than small stones and pebbles,
crudely split and shaped, but they placed Africa at the centre of human
development for most of its subsequent span. Some three hundred thousand years ago, the 'pebble tool' began giving way to the more sophisticated 'hand-axe', a pear-shaped tool of stone, and though examples of
these have been found in most parts of the world, the richest sites by far
are African. Then, some two hundred thousand years ago, the use of fire
for warmth was discovered by man in the farthest reaches of Asia, and it
took one hundred and fifty thousand years before this new human stride
reached Africa and Europe. The heavy 'hand-axe' gave way in turn to a
multitude of more complex tools, with wood and skin and bone, gums

[1] *A Short History of Africa* by Roland Oliver and J. D. Fage (Penguin Books, 1962), p. 14.

and fibres as material. Thirty thousand years or so ago, began that process of rapid inventiveness which brought the needle and thread, the bow and arrow, the red ochre of cosmetics, announcing the arrival of known and knowledgeable man.

The four racial types existing in Africa today gradually took distinct shape. There were the ancestors of the modern Bushmen, hunting through the drier and more open stretches from the Sahara to the Cape and destined to be driven, by other African and European aggressions, to a precarious survival in the deserts of the South, with a scattering of rock paintings illuminating their tracks. There were, along the forest margins in the west and centre of Africa, the first Negroes, who would enter history as settled fishermen and multiply with the coming of agriculture to dominate much of the continent. There were the ancestors of the contemporary equatorial Pygmies – Negro or Bushmen in type, it is still not certain. And there were, making their appearance in northern and eastern Africa some ten thousand years ago, members of a new race, kin to the Caucasian and now called 'proto-Hamite', who had probably migrated from south-west Asia. It was these men, with a culture – it seems likely – of Palestinian origin, who made the earliest pottery some six or seven thousand years before the birth of Christ.

If the manufacture of tools was the first huge leap in the development of man, and the control of fire the second, the third was the production of food – the cultivation of plants and the breeding of animals – which replaced the vicissitudes of the hunt by the leisure of settlement and allowed the accumulation of people, possessions and ideas. Some ten thousand years ago the first food-producing community developed at a spring by the rim of the Jordan Valley, in a place that would become known as Jericho, and from there agriculture spread, between six and seven thousand years ago, across the Isthmus of Suez to the Nile Delta. By the first millennium before Christ, with all but a thin horizon of Europe benighted, civilization had spread to northern Nigeria, where the Negroes of the Nok culture lived in villages and produced stone tools, jewellery and terra cotta sculpture of a high standard. The forest regions required different plants from the wheat and barley of Egypt, however, and it was not till the arrival of the banana and yam from south-east Asia, brought by Indonesian peoples in the early years of the Christian era, that the Negroes developed and spread their culture across so much of the continent.

Contemporary Ghana has excited much Western ridicule with its more extravagant efforts to redress the racial imbalance of the history books. Decorations on public buildings that lay an African claim to almost every important human achievement may properly be derided; but no more so, surely, than Western efforts of a similar kind. The practice by which ancient Egypt is blandly annexed by the West, and modern Egypt, apparently less valuable an acquisition, relegated to Africa, is a by no means singular – though notable – manifestation of that racial or regional derangement which so often afflicts the writing of history. Whatever else the centuries may have done, they did not shift Egypt from Africa to Europe and then suddenly back again, and if ancient Greece is part of the Western contribution to human culture, ancient Egypt is no less part of the African one. The pyramid and the pharaoh were not carried to the Nile Valley on the shoulders of immigrant agriculturalists; they developed, with all that was individual in the Egyptian achievement, from an African environment.

The fertility of the Nile flood-plain was such that it provided both for a vast increase in population and for a substantial surplus of production over the needs of survival. Villages became towns and towns became cities, while assiduous exploitation sluiced the efforts of the peasantry to the support of a leisured governing class, an abundance of public building, and the cultivation of arts and sciences. In 3200 B.C. Menses combined the kingdoms of Upper and Lower Egypt, and the dynastic period, with its system of divine kingship informing an intricately organized society of several million people, began.

Pre-dynastic Egypt had stretched for its gold and copper southwards, among the Red Sea hills, and sent its ships of sixty oars across the Mediterranean, to the Aegean islands, for silver and lead. With the development of political unity in Egypt, the resources for engagement in more distant trade grew alongside the need for raw materials and the appetite for foreign manufactures, and while ships searched the wastes of southern Arabia and present-day Somalia for incense to burn in Egypt's multitude of temples, land expeditions penetrated the interior of the continent southwards for ivory and hardwood and metals. An inscription of 2275 B.C. celebrates ventures as far as southern Ethiopia, which brought back ivory, ebony, animal skins, boomerangs and even, as an offering of the exotic, a pygmy.

Such exploration and trade inevitably scattered wide the achievements of Egyptian experience. Expeditions into the unknown would doubtless have taken along animals and seed, so initiating new peoples into the mysteries of food production; Egyptian musical instruments and baskets would in time have been copied by those who first viewed them with wonder; and seeping through the centuries over vast stretches of the

African interior, there spread Egyptian religious and political ideas, the whole concept of the complex state formed around the person of a divine king.

With Egypt beginning its long political decline around 1000 B.C., there rose to pre-eminence the kingdom of Kush, in what is now the Sudan Republic, with its capital at Napata. By the eighth century B.C. this new African state was strong enough to conquer Egypt itself, its rulers becoming the twenty-fifth Dynasty of Pharaohs, and while Egypt then fell victim successively to the Assyrians, the Persians, the Greeks, and the Romans, Kush flourished to tend, transform and transmit Egyptian civilization. Like Dynastic Egypt, the early Kush kingdom was inhabited in the main by light-skinned Caucasians, but around the sixth century B.C. it began to push its frontiers southwards into the land of the blacks, where desert gave place to forest, and both ore and fuel abundantly existed for the new techniques of iron-working introduced by the Assyrian enemy. From the new capital of Meroe, between the Fifth and Sixth Cataracts of the Nile, where mountains of slag today testify to a once huge iron industry, the now predominantly Negro empire sent its power and influence across the Sudanic belt of Africa, from the Ethiopian highlands to the Niger, while its trade stretched to the Mediterranean and even the East. And when Kush began to decline, by the middle of the first century A.D., it was in response to the rise of a rival trading empire in Africa, with its centre at Axum in the northern corner of the Ethiopian highlands. A city of stone palaces and temples, with towering carved obelisks, Axum controlled the ivory trade of north-east Africa and supported a dynasty of kings in golden splendour. In the middle of the sixth century, the kings of Axum sent their armies into Kush and fired Meroe itself, scattering refugees and ideas westwards to Lake Chad and beyond.

Certainly there emerged in the period known to European history as the Middle Ages, south of the Sahara across the whole highland belt of Negro Africa, centralized states of varying sizes, with an intricate and hierarchical bureaucracy dependent upon the person of a divine king. The success of agriculture was tied to royal ritual; trade was typically a royal monopoly; artists and craftsmen lived in the royal capital under royal control. An Arab author of the eighth century, Al Fazari, first mentioned Ghana, with its centre in modern Mauritania, and for three centuries the kingdom was widely known in the Muslim world as a rich trade source of gold. The kingdom of Kanem, north-east of Lake Chad, was described by ninth- and tenth-century Arab writers, and Al Masudi of Baghdad, traveller and geographer, who sailed down the east coast of Africa about

A.D. 922, reported the considerable flow of gold and ivory from an empire in present-day Rhodesia – probably the one whose monuments at Zimbabwe so disturbed subsequent European assumptions – through the port of Sofala, in present-day Moçambique, to Oman, and from there to India and China. These were, moreover, merely the states which caught the attention of contemporary Arab writers.

Extensive cemeteries of the eighth and ninth centuries on the banks of the upper Lualaba river in the Congo reveal that Katanga copper was already being mined then, and made into jewellery or small H-shaped ingots for currency, by subjects of a state with advanced technology, while northwards, in the region of the present-day Congo and Uganda, evidence is accumulating of similarly developed states at that time. What matters to the prejudices of the present is that, whether carved out by conquest or developed by ideas from the Egyptianized north-west of the continent, civilized states preserving order by ritual and a ubiquitous bureaucracy, nourishing the arts and conducting trade with far areas of the earth, existed in the centre of black Africa at a time when Europe was still in the grey hours following the Roman collapse.

Both Asia and Europe, of course, culturally interacted with Africa as well as with each other over the centuries, sometimes clearly and closely, more often darkly and at countless removes. The civilization of classical Greece flooding into Egypt with the conquering armies of Alexander the Great in 332 B.C., made the new city of Alexandria a centre for the fusion of Greek and Eastern, especially Semitic, cultures. While the ruling Ptolemies enriched themselves by taxing the trade in luxuries between Asia and Europe, philosophy, science, religion and scholarship flourished in the confluence of ideas from three continents.

From their base in the prosperous trading ports of Syria, Phoenician merchants in the eighth century B.C. had begun colonizing the North African coast to establish in Carthage a settlement that would grow into a city of half a million inhabitants, with a rich agricultural hinterland in the Tunisian plains. Carthage soon, however, came into conflict with the growing power of Rome, and by the middle of the second century B.C. had been destroyed by it. Rome itself then continued its course of African conquest, and eventually carved out an empire nearly four thousand miles in extent and comprising all the cultivable land north of the Sahara. It was not an altogether fortunate dominion. The Romans treated Egypt as other European powers would, many centuries later, treat their African colonies; they ruthlessly exploited it in their own interests, and when at last they were forced to withdraw their rule, left an exhausted economy and impoverished culture in their wake. Farther westwards, however, along the coast of the Maghrib, the need to feed Rome absorbed a multitude of Berbers into agricultural, even urban settlement, and when the Mediterranean empire itself had departed, its traces were not merely the ruins of theatres and temples. Though the nomads overran the settlements, settlement survived, and the ideas implanted by conquest – not the least of them, those of Christianity – proceeded to a due if distant growth.

The new confluence of Europe and Africa, moreover, reached into the Western Sudan. The Berbers themselves had been in contact with the Negroes of the far south long before the coming of Mediterranean civilization, and the ravenous appetite of Rome excited trade across the desert. Gold, ivory, ostrich feathers, hides and slaves were carried northwards by Berber merchants, and mainly salt, rare in the Sudan but common in the Sahara, carried southwards in exchange. The arts and sciences of the empire may not have lasted the distance, but the trade itself, with the vast wealth to be sluiced off by taxing it, must have combined with the concept of divine kingship filtering from the east to promote and sustain substantial African states like Ghana.

Between A.D. 622 and 632 Muhammad preached his message to the tribes of Arabia, a doctrine of the single God and his single prophet which transcended traditional conflict and division, and led, with the problem of population in a largely desert area, to one of the great cultural aggressions of history. In A.D. 639 the Muslim Arabs plunged into Egypt, and by the start of the next century had conquered all Africa north of the Sahara, to invade Europe itself. The new empire, however, did not long survive tribal and doctrinal antagonisms; while the Abbasid dynasty of Caliphs ruled from the new city of Baghdad, built out of the wealth of Mesopotamian agriculture and commerce, the Muslims in al-Maghrib, the west, began forming kingdoms of their own. A Moroccan dynasty ruled from the new capital of Fez, and a Tunisian one reconstructed the prosperity of its Roman period on Islamic foundations.

For five centuries, from about A.D. 800 to 1300, Islamic civilization, with its strides in art, science and government, far outstripped the slow progress of Europe. But Islam itself had long ceased to be dominantly Arab. The Muslimized Berber tribes swept out of the North African desert, and put their own Muslim sects to the service of empire-building by the second half of the twelfth century. Berber government, with a professional civil service and cities of much splendour like Marrakech and Rabat, stretched from Spain as far east as Tunis across a united Maghrib.

Berber expansionism, however, not only claimed the coast, but turned southwards too, and bit deep into Africa. In 1076 its forces captured and sacked the capital of ancient Ghana, after fourteen years of fighting that testified to the resources of its new victim; but the desert tribes were soon squabbling over the spoils and lost the substance of their success. The prospects of stable Negro empire meanwhile migrated farther south, into richer agricultural land remote from the possibility of Berber attack, and by the middle of the thirteenth century Mali rose to prominence among the Mande clans of the upper Niger valley.

Sundiata, the founder of the empire, who reigned from 1230 to 1255, saw obvious advantages in the adoption of Islam and became at least a nominal convert; many of his successors as Mansa or Emperor were devout, and their example was followed widely by other candidates for rule. Inclusion in the Islamic fold earned for the Negro states and their merchants a new legitimacy and trust from the governments and merchants of the Maghrib, while Islamic doctrine and culture helped to confirm the sway of a Sudanic ruler beyond his own clan to the alien subjects of conquest. In particular the establishment and spread of Muslim schools produced a class of educated officials who could administer government and trade efficiently, submerging their kinship loyalties in an imperial interest.

These West African empires, like Mali and Songhai, were no pocket kingdoms; they covered vast areas, included considerable populations, and depended upon a complex administration. They were also rich. Mansa Musa, the most celebrated of the Mali emperors, went on a pilgrimage to Mecca in the middle of the fourteenth century and carried so much gold in his train that the price of the metal in Egypt, through which he passed, fell resoundingly. The trip, indeed, had European reverberations, and Mali, with its 'Lord of the Negroes', appeared in 1375 on the first map of West Africa ever drawn in Europe.

The power, prosperity and ordered government of these empires impressed even sophisticated visitors from the capitals of the Islamic world, and the renowned traveller, Ibn Battuta, who toured Mali in 1352-3, remarked on its flourishing agriculture and trade, with the ease and safety of travel because of the always certain access to food and good lodgings for the night. The Negroes, he stressed, 'are seldom unjust, and have a greater horror of injustice than other people ... There is complete security in their country. Neither traveller nor inhabitant in it has anything to fear from robbers or men of violence.'

The mosques and schools of the western Sudan attracted divines and scholars from all over the Islamic world, and even maintained hostels for their students in centres of Muslim culture like Cairo. Timbuctu was widely known as a city of scholarship and learning, and neither Paris nor Padua could seriously have claimed to excel it. If the Negro Sudan became in later centuries a relative wilderness, the blighting expansionism of Europe was not without responsibility.

Guinea, the tropical forest region of West Africa to the south of the savanna, lay beyond the limit of Islamic travel in the Middle Ages, and its early development is accordingly obscure. But it is clear that by the thirteenth century at the latest the Negroes of the area had started to establish states similar to those in the Sudan, partly at least in response to immigration, of people as well as ideas, from the north. These were, like their models, founded on agriculture but urban in character, with their nucleus in a large town surrounded by a wall where members of different clans lived in distinct wards around the royal palace. One such town, Benin in present-day Western Nigeria, impressed European visitors of the sixteenth and seventeenth centuries as comparable with the major European cities of the time. A Dutch writer remarked in 1602:[1]

> The town seemeth to be very great; when you enter into it, you go into a great broad street, not paved, which seems to be seven or eight times broader than the Warmoes street in Amsterdam; which goeth right out and never crooks ... When you are in the great street aforesaid, you see many great streets on the sides thereof, which also go right forth ... The houses in this town stand in good order one close and even with the other, as the houses in Holland stand ...
>
> The King's Court is very great, within it having many great four-square plains, which round about them have galleries, wherein there is always kept watch. I was so far within the Court that I passed over four such great plains, and wherever I looked, still I saw gates upon gates to go into other places ...

The existence of such organized states produced a thriving commerce which, long before the arrival of European enterprise, linked towns and villages throughout West Africa. Most communities grew or manufactured sufficient for their basic needs, and the cost of transport, especially in the forests, was high, so that the staples of long-distance trade were generally luxuries. But kings and their courts, supporting a retinue of civil servants, soldiers, artists and craftsmen on the taxed surplus of their subjects, provided the demand and the means of satisfying it. Moreover,

[1] R. Oliver and J. D. Fage, op. cit., pp. 106–7.

trade itself produced wealth and so more trade; the merchants of the Sudan traded with Guinea in part to satisfy their own demands as a new class of wealthy consumers, while the Guinea states, where the merchants were in the main mere agents of the kings, began to see trade as a source of enrichment in itself. Such widespread commerce implies, of course, a widely recognized medium of exchange no less than a well-developed system of weights and measures, and cowrie shells, gold dust, blocks of salt, pieces of iron and copper and even cloth were used as money.

To Guinea came salt from the Sahara and the sea; cattle and horses from the Sudan; beads, trinkets, cutlasses, cloth and scarce metals like copper, from the Sudan, North Africa and the Mediterranean; cowrie shells from the Indian Ocean through Egypt. Northwards to the Sudan, the Maghrib and the Mediterranean, went gold dust from workings in the area of present-day Ghana, kola nuts and ivory. Nor was the trade wholly remote. Within Guinea itself stone and glass beads, cloth and trinkets were manufactured, especially in Yorubaland, for sale to communities elsewhere in the area. What seems to be significantly missing as a major item in early Guinea trade is the slave. Certainly there were slaves in the forest regions, as agricultural labourers, porters and domestic servants; but trade in slaves on any significant scale seems only to have begun after the growth of Islam in the Sudan and to have reached the coastlands only with the development of the European demand from the sixteenth century onwards.

On the east coast of Africa, the Christianized – if, in the eyes of Rome, heretical – kingdom of Abyssinia escaped Islamic domination, and it was from the pagan south that menace in the Middle Ages arose. In the late tenth century the kingdom was almost overwhelmed, and only a new dynasty of soldier kings, the Zagwe, were able to defeat the invaders and take the offensive, pushing their frontier southwards steadily through two and a half centuries, and leaving as their monument the startling rock churches of Roha.

In the thirteenth century the bulk of the Indian Ocean trading system passed into Muslim hands with the second great wave of Islamic expansionism, stretching down the coast of East Africa and reaching into India, Malaya and Indonesia. All along the seaboard of Somalia, Kenya and Tanganyika, Islamic communities took urban root, building in stone and rich enough to import porcelain from late Sung and early Ming China. At Kilwa (in present-day Tanzania), rich on the gold trade from the region of the Zambezi and the copper from Luba workings in Katanga, the sultans produced their own copper coinage in the earliest mint to be established south of the Sahara, placed governors over the old part of

Sofala (in present-day Moçambique), and levied large duties on the ocean trade to and from the East. Maindi and Mombassa (in present-day Kenya) exported iron ore to India for the manufacture of steel swords and daggers, and from Mogadishu (in present-day Somalia) went cottons and camel-hair cloth for the Egyptian market, while from most of the coastal settlements flowed steady streams of ivory and slaves. Neither the prosperity nor the cultural florescence along the coast were, however, to last, for a new imperialism was rising, and, for the first time since the fall of Rome a thousand years before, in Europe.

The Crusades had stimulated trade between Europe and the outside world, and Venetian merchants had been quick to accomplish control of the European side by establishing friendly relations with the Muslim world. In the west, however, Portugal and Spain, having driven Islam from most of the peninsula, began in 1415 to carry the war into Africa itself, and though they failed in their attempt to conquer Morocco, their irruption into the world beyond Europe would soon carry their rule to three continents. From their involvement in the Maghrib the Portuguese learnt of the lands on the other side of the Sahara, and of Arab geography, with its belief that Africa was surrounded by sea. Assisted by mariners and merchants from the Italian cities anxious to break the Venetian trade monopoly, they conceived the design of outflanking Islam by sea, exploiting the gold of Guinea themselves, and by sailing to India, importing Asian commodities like spices at a price which Venice could not match.

Portugal made contact with Negro Africa in 1444–5, and soon afterwards began colonizing the Cape Verde Islands as a base for trade with Mali; by 1471 Portuguese ships had reached the Gold Coast, by the early 'eighties the mouth of the Congo, by 1488 had rounded the Cape, and by 1497–9 had made, under Vasco da Gama, the voyage to India and back. The Ottoman Turks, who occupied Egypt in 1517 and struck out west to conquer all the Maghrib but Morocco, failed to crush Portuguese sea power and at Lepanto in 1571 were decisively beaten by a combined Christian fleet. More and more, African trade was diverted, from the traditional routes across the Sahara, to the coast, where the European states established forts to secure their various spheres of influence.

At first the European merchants were far more interested in Asia and the newly discovered Americas than in Africa. The luxuries they sought, like silk, drugs, perfumes, spices and sugar, were not obtainable in Africa, which could provide only ivory in diminishing supplies, and gold from a few established sources, while the problems of climate, disease and communications combined with the density and vigour of African population to discourage European settlement. The plantation system, therefore, first tried on the accessible offshore islands of West Africa, was from there shipped across the Atlantic by the Spaniards to the West Indies and by the Portuguese to Brazil. The American Indians, however, were unable to provide sufficient labour for the fast multiplying plantations and revealed an unfortunate incapacity to survive in servitude. Since Europe could not transport the American plantations to Africa's labour supply, it accordingly set out to transport the African labour supply to America's plantations.

What followed was a racial war, conducted for commercial profit, without precedent in human cost. The doctrine of inherent Negro inferiority was developed to excuse conduct which the teachings of Christianity and the twinges of traditional conscience alike disparaged, and a civilization which had barely emerged from the sick-bed pronounced itself the only one sound and capable of uplifting humanity. There was, it is clear, a system of slavery already existing within Africa mainly as a punishment for crime or payment for debt, and in some areas slaves had been a component of trade with the Islamic world for centuries. But neither indigenous slavery nor the customary slave trade, though doubtless disreputable, was more than a social by-product; nowhere does slavery seem to have been intrinsic to the character of an African culture, or the slave trade basic to the survival of an African state. The irruption of European slave traders into Africa, however, produced an entirely different situation. The European appetite for slaves was insatiable, and when African states near the coast had disposed of the slaves in their keeping, they used the guns they had received in exchange to penetrate the interior and there seize slaves for export. The widespread warfare which resulted and the cultural decay produced both by that warfare and by the huge loss of population to the slave ships, were then seen not as a responsibility of European ravages, but as evidence of an inherent African inferiority, which excused still further ravaging in the cause of cultural redemption.

Some 900,000 Africans were actually landed in the Americas during the sixteenth century; at least 2,750,000 during the seventeenth; 7,000,000 during the eighteenth; and 4,000,000 during the nineteenth – a total of nearly 15,000,000 slaves. These figures, of course, take no account of the numbers lost during the transatlantic crossing or 'middle passage', when overcrowding and ill-treatment, disease and despair took a toll seldom less than one in five; of the numbers lost in the warfare that produced the slaves; and of the numbers lost in the unborn and unfed, since it was the able-bodied men and women who were taken, leaving the unproductive young and old behind.

At first the trade was in the hands of the Portuguese, who supplied the Spanish colonies as well as their own; but the enormous profits made out of slaving, with the mounting demand for plantation labour produced by the colonial endeavours of other European states, soon provoked ferocious competition. The Dutch ousted the Portuguese from the Gold Coast in 1642 and for a short time enjoyed a virtual monopoly of the transatlantic trade; but then the English and the French intervened, and by the end of the eighteenth century Britain had outstripped all her rivals, to carry in her own ships more than half the slaves who crossed the Atlantic.

The three staples of colonial production in the spreading British empire – tobacco and cotton on the North American mainland, sugar on the islands of the Caribbean – required cheap labour, with a substantial invest-ment in the land and equipment, to provide proper profits. This was especially true of sugar, which soon became the major field of capitalist effort abroad, and as the black slave displaced the more demanding inden-tured white servant, so the plantation – often run by a professional manager – dispossessed the small owner-worked farm. The changes were rapid and immense: Barbados in 1645 had 11,200 white farmers and 5,680 Negro slaves; in 1667 there were 745 plantation owners and 82,023 slaves. 'The increase of wealth for a few whites was as phenomenal as the increase of misery for the many blacks. The Barbados crops in 1650, over a twenty-month period, were worth over three million pounds',[1] a sum worth ten times as much today. The British Empire was, as a contemporary source described it, 'a magnificent superstructure of American commerce and naval power on an African foundation'.[2] In 1788 the sugar planters in the West Indies valued their holdings at £70,000,000, and in 1798 Pitt assessed the annual income from the West Indian plantations at £4,000,000 compared with £1,000,000 from the rest of the world.

The slave trade was more than the hinge of colonial exploitation, how-ever; it was the basis of British – as well as French and American – mercan-tile prosperity and the source of industrial expansion. The slave ship sailed from its home port with a cargo of manufactured goods – cloth, firearms, beads, spirits, kettles, hats, glass – which it exchanged on the African coast for slaves at a profit; it then crossed the Atlantic and traded the slaves, at a

[1] *Capitalism and Slavery*, by Eric Williams (The University of North Carolina Press, 1944), p. 25.
[2] *The African Trade, the Great Pillar and Support of the British Plantation Trade in North America*, by M. Postlethwayt (London, 1745), pp. 4, 6.

further profit, for colonial produce; finally, home again, it sold its cargo, at a profit once more, for processing and domestic consumption or manufacture into articles of trade. Bristol became the second city of England for most of the eighteenth century on the success of the slave and sugar trades; customs duties rose from £10,000 in 1634 to £334,000 in 1785. Liverpool, the greatest of the slaving ports in the late eighteenth century, grew in population from 5,000 in 1700 to 34,000 in 1773, while customs receipts rocketed from an average £51,000 a year for 1750–57 to £648,000 in 1785.[1] It was the huge profits from the slave and sugar trades which produced much of the capital for Britain's industrial revolution; the ships of Liverpool paid for the factories of Manchester. The technological achievements which were to give the West political and economic dominance over so wide an area of the world were made possible by the miseries of the middle passage.

The slave trade enriched – and sometimes ennobled – men to the upper reaches of social acceptability and political influence. The Earl of Westmorland told his peers in the early nineteenth century that many of them owed their place to slaving and that cries for the abolition of the trade were nothing less than Jacobinism. Some of these English merchants were widely renowned for their good works in establishing schools for the poor, homes for the aged, libraries and associations for the learned. Like their moral kinsmen in the slave states of America, or their twentieth-century descendants in the City of London with their mining and industrial interests in Southern Africa, they saw charity as beginning – and ending – at home, within whitewashed walls.

The effects of the slave trade on Africa itself reached far beyond the contemporary cost. At the start of the slave-trading era in the early years of the sixteenth century, Africa was on the whole culturally no more backward – or advanced – than Europe was; if there were still communities on the continent existing as they had done for thousands of years, this was true too of Europe. The African states were doubtless inferior to European society in some respects, but in others they may well have been superior; it is certainly improbable on the evidence that they were given to such fierce religious conflict, with the torture and public burning of citizens on flimsy differences of doctrine. Yet three and a half centuries later, at the start of the colonial era, Europe was undisputed master of the world, with its machines producing unprecedented power and wealth, while Africa lay relatively primitive, largely distracted and all but helpless against those planning to plunder it again. Even the ruins of great cities that it had borne

[1] E. Williams, op. cit., p. 63.

no longer existed, and whites of sense and wide education could seriously suppose that its history was all that could be seen on its wasted surface. The stages and character of this terrible decline are not without record. When the Portuguese reached the mouth of the Congo in 1482, they encountered the country of the Bakongo, with its capital at Mbanzakongo, the modern San Salvador in northern Angola. With a population estimated by a seventeenth-century missionary at two and a half million, it was ruled by the Manikongo, an emperor who claimed allegiance from neighbouring kings and governed through a hierarchy of appointed chiefs. The Bakongo themselves knew how to work metals, including iron and copper, and wove mats and clothing from raffia tissues or palm-cloth with a skill that excited Portuguese remark. Their society was not as developed as the great West African states, but it was peaceful and receptive, and the Portuguese were welcomed for what they could teach. At first, indeed, the Portuguese king treated with the Manikongo as an equal, receiving many young Congolese at his court for instruction, and sending missionaries, masons, carpenters, bricklayers, and even several white women to give lessons in European domesticity. Nzinga Mbemba, baptized as Affonso I in 1491, succeeded as Manikongo in 1507 and ruled as an ardent Christian till his death in 1543; he built a cathedral and other stone churches in his capital, together with schools; he modelled his court on Lisbon and studied Portuguese laws, though without adopting the savage penalties inflicted in Portugal for the most trivial offences. 'What', he asked the Portuguese envoy on one occasion, 'is the penalty in Portugal for anyone who puts his feet on the ground?'[1]

The confluence of African and European cultures promised a new florescence. But Portugal was more interested in acquiring slaves for her plantations in Brazil than in the spread of her civilization or faith; the priests dispatched in 1508 found trading in slaves far more lucrative a labour than the saving of souls; and letters of appeal or complaint sent by Affonso to Lisbon were carefully lost on the way or disregarded when they arrived. In 1575 Paulo Dias de Novais arrived to command a new phase of Portuguese policy, planted his base a little to the south of the Bakongo frontier at Loanda, and began a war of conquest against the Ngola people. Before long African 'allies', trained and armed by the Portuguese to help supply the slave trade, were plundering the southern provinces of the Bakongo; the Manikongos, all of them nominally and some devoutly Christian, appealed to Rome, but even the concern

[1] Quoted in 'The Old Kingdom of Congo', by C. R. Boxer, in *The Dawn of African History*, ed. Roland Oliver (Oxford University Press, 1961), p. 78.

expressed by several Popes could not deflect the Portuguese from their mission. At last, in 1660, the Bakongo turned to war and were crushed; the kingdom began to disintegrate and by the end of the eighteenth century had become a scattering of villages around San Salvador.

On the east coast of Africa at the beginning of the sixteenth century the Portuguese seized Sofala in an attempt to take control of the gold and ivory trade from the interior. A hundred miles to the north of present-day Salisbury lay the capital of the Karanga kingdom, whose ruler was called the *Mwenemutapa* – or as the Portuguese spelt it, Monomatapa – and whose inhabitants had moved towards the middle of the previous century, with the failure of their salt supplies, from a royal village or *Zimbabwe* built of stone nearly three hundred miles to the south. The Monomatapas ruled the Zambezi valley for some seven hundred miles of its length, from the Kariba gorge to the sea, and the new Portuguese power soon erupted into their domain. A series of military expeditions, from 1560 to 1575, forced treaty relations upon the kingdom, and the establishment of private slave-run concessions or *prazos* ate away at the control of the Monomatapas in the lower Zambezi valley. By the close of the seventeenth century, under assault by the rising power of the Changamire kings at Great Zimbabwe and ruthlessly plundered by the Portuguese, the Monomatapas were reduced to a tiny relic of their former possessions and to survival only as puppets of Portuguese rule.

For as long as the slave trade was considered essential to their enrichment, the leading states of Europe, with Britain foremost among them, ignored all appeals for its abolition from religious enthusiasts. There were doubtless profits of a kind in pursuing the kingdom of God, but they were neither as evident nor easy as those to be found along the coasts of Africa and in the plantations of the Americas. Even official spokesmen for the Christian conscience of Britain condoned the slave trade; the Society for the Propagation of the Gospel branded its new slaves with the word 'Society' to distinguish their ownership, and the churches of Bristol pealed their rejoicing at Parliament's rejection of abolitionism. Nor was this only a British heresy. The Spanish Jesuits, Dominicans and Franciscans invested considerable resources in slave-worked sugar plantations, and a slave ship named *The Willing Quaker* plied between Boston and Sierra Leone.

Yet the slave trade was all the while busily arming an enemy to defeat it. From the profits of slavery, Britain was equipping herself with machines to become the first industrial power of the world, and as Manchester and Birmingham clanged and sizzled with the products of a new age, the planters of the British West Indies receded in political influence. From

1785 to 1830 exports of British cotton manufactures soared in value from £1,000,000 to £31,000,000, and the output of pig-iron multiplied ten times. The factory cities were more interested in markets than in colonies, for Brazil or the United States would buy British cloth or kettles as readily as would coddled Jamaica or Barbados, and in far larger quantities. Indeed, after the successful revolt of the colonies on the American main-land, British trade with them expanded enormously. The traffic in slaves suddenly became the blind plundering of a continent that might otherwise prove a profitable market for British manufactures, and a plundering, moreover, which was of far greater benefit to Britain's competitors than to Britain herself. Other European states had discovered the riches to be made out of sugar; the French in Saint Domingue, an island larger and more fertile than any British West Indian colony, were taking the Euro-pean sugar market away from Britain, but needed thousands of slaves each year from British traders to sustain and augment the labour force. As one eighteenth-century writer saw it: 'We may confidently conclude that the African trade is more confined in its utility than is generally imagined and that of later years it has contributed more to the aggrandisement of our rivals than of our national wealth'.[1] The British islands, with their ex-hausted soil, were producing sugar at a higher cost than their rivals, while the price of protection, by which their output enjoyed a monopoly market in Britain, was increasingly burdensome. Abolition of the slave trade accordingly recommended itself as an exercise in the shrewd management of costly colonies, of pressing competitors, and of Christian morality all at the same time.

The radical Christians and humanists – and there were certainly some provoked less by economic than by moral argument – owed their first victory to the arrogance of the West Indian planters themselves, who failed to recognize that distance helped to make slavery a tolerable insti-tution and who brought their household slaves to England as ornaments of their opulence. A few slaves seized the occasion to desert their masters, and their recapture on English soil provided the abolitionists with the chance to test the legal standing of slavery. In 1772 Lord Chief Justice Mansfield, not without reference to the condition of public opinion, ruled that 'the seizure and sale of a man was so high an act of dominion, and the state of slavery was so odious in itself that nothing could justify the one or the other but positive law'.[2] Since no such positive law existed, neither did

[1] J. Ramsay, An Inquiry into the Effects of Putting a Stop to the African Slave Trade (London, 1784), p. 24.
[2] Freedom from Fear, by O. A. Sherrard (The Bodley Head, 1959), p. 110.

slavery within the frontiers of Britain. It was a beginning. Thirty-five years later, in 1807, Parliament at last outlawed the slave trade for British subjects, and in 1811 imposed severe penalties on anyone engaging in it.

Having herself abandoned it, Britain had no intention of standing by while other states enriched themselves on the slave trade, ruining Africa for more constructive commerce in the process. Under the combination of moral incitement and British pressure, which took the form of naval patrols as well as the more conventional methods of diplomacy, almost all the maritime nations fell into line by 1842. This, however, did not put a stop to the trade, for while slave labour was needed by the plantations in the United States, Cuba and Brazil, there were seamen ready to run the risk of prosecution for adequate reward. The end came with the drying up of the demand from the United States, after the victory of the abolitionist North in 1865, and from Cuba and Brazil, after the abolition of slavery there at last in the 1880s.

The moral arousal which had excited the apostles of abolitionism excited too a new concern for the conversion of the heathen, and from the early eighteenth century a number of important missionary societies were founded, with Africa as the main field of their activity. They were not alone in their interest. Africa was by now the 'dark continent', known as little more than an outline on the map, and its mysteries tempted explorers, scientists and adventurous traders. British, French and German expeditions, financed by private associations and governments, set out to establish the direction in which a river flowed, the source of a legend, or simply the character of region where no white had been. The specific purposes varied according to sponsor and participant, but the general impetus was an association of the philanthropic, the pious and the profitable. Africa was to be introduced to the market-place of human progress, where ideas and goods were so usefully exchanged; its peoples would be converted to an industrious Christianity, their ignorance relieved by literacy, their diseases by medicine, their hunger by improved cultivation, and their needs by the manufactures of Europe. That there was greed and self-righteousness at work does not cancel the existence, too, of generosity and self-sacrifice. But the era of penetration and philanthropy soon gave place to the era of colonization. It is not without significance that H. M. Stanley, the architect of King Leopold's Congo, found Dr David Livingstone, and survived him.

European settlement, indeed, had already taken firm root in the south of the continent long before Mungo Park, the first of the celebrated modern explorers, journeyed to the upper Niger in 1795–7. The Portuguese were the first to reach the Cape – under Bartholomew Diaz in 1488 – but they did not stop there, preferring the less tempestuous harbours of the east coast before catching the monsoon to Goa. It was only in 1652, after the Dutch had discovered how to sail east on the trade winds, that three ships of the Dutch East India Company, under the command of Jan van Riebeeck, dropped anchor in Table Bay to establish a refreshment station at the Cape.

The soldiers who accompanied van Riebeeck were grudging and occasionally mutinous labourers, however, and in 1657 the Company released nine married men from its service to take up residence at the Cape as free farmers. One year later the first large supply of slaves arrived, and by the end of the seventeenth century a rigid stratification by race had taken shape, reinforced by the Calvinist doctrine of predestination which encouraged the whites to regard their own colour as a sign of God's considerate grace. The shrewd settlers were already developing the policy of selective segregation, by which white and non-white might live alongside each other, but only within the relationship of master and servant. Regulations prohibited slaves from wearing shoes or smoking in the street, though not from cooking white food or nursing white children, and since the offspring of a slave woman became a slave, miscegenation – common from the first – continued to be allowed, and was even fostered. 'The Dutch ladies', an early nineteenth-century writer remarked, 'have no reluctance to their slave girls having connection with their guests, in hopes of profiting by it, by their being got with child. I myself know instances where they have been ordered to wait on such a gentleman to his bedroom.'[1]

The demand of passing ships for meat and the irritations of official control sent the settlers into the interior, where the Company pursued them by pushing the formal frontier of the colony farther and farther into the cattle pastures of the Khoi-Khoin or Hottentots and the hunting grounds of the Bushmen. The *trekboers* (literally 'migrant farmers') themselves dismissed the possibility, if they considered it at all, that the indigenous peoples had any right to the land, or even to cattle, which they stole without compunction and pursued, when stolen back, with righteous rage. The Bushmen, indeed, they viewed as little different from vermin, and Boer commandos competed in shooting as many as possible. That a few thousand Bushmen did, in the end, manage to survive must be attributed less to a lapse in settler ferocity than to the capacity of the Bushmen

[1] *An Account of the Cape of Good Hope*, by Robert Percival (C. and R. Baldwin, London, 1804), p. 291.

themselves to retreat into desert regions, like the Kalahari, where they
were unlikely to be followed by any but the most fervent anthropologist.
The Hottentots were somewhat less persecuted because, as pastoralists
themselves, they could be made more useful, and many, their lands and
herds taken from them, settled as labourers on white farms or moved to
Cape Town. Those who survived white warfare and the subsequent
ravages of white drink and disease – several smallpox epidemics seriously
thinned their numbers – mingled with the slaves, East Indian political
exiles, and the products of miscegenation to swell the fast-growing
coloured population of the colony.

At last, in 1775, the *trekboers*, moving east along the fertile coastal belt,
reached the Great Fish River, some halfway between the modern cities of
Port Elizabeth and East London, where they encountered an enemy much
less manageable than the Hottentot or Bushman. The Bantu-speaking
Africans, a pastoral people like the Boers themselves, were organized into
large cohesive nations, with a complex political and military character,
and their numbers all but cancelled the advantages which the rifle and the
horse gave the whites. A series of racial collisions, still called the 'Kaffir[1]
Wars' in South Africa, resulted; but the white frontier advanced only a
little, and a virtual deadlock, that would last for some forty years,
developed.[2]

The first strains appeared among the African nations themselves, suddenly cut off from expansion and able to enlarge their pasture lands only
at each other's expense. By the beginning of the nineteenth century the
Zulus in Natal had produced a formidable war machine under the direction of Shaka, a military genius who organized regular regiments to fight
at close quarters, and they fell upon their neighbours, capturing cattle and
incorporating the young of the defeated peoples into their own society.
Shaka himself was assassinated after ten years of dictatorship in 1828, but
his half-brother Dingane proved no less ruthless or – for a while – successful. The whole of southern Africa outside of the white colony was thrown
into turmoil by Zulu power, some peoples setting out on careers of conquest themselves, and others merging with refugees from the Zulu wars

[1] 'Kaffir', originally an Arab word meaning 'infidel', is used as a term of contempt or abuse by
whites of Africans, and generally avoided today, outside the history books, by the more
educated and rational white South Africans – which is not, of course, to say that it has ceased
to be in common use.
[2] Despite the passion with which current white South African propaganda claims that white
and Bantu entered the territory of present-day South Africa at the same time, the Bantu – on
the evidence of shipwrecked Portuguese sailors – had been settled in the eastern Cape as far
south as the sea well before the arrival of van Riebeeck's three ships.

to form, under chiefs of vision and exceptional ability – like Sobhuza, founder of the Swazi kingdom, and Moshesh, founder of the Basuto one – new nations strong enough to secure their survival.

Within the colony itself, change was also taking place. As a result of the Napoleonic wars, the Cape passed from Dutch to British control, at a time when public opinion in Britain, stirred by the abolitionist movement, was beginning to concede some human claims to those who had not been born white. Rule by Britain was clearly going to be even more distasteful to settler sensibilities than rule by the Company had been. The new government soon started meddling with the 'trekboer' trinity of land, labour and security. It planted British settlers on the frontier to prevent both African and Boer aggressions; it auctioned Crown land instead of presenting it on request; and it attempted to curb the activities of Boer cattle-raiding parties. All this was wickedness enough in a community where younger sons were finding it increasingly difficult to get new farms of the 6,000-acre size needed for raising a family. But it was the British attitude to colour, and its consequences for the labour supply, that neither righteousness nor reason would endure. In 1828 the Cape government, prompted by the London Missionary Society and its indefatigable superintendent in South Africa, Dr John Philip, gave 'all free persons of colour' the same civil and legal rights that whites enjoyed, and in 1833 Britain abolished slavery throughout her empire, with what the Boers regarded as inadequate compensation and without the provision of laws to control the movements of liberated slaves. Anna Steenkamp, a niece of the Voortrekker leader, Piet Retief, succinctly described in 1876 the main cause of the movement known to South African history as the Great Trek.

The shameful and unjust proceedings with reference to the freedom of our slaves; and yet it is not so much their freedom which drove us to such lengths, as their being placed on an equal footing with Christians, contrary to the laws of God, and the natural distinction of race and colour, so that it was intolerable for any decent Christian to bow down beneath such a yoke; wherefore we rather withdrew in order thus to preserve our doctrines in purity.[1]

From the end of 1835 organized parties of Boers began leaving the colony, most of them moving across the Drakensberg to Natal. The Zulus had no intention of permitting any white occupation of their rich

[1] Quoted in *The Making of South Africa* by M. S. Geen (Maskew Miller Ltd, Cape Town, 1958), p. 91.

grassland, however; sent their impis against the interlopers; and at a place later called Weenen – after the Dutch for 'weeping' – killed nearly three hundred settlers. Under the leadership of Andries Pretorius, the trekkers gathered a force almost five hundred strong, and having promised God to keep the day of victory as one of thanksgiving for ever, met the Zulus on December 16th, 1838, at a stream later called Blood River. The victory was crushing – Boer rifles killed at least three thousand Zulus – and on December 16th every year now, white South Africa celebrates the Day of the Covenant as a public holiday, with racial rallies and calls to the spirit of the past.

In 1839 Pretorius proclaimed a republic in Natal, but the British government firmly set its face against a Boer state with access to Indian Ocean harbours and an appetite for other people's land that would soon lead to an increase in African pressure on the frontier of the Cape. Natal was accordingly annexed by Britain in 1845, and many trekkers moved back across the Drakensberg, to join others already pursuing a scattered independence on the High Veld north of the Orange River. There, forced by the need for co-ordinated action against the Africans, the isolated communities reluctantly combined into two major republics – the Orange Free State, between the Orange and Vaal Rivers, and the South African Republic, between the Vaal and the Limpopo – each governed by a Volksraad or People's Council, and a President, elected by white men only. The British government was tired of constantly having to extend its administration in an area that sucked up money like rain, with even less return, and in the early 1850s it formally recognized the independence of the two poor and land-locked Boer states.

The Great Trek had dispersed white settlement across most of present-day South Africa. But it was to do much more than that. In turning their backs on the Cape, the trekkers turned their backs as well on the nineteenth century, taking with them into the isolated High Veld the economic and intellectual backwardness of a frontier culture. Moreover, the land which the trekkers occupied was not empty, and uncounted thousands of Africans, plundered of their cattle and pasture, were forced to become squatters on white-owned farms in order to survive. The two northern republics established the intransigent serf society, with its land-owning white citizenship, its landless black proletariat deprived alike of political and economic rights, and its statutory colour bar, which would in time envelop the whole of South Africa.

While the economy of the Cape expanded during the 1860s with the development of sheep-farming, and Natal began to prosper from the growing of sugar with indentured Indian labour, the two republics stag-nated in a primitive poverty, unable to raise sufficient revenue through the long refusal of their citizens to pay any tax on land. Then, in the late 1860s, diamonds were discovered in Griqualand West, an area to the north of the Cape, to which its Griqua inhabitants – Hottentot in ancestry – and the Orange Free State both laid immediate claim. Never one to stand on excessive ceremony where such potential profit was in question, Britain engaged in some tortuous negotiations about the proper owner-ship and in 1871 annexed the area, accepting the rage of the two republics as a necessary risk in the exercise of imperial responsibility. Within ten years the new mines had produced £20,000,000 worth of diamonds, and by 1885 the new town of Kimberley, with its 20,000 whites and 10,000 Africans, was linked to Cape Town and Port Elizabeth by rail. To prevent illicit trading in stolen diamonds, African workers in the mines were imprisoned in compounds for the duration of their service contracts, and a 'pass' system was introduced by Proclamation 14 of 1872 to control labour to and from the mining area. The organization of mine labour in the Republic of South Africa today, with its migrant male workers in closely guarded compounds, was developed by British capital in Kimberley.

Britain began now to press for federation of the four white states as the best way of ensuring profitable development of the country and a co-ordinated policy towards the Africans within and beyond the various borders. In 1872 the Cape was granted internal self-government, with a parliament elected on a non-racial, if financially much qualified, franchise. Such a system, the British government supposed, if adopted by the rest of South Africa, would produce in time a common society, and would meanwhile enable Britain herself to reduce the costs and confusion of imperial administration. It was a delusion. The Cape had no intention of sharing its new-found prosperity with its poor neighbours or of surrender-ing its comfortable racial ratio – almost half its population was white – by acquiring the large African populations of Natal and the republics. The Orange Free State and the South African Republic, already antagonized by the annexation of Griqualand West, suspected, not unreasonably, an imperial itch along the proffered hand of collaboration, and in any event would reject any scheme that promised to erode white supremacy.

The South African Republic, however, was bankrupt and unable to cope with the restless Africans on its frontiers. Indeed, independent Zulu-land, under the dynamic rule of Cetshwayo, had raised a substantial army and was threatening to show the Boers that expansionism was not their monopoly. Seeing in the situation an opportunity to win support from the Boers by tackling their frontier problems for them, Britain annexed the republic in 1877. In January 1879 the Great Zulu War broke out, and after a severe defeat by an army of 24,000 Zulus at Isandhlwana, the British at last broke the back of Zulu power. The Boers in the Transvaal were suitably pleased, but no more reconciled to British rule, which provokingly forced them to pay their taxes. On the hallowed 16th of December, in 1880, the First Anglo-Boer War, or the Eerste Vryheidsoorlog (First Freedom-war) as it became known among the Afrikaners,[1] began. The British immediately opened negotiations for a settlement, and undeterred by the Boer victory at Majuba, recognized the independence of the republic, subject only to a vague British suzerainty. It was a humiliating – and dangerous – end to a ramshackle policy. Had Britain forced a federation on the four white-ruled states in Southern Africa and directed them firmly towards inter-racial democratic government, she would have involved herself in conflict and, doubtless even worse, some immediate cost, but she would have laid the basis for a sane and stable society. Had she committed herself to developing properly the Cape and Natal alone, absorbing the African territories at the edges into a state that could command the loyalty of different races, the Boer republics might well in time have been forced to succumb. As it was, she was ruthless only in her subjugation of African interests; the whites she fought with neither mind nor heart. Her annexation of the South African Republic displayed a purely imperial purpose, and her subsequent recognition of the Republic's independence, after the Majuba defeat, made the purpose appear incoherent and infirm. It would be remembered.

Meanwhile, European power was entering other parts of Africa. The Napoleonic wars had given Britain control of the oceans, and France turned to empire-building in the Mediterranean. Command of Egypt herself, over which both countries had fought, passed effectively, in 1811, to the Albanian troops of an Ottoman army under Muhammad Ali, whose ability and vision turned a stagnant province of the Ottoman Turks into a relatively prosperous and virtually independent state. Muhammad Ali's heirs, however, were less able. European merchants and money-lenders descended on the economy; and in 1869 the Suez Canal, planned and built under the direction of a former French consul, De Lesseps, was opened, to place Egyptian independence at the mercy of the European maritime

---

[1] The Boers, overwhelmingly Dutch in origin but with an early and important Huguenot infusion, gradually began to speak of themselves as Afrikaners, and of their language, increasingly distinguishable from its parent Dutch, as Afrikaans.

powers who used it. By 1879, the Egyptian government, having borrowed at predatory rates in Europe to finance a multitude of prestige projects, was bankrupt, and control of the Egyptian revenue, with command of the country, fell into the hands of British and French nominees.

In 1830, on the pretext of crushing piracy, France occupied Algiers, and then set out to expel the hostile Arab and Berber tribes from the coastal plain, replacing them by European colonists. Effective Algerian resistance, however, ceased only in 1879, at a cost to France of some 150,000 soldiers and with the Muslim tribesmen conciliated by indirect rule through chiefs and councils. France herself was unable to provide sufficient settlers for the colonized northern plains, and of the 350,000 Europeans living in Algeria by 1880, nearly half were Spaniards, Italians and Maltese. The Egyptian extravagance of the Beys at Tunis then gave France the occasion to proclaim a protectorate there in 1881, and only Morocco in the Maghrib was able to preserve her independence into the twentieth century, less through the resistance of her people than through her strategic position at the entrance to the Mediterranean, which kept France, Britain and Spain jealously preventing each other's intervention.

On the west coast, France sought to strengthen and extend her sphere of influence in the region of the Senegal River, acquired during the heyday of the slave trade. From 1854 onwards the basin of the Senegal was systematically conquered, and its inhabitants were converted to producing crops, such as groundnuts, of value to France. In 1857 the French occupied Cape Verde, on which the city of Dakar, the capital of the French West African empire, was later to rise, and by the mid'sixties they had acquired a secure base for the subsequent conquest of the western Sudan with the help of Senegalese soldiers. Farther south, on the coast of present-day Gabon, France established in 1849 the settlement of Libreville, as a home for liberated slaves, but it developed little until the European scramble for colonies in the 'eighties, when the French seized a vast area of equatorial Africa.

At the end of the eighteenth century a group of British philanthropists had established Freetown on the coast of Sierra Leone, as a refuge for former slaves and a footing for legitimate trade, but the colony barely survived until 1808, when it was taken over by the British government as a base for naval patrols against illegal slaving. In the next forty years, some 70,000 Africans captured from slave-ships were freed and resettled in Sierra Leone, and a successful colony, with a significant proportion of African traders, priests, doctors, lawyers and teachers, spread outwards from the capital. The British government gradually became convinced that the most effective way of stopping the slave trade and nourishing a proper yet profitable commerce in its place was to extend protection or even direct rule to the principal slaving coasts. It took control of the British forts on the Gold Coast from private merchants, warned off the Ashanti by sacking their capital, Kumasi, and declared the area a British colony in 1874. Eastwards, along the coast of present-day Nigeria, where an export business in palm oil was being developed by European – mainly British – merchants, but where the slave trade with Cuba and Brazil was flourishing as never before, Britain captured the port of Lagos in 1851 and ten years later formally constituted it a colony. The basis for Britain's subsequent West African empire was securely laid.

On the East Coast of Africa, the chief foreign factor was Arab and not European for the first three-quarters of the nineteenth century. From his capital at Muscat on the Arabian peninsula, the ruler of Oman, Imam Seyyid Said, sent his small but efficient navy to seize control of the East African trading ports, using Zanzibar as his operational base, and having planted cloves on the island, to develop it into the world's largest producer of the spice, established his capital there in 1840. Around him gathered Arab planters and merchants, who with credit provided by Indian financiers then cornered the trade of the mainland opposite, sending caravans of cloth, beads and firearms into the far interior and receiving back ivory and slaves. As had happened elsewhere in Africa under European direction, the arrival of firearms and the departure of slaves led to a disruption of traditional power patterns and the impoverishment of African society by rival aggressions. Then, from 1822, Britain began to interfere in Arab slaving operations and at last, in 1873, forced Sultan Barghash of Zanzibar, under threat of naval bombardment, to outlaw the slave trade in his dominions; the huge slave market on the island was closed, and a Christian cathedral rose on the site. Within a few years the rush for European colonies in Africa had begun, and Arab power along the coast came to an end.

European interest in Africa had, since the end of the slave trade, been fastidious; now, all at once, it was to become frenzied. Within a mere twenty years, the principal powers of Europe would swallow almost the whole of the continent, snatching what they could in a frantic fear of each other. They had scarcely considered their rival appetites, when the greed of an outsider suddenly alarmed them. King Leopold II of the Belgians was discontented with the extent of his possessions and hungered after an overseas empire. Carefully festooning his motives with the philanthropic platitudes of the time, he established in 1876 the African International

Association to plant across central Africa a series of commercial and scientific stations, with garrisons to attack the slave trade and protect Christian missions. Then swiftly his attention centred on the Congo basin, and with the help of Stanley, the explorer, who took service with him in 1879 and established the existence of a practicable transport system along the Congo, he set out to win international recognition of the area as a zone of free trade under his control. His diplomacy was skilled and successful, but it was not long solitary.

In 1881 the Egyptian army, under the leadership of a senior officer, Arabi Pasha, rose up against foreign command of the country; and anxious to secure the Suez route to India, Britain invaded Egypt in the following year, remaining in occupation despite promises to France that she would withdraw. Germany at once took advantage of the souring in relations between her rivals to play up one against the other in Africa, meanwhile seizing what she could for herself; in a bare eighteen months between 1883 and 1885, she annexed sizeable stretches of territory in four different parts of the continent – South-west Africa, Togoland, the Cameroons, and Tanganyika. When, accordingly, the European powers met on Bismarck's initiative at Berlin in December 1884, ostensibly to settle the status of the 'Congo Free State', the participants were already aware that a partition of the whole continent was inevitable, and though they joined in stressing the need to prove effective occupation before annexing any fresh territory, they eyed the map of Africa with obvious impatience.

The French, who had already begun expanding from Senegal in 1879, reached Timbuctu in 1893, their advance slowed by the resistance of the Mande people under the brilliant leadership of Samori. Farther south, following the explorations of de Brazza, they negotiated a network of treaties in the region of what was to become the French Congo and, in the 'nineties, began pushing northwards to meet the expansion of their West African empire at Lake Chad. The British hastily annexed Bechuanaland in 1885 to cut off the Germans in South-west Africa and in 1888 declared a sphere of interest from there to the Zambezi, delegating the functions of government in the area to the British South Africa Company of Cecil Rhodes. Though West Africa was economically more alluring, East Africa lay along the Suez route to India, and it was around the strategic importance of Egypt that Britain built her African policy. In 1886 the British acquired control over the region of present-day Kenya, with the possibility of expansion westwards into Uganda and command of the back entrance to the Sudan and Egypt; in 1889–90 they claimed Northern

Rhodesia (the modern Zambia) and Nyasaland (the modern Malawi), and
soon afterwards acquired Zanzibar from Germany in return for Heligo-
land. Agreements imposed by Britain on Portugal in 1890–91 fixed the
frontiers between British Central Africa and its Portuguese neighbours,
while a further agreement settled the border between British East Africa
and Italy's new colony in Somalia.

At first the predators went to work mainly in Europe, needing at most
a few treaties from bewildered or intimidated, frequently bogus chiefs to
establish their claims, and resolving any conflict amongst themselves by
diplomatic haggling and a sudden scratch somewhere on the map. But as
the extent of unseized territory diminished and claims collided around
interior frontiers, the struggle switched to Africa itself. After French
forces had taken the kingdom of Dahomey in 1893, the British acted
swiftly with force to conquer large areas of Nigeria; in the late 'nineties
France began pushing towards the Sudan, and Britain, anxious as ever to
secure her control over Egypt, moved into the territory first, to accomplish her conquest at a cost of at least 20,000 Sudanese dead. The partition
of Africa was an affair of men as well as of maps, and if it sometimes
occurred bloodlessly, its prey made helpless by surprise and ignorance of
the consequences, it was often cruel, a hideous alliance of violence and
deceit.

In the south of the continent the expansion of British power alarmed
the two Boer republics and excited Cecil Rhodes – a passionate imperialist
who had acquired riches and influence by consolidating the Kimberley
diamond mines – with the prospect of expanding it still further. The discovery in 1886 of gold on the Witwatersrand, where Rhodes immediately
extended his mining interests, had the unhappy consequence as well of
enormously enriching the South African Republic, whose dour President,
Paul Kruger, inveighed regularly against the menace of all this new wealth,
but revealed little eagerness to leave it decently in the ground. For the
time being, therefore, Rhodes devoted his attention to confirming – and
exploiting – British control in the north. In 1890, the same year that he
became Prime Minister of the Cape, he sent his pioneer column of police
and settlers into the Mashona territories of present-day Rhodesia, armed
with the Royal Charter given to his British South Africa Company and a
large supply of rifles for good measure. It was for Rhodes a disappointing
venture. The Mashona and more powerful Matabele regarded British
rule as an inadequate substitute for the loss of their land and the insatiable
settler demands on their labour; they fought fiercely if hopelessly till 1897.
The gold of the Monomatapas was more traditional than real, and such of

it as existed proved expensive to extract. Kruger had taken fright at the manœuvres to outflank him and rushed the completion of a railway from the republic to the Portuguese port at Delagoa Bay in Moçambique.

Gold had meanwhile attracted to the republic so many white immigrants – the black ones, of course, counted only as labour statistics – that by 1895 there were seven such *Uitlanders* to every three free-born burghers. Kruger, experiencing some relatively liberal opposition within his own community, the *volk*, had no intention of strengthening this by permitting the Uitlanders a share of political power, while the Uitlanders themselves, who provided most of the revenue, demanded with increasing vigour that they should qualify for votes as well as taxes. Rhodes saw an opportunity to further his designs in provoking an Uitlander revolt, and on December 29th, 1895, Dr Starr Jameson, who administered Southern Rhodesia for the British South Africa Company, entered the republic from Bechuanaland with a force of five hundred police. The adventure was initially a fiasco. The raiders were captured by republican troops; the planned Uitlander uprising never took place; and Afrikaner sentiment throughout South Africa was so antagonized that Rhodes had to resign as Prime Minister of the Cape. But the ultimate objective of the Jameson Raid was soon to be realized. In 1897 Sir Alfred Milner, with the backing of the aggressive British Colonial Secretary, Joseph Chamberlain, became High Commissioner, and his own hard attitude combined with the heady intransigence of Kruger, who expected help from Britain's European rivals in the event of a clash, to bring war at last in October 1899. Public opinion in Europe and the United States, so indifferent to the coloured victims of imperial appetite, attached itself strongly to the cause of the white ones; but only the Orange Free State came to the help of the South African Republic, and 87,000 Boers were eventually faced by a British force of 450,000 men. By June 1900 Pretoria had been taken, but the Boers then formed small mobile commandos and waged guerilla warfare. In response the British, under the direction of Lord Kitchener, built blockhouses for the protection of communications, burnt farmhouses as partisan sources of supply and centres of resistance, established refugee camps for the homeless – where dirt and disease killed several thousand women and children – and sent Boer prisoners to Ceylon and St Helena. (This whole scorched-earth policy of Kitchener's, which the Boers would themselves happily have followed in crushing guerilla warfare by Africans, soon became part of Afrikaner folklore, a running ulcer of resentment that would contribute to the subsequent rise of a monolithic Afrikanerdom to power.) Eventually, the Boers had had enough and sued for peace at Vereeniging in

May 1902. The two republics surrendered their independence and in return were promised full responsible government before the issue of votes for Africans was settled. As before, and afterwards in the Act of Union, Britain saw only her own immediate interests, not those of the Africans whose cause she flaunted as periodic propaganda required.

With the British conquest of the republics, all Africa but Ethiopia, Morocco, Libya and Liberia was in European hands. Italy seized Libya from the dying clutch of the Turkish empire in 1911; Morocco was partitioned between Spain and France in 1912; and the independence of Liberia – established by American philanthropists as a home for freed slaves in 1821, and formally constituted a republic twenty-six years later – survived as the sluggish prey of European moneylenders. Only Ethiopia withstood European assault with success for a few more years, keeping the Italians to the coastlands of Eritrea and Somalia, and she would fall at last, also, to the shoddily late imperialism of Mussolini, in 1935.

Now that they had duly apportioned the available territory and peoples, the new rulers of Africa had to decide what to do with their shares. King Leopold II of the Belgians had no doubt himself of the form that his regime should take; it was 'absolute ownership, uncontested, of the Congo and its riches'.[1] In a vast area of the Congo he outlawed private trade, giving monopoly rights over the collection of rubber, ivory, palm oil and other profitable products to his own agents or concessionaires, and pressing them relentlessly to increase their exactions. Whole districts were depopulated by raids for labour that taxes could no longer produce, while the diligence of the chain-gangs was excited by the killing or mutilation of those who did not fulfil their quotas.

With a part of his profits, Leopold undertook an extensive programme of public works in Belgium, and this, combined with the prosperity of many private citizens involved in some part of the Congo trade, kept Belgian opinion generally unmoved by the mounting reports of atrocities. As E. D. Morel, the most important of those agitating against Leopold's private empire, wrote in 1909:

> Sections of the upper and middle class secured handsome returns; contractors did a flourishing business for a time; much wealth accrued to Antwerp in particular ... The Belgian people thus became *de facto* although not *de jure* identified with a system of colonial government recalling, but surpassing, the worst example of medieval history. To a people wholly ignorant of the problems incidental to the government

[1] Quoted in *King Leopold's Congo*, by Ruth Slade (O.U.P., 1962), p. 175.

of coloured races, the African was represented as a brute beast with no rights in his soil, in his labour, or in his person. And this pestilent doctrine was popularized by a mechanism of financial, political, and Press corruption which for comprehensiveness has seldom been equalled, and which bit deep into the national life of Belgium. It was a double wrong; upon the people of the Congo, and upon the people of Belgium.[1]

Fifty-one years after those words were published, King Baudouin of the Belgians opened the independence day celebrations of the Congo Republic in Leopoldville with a speech that praised the early Belgian colonizers, and in particular King Leopold II. Patrice Lumumba, the new Congolese Premier, changed the draft of his own speech as he listened and when he was called upon to reply, stressed the humiliations which the Congolese had suffered under Belgian rule. The incident was not trivial. Belgian public opinion was deeply shaken – *Libre Belgique* in Brussels called the speech 'an affront to the King and to Belgium' – and newspapers elsewhere in the West regarded Lumumba's conduct as provocative and irresponsible. In the crisis that would soon convulse the Congo, Lumumba's remarks were not forgotten.[2] Yet who, if not King Baudouin himself, had been provocative and irresponsible? Could he reasonably have supposed that a speech praising Leopold II would be suitable to the celebration of Congolese independence? Or was his speech no more than a spontaneous gush of that racial arrogance which now sees even the most destructive periods of the past as contributions to civilization?

Certainly the rule of Leopold was such that even a Europe that had just emerged from the necessary cruelties involved in conquering a continent was shocked. The British House of Commons, not easily troubled by colonial distresses, was so stirred by reports of murder and mutilation in the Congo that it agreed in 1903, without dividing, to consult with the signatory powers of the Berlin Act on 'measures ... to abate the evils in that state'. The publication in the following year of an official and corrosive report by Roger Casement, British consul at Boma, and the formation soon afterwards of Morel's Congo Reform Association provoked further public concern, and after a series of careful delays for Commissions of Inquiry and advertised reforms, Leopold at last surrendered possession of

[1] *Africa and the Peace of Europe*, by E. D. Morel (London, 1909), quoted in *Congo Disaster*, by Colin Legum (Penguin Books, 1961), p. 33.
[2] For a careful treatment of the speeches and their effects, see *The Congo since Independence, January 1960–December 1961*, by Catherine Hoskyns (O.U.P., 1965), pp. 85-6.

the Congo to the Belgian government in 1908. There was, however, no sudden change in the impact of white rule; the Belgian government dismantled Leopold's structure of enterprise with cautious deliberation, substituting a far less crude model of its own, and the Congo Reform Association wound up its affairs only in 1913.

The other colonial powers of Europe were glad to have Leopold out of the way; his excesses had excited a regard for conditions in Africa that promised to prove expensive if it moved beyond the borders of the Congo. And it was precisely expense that the colonial powers wished to avoid. They had not seized Africa for the benefit of the Africans, and if they were not themselves prepared – or by public opinion permitted – to extract immediate profits by methods such as Leopold had used, they had no intention of sustaining an uncomfortable loss. In time African raw materials would feed European factories, and African markets would be developed for European manufactures, but this would have to wait upon effective administration, and meanwhile the price of establishing such an administration would as far as possible have to be paid by the colonies themselves.

There were four main methods of meeting the initial costs: land could be leased to private companies, for an immediate capital payment and a subsequent share of profits; settlers could be introduced, and their mining or farming operations taxed; customs duties could be levied where economic crops and easy communication already existed; and – least satisfactory of all – the colonial power itself could provide the money for essential investment until a taxable African population was developed. In 1898–9 France granted huge tracts of land in her equatorial empire to concessionaire companies, and their blind exploitation of the ivory and rubber trade soon reduced the area to a state of quiet decay. In colonies like Kenya and Southern Rhodesia, Angola and South West Africa, where climate and metropolitan policy nourished white settlement, land was rapidly alienated to immigrant ownership, with the displaced Africans forced into 'native reserves' or virtual serfdom. In Eastern Nigeria, palm oil and the Delta waterways provided immediately taxable trade. And in Uganda, the protectorate government was supported by grudging British grants-in-aid, till the railway from the coast reached Lake Victoria and brought the commercial possibilities of cotton and coffee.

But whatever the form of achieving cheap administrative control, it involved the use of forced labour – for porterage and building, for the construction of roads and railways, for service on plantations and in mines. Sometimes the force was naked, but in the main it was modestly covered by a tax, which could be paid by working a set period for the administration or by earning the cash value through work for a settler enterprise. In 1896 Sir Harry Johnston explained his course of conduct in Nyasaland to the British Foreign Office. 'All that needs to be done is for the Administration to act as friends of both sides, and introduce the Native labourer to the European capitalist. A gentle insistence that the Native should contribute his fair share to the revenue of the country by paying his tax is all that is necessary on our part to ensure his taking a share in life's labour which no human being should avoid.'[1] All the colonial powers imposed such taxes, under a variety of titles and sanctimonious excuses. The French had the 'prestation', which was levied throughout their African empire – to produce millions of forced labourers each year – and was formally abolished only in 1946. The Portuguese issued a labour code in 1899 which provided for a few exemptions by age or class and then roundly declared: 'All others who do not fulfil voluntarily the obligation to work ... will be compelled by the authorities to do so.'[2] And compelled, by taxes and simple force, they still are today.

By the outbreak of the First World War, colonial occupation was complete, with indigenous resistance crushed and civil administration firmly established in all but the most distant districts. Some governments, like the Belgian and French, deposed most of the important traditional rulers and, having broken up the larger political entities, commanded the pieces through nominated chiefs. Others, like the British and the German, preferred to keep the larger entities and control them through their traditional authorities. But whatever the structure of power, it was productive of little more than the provision of essential communications and the building of offices and homes for the expatriate rulers. Education and health were left to the Christian missions, and economic development to individual settler or private company initiative. The colonial officials, from governor to district administrator, were concerned merely to preserve order and raise sufficient revenue for the running costs of rule.

Rule, of course, requires an excuse, both to dazzle the ruled and to give the rulers themselves a sense of security, if not of purpose. In the world of the early twentieth century, the representatives of imperial power felt small need of hypocrisy. The whites had conquered Africa because they belonged to a superior race; their authority was part of the natural order. What, after all, had the black race produced to command a place in the

---

[1] *Trade and General Conditions Report*, 1895-6, quoted in *Africa – The Roots of Revolt*, by Jack Woddis (Lawrence & Wishart, 1960), pp. 50-51.
[2] *Portugal in Africa*, by James Duffy (Penguin Books, 1962), p. 132.

community of the self-governing? If Europe had ever been aware that African empires, too, once conquered and exacted tribute, traded far and amassed gold, sustained resplendent courts with resident musicians, sculptors, poets, architects and scientists, all this had been forgotten alongside the ravages of the slave trade. The European administrators themselves came from the wealthier and educated classes, and were generally almost as ignorant of the cultural level reached by the mass of the people in their own countries, as of the cultural content in the far more alien African practices that they now encountered. What they saw was a continent isolated from centuries of material progress in the West and plundered even of such clear imperial traces as might reluctantly have commanded a Western regard. (Mysterious monuments, like those at Zimbabwe, were quickly ascribed to colonists of some unindigenous race lost in the past, while examples of the most sophisticated African art excited bewilderment and horror.) By the material standards which the European middle-class administrators employed as the main measure of civilization, the Africans were undeniably primitive, and to search for some explanation under the floor-boards of history when the difference in race was so agreeably apparent at eye-level, would have been the mark of an unhealthy temperament.

Personal relationships between black and white beyond the rapid grapplings of sex were unthinkable. What could the civilized and the savage mind have in common? Besides, rule required a deliberate remoteness, so as to protect the rulers themselves from any display of inadequacy or weakness. It would never have done for any Africans but a few essential servants to see their masters drunk and even disorderly, differing with each other and even plainly dissatisfied with their condition. Moreover, as times and strides in tropical medicine allowed, their white wives joined the colonial officials and settlers to make more rigid the separation of club and residence. Whether they doubted their capacity to rival African women in sexual attraction or saw themselves as the peculiar custodians of the home and its racial heritage, the white women brought a special passion to the development of the social colour bar. Inevitably, the British, with their sexual and class obsessions, were more energetic in practising social discrimination than the other European rulers; but Belgians, French, Germans, Italians and Portuguese were in their varying degrees all dedicated to the preservation of social distance.

The racial egoism of the age was nowhere more crudely and cruelly exhibited than in the form taken by the union of the two British colonies in South Africa with the two Boer republics. In 1899 Lord Milner had given his own influential interpretation of British policy in the area: 'The ultimate end is a self-governing white community supported by well-treated and justly governed black labour.'[1] Now, having beaten the republics in war and soothed them in peace, Britain was ready to promote a single white-controlled South African state strong enough to tackle the growing 'native problem' without too scrupulous a concern for the interests of the 'black labour' involved. In 1906 the Transvaal, and in 1907 the Orange Free State were given responsible government despite their racially repressive characters, and in 1908-9 their representatives met with those of the Cape and Natal in a National Convention.

The whites from republic and colony rejoiced in their reconciliation. The delegates chose a union rather than a federation, made English and Dutch[2] joint official languages, and agreed to limit the vote to whites outside of the Cape (where income and property qualifications in any event kept non-white voters to a manageable minority). The non-white franchise in the Cape itself was protected by an entrenched clause of the Constitution, but the share of each province in the membership of the Assembly was to be calculated on the number of white adult males in its population. It was so racialist an agreement that even Britain felt it prudent to exclude the three protected territories of Basutoland, Bechuanaland and Swaziland from the new state.

W. P. Shreiner, a former Prime Minister of the Cape, led a small group of liberals in opposing union on such terms and joined the Reverend Walter Rubusana and John Tengo Jabavu, editors of African newspapers, in heading a protest delegation to London. The House of Commons was overwhelmingly unimpressed. Some whose sense of fitness was a little disturbed were soon persuaded that the threat of war with Germany made a friendly white population in South Africa of much more moment than a justly treated African one. Only the small Labour Party and some thirty Liberals opposed the colour bar in the South African constitution. The South Africa Act was signed by King Edward VII in September 1909, and Union took place on May 31st, 1910, the eighth anniversary of the Treaty of Vereeniging. In 1911 the Union Parliament passed the Mine and Works Act, closing to all African workers the skilled jobs that carried high wages, and the course of statutory oppression, so long pursued by four separate states, took its far more effective single form.

The First World War gave imperial self-assurance a jolt. The more

[1] Quoted in *The African Patriots*, by Mary Benson (Faber & Faber, 1963), p. 20.
[2] Afrikaans took the place of Dutch as one of the two official languages by Act of Parliament in 1925.

intelligent and honest Europeans suspected – however dimly – that their
own battlefields might well have recorded a barbarism to stagger the most
exaggerated accounts of tribal warfare in Africa. Furthermore, the society
of the new peace was very different from the society of the old one; the
effort of waging such war had produced an economic and political upheaval from which traditional attitudes could not escape unscathed.
Though the war itself had begun as a clash of power, patriotism alone had
been unable to supply sufficient fervour, and propaganda had moved into
the trenches of ideology. In 1917 a communist revolution had overwhelmed Russia, and its cries increasingly resounded through the streets
of European cities. When the representatives of the Allies met at Ver-
sailles, therefore, to consider a peace treaty, establish the League of
Nations and distribute Germany's African possessions, they issued their
decisions in moral wrapping paper. France and Britain divided Germany's
West African colonies, Togoland and the Cameroons; the Union of
South Africa got German South-west Africa; and Britain and Belgium
split German East Africa. But they accepted the territories as mandates
from the League, to govern them as 'a sacred trust of civilization' and
'promote to the utmost the material and moral well-being and the social
progress of the inhabitants'.

There was patently more pretence than purpose in such declarations,
but the very pretence stressed the need now to justify colonialism.
European governments spoke of their obligations not merely to secure the
peace but to better the condition of their imperial subjects, and if they
were hardly more eager than they had been before to provide the money
themselves, they encouraged their colonial administrations, with varying
degrees of energy, to spend any excess revenue on agricultural development, medical services and schools. The Portuguese, as ever, did little more
than turn on their other side and go to sleep again. The Belgians subsidized
and improved the existing missionary enterprises, but carefully limited
their encouragement of education to the primary and technical levels. The
French established state schools with high metropolitan standards to produce an African elite, small in number but increasingly able to exploit the
intricate processes of metropolitan power. The British, like the Belgians,
supported missionary enterprise rather than developing a separate educational system; but they encouraged secondary as well as primary schooling, and if the African elite they produced was generally less cultivated
than its counterpart in the French territories, it proved itself more advanced and radical in its discontent.

The new concern with objective fed the development of a colonial philosophy. France, Belgium, Portugal and Italy each maintained that her overseas territories were, with the metropolitan area, integral parts of a single state, and that their inhabitants would, with time and assimilation, acquire full citizenship rights. In the event, however, only the French permitted any real participation by Africans in metropolitan politics, and then only – until the reforms produced by the Second World War – from four communes in Senegal. The Belgians denied the Africans and even the economically privileged colonial whites all political rights, while the Portuguese and Italians, pursuing their policy of assimilation little beyond the limits of propaganda, soon acquired fascist regimes at home and further faith in the efficacy of force. The British themselves uniquely rejected the doctrine of assimilation, envisaging – when they considered any ultimate at all – self-government on the Westminster pattern for their colonies, but they moved so slowly and erratically that it was difficult to establish any sense of direction at all.

The decisive factor in political development was generally the white settler. Where he existed in substantial numbers and racial discrimination raged within the colony itself, such political advances as the imperial government allowed were pre-empted by the whites. In Southern Rhodesia, Britain yielded internal autonomy in 1923, on an income suffrage high enough to exclude all but a few Africans, and steadily the white settlers, effectively free from any supervision but that of their own appetites, increased their economic and political dominion. The Algerian settlers more and more commanded political power not only at home but, through their efficient lobbies, in the metropolitan capital. In Kenya, where well-connected white colonists under the leadership of Lord Delamere arrived before the First World War, a British government pronouncement of 1923, that African interests in the territory, as in Uganda and Tanganyika, were to be paramount, had little effect on local white sway till the African rebellions of the early 'fifties. In many other colonies, white settlers did not so much assume power as control, delaying political advance for the indigenous people and even blocking reforms ordered by the imperial authority. When the Popular Front government of France in the 1930s attempted to end forced labour, the white planters in French Africa simply refused to comply, and in the Ivory Coast even forced the recall of the Lieutenant-Governor for taking his instructions seriously. The theory of colonial development was flourishing; it was the practice that lay still in the seed.

Though strategic railways encouraged trade, and trade encouraged the production of new cash crops like tea and cocoa, coffee and tobacco,

Africa needed money to develop her resources, and Europe had money only for investment in white-owned plantations or, much more generously, in mines, where large and rapid returns could be ensured. Imperial powers and the private capitalists under their protection were naturally not quite as interested in the 'sacred trust of civilization' as in the more negotiable rewards of effort. In 1938 Professor S. H. Frankel reported that of the £1,222 million – about half in private capital and half in public loans – so far invested in Africa south of the Sahara, £555 million had gone to South Africa, £143 million to the Congo and £102 million to the two Rhodesias. Some two-thirds of all European investment, therefore, had been poured into only four territories, all economically rooted in mining. The profits were spectacular. De Beers Consolidated Mines, in the fifty years from 1888 to 1937, produced diamonds worth over £170 million, paid £7,125,000 in taxation, and £71, 901,000 in dividends.[1] By 1934, in a period of fifty years, gold valued at £1,227 million had been extracted from the Witwatersrand.[2] One Witwatersrand mine, Meyer & Charlton, owned by the General Mining & Finance Corporation, was formed in 1888 with a capital of £40,000, which was subsequently increased but never exceeded £200,000. In its forty-four-year career till 1932, when it was worked out, it:

produced gold worth	...	...	...	...	£11,640,000
spent in working costs	...	...	...	...	£6,110,000
paid in taxation	...	...	...	...	£1,040,000
and distributed to shareholders	...	...	...	£3,855,309

Each £1 share accordingly produced a return of over £26, or a dividend of roughly 60 per cent a year.[3] By the end of 1959, the value of minerals extracted from South Africa since mining began would amount to no less than £5,976 million – £4,655 million in gold, £525 million in diamonds, £385 million in coal, and £149 million in copper[4] – and foreign, especially British, investment would have recovered several times its stake.

The mines attracted white settlement and an industrial enterprise which then attracted still further white settlement. Johannesburg alone, which had fifty inhabitants in 1885, had 381,000, of whom 203,000 were white,

[1] *The Story of De Beers*, by Hedley A. Chilvers (Cassell & Co., 1939), p. 326.
[2] *Randlords*, by Paul H. Emden (Hodder & Stoughton, 1935), p. 354.
[3] Ibid., p. 343.
[4] *Year Book & Guide to Southern Africa, 1962* (Robert Hale, London), p. 163.

in 1934; throughout the rest of the continent south of Algeria, there were in 1934 only 60,000 whites, or less than a third as many. Inevitably, too, the mines needed Africans – for who else would do the unskilled work at so small a wage? But in South Africa, as in the Rhodesias, government discouraged permanent settlement by Africans in white areas, while the white trade unionists themselves saw in a stable African labour force a menace to their monopoly of skills. The mines, therefore, promoted a system of migrant labour, by which males were recruited on short-term contracts and kept in special compounds near their work. The recruiting agents went far afield, through the three High Commission territories to the Portuguese colonies, the Rhodesias and even beyond, but they found the bulk of their supply still in the African Reserves of the Union itself, where taxes and insufficient land made migratory labour the only alternative to imprisonment or starvation. Official South African propaganda today stresses the accomplishment of white capital and enterprise in exploiting the mines; yet no mines would ever have existed without the unceasing exploitation of black labour as well. Certainly white capital and enterprise received a more than adequate return. The dividends paid to black labour were the shattered Reserves, where women and children, the sick and the old, were left to diminish yet further the diminishing nourishment of the land; the economies of Portuguese Africa, the three High Commission Territories and wide areas of Central Africa, where government found it more profitable to sell labour to the mines than invest sufficient resources to keep labour at home; the denial of skills and, above all, a natural family life to generations of Africans.

The mines could prosper on the use of cheap migrant workers, but manufacturing industry required a stable labour force, while white privilege demanded service in the kitchen as well as the factory. Despite a rigid system of control, therefore, aimed at preventing the settlement of a sizeable African community in the towns, the black population there irresistibly increased, establishing shanty slums on the outskirts, and hiding wives and children – generally forbidden to enter – in their confusion. In 1911 there were 510,000 Africans (12.7 per cent of the total African population) in the urban areas: 1,750,000 (43.4 per cent) on the white-owned farms; and 1,768,000 (43.9 per cent) in the Reserves. In 1951 there were 2,312,000 (27.1 per cent) in the urban areas; 2,590,000 (30.3 per cent) on the white-owned farms; and 3,633,000 (42.6 per cent) in the Reserves.[1]

The industrialization that resulted from the prosperity of the mines in

[1] *South Africa, A Study in Conflict*, by Pierre L. van den Berghe (Wesleyan University Press, Middletown, Connecticut), p. 290.

South Africa widened still further the gap between economic development there and in the rest of Africa south of the Sahara. Throughout the
world slump of the 'thirties, the colonial economies stagnated, though the
metropolitan governments, hungry now for foreign trade, began investing
small sums of money in development.

It was the Second World War that suddenly brought the colonies to
life. While the conflict itself was raging, strategic raw materials were in
desperate demand, and when it was over, a Europe of devastated industry
and agriculture needed all the African produce it could obtain, if not for
domestic consumption then for trade with the United States to provide
the means for industrial rehabilitation. For the first time since the eighteenth century, colonies, and Africa in particular, assumed supreme economic importance. As Sir Stafford Cripps, Britain's Chancellor of the
Exchequer, told a conference of colonial governors in November 1947:
'The whole future of the sterling group and its ability to survive depends
in my view upon a quick and extensive development of our African
resources.' Cripps expressed hope for 'a really marked increase' within two
to five years of all raw materials able to save or earn American currency.[1]
The appetite for dollars stimulated massive investment in the colonial
economies, which flourished on the transatlantic trade.

	Exports to U.S. in thousands of dollars		Approximate % increase
	1937	1949	
Tanganyika	1,147	9,436	850
Northern Rhodesia	620	18,028	3,000
Belgian Congo & Ruanda-Urundi	1,471	21,895	1,500
Nigeria	11,589	26,875	230
Gold Coast	17,937	45,290	250
French West Africa	2,434	5,609	230
Kenya & Uganda	1,523	7,428	500
Angola	191	8,646	4,300
Moçambique	212	3,831	1,900[2]

Europe's recovery from the war was in large measure due to the effective
exploitation of African resources.

Britain's Colonial Development and Welfare Act, passed in 1940,
broke the long tradition that the colonies should finance their own

[1] *Common Sense and Colonial Development*, by Rita Hinden (Gollancz, 1949), p. 9.
[2] J. Woddis, op. cit., p. 229.

development and provided a sum of £5 million a year for ten years as a direct grant towards the cost of communications, housing, education and social services in the colonies; in 1945 the sum was raised to £12 million a year. With their own enhanced resources, the British colonies were accordingly able to undertake development plans costing £210 million in the ten years 1946–55. France's West African territories alone, with greater help from the metropolitan government, spent £277 million on development in the same period.

The returns on investment, both private and public, especially in mines, were phenomenal outside South Africa as well. The Union Minière du Haute Katanga in the Belgian Congo, with a capital of 1,000 million francs, made a profit of 600 million francs in 1946; 1,838 million francs in 1950; 4,093 million francs in 1955; and 4,571 million francs in 1956.[1] In 1919 the British South Africa Company of the Rhodesias had earned mineral royalties of £13,000;[2] by 1957 these reached £8,800,000. In 1938, Northern Rhodesia exported goods worth £10 million; in 1946, £12·8 million; in 1949, £32·9 million; in 1952, £81·7 million; in 1953, £93·7 million.[3] The value of copper produced in Northern Rhodesia from the commencement of mining operations to the start of 1960 exceeded £1,000 million.

But the economic return on investment was no longer the sole criterion. The European imperial states emerged from the war into a world dominated by two great powers, the United States and the Soviet Union, both of whom – whatever their conduct – denounced the colonial relationship, and each of whom saw in a subjugated Africa the opportunity of the other. Colonial discontent could not easily be contained any more in the old way by a salutary lesson in the eloquence of force. The United Nations Organization was a new and unknown quantity; discretion suggested a lip service at least to the platitudes of the Charter. And the idealism of the European Allies had not yet evaporated altogether in the ardour of the old power game. If there was no intention of permitting political independence, plans for the social as well as economic progress of the colonies seemed both proper and shrewd.

University lecturers, schoolteachers, social welfare officers, trade union and co-operative organizers, engineers and surveyors, doctors and economists settled in Africa – alongside less altruistic white immigrants, attracted to the areas of easiest prosperity – to expand the education services,

---

[1] *The Economist*, April 20th, 1957; *East Africa and Rhodesia*, May 16th, 1957.
[2] *The Politics of Partnership*, by Patrick Keatley (Penguin Books, 1963), p. 212.
[3] *The Two Nations*, by Richard Gray (O.U.P., 1960), p. 201.

plan housing, encourage industrial development and establish marketing boards, build dams and roads, staff hospitals, and advise on the employment of resources. Inevitably, change produced desire for still more change, and the existence of an unexpected promise excited a reach for the promise beyond and denied. Revolutions are not commonly promoted by the blind, but by those who see what they want and the bars in between. If schools and roads and hospitals could be built by a colonial administration, for some advantage of its own, how many more schools, roads and hospitals might not be built by a popular government? The very experts sent from those far-away countries drew salaries and services that no African, whatever his talents, could command. The money available for development, so much of it earned by African endeavour, seemed more and more to be spent not on improving the condition of the Africans themselves, but on keeping whites at a level of extravagant superiority. If whites could live like that why could not Africans? And there were leaders enough – many of them students recently returned from the rich and assertively free societies of the white West – to fire general rebellion with demands for freedom at home.

The Second World War itself cleared Ethiopia from Italian rule in 1941, and put Eritrea and Italian Somaliland under British military government; in 1952 Eritrea federated with Ethiopia, and in 1960, after ten years of United Nations trusteeship and Italian administration, Italian Somaliland joined British Somaliland in the independent Somali Republic. Libya, captured from Italy in 1942, was administered by Britain to become an independent kingdom nine years later.

The British had withdrawn their formal protection from Egypt in 1922 and allowed the establishment of an independent monarchy; but the independence was nominal, for British troops stayed, ostensibly to guard the Suez Canal and materially to prevent the pursuit of policies to which Britain was opposed. There followed a sterile round of political changes. The palace would attempt direct rule, and then capitulate under public pressure to elections and government by the nationalist Wafd. The Wafd, however, was too conservative for the programme of agrarian reform that would have given it a powerful popular base, and too radical in its hostility to the British presence for long survival. British power and the palace would then combine to produce royal rule again, and this would last till public discontent forced elections and another Wafd government. Though British dominance had, in the past, done much to streamline Egypt's administration and develop her economy, it had only further enriched the traditional upper class, which expanded its interests to industry, while the peasants and swelling city mass hungered and huddled in neglect. The expansion in manufacturing was claimed as a victory for nationalism, but in fact was largely commanded by foreign capital. In 1948 more than 60 per cent of the capital invested in Egyptian limited companies was held by foreigners.[1]

Mussolini's appetite for an African empire brought the British and the Wafd together in 1936 for an agreement that retired British troops to the immediate area of the Canal; but in 1942, when German forces under Rommel were advancing into Egypt, and the young King Farouk seemed likely to summon as Prime Minister a politician friendly to the Axis, British troops surrounded the palace and forced the king to appoint a Wafdist administration friendly to the Allies instead. It was an outrage to nationalist susceptibilities that would ultimately destroy the monarchy and the Wafd as well as British power in Egypt. The war against the new state of Israel in 1948 led to fresh humiliation and nationalist fury; Egyptian troops were defeated by much smaller Israeli forces, and investigation disclosed the incompetence of senior officers and the supply of faulty equipment to the Egyptian army by the cynical regime of profiteers in Cairo.

The wealth of the corrupt and flaunting upper class jostled the ever deepening poverty of the peasants. The population steadily increased while the area of cultivated land stayed the same, and as rents and prices rose, more and more of the poorer farmers were forced into labouring for the larger estates. At last, on July 23rd, 1952, a group of army officers led by Colonel Gamal Abdul Nasser seized power, to sweep away both parliament and the monarchy. The new regime agreed with the British government that the Sudanese should be allowed to decide their own future, after three years of self-rule under international supervision, and in 1956 the Sudan voted to become an independent republic.

In the Maghrib, a militant nationalism had begun to oppose French rule before the outbreak of the Second World War, and the collapse of France herself in 1940 enormously strengthened nationalist resolve and self-assurance. In March 1934 Habib Bourguiba had formed the Neo-Destour as the radical movement for Tunisian liberation; he had been arrested six months later, released in May 1936 by the Popular Front government, and then arrested again in April 1938, to be sent by the Germans from France to a cajoling Rome in January 1943. Holding high hopes of a change in French policy with the Allied commitment to democracy, he refused to collaborate with the Axis; but the Fourth Republic that succeeded to the

[1] *Nasser's Egypt*, by Peter Mansfield (Penguin Books, 1965), p. 29.

peace was no more ready to concede Tunisian independence than the Third Republic had been. The 250,000 whites in Tunisia resisted all prospect of reform and were supported by the Algerian lobby in Paris, which feared the effect of concessions to Tunisian nationalism on the increasingly restless Muslims of Algeria. In January 1952 Bourguiba was arrested again, and the country exploded into strikes and guerilla warfare. At last, facing rebellion in Morocco and Algeria as well, the French began to measure the cost of their intransigence and in June 1955 granted internal autonomy to Tunisia.

The Moroccan struggle did not lag far behind. In January 1944 nationalist sentiment coalesced around the formation of the Istiqlal or Independence Party, which demanded the abrogation of the protectorate treaty and the recognition of Moroccan independence. In 1947 the Sultan, Mohammed V, associated himself with these demands, proclaiming the affiliation of Morocco with the Arab world, and so rallied the traditionalist peasantry to the cause. Having tried unsuccessfully to intimidate or circumvent the Sultan, the French, egged on by the 400,000 whites in the territory, deposed and exiled him in 1953, but this only infuriated the Moroccan masses, and violence began under an Army of Liberation. By 1955 the French had had enough; the Sultan returned to the throne in November; and in March 1956 Morocco obtained her independence. Tunisia could hardly be expected to content herself with less, and later in the same month became independent as well.

It was in Algeria, with her nine million Muslims and one million whites, that race war took by far its most terrible toll. Constitutionally Algeria was an integral part of France, but Muslims could not acquire the status and rights of French citizens unless they abandoned Muslim law; it was a religious, cultural, and ultimately nationalist barrier, but others would soon have been added if enough Muslims showed themselves willing to surmount it. In practice, Algeria was governed in the interests and by the pressures of her whites, the *colons*, who – especially the poorer amongst them – comforted their sense of inferiority before the metropolitan French by a strident sense of superiority towards the Muslims. In 1892 Jules Ferry, one of France's staunchest imperialists, wrote of Algeria:

> It is difficult to try and convince the European settler that there are rights other than his own in Arab country and that the native is not a race to be taxed and exploited to the utmost limits ... the settlers proclaim that [the conquered Arabs] are totally incorrigible and utterly incapable of education, without ever having attempted, over the past

thirty years, to do anything to drag them out of their moral and intellectual misery.[1]

It was an attitude that would persist, through rebellion and war, to the independence of Algeria and the mass flight of the whites. The *colons* were confident in the ease with which they could influence metropolitan policy, through their parliamentary representation in Paris and, when necessary, the open threat of rebellion.

Algerian nationalism itself had first taken significant shape in 1937 with the founding by Messali Hadj of the Parti Populaire Algérien, which was banned two years later and continued underground, persistently strengthened by the rigid refusal of the settlers to countenance concessions. The war excited hopes for change, and the armistice in May 1945 was greeted by nationalist demonstrations. Police fired on the crowds, however; the storm of Muslim fury that followed left over one hundred whites dead; and the French government, with eager assistance from the settlers, set out to re-establish control. Official figures subsequently admitted to 1,500 Muslims killed in 'pacification', but reliable estimates, frequently quoted in the French parliament, set the figure ten times as high.

The P.P.A. reformed itself into the Mouvement pour le Triomphe des Libertés Démocratiques, while the more moderate Muslims under the leadership of Ferhat Abbas, who had once believed passionately in a French – if emancipated – Algeria, began to demand independence and no longer merely reform. While French politicians discoursed ceaselessly of French liberties and values and benefits, the *colons* busied themselves in securing their privileges by rigging elections and ruthlessly attempting to intimidate dissent. At last a group within the M.T.L.D. formed itself into the Organisation Secrète to plan an armed uprising, and on All Saints Day, November 1st, 1954, what was to become the Algerian war broke out with attacks on police stations, garages and gas works. The revolutionaries established the Front de Libération Nationale (F.L.N.), and in April 1956 Ferhat Abbas formally associated himself with it, to reflect a nationalist unity that transcended class and political divisions.

The cost of keeping Algeria captive was belittled by French resolve; but soon even the most feverish patriotism could not conceal the drain in men and money that would be involved. Algerian resistance had not been easy to crush in the era of imperial expansion, and now it was not alone but furnished with moral and even material subsidy by Muslim states, the

[1] *Le Gouvernement de l'Algérie*, 1892, quoted in *The Algerian Problem*, by Edward Behr (Penguin Books, 1961), p. 29.

steadily spreading extent of decolonized Africa, and the communist bloc. From 1956, with the achievement of their independence, Algeria's neighbours, Morocco and Tunisia, became not only channels of supply, but sanctuaries from French pursuit and training camps for F.L.N. Forces. Yet it was Egypt – considered by France, rather as China is considered by the United States today, the centre and sustenance of subversion, violence and enmity – that attracted serious reprisal.

The new Egypt was not behaving well. She was taking her independence seriously, projecting a policy of international non-alignment and even, when the West refused to supply her with the arms she wanted, getting them from the Soviet bloc instead. Moreover, the West, and especially Britain, supported the monarchies of the Middle East as manageable and safe regimes, while Nasser undermined them – and so British oil interests – with his revolutionary propaganda and the example of his agrarian reforms. The French Foreign Minister visited Cairo in an effort to stop Nasser's support for the Algerian rebels, but failed.[1] Then, in the spring of 1956, Egypt recognized the People's Republic of China, and there were reports that she had concluded further armament deals with the Soviet bloc. The United States and Britain announced that they were withdrawing their promise of aid for the construction of the Aswan High Dam, and on July 26th Nasser replied by nationalizing the Suez Canal Company. Though there was no legal ground on which the nationalization could be challenged, especially since Nasser offered compensation to the Company's shareholders, Britain, France and the United States were enraged and froze all Egyptian assets in their keeping. At last, on October 29th, Israeli forces – with the collusion, there can be no doubt now, of the French and British governments – invaded Egypt. On the following day, Anthony Eden, the British Prime Minister, announced: 'In order to separate the belligerents and to guarantee freedom of transit through the canal by the ships of all nations, we have asked the Egyptian government to agree that Anglo-French forces should move temporarily into key positions at Port Said, Ismailia and Suez ... British and French forces will intervene in whatever strength may be necessary to secure compliance.' It was an absurd demand, immediately rejected, and on October 31st British and French planes began bombing military targets in Egypt.

International opinion was roused by so arrogant and obvious an act of aggression; the United States denounced it, the Soviet Union threatened to intervene, and Britain herself was divided more bitterly than she had

[1] *Nasser's New Egypt*, by Keith Wheelock (Stevens & Sons, London, 1960), p. 235.

been over any foreign issue for decades. By November 6th, when their forces landed at Port Said to meet unexpectedly fierce civilian resistance, Britain and France were ready for retreat, and the victory was Nasser's, despite the costly defeat of his troops by the Israelis in Sinai. Egypt acquired complete control of the Canal, confiscated Britain's large military stores in the zone, and sequestered all British and French property in the country. Above all, the two major imperial powers of Europe had been humiliated; their ability to enforce their will would never be feared in the same way again.

British Africa was already in ferment. West African intellectuals had begun agitating against British rule, with circumspect mildness and limited objectives, in the 1890s, and had attended the early Pan-African Conferences in Europe after the First World War. Influenced by the Africanist movement among Negroes in the United States under the leadership of Marcus Garvey and by the growth of Congress in India, they had established the National Congress of British West Africa in 1920 and, five years later, the West African Students' Union in London, which had rapidly become a training ground for nationalist leaders. In 1934 Nnamdi Azikiwe, a young Nigerian, had returned to Africa from his studies in the United States, and after editing a newspaper in the Gold Coast for three years, had started a chain of nationalist newspapers in Nigeria. He had flung himself into the work of the new Nigerian Youth Movement, and by the end of 1938 this source of vigorous nationalism possessed a membership of ten thousand.

The Second World War produced in British Africa, no less than in other parts of the continent, a new turbulence. The success of the Japanese against white forces in Asia sapped imperial prestige and stirred nationalist self-assurance. Many West Africans served on equal terms with British troops in other parts of the world and found them far less formidable than colonial mythology had suggested. Indeed, the Allies seemed, in the Atlantic Charter, to have discarded the very basis of imperial rule by recognizing 'the right of all peoples to choose the form of government under which they will live'. The war was also bringing, alongside a new prosperity, considerable economic dislocation. The rise in the cost of living had not been accompanied by a corresponding rise in wages, and in 1945, with the support of Azikiwe's recently formed National Council of Nigeria and the Cameroons, labour unrest in Nigeria led to a general strike, involving 30,000 workers and lasting a month.

The wake of the war was scarcely less unsettling. The British finally withdrew from India, the imperial current around which African colonies

had for so long been wound as strategic insulation. That Britain should
now find her African possessions more profitable than her Asian ones
hardly reconciled their peoples to an indefinite perpetuation of British
rule. If Indians could govern themselves, why not Africans? In August
1947 a group of intellectuals in the Gold Coast formed the United Gold
Coast Convention to work for further constitutional reform and appointed
to the post of General Secretary Kwame Nkrumah, who had studied
abroad and played a crucial role in the Pan-African Conference at
Manchester in 1945. There was already widespread unrest in the colony,
which Nkrumah increased by mass recruitment, and in February 1948
disaffection erupted in rioting. The British administration restored temporary order, with the loss of twenty-nine African lives, and arrested the
Convention leaders, but was aware that it could not contain popular discontent by such measures and in 1949 instituted consideration of political
reforms. Nkrumah, however, was not satisfied, and formed the Convention People's Party to fight for 'Self-Government Now'. He was arrested
again, for sedition, but in the 1951 general election held under the new
constitution, he and his party received an overwhelming popular vote.
The British government, unwilling to face the consequences of defying
such awakened nationalism, released Nkrumah, to give him and his
colleagues leading posts in the colonial administration. Six years later,
after a series of elections which confirmed Nkrumah's leadership and –
despite disturbances largely fomented by an alarmed tribalism – produced
a unitary constitution, the Gold Coast became independent, under the
name of Ghana.

A similar imperial retreat could hardly be denied Britain's other
possessions in West Africa. The size and diversity of Nigeria nourished
the development of a federal system first, but by 1952 Azikiwe had become Premier of the Eastern Region, and in 1960 the country achieved its
independence, with the traditionalist leadership of the North – much to
British pleasure – in major command. Sierra Leone became independent
soon afterwards.

It was in East Africa, where white settlement was so much more substantial, that British policy relentlessly provoked rebellion. The Africans
in Kenya, especially the dominant Kikuyu, grew more and more resentful
at the alienation of their land to white ownership and the all but complete
possession of the Legislative Council by white officials and settler representatives. The Second World War, with the heightened economic
activity that it caused, brought a swelling number of Africans from the
overcrowded Reserves into the slums of the cities, where they acquired

Western appetites without the means of satisfying them. African nationalism had sprouted among the Kikuyu as early as 1921, when the Kikuyu Association had been founded mainly by chiefs to plead for land reform, and its successor, the Kenya African Union, formed in 1946, revealed by its militancy and mass support the growth of frustration and bitterness in the quarter-century between. In 1946, too, Jomo Kenyatta returned from Britain, where he had been active with Nkrumah in the Pan-African movement, and under his leadership the K.A.U. made rapid strides, reaching a proclaimed membership of 150,000 in 1951. In 1947 labour unrest detonated in strikes, ruthlessly suppressed, and the government – apparently unconcerned with the increasing land hunger of the Kikuyu – began to enforce more strictly the regulations against African squatting in the white farming areas. Secret societies – one of which, the government declared, was called 'Mau Mau' – proliferated in consequence, sometimes securing the allegiance of their recruits by oaths and ceremonies of a deliberately debasing kind. Yet this dependence on deformed tribal tradition, while not an unexpected outcome of resentment driven underground, was far less common an aspect of African resistance than government propaganda maintained. The K.A.U. was the major medium of African protest, and if its leaders increasingly felt the hopelessness of constitutional struggle and turned to the consideration of violence, they were behaving no differently from the Algerians in a similar situation.

The government had eyes only for the fact of rising African unrest, not for its causes; in 1951 it banned 'Mau Mau', and in October 1952 declared a state of emergency. Kenyatta and other leaders of the K.A.U. were arrested and subsequently sentenced to long terms of imprisonment for managing 'Mau Mau'. Widespread violence broke out, British troops arrived in strength, and the colony was at war. The rebellion undoubtedly had the overwhelming support of the Kikuyu masses as well as many Africans from other tribes, and the government was driven to undertake a general repression. Some 26,000 Kikuyu men were rounded up in Nairobi alone for individual screening, and 100,000 Africans thrust into the already packed Reserves for apportionment to 'emergency villages' under strict curfew regulations. Pitched battles took place between rebel and government forces, though the Kikuyu generally pursued guerilla tactics, and terrorism was widely used by both sides. Indeed, the conduct of government troops, no less in the interrogation and detention centres than in the field, provided a singularly unpersuasive display of the civilization for which Britain was supposed to be securing Africa.

By the end of 1955 the war was virtually over, though African guerilla fighters survived in the forests and the state of emergency was lifted only in 1960. The cost in money exceeded £50 million; the cost to humanity far exceeded even the few whites and the many Africans killed. White public opinion abroad was subjected to atrocity propaganda of a kind that brutalized the minds of those who took it seriously, while fury and despair had driven thousands of Africans into practices that would normally have appalled them. And for what? After five years of violence, the government set constitutional progress on the path to African majority rule and the independence of Kenya under Kenyatta's leadership in 1963. Not the least corrosive comment on those years of stupidity is that Kenyatta himself, execrated for so long by the British press and government as well as by the white settlers in Kenya, should now be treated with such respect and trust as a 'moderate' by them all.

The nationalist struggle in the rest of British East Africa was much easier – in large measure, of course, because the brunt had been borne by Kenya; the British government had learnt much by the time that it encountered significant African pressures in Tanganyika and Uganda. Tanganyika was, in any event, a United Nations Trust Territory, and British administration was subject to international accountancy. In July 1954 Julius Nyerere founded the Tanganyika African National Union to press for independence, took his demands to the U.N. itself in the following year, and in 1960 became Chief Minister with the grant of responsible self-government; at the end of 1961 Tanganyika became an independent state and one year later a republic under Nyerere as President. The struggle in Uganda was complicated by the relationship of Buganda, the dominant and richest area, with the rest of the country. Indeed, it was with Buganda nationalism, in the person of the Kabaka or king, Mutesa II, that Britain first collided in October 1953. The government exiled the Kabaka to London and declared a state of emergency, but the disturbances in Buganda only increased, the prestige of the Kabaka flared amongst all nationalists, and two years later he was allowed to return in triumph. A federal relationship was developed between Buganda and the rest of the country, and in October 1962 Uganda became independent.

Such developments in Britain's African empire, especially along the West Coast, did not leave France's many possessions south of the Sahara unmoved. The Second World War itself had already shaken the French imperial hold. The fall of France in 1940, with the subsequent conflict between white Frenchmen who were loyal to Vichy and white Frenchmen who followed General de Gaulle, eroded French prestige, not least

because most of the French administrators associated themselves with
Vichy and the Nazi racism which only a short while before they had
publicly deplored. Under the leadership of Felix Éboué, a Negro from the
West Indies who was Governor of Tchad, however, the less developed
French Equatorial colonies swung to de Gaulle and became a centre of
Free French operations. Partly in response, Free French politicians and
administrators met at Brazzaville in 1944 and decided that African representatives should help draw up the post-war constitution for France. But
the new liberal euphoria soon evaporated with victory. The constitution
of the Fourth Republic established a French Union, with the 'overseas
territories' made 'partners' of France, and all Africans became citizens
with a share in French parliamentary elections; but the share was a small
one, and the colonial administrations were left hardly less powerful than
they had been before.

Most of the African parliamentarians met at Bamako, capital of French
Soudan, in October 1946 and formed the Rassemblement Démocratique
African (R.D.A.) under the leadership of Félix Houphouet-Boigny, a
deputy from the Ivory Coast, to organize the struggle against French rule.
The new movement was advised and supported by the Communists in
Paris, and this, combined with its own increasing militancy, soon incited
the authorities to repression. Resistance spread with demonstrations, boycotts and strikes, and by 1951 over fifty Africans had been killed, several
hundred wounded and thousands imprisoned. Houphouet-Boigny led the
R.D.A. out of its association with the Communist Party, which was itself
fervently discouraging nationalist trade unionism, and turned to nourishing the trust of the French business community. In 1956 he even became a
Minister in the Socialist government of Guy Mollet, and though he was
accordingly involved in the Suez adventure, he also used his influence to
promote the passing of the loi-cadre, an outline law which permitted the
French African territories a significant measure of local self-government.
His own accommodation, however, had not smoothed the path of imperial control. In Guinea, Sékou Touré had created a radical movement
with mass support, and in the loi-cadre elections of March 1957 swept the
polls to become Vice-President of the territory and leader of the radicals
in the R.D.A.

The 1956 invasion of Egypt had neither toppled Nasser nor stopped – as
how could it, even if it had succeeded? – the Algerian war. Angry at the
apparent weakness and vacillation of successive parliamentary governments, the Algerian colons rebelled in May 1958, to receive the support of
the army, and fear of civil war thrust General de Gaulle to power over the

ruins of the Fourth Republic. Aware of African unrest, which the British policy of formal retreat was only further exciting, de Gaulle boldly toured France's possessions in West and Equatorial Africa, to offer them a choice by referendum between independence and autonomous membership of a French Community. Since he made clear that the independence would be complete, with a severing of aid from France, all but one territory voted in September for autonomy. Guinea, however, overwhelmingly chose independence, and with help from Ghana and the communist states survived the abrupt recall of all French administrators, teachers and technicians, the removal of much capital equipment, the disruption of nearly all her trade, and the blocking of the financial flow from France. A colonial record begun in cruelty and greed was ending in spite. Yet if Ghana had taken independence, how far behind could the other African territories lag? In 1959 Senegal and Soudan asked and received their independence inside the Community, and in 1960 the Ivory Coast, Niger, Dahomey and Upper Volta, not to be outdone, successfully applied for independence outside. By the end of the year all her former colonies in West and Equatorial Africa had become independent of France, though in most instances no more than technically so. De Gaulle did not repeat his mistake over Guinea, and though France withdrew her remaining powers, she left her financial and administrative support, and so an ultimate control, behind.

It was in Algeria that de Gaulle registered his most astonishing achievement, moving France, painfully but relentlessly, to accept Algerian independence. Those who had acclaimed him first were soon to execrate him; in September 1959 he recognized the right of the Algerians to self-determination, and the *colons* staged another – this time unsuccessful – uprising. In April 1961 a section of the army in Algeria rebelled, but this, too, de Gaulle survived, and in March 1962 the French government signed a cease-fire agreement with the F.L.N. A war which had cost France more than £2,500 million and killed, by official French estimates, some 70,000 French soldiers and 140,000 Algerian nationalists, was over. The F.L.N. estimated the Algerian dead at more than one million, many killed in the concentration camps and military swoops on villages, but most killed unnoticed, in the open, under French protection, by hunger. And still the killing was not at an end. The *colon* extremists had formed the Organisation de l'Armée Secrète (O.A.S.) to shatter all administration and authority in Algeria by indiscriminate acts of terrorism, and the cease-fire only intensified their frenzy. A whole society seemed to have gone race mad as whites, with hideous irrelevance now, hurled bombs into Arab hospitals and schools, markets and street crowds. By the beginning of August 1962, half the *colons* had left for France; in October, Algeria at last became independent; and within another six months, the white population had dwindled to a tiny remnant.

At the other end of the continent, however, white rule steadily fortified itself against change. In the new Union of South Africa, an alliance of 'reconciled' English- and Afrikaans-speaking whites, first under one former Boer general, Louis Botha, and then, from 1919, under another, Jan Christian Smuts, constituted the government, while the recalcitrant Afrikaners formed themselves into the opposition National Party under a third, J. B. M. Hertzog. This 'reconciliation', which ignored the non-white majority for all purposes but those of repression, brought South Africa into the First World War on Britain's side, crushing a rebellion by Afrikaner militants in the process; received control of neighbouring German South-west Africa, as a mandate from the new League of Nations, in recompense; and entered the peace arm-in-arm with British capital.

The mining houses saw no virtue in paying skilled white labour at high rates if they could employ skilled black labour at low rates instead. But such exclusive concern with profit threatened to sell the pass of white supremacy. Smuts ruthlessly broke the white miners' strike on the Rand in 1922; but the Labour Party formed an election pact with the National Party, and in 1924 General Hertzog swept to power at the head of an alliance between English and Afrikaner racists. The new Pact Government closed many skilled and semi-skilled trades to Africans and Indians by law, and reduced still further the force of the non-white vote by en-franchising white women and then removing all educational and financial qualifications for the vote from white men. By 1932 there were, therefore, some 39,000 non-white voters to 850,000 white ones. It was a ratio of less than one to twenty, but it was none the less far too high for the custodians of Western Christian civilization.

Battered by the Depression and demands from many of their supporters for a new reconciliation of English and Afrikaner, Hertzog and Smuts formed the Fusion Government in 1933, with a final solution to the ever-present 'native problem' as a primary objective. But the more militant Afrikaners saw this compromise as a conspiracy of British capitalism, securing power once again through the sacrifice of only some non-white rights, and under the leadership of Dr Malan they withdrew in 1934 to form the Purified National Party. Two years later the new Hertzog government used its now overwhelming majority in parliament to alter the constitution and deprive the African in the Cape of his vote on the common roll.

With the Nazis, now in control of Germany, putting into effect their racist doctrines against the Jews, Dr Malan's National Party worked itself up into an anti-Semitic hysteria, while various fascist groups – the Grey-shirts, the Blackshirts, the Brownshirts – sprouted in its shade. In 1938 the centenary celebrations of the Great Trek swept Afrikanerdom with racist fervour, and Dr Malan appealed to the spirit of Blood River in a new Great Trek to assure white civilization. When, at the beginning of September 1939, German forces invaded Poland, the government split, with Hertzog favouring neutrality and Smuts a declaration of war; Hertzog submitted his policy to parliament, in a speech that defended the German invasion, and was defeated by 80 votes to 67.[1]

While the new government under Smuts prosecuted the war, Hertzog and Malan led the Reunited National Party in parliament, and the Ossewabrandwag,[2] founded in 1938 to perpetuate the spirit of the Great Trek and now a movement of semi-secret subversion, recruited some 300,000 members. The National Party itself fathered a draft constitution for a totalitarian republic, and though the prosperity brought by the war gave Smuts a massive victory in the 1943 elections, Malan's parliamentary following – Hertzog himself had died an abandoned and bitter man in 1942 – substantially increased. With peace declared, white South Africa returned whole-heartedly to its racial preoccupations, but found itself in a somewhat different world. The Smuts government's move in 1946 to restrict the purchase of land by Indians led to a trade boycott by India, and criticism of the country's racial policies, in South-west Africa no less than at home, was raised in the United Nations Organization.

The National Party campaigned in the 1948 election on the policy of 'apartheid' – a yet more rigorous separation of the various racial groups from each other – and won, with its allies, a narrow majority. A spate of racist laws followed, forbidding sexual relations or marriage between white and non-white, enforcing the segregation of residential areas, introducing racial identity cards, and still further controlling the movements of Africans. The African National Congress, which since its establishment in 1912 had confined itself to entreaty and constitutional protest, joined with the South African Indian Congress to launch in 1952 a Defiance of Unjust Laws Campaign, during which some 8,000 volunteers went to prison for

[1] For an excellent treatment of the years from Fusion to the outbreak of war, read *Hofmeyr*, by Alan Paton (O.U.P., 1965), pp. 198–323.
[2] Literally, 'oxwaggon-guard'.

having deliberately broken one or other of the racist laws. The government responded by introducing fierce new penalties, and the campaign spluttered to a close in rioting and gunfire.

In 1955 Dr Malan gave way to J. G. Strijdom and a new phase of racist repression. Mounting non-white unrest was ruthlessly crushed; new laws were passed to protect white command of skills; and parliament was packed to remove the coloured voter from the common roll. Then, in 1958, Dr Verwoerd, Minister of Native Affairs since 1950, who had openly published Nazi propaganda in his newspaper during the war, succeeded to the Nationalist leadership. The new administration, concerned both about increasing hostility abroad and continuing non-white unrest at home, applied itself more diligently than its predecessors had done to dressing up the practice of white supremacy in the propaganda of 'separate development'. Official doctrine emerged as the establishment of tribal homelands or 'Bantustans' for the Africans in the existing Reserves; but official policy remained, as ever, the provision of cheap labour to the white areas, with the rigid denial of all civil rights to the non-whites and the containment of their disaffection by force.

The commitment to intimidating force was stridently displayed in March 1960 at Sharpeville, some forty miles from Johannesburg, when police fired repeatedly into a peaceful African protest meeting, killing nearly seventy men, women and children. Even the white West was stirred for a moment out of its indifference, and widespread non-white demonstrations erupted in several South African cities. The government declared a state of emergency, outlawed the African political movements, and detained several thousand men and women. Within a few months, this repression had begun to restore the confidence of foreign investors, but it had also confirmed the younger African leadership in their belief that violent resistance was necessary. In December 1961 several acts of sabotage announced the existence of 'The Spear of the Nation', a movement allied to the African National Congress.

By now, however, white opposition to the Nationalist government had all but ceased to exist beyond the formalities of parliamentary debate. Successive general elections had only increased the Nationalist majority in parliament, while the distracted opposition United Party was reduced to trying to rake the government from the right. In November 1960, an all-white referendum had given Afrikanerdom its long-wanted republic, by 850,000 to 775,000 white votes, and the subsequent departure of South Africa from the Commonwealth had produced little more than a few wary demonstrations of English-speaking distress. B. J. Vorster, who had been interned during the war as a member of the Ossewabrandwag, was made Minister of Justice, and his hand could be detected in the new efficiency of the political police, with the new techniques of torture that they employed. Against the increasingly hostile front of the non-white world and its majority in the United Nations General Assembly, white South Africa put its trust in the indulgence of the white West – whose investors continued to receive a comforting return on their confidence – and in its own rearmament programme. A defence budget which had stood at £18 million in 1958–9, reached £60 million in 1962–3, and in 1965–6 some £115 million, or ten times the average expenditure a year promised for the whole policy of separate development.

Portugal, too, was finding it necessary to use more and more force in protecting her rule. The years before the Second World War had produced little change in the primitive exploitation of the African empire, though Portugal had increased her income from the export of labourers to the South African mines. It was the war and above all the booming commodity markets of its aftermath – Angolan coffee at one stage produced 60 per cent of Portugal's foreign exchange – that brought bustle at last to the colonies, and with it the flow of white immigrants. In 1940 there were 44,000 whites in Angola; ten years later, 79,000; and ten years later again, 200,000. In Moçambique, white settlement rose from 27,500 in 1940 to 48,000 in 1950 and 85,000 in 1960. But this prosperity, with the proliferation of settler estates and labour needs, increased rather than diminished African distress. In Angola alone, labour recruiters received licences for 180,000 men in 1959, and 190,000 in 1960.

The presence of so many new white settlers, mainly from among the poor and uneducated Portuguese, inevitably hardened the racist mood in the territories, and the colour bar was raised everywhere, while informal curfews savaged the lives of Africans in the towns. Imperial mythology projected the colonies as 'overseas provinces' of Portugal, with citizenship rights – such as they were in the New State of Salazar – open to Africans who qualified as civilized. But the policy of assimilation clearly suffered from a congenital lassitude; after four hundred years of activity, the percentage of Africans in 1950 whose civilization had been officially acknowledged was 0.74 in Angola, 0.44 in Moçambique, and 0.29 in Portuguese Guinea.

African despair first exploded in Luanda on February 4th, 1961, when Africans stormed the jail and police barracks. Portuguese security forces crushed the rioting, but this did not console the settlers for their shaken self-assurance, and white gangs repeatedly raided the African slums, killing and pillaging, or roamed the streets at night attacking all Africans they found. Then, on March 15th, African labourers organized by the União das Populacões de Angola (U.P.A.), an illegal, largely peasant movement, attacked white settlers on a coffee plantation in the north of Angola. Settlers near by shot at their suddenly rebellious serfs, and Africans throughout the region rose in organized bands to attack all whites they could find. Troops arrived to put down the rebellion, and the Angolan war had begun.

The Portuguese government blamed the rebellion on Communists without and Protestant missionaries within, and applied its propaganda efforts to establishing the image of a civilized and white Christian Portugal confronted by a savage heathen and black Africa. This was race war, undisguised. There were public references to a war of extermination,[1] and the Minister of Defence, presiding at the embarkation of soldiers for Angola, proclaimed: 'You are not going to fight against human beings, but against savages and wild beasts.'[2] By the end of the year, estimates for the number of Africans killed ranged from 10,000 to 30,000, while more than 150,000 had fled across the border into the Congo, many of them arriving mutilated, severely burnt or shot. Slowly Portugal pacified most of the coffee areas, but even her 50,000 troops in the territory[3] could not crush the rebellion altogether, and guerilla soldiers continued to operate from the forests along the Congolese frontier.

Rebellion broke out, too, thousands of miles to the north-west, in Portuguese Guinea – at first, in July 1960, on a small and manageable scale, and then, from 1963, on a much wider front, till insurgents could claim 40 per cent of the territory and the Portuguese government itself concede a figure of 20 per cent.[4] Then, in September 1964, African unrest in Moçambique caught fire, and though Portuguese troops were able to prevent any serious spread, rebels with support from training camps in neighbouring Tanganyika soon held a substantial stretch of the frontier north, while acts of terrorism – if still sparse – occurred in the centre of the territory.

By 1964, Portugal, a backward country with one of the highest infant mortality rates (73 per 1,000) in Europe, was spending well over a third of her total budget on the armed forces. But wars in three colonies did not discourage Western support for a member of the North Atlantic Treaty

[1] J. Duffy, op. cit., p. 216.
[2] 'The Torment of Angola', by the Rev. Clifford J. Parsons, in *Africa South*, Vol. 5, No. 4, July–Sept., 1961, p. 80.
[3] *The Economist*, March 28th, 1964, p. 1198.
[4] *The Economist*, August 7th, 1965, p. xxvi.

Organization, whose signatories are 'determined to safeguard the freedom, common heritage and civilization of their peoples, founded on the
principles of democracy, individual liberty and the rule of law'. While
the black states of Africa were assisting the black rebels with money,
equipment and training facilities, the white states of the West, collectively
through NATO or individually through loans and investments, were shoring up the white military power of imperial Portugal. After reporting the
fortification of 'considerable foreign credits', The Times of London saw
Dr Salazar as 'able to begin his new year with certain optimism – and no
doubt with a justifiably cynical glance at his detractors'.[1] The Africans,
rebels and allies, were no doubt casting an equally cynical glance at the
dedication of white men to democracy, individual liberty and the rule of
law.

Certainly, there can be few instances in African history of a cynicism so
bland as that which produced the white-dominated federation in Central
Africa. As early as 1936 settler representatives from the two Rhodesias had
met and demanded the amalgamation of the two territories; but the
Bledisloe Commission, appointed two years later, had reported too strong
an opposition from Africans. The war with its tumultuous aftermath had
then brought unprecedented prosperity – and thousands of whites – to the
Northern Rhodesia Copperbelt, and the settler support for some form of
Rhodesian union grew; the whites in the South would be able to command the wealth of the Copperbelt, and the whites in the North would
loose themselves from Colonial Office control by association with the
self-governing colony of Southern Rhodesia. The British Labour government saw substantial economic advantages in a federation of the two
Rhodesias and the tediously poor Nyasaland, but found some difficulty in
ignoring the open display of African antagonism; the Conservative
government, elected in 1951, was less sensitive, and hastened decision. To
protests that Africans in the two Northern territories were united in their
opposition; that Africans in Southern Rhodesia had not even been consulted; and that Britain was intending to do now what she had done so
calamitously in South Africa over forty years before – surrender African
interests to the control of white settlers – government spokesmen argued
that the new state would be committed to a policy of racial 'partnership'
and that the duty of a trustee was to act for the benefit of his ward, even if
the ward had his own very different ideas.[2]

The proposed Federal parliament would have thirty-five members, of

---

[1] April 22nd, 1965.
[2] Said also by The Times in a leader of January 22nd, 1952.

whom only nine would represent Africans (too few to block any constitutional change), while an African Affairs Board (which Sir Godfrey
Huggins, Prime Minister of Southern Rhodesia, called 'a little piece of
Gilbert and Sullivan'[1]) would refer laws which discriminated against
Africans to Britain for final decision. Last-minute appeals and deputations
from Africans had no effect; a Labour amendment disapproving of the
scheme because it provided inadequate safeguards for African interests and
was being promoted 'against the will of the African people', was defeated
in the House of Commons; and Southern Rhodesia, in a referendum
effectively limited to whites, voted by some 25,500 to 14,700 for membership of the Federation. The large white opposition vote in Southern
Rhodesia, rejecting even the façade of racial partnership in the Federal
constitution, hardly boded well for African advancement.

Power soon scattered whatever illusions still lingered. By 1956, Sir
Roy Welensky, Federal Prime Minister, felt secure enough to dispense
with the humbug. 'We Europeans have no intention of handing over the
Federation to anyone, because we have no intention of getting out. We
believe that the African should be given more say in the running of his
country, as and when he shows his ability to contribute more to the
general good, but we must make it clear that even when that day comes,
in a hundred or two hundred years' time, he can never hope to dominate
the partnership.'[2] In 1957, changes in the Federal parliament, which effectively reduced African representation and were referred by the African
Affairs Board to Westminster, were allowed by the British government.

On the Copperbelt, where African miners earned a tenth of what
white miners did and were shut out by white trade union hostility from
the main skilled jobs, unrest spread from strikes to demonstrations. In
Southern Rhodesia, an African National Congress was established in 1957
to agitate for change, and African disaffection broke the long-still surface
of apathy with meetings and protests. Then, in July 1958, Dr Banda
arrived in Nyasaland to take over the leadership of the African National
Congress in the territory, and dedicate himself publicly to break the
Federation; popular resentment centred round him, tension steadily
increased, and by the early months of 1959 there was intermittent rioting.
The Governor summoned white troops from Southern Rhodesia, declared a state of emergency, and arrested several hundred Congress
leaders. Widespread demonstrations followed, and before they were

[1] *The Times*, October 13th, 1952.
[2] Speaking at an election meeting in Que Que on March 2nd, 1956. Quoted in *Year of
Decision*, by Philip Mason (O.U.P., 1960), p. 69.

reduced, some fifty Africans had been killed and many more injured. In Southern Rhodesia, the government declared a state of emergency, outlawed the African National Congress, detained hundreds of its leaders and sympathizers, and rushed through parliament a series of crudely repressive laws. In Northern Rhodesia the Governor banned the militant Zambia African National Congress, arrested its leaders and rusticated them to remote parts of the territory. The edifice of racial partnership was in unmistakable ruins.

The British government made much of a plot by the Nyasaland Congress to murder whites, but its evidence was so threadbare and its declarations so theatrical that it could scarcely disguise its own embarrassment. Britain was still ultimately responsible for both Nyasaland and Northern Rhodesia, and 1959 was late in history for another Kenyan adventure. Nor would complete abdication to white settlerdom suit surviving African interests or the overall strategy of the West. Moreover, liberal and Church opinion at home was growing restless; the promise of federation had not encompassed mass detentions and rule by rifle. The British government decided to switch course. The Devlin Commission of Inquiry, which it appointed to consider the Nyasaland disturbances, uncovered no evidence of a murder plot, but reported much popular hostility to federation and criticized Nyasaland as 'a police state'. The Monckton Commission, appointed to advise on any constitutional changes for the federation, recommended drastic franchise reforms to produce the substance of partnership, and the right of secession by any individual territory as a last resort. In Welensky's own rancorous words, 'those who had created the Federation ... passed sentence of death on it ... The British Government wanted it all done smoothly, with a lot of noble sentiments ... and the minimum financial cost and moral and political discredit for themselves.'[1] While the federal leadership issued sporadic – and empty – threats of a settler rebellion, the British government speedily set about transferring to African hands the power it had previously given to white ones.

In November 1962 agreement on a constitution for a self-governing Nyasaland was reached in London, and in February of the following year Banda became the territory's first Prime Minister. In Northern Rhodesia, with its copper wealth and large white settler community, progress was slower and more insidious. By the end of 1962, a nationalist African coalition was in command of the territory, and at the end of the following year the Federation disintegrated. With Nyasaland (as Malawi) and Northern Rhodesia (as Zambia) both assuming independence, by the end

[1] *4,000 Days*, by Sir Roy Welensky (Collins, 1964), pp. 283–4.

of 1964 almost all Africa north of Southern Rhodesia had been formally decolonized. But the meaning of such decolonization, the independence and security of African government, remained uncertain. Affecting opinion and events not only in Africa but all over the world was the course of the Congo crisis.

Belgium herself never contemplated independence for the Congo; she simply supposed that she would somehow always have final responsibility. She was, therefore, at best warily paternalist, encouraging primary education or technical training, and providing in her colonial cities better African housing than most other territories could boast, but neglecting secondary and higher education – there were only twenty African university graduates among some 13,500,000 Congolese in 1960 – and admitting Africans as a rule only to the lower ranks of administration. The thousands of white settlers were denied any formal role in government as well but they constituted a class of obvious privilege none the less, with their informal influence on the administration, their high living standards, and the multitude of social barriers that they raised to secure their sense of superiority. Even many of the 7,000 missionaries, while performing determined service in hospital and school, displayed their contempt for Africans so culturally remote that the less polished settlers commonly called them *macaques* or monkeys.

Yet the continental currents of African nationalism did not bypass the Congo. In 1950 a group of Bakongo, in Leopoldville Province, formed a cultural association known as *Abako*, which within six years, under the leadership of Joseph Kasavubu, became a political party in all but name. The Belgians attempted to meet the mounting political pressures by introducing popular elections for the major urban councils, but these did no more than excite the appetite for significant advance. Then, in August 1958, General de Gaulle visited Brazzaville, just across the river from the capital, and offered the French Congo a choice by free vote between independence and autonomous membership of a French Community. The effect on African opinion in the Belgian Congo was massive and immediate; prominent *évolués*, led by Patrice Lumumba, demanded moves towards independence and formed the Mouvement National Congolais (M.N.C.) to promote their demands. The governing party of Ghana was meanwhile organizing an All-African Peoples' Conference in Accra to co-ordinate the struggle for independence in the surviving colonies, and this Lumumba attended in December, to be deeply impressed by the mass movement which Nkrumah had created and the unitary state which he had, despite tribal divisions, shaped. On his return to Leopoldville,

Lumumba addressed a frantic meeting and called for independence as a right, not a gift; violent rioting in the city followed on January 4th, 1959, set off by a march of several thousand unemployed, and some two hundred Africans were killed in firing by the Force Publique. With disorders spreading in the months following to different parts of the country, the Belgian government at last agreed to call a Round Table Conference at Brussels in January 1960.

In Katanga, the copper-rich province which accounted for a third of the country's whole domestic production, 40–50 per cent of its foreign trade, and 40 per cent of the public revenue, the dominant settler community viewed developments with alarm. In October 1958 *Conakat* was formed, with the base of its popular support among the Balunda of southern Katanga but with close supervision and assistance from the local whites,[1] and in 1959 this began to advocate provincial autonomy for Katanga and close ties with Belgium.

The Congolese delegates to the Round Table Conference, though from different and even hotly rival parties, formed a common front and so wrested from the Belgian government a promise of independence by the end of June 1960. The delegates differed sharply, however, over the proposed constitution; *Conakat*, at the one extreme, demanded a confederation, with each province in control particularly of its natural resources, while the M.N.C., at the other, demanded a strong unitary state with command of all the riches in it. In the end, though the six provinces were given minor powers the central government was invested with the major and all residual ones. The Congo was to be a single state because the Belgians had developed it as such; the provinces were economically interdependent, with an overall system of communications, so that even Katanga copper was shipped from Matadi near Leopoldville, not through the nearer Portuguese ports, and industry was centred in Leopoldville and Elisabethville to supply the whole country.

The Belgians had decided in panic to yield. They were not prepared to face the prospect of a costly and endless colonial war; but they were not prepared either to make the massive effort of help which so many years of

---

[1] To what degree *Conakat* was controlled by white settlers from the beginning is disputed. Catherine Hoskyns in *The Congo Since Independence* suggests that the movement was founded because of tribal rivalries and then 'worked closely with the various European organizations'. Conor Cruise O'Brien (*New Left Review*, No. 31, May–June 1965, London, p. 6) agrees with the Belgian journalist, Pierre Davister, who supported Katangese separatism and claimed that the Europeans virtually established *Conakat* themselves to provide in tribal rivalries an answer to black nationalism (*Katanga; enjeu du monde*, Editions Europe-Afrique, Brussels, 1960, pp. 52–3, 67).

complacency and neglect now made necessary. Nowhere was this more evident than in their attitude to the Force Publique, the 25,000-strong army responsible for maintaining internal order, where all the positions of command were held by Belgians and no steps were taken to counter rising African unrest by appointing African officers. The commander himself, General Emile Janssens, was a fervent paternalist and did little to conceal the disquiet with which he viewed the transfer of power to a pack of black politicians. The Belgians were concerned now only to protect their huge financial stake in the Congo – variously estimated, but certainly in excess of £1,500 million – and hoped that the Parti National du Progrès (P.N.P.), a federation of 'moderate' tribal and traditionalist groups financed and guided by the administration, would win the general election of May 1960.

The P.N.P., however, did badly, and it was Lumumba's M.N.C., with almost twice as many votes as its nearest contender, and with support in several provinces, that emerged as the dominant political party. But the results also showed firm regional differences, with *Abako* successful in the Leopoldville area and *Conakat* successful in Katanga. The Belgians might yet have prevented the worst consequences of their errors by throwing their support whole-heartedly behind Lumumba; instead, they tried to manœuvre Kasavubu into the premiership and gave up only when it was apparent that Lumumba controlled a majority in Parliament. When at last a compromise was reached by which Kasavubu became President and Lumumba Prime Minister, trust in Belgian intentions, already worn thin by events in Katanga, had all but gone.

Of the sixty seats in the provincial assembly of Katanga, *Conakat* controlled thirty-eight, and the opposition *Balubakat* the remainder; but under the constitution, the assembly could not operate if less than two-thirds of the members were present, and the *Balubakat* deputies, convinced that *Conakat* was plotting secession, refused to take their seats. The Belgian parliament then amended the constitution on June 15th, without consulting the Congolese leaders, to enable a provincial assembly to elect its government with only a majority of the members present, and on the following day Moise Tshombe formed a wholly *Conakat* administration.

On June 30th the Congo celebrated independence, and on July 4th the disaffection in the African ranks of the Force Publique, detonated by a lecture from General Janssens, which ordered absolute obedience and offered no reforms,[1] became mutiny. There were attacks on whites, a few cases of rape, but no widespread violence, and the dismissal of Janssens

[1] Janssens actually wrote on a blackboard: 'before independence = after independence'.

with the promotion of Africans seemed to calm the soldiers. But reports exaggerated the violence; whites began leaving or arming themselves; incidents multiplied as units of the Force Publique were swept by rumours of white plans to seize power; and on July 10th the first Belgian troops intervened. Lumumba, who with Kasavubu had succeeded in restoring order among the soldiers in the Lower Congo and was convinced that negotiation would suffice, was furious and broadcast his protest. Peace might even yet have been restored, but then, on July 11th, Belgian forces entered the port of Matadi – though the situation there was quiet now – and in the fighting that followed killed twelve Congolese soldiers. That evening Tshombe declared Katanga independent, and though Belgian forces controlled the Elisabethville airport, Lumumba and Kasavubu were refused permission to land. The Congolese leaders became convinced that the Belgians were attempting to seize control of the country, and they appealed to the United Nations for help.

In the United Nations Security Council the two Afro-Asian states (Tunisia and Ceylon), supported by the two communist members and Ecuador, clearly considered that Belgium was guilty of aggression; the four Western representatives (the permanent three and Italy) did not. In the end, a Tunisian resolution, calling upon Belgium to withdraw her troops and authorizing military assistance to the Congolese government, was passed, with Britain, France and China (Taiwan) abstaining. Meanwhile the Matadi intervention had inflamed Force Publique units throughout the country, and the soldiers set out not only to disarm the whites, but hurt and humiliate them. Atrocities certainly occurred, but they were not limited to the Congo; most of the major Western newspapers went on the rampage, devoting more attention to the violence of black against white in the Congo than they had ever done to the decades of white violence against black there. There is no attempt to diminish the anguish of those involved, of course, in recording that violence reached nothing like the extent so authoritatively reported; a subsequent Belgian Commission of Inquiry established fifty-two cases of rape in this whole period of turbulence. It is, indeed, reasonable to argue on the evidence that Belgian intervention sacrificed more lives – even white ones – than it saved, by provoking the very racial passions that it was apparently initiated to control. That the intervention itself was without justification in terms of the new constitutional relationship between Belgium and the Congo, the Belgians themselves admitted by arguing instead that they had the right under international law to act in a foreign country for the protection of their nationals. There is little doubt that the West would have denounced such a doctrine had the colours of the two peoples concerned in these events been switched.

The secession of Katanga received wide public support in Belgium, but the government, aware of the international repercussions that recognition might produce, contented itself with giving all possible military and administrative assistance to the Tshombe regime. Soldiers and officials loyal to the central government were arrested or dismissed, and critical civilians expelled, with the use of Belgian troops. Even the right-wing *Daily Telegraph* in London,[1] importunately sympathetic to Katangese independence, called it a 'masquerade', with Tshombe 'under the domination of Belgian officials', and his regime entirely dependent on 'Belgian arms, men and money'. By the end of July, U.N. troops had entered every province of the Congo but Katanga, and the central government under Lumumba, with support from the more radical Afro-Asian states and the communist bloc, was accusing the U.N. Secretariat of too avid a concern with Belgian and other Western susceptibilities. A Security Council resolution of August 9th, sponsored by Tunisia and Ceylon and passed with only France and Italy abstaining, called for the withdrawal of Belgian troops from Katanga but reaffirmed that the U.N. should not intervene in any internal conflict. Relations between Hammarskjöld and Lumumba deteriorated further, especially after Hammarskjöld visited Elisabethville without consulting the central government. The U.N. was certainly acting in the Congo more and more as an independent agency, though the crucial Security Council resolution of July 14th had authorized the Secretary-General to act 'in consultation with' the central government, providing it with technical and military assistance till 'the national security forces may be able, in the opinion of the government, to meet fully their tasks'. Hammarskjöld's report to the Council that the dispute with Katanga 'did not have its root in the Belgian attitude' was clearly absurd, and his treatment of the Tshombe regime as a factor outside the scope of the central government was a virtual accession to the wishes of the West. The truth is that the Secretariat, for all its outward deference to the Afro-Asian states during the Congo crisis, was dominated by the West, especially the United States, and responsive to its view of events.

Lumumba resolved to take the necessary action himself. The Congolese army, with some urgently supplied Soviet equipment, invaded Katanga and diamond-rich Kasai (which had also seceded), and its many acts of gratuitous violence against civilians were carefully recorded in the Western press. The Tshombe regime in Katanga set out, with Belgian

[1] July 27th, 1960.

troops, to pacify the hostile Baluba north; its assaults on villages were carefully ignored in the West. The employment by Lumumba of Soviet support widely inflamed Western opinion as importing the Cold War into Africa; the continuing presence of Belgian troops and administrators in Katanga was, for the same wide stretch of Western opinion, part of a popular struggle to sustain peace and good government in the ocean of Congo chaos.

Kasavubu and Lumumba were meanwhile drawing apart – there can be no doubt that Western hostility to Lumumba was at least in part responsible – and on September 5th Kasavubu invoked his powers under the constitution to dismiss Lumumba as Prime Minister. Lumumba then dismissed Kasavubu as President, and with the two Congolese leaders in open conflict, the U.N. Command seized control of the airport and radio station in Leopoldville. Whether or not such was its deliberate purpose, the U.N. action clearly favoured Kasavubu, whose source of power was in the city and whose friendship with the President of the formerly French Congo gave him access to the near-by Radio Brazzaville. The U.N. had refused to involve itself in the Katanga dispute, since this was an internal conflict, and had then openly involved itself in the dispute between Lumumba and Kasavubu on the pretext of preventing civil war. The Congolese parliament speedily intervened to resolve the crisis and confirm both Lumumba and Kasavubu in their offices. Lumumba seemed to have successfully survived the sudden threat to his position. But the Congolese army was growing uneasy meanwhile, since the soldiers had not been paid for some time; on September 10th Colonel Joseph Mobutu presided at a pay parade with money provided by the U.N., and four days later announced that he was assuming power. U.N. and Western embassy officials, some of whom seem to have expected, if not nourished, something of the sort, were delighted. Constitutional government was at an end in the Congo, and Lumumba ousted at last from power.

Radical African states like Guinea, Ghana and the United Arab Republic, with troops in the U.N. Force, were reluctant to assail the United Nations, which they saw as a protection against the great powers, but they showed themselves increasingly disturbed. The Soviet Union was by now openly hostile to Hammarskjöld and the conduct of the U.N. in the Congo, and vetoed compromise resolutions before the Security Council. The General Assembly was therefore summoned under the 'Uniting for Peace' formula on September 17th, and an Afro-Asian resolution adopted which saved the face of the Secretary-General but requested him to 'assist the Central Government of the Congo in the restoration and maintenance of law and order throughout the Republic of the Congo and to safeguard its unity, territorial integrity and political independence'. Hammarskjöld, smarting under Afro-Asian suspicions, set about trying to achieve the removal of Belgian forces from Katanga but met with no response from Brussels, and when the Secretariat began moving towards some accommodation with Lumumba, the U.S. State Department protested. It was clearly one thing to support the U.N. when it acted as the West desired, and quite another when it took uncongenial directions. After a General Assembly vote, produced by intense Western lobbying and pressures, to seat a Kasavubu delegation, not a Lumumba one, as officially representing the Congo, Lumumba seems to have given up all hope of a constitutional return to power and, on November 27th, fled from Leopoldville, hoping to reach Stanleyville, his stronghold, and organize his national support from there. He was captured by Congolese soldiers in Kasai, and when Ghanaian troops in the area requested U.N. permission to rescue him, this was refused. Several Afro-Asian states subsequently demanded to know why a U.N. Command that had closed the Leopoldville airport and radio in the interests of law and order could not rescue and protect Lumumba for the same reason.

Mobutu's authority was crumbling, and even in Leopoldville Province, crowds were shouting for Lumumba. On January 17th, 1961, Lumumba was flown to Katanga, apparently on the orders of Kasavubu, and there killed 'in the presence' – according to the subsequent U.N. Commission of Investigation – 'of high officials of the government of Katanga province'. The murder led to much more than marches and demonstrations in thirty cities, expressions of outrage by Afro-Asian governments, and a further sapping of confidence in the United Nations by many of the newly independent states. Lumumba may have been killed by blacks, but they were blacks ultimately under the control of whites, while the situation out of which the murder almost inevitably arose had been shaped in major measure by the policies of the white West inside and outside the United Nations. At the Security Council meeting of February 15th, a group of American Negroes demonstrated from the public gallery against their government's policy over the Congo.

The more militant of the Afro-Asian states were beginning to withdraw their troops from the U.N. Congo Command or threatening to do so, while Antoine Gizenga, Deputy Premier in Lumumba's government, was in firm control of the Stanleyville regime. The United States, which had acquired a Democratic administration in the previous November, now viewed with alarm the possibility of a civil war in the Congo, with the Lumumbists supported by a number of African states and the Soviet bloc. The American government accordingly supported the Afro-Asian sponsored Security Council resolution of February 21st, which authorized the U.N. to use force as a last resort to prevent civil war; urged the U.N. to take measures for the immediate removal from the Congo of 'all Belgian and other foreign military and paramilitary personnel and political advisers not under the U.N. Command'; and urged the convening of the Congolese parliament. After all, Lumumba himself was now dead.

Parliament met at last under U.N. protection, but without the participation of the Tshombe deputies, in July. The sessions disclosed a small Lumumbist majority but elected a compromise candidate, Cyrille Adoula, as Prime Minister, and Stanleyville recognized the new government as one pledged to end the secession of Katanga. Meanwhile, however, the Katanga secessionists, far from encouraging reconciliation, were hastily adding to their resources of Belgian military and technical personnel several hundred white mercenaries, mainly from Southern Africa but also from among the French diehards in Algeria, who were known even among local whites as 'les affreux', the terrible ones.[1] Negotiations with the Tshombe regime to expel all foreign personnel encountered in the main refusals or evasions, and on August 28th U.N. forces in Katanga began arresting white advisers and mercenaries. Though such action had clearly been implied by the Security Council resolution of February, a shrill protest rose from Tshombe's assemblage of allies from Salisbury to London. The British government complained to Hammarksjöld that 'there was no mandate for the removal of essential foreign civilians which might lead to a breakdown of the administration of the Katanga', while the Western diplomatic representatives in Elisabethville, with the exception of the Americans who were now backing the U.N., made clear their support for Tshombe. The significance was lost neither on Tshombe himself nor on his white advisers, now in hiding, whose incipient co-operation gave way to violent hostility. While more than 20,000 Baluba refugees from the Tshombe regime sought U.N. protection at a camp in Elisabethville, Western newspapers trumpeted the cause of Katanga democracy. Tshombe's gendarmerie increasingly attacked U.N. personnel, and on September 13th, 1961, U.N. forces moved to take control of the

---

[1] The *Sunday Telegraph*, November 26th, 1961, preferred to call them 'unlikely unshaven Galahads [who] alone in this tortured continent are ready to shed their blood in the cause of non-racialism'.

most important public buildings. Fighting broke out; Tshombe visited the British consul and emerged with a determination to resist. Hammar-skjöld himself decided to meet Tshombe in Northern Rhodesia to discuss a cease-fire, but his plane crashed near Ndola on September 17th. A cease-fire was subsequently agreed, and Katanga secessionists settled down to enjoy their triumph over the U.N.

Even the generally moderate African states like Ethiopia and Nigeria were now demanding strong action against Tshombe; the United States saw a continuing danger in Stanleyville, but could hardly expect moves against the regime there, while the foreign-backed secession in Elisabeth-ville continued to prosper; and Britain was at last listening less to the copper lobby in London and more to the outrage at her Congo policies among the non-white members of the Commonwealth. On November 24th the Security Council passed a new resolution, with the abstention of Britain and France, strongly deprecating 'the secessionist activities illegally carried out by the provincial administration of Katanga, with the aid of external resources and manned by foreign mercenaries'; declared that such activities should cease; and authorized vigorous action to expel, with force if necessary, foreign personnel and mercenaries. After a series of incidents U.N. forces on December 4th, with the help of American air-craft, began military measures against the Tshombe regime, and this time the outcry in Britain, France and Belgium did not halt operations. On December 21st Tshombe signed a declaration which effectively renounced Katanga's secession, and troops of the central government then arrested Gizenga in Stanleyville.

While Gizenga was in jail, however, Tshombe was at liberty in Elisa-bethville and soon enough again in command, with the huge copper revenues of Katanga paying the host of white advisers who staffed his administration and the mercenaries who officered his gendarmerie. More-over, though American aid streamed into Leopoldville, the Adoula regime revealed only a diminishing ability to maintain law and order or mobilize popular support. Lumumbist resistance persisted in many areas, encouraging a dangerously unWestern intervention, and no pretence at stability or independence could be projected while Katanga secession effectively survived. Talks between Tshombe and Adoula, repeatedly interrupted, broke down altogether in June 1962, and the U.N. Secre-tariat, under the control now of U Thant, proposed economic pressures to end 'the delays and evasive tactics so artfully deployed by M. Tshombe'. At last, on December 27th, heavy fighting broke out in Elisabethville between Katanga forces and U.N. troops, and despite Tshombe's threats that the people of Katanga would defend their independence at all costs, the Katanga gendarmerie dispersed into the bush or, with most of the mercenaries, retreated to Angola. On January 15th, 1963, Tshombe himself, who had taken sanctuary in Salisbury, announced that he was ready to end the secession of Katanga, and this time was given no chance to do anything else.

If the West now supposed that the Congo under Adoula's supervision would be a manageable client, however, it was seriously mistaken. Lumumba dead was proving to be much less destructible than Lumumba alive, and political heirs proclaimed themselves everywhere, sapping what little stability the regime still possessed. In September 1963 Kasavubu abruptly dissolved parliament, and a number of Lumumbist deputies, including Christophe Gbenye, fled across the river to Brazzaville, where rebellion had displaced the regime so friendly to Tshombe and the West by a much more radical one. There the Lumumbists established the Committee of National Liberation, and in the following months insurrection, not always connected with the C.N.L., spread beyond the capacity of the central government to control. By July 1964, with large areas of Leopoldville Province, Kasai, Kivu and Katanga in rebel hands, and with the U.N. forces withdrawn by the financial crisis facing the organization, the Leopoldville regime was distraught. At last, with the West in search of anyone politically congenial who seemed able to produce stability by compromise, cunning, or force, Tshombe himself became Kasavubu's new nominee as Prime Minister. His promise to reconcile the Congolese contenders, however, went little further than the release of Gizenga – who was subsequently to be placed under house arrest – and a visit to Stanleyville, where Tshombe laid a wreath at the Lumumba monument. But Tshombe's sudden appreciation of Lumumba left – not surprisingly – the rebels unaffected. In August Stanleyville fell to rebel forces, with many of the central government troops in the Eastern Province deserting to the enemy, and Washington grew alarmed at reports of Chinese assistance through embassies at Burundi and Brazzaville, as well as open support for the rebels by African states like Algeria and the United Arab Republic.

Tshombe increasingly resorted to the techniques which had proved so successful during the dog-days of Katanga secession; he recruited white mercenaries, repatriated many of his gendarmes from their refuge in Angola, and sought Western help for his bulwark against Communism. He solicited and received from Belgium the official services of Colonel Vanderwalle, who had been Consul-General at Elisabethville during secession, to reorganize the government forces, and put to effective use the planes and Cuban refugee pilots he received from the United States. By the late autumn, the mercenary commandos, with air support, were leaving in their wake a smoking desolation. The rebels in the Stanleyville area seized the 1,300 whites there as hostages and threatened to take reprisals unless a cease-fire was proclaimed. The Congo Reconciliation Commission appointed by the Organization of African Unity, with Kenya's Kenyatta at its head, excited negotiations, and then suddenly, on November 24th, 1964, Belgian paratroops, flown from British-controlled Ascension Island in American planes, were dropped on Stanleyville, to rescue the hostages. In the panic that followed, rebels killed some sixty whites.

While the Western press flung itself again into atrocity accounts and a general censure of African savagery, a group of states, mainly African and including such admitted moderates as Dahomey, Ethiopia, Malawi, the Sudan, and Uganda, summoned a meeting of the Security Council to discuss the Western intervention. In the debate that followed, one African representative after the other gave expression to a racial outrage with a bitterness and anger that showed how far the euphoria of decolonization had evaporated and how deeply the uninnocent realities of white power were resented.

'How can one speak of a blood bath which one has designed and caused, in one breath, and of humanitarianism in the other?' asked Mr Murumbi of Kenya. 'Where is this humanitarianism when the white mercenaries are allowed full licence to murder innocent African men, women and children? Where was this humanitarianism when Patrice Lumumba, later brutally done to death, was held hostage? ... What happened to this self-same humanitarianism when innocent Africans were butchered in Sharpeville in South Africa? Where is this humanitarianism when American Negroes are brutally done to death in Mississippi and elsewhere? It is a peculiar brand of humanitarianism coming from countries whose record and international behaviour do not entitle them to boast about their achievements.'[1]

Mr Mahgoub, of the Sudan, reminded the Council that his country had contributed troops to the U.N. Congo Command. 'But after all this, where do we find ourselves today? The answer is as simple as it is cruel; developments in the Congo have come full circle. The foreign mercenaries whom the United Nations took so much pain for so long to dislodge from their entrenched positions in the Congo are back; and they are back

[1] Security Council Debate, December 15th, 1964.

even in possibly greater numbers than ever before ... Conciliation and peace are definitely no part of their concepts.'[1]

African delegate after delegate took the floor to stress that the rescue operation had provoked, not prevented, the violence; that the negotiations being conducted by the O.A.U. Commission may well have succeeded; that the whites had been killed after the paratroops landed; and that the escape of the survivors had been ensured at the cost of killing numberless blacks. To the legal pretext for the intervention, the request for help made by the Congolese government, African delegates reminded the Council that the existence of the Tshombe regime depended not upon the approval of parliament, but upon the guns of the white mercenary commandos. And to the complaint that the rebels were receiving aid from outside the Congo came the repeated reply that aid had been streaming from outside to regimes without popular support in the Congo since independence.

That the killing – in some instances, mutilation – of unarmed whites by rebels in the Congo defied any excuse beyond the sheer human explanations of hatred and panic was nowhere denied by the Africans who spoke in the Security Council debate. But what civilized fastidiousness was this, that selected sixty whites for the sudden expression of outrage? What might not properly be said of a white West that made so much of so few now, and so little of so many in the months and years before? If the killing of sixty whites could be seen as so deep a descent by blacks into savagery, how were blacks to see the record of white rule in Africa, even yet being written in violence?

The past, of course, is the shrugged shoulders of another's responsibility. But what of the present? What 'mercy missions' are being mounted by the West to save the lives not of a few hundred, but of many thousand unarmed Africans under Portuguese fire in Angola? It is not even as though the principal representatives of the West at the United Nations admit any excuse for Portuguese rule. Yet they act none the less to sustain Portuguese violence, not only by supplies of credit and military equipment, but by concerted pressure to prevent the United Nations from intervening. How many innocent black victims of Portuguese terror have decorated the cover of *Time* or excited the moral sensibilities of the American State Department?

Mounting pressure by the world's coloured peoples for decisive action against South Africa is assiduously blocked by the West. Overwhelming votes at the United Nations condemn the South African government –

[1] Security Council Debate, December 9th, 1964.

for its racial persecution of the country's Indian community; its defiant refusal to surrender South-west Africa to international trusteeship; its open, indeed proud dedication to the principles and practice of white supremacy. In the debates on South African policy, no governments outstrip those of the West in the force of formal condemnation, even disgust. The racial provocation and human cost of 'apartheid' are not denied, are indeed even eagerly proclaimed by the West. In August 1963 the Security Council went so far as to declare itself convinced that 'the situation in South Africa is seriously disturbing international peace and security'. Yet to any demands for effective international intervention, the principal powers of the West oppose their votes or, where these do not suffice, their simple refusal to co-operate. In November 1962 the General Assembly called by 67 votes to 16, with 23 abstentions, for punitive measures – mainly economic sanctions – against South Africa. The West has ignored the call.

If any country on earth, by repeated Western admission, is guilty of racial violence, South Africa is. Yet what 'mercy missions' are being mounted by Western power to save the victims? The doctrine of domestic jurisdiction has not deterred intervention, covert and overt alike, when Western interests have demanded it, and in any event can scarcely be applied to a situation recognized by the Security Council as 'seriously disturbing international peace'. Moreover, the persistent refusal of South Africa to loosen its grip on the international mandate of South-west Africa – that 'sacred trust of civilization' – would provide the most tender conscience with an adequate moral and legal excuse. The truth is that, whatever their recorded opinions to the contrary, the principal powers of the West consider white persecution of blacks in South Africa far less culpable than they would any similar black persecution of whites. Can it reasonably be supposed, were the colours of oppressor and oppressed in South Africa switched, that the West would hesitate a moment to intervene?

This racially selective humanitarianism of the West, repeatedly displayed during the tumultuous years of 'decolonization', reached another peak of blatancy in the Rhodesian crisis. As far back as 1923 Britain effectively handed power in Southern Rhodesia to the small white settler minority, and though she retained the right to veto legislation, she never exercised it, even against the Land Apportionment Act of 1930 which set aside the best land in the territory for whites and totally excluded Africans from owning urban property. The federation with Northern Rhodesia and Nyasaland, advertised by its proponents as likely to produce a more liberal mood in the south, simply fidgeted with settler rule. When Garfield Todd, a former missionary who became Prime Minister of Southern Rhodesia, proposed that Africans elect five of the thirty-five members of parliament, he was driven from office, and his successor, Sir Edgar Whitehead, having used the Nyasaland emergency of 1959 to ban the territory's African National Congress and detain the leaders, introduced in 1960 a law which exacted the most savage penalties for the expression of African resistance. In the search for complete territorial independence from Britain, the Whitehead government negotiated in 1961 a new constitution, giving Africans fifteen of the sixty-five seats in parliament – a concession rejected as ultimately meaningless by the African nationalist leadership – and campaigned for the gradual dismantling of the Land Apportionment Act. But the white settler electorate was moving steadily to the right, and in 1962 swept to power the Rhodesian Front, a party dedicated to securing white rule and privilege for the indefinite future. With the collapse of the Federation at the end of 1963, therefore, independence in all but name – and, with British compliance, almost the whole strong Federal Air Force – went to a racial government in Rhodesia drawing ever closer to the South African pattern.

Within the Commonwealth and, more clamorously, at the United Nations, coloured and especially African states demanded intervention against the growing persecution of black by white in Southern Rhodesia. But to every demand Britain, strongly supported by her white allies, opposed the argument, careless of its inconsistency, that Rhodesia was a domestic British concern, since the territory was ultimately subject to the British parliament, and that the British parliament could not interfere, since Rhodesia was by long-established practice in control of her internal policies. Prevailing Western opinion seemed able easily enough to accommodate itself to the detention of some Africans, without charge or trial, for leadership of the opposition to white rule, and the imprisonment – or execution – of others for acts of resistance.

The regime of white domination in Rhodesia might accordingly well have survived for some years to come, under British protection and the United States desire for anti-communist stability in Africa, had the settlers themselves been satisfied with their effective independence. But the white electorate, impatient of any restraint, even on paper, and in haste to follow the prospering intransigence of South Africa, insisted on possessing the shadow as well as the substance. Britain, hard pressed by Afro-Asian opinion as she was, could scarcely withdraw her ultimate authority without seeming to ensure constitutional advance to majority rule. What had been done in South Africa more than half a century before could not be done with political safety now in the world of the 'sixties. But the settler leadership was obdurate; despite threats from Britain that any attempt to seize independence would be an act of rebellion, requiring immediate measures to restore constitutional government, it unilaterally declared Rhodesia independent on November 11th, 1965.

Acting swiftly to prevent a United Nations initiative, the British government, with ready support from the Western alliance, imposed economic sanctions on the rebel colony. Why – coloured and especially African nations wanted to know – did Britain refuse to use force? Rebellion in Kenya had found her less considerate of the human costs. Racial violence in British Guiana had, not long before, led to the unilateral suspension of a democratic constitution and the speedy dispatch of British troops. A short while before the Rhodesian rebellion, Britain had suspended the constitution of Aden, and had ever since been governing by martial law. Why, in any event, should economic sanctions be regarded as an effective substitute for force? When economic sanctions had been advocated at the United Nations as a way of dealing with the recalcitrant racism of South Africa, Britain had been foremost among the main Western states in questioning their efficacy. Had not sanctions, Britain had proclaimed, always failed? Could the clandestine activities of uncooperative nations, companies and individuals ever be adequately controlled? Could sanctions ever hope to succeed without an oil embargo, and was an oil embargo remotely practical? (Within a few weeks of the Rhodesian rebellion, Britain extended her economic sanctions to an oil embargo, and patrolled the Moçambique coast to note infringements.)

In anger at Britain's refusal to use force, and following a decision by foreign ministers in the Organization of African Unity, several African states, including Ghana and Tanzania from the Commonwealth, broke off diplomatic relations with her. And when in December the British Prime Minister, Harold Wilson, addressed the United Nations General Assembly, all but a handful of African delegations absented themselves or walked out of the chamber in protest. The black world of Africa, no less than the white world of Britain and her allies in the West, understood the racial bias which informed British government policy, whether Labour or Conservative in complexion.

The era of decolonization was revealing two – not unrelated – characteristics of Western policy towards Africa, both of them challenges to the whole meaning of African independence. The first was fundamentally racial. 'In international law', Mr Botsio of Ghana declared in the Security

Council debate on the Congo paratroop mission, 'the United States is no more entitled to intervention than would, say, Ghana be entitled to intervention in the Southern states of the United States of America to protect lives of Afro-American inhabitants of those states, who are, from time to time, tortured and murdered for asserting their legitimate rights and whose lives are entrusted to the United States government … If great powers can intervene at will if their nationals are experiencing any hardship in any country, then where is the security for smaller countries? If that is permissible, then not only the Congo but all Africa is exposed.'[1] The warning of Conor Cruise O'Brien[2] is ruthlessly relevant. 'Are white people in Africa to be regarded as covered by a sort of Caucasian providence insurance policy, with a guarantee that if the natives get rough, the metropolitan forces will once again come to the rescue? And if so, will this doctrine, in the long run, increase or decrease the security of white people in Africa and elsewhere? Similar policies in China contributed eventually to the total exclusion of all white influence, missionary or other, from that country.'

The second characteristic was a near-sighted attention to Western interests and influence. Lumumba's heady nationalism and Pan-Africanist commitment seemed to threaten at the time the security of the West's important economic stake in the Congo and the stability of countries to the south. The white settlers in Katanga, with the connivance – some would say, the material encouragement – of Union Minière, the huge Belgian mining company whose profits and influence stretch wide in the West, may well have been initially responsible for the province's secession; but it was the West itself, from the pressure of its press and financial lobbies on public opinion to the pressure of its government representatives at the United Nations, that allowed the secession to survive. Can it reasonably be supposed that Western power would have permitted the secession of Katanga for a few days, let alone years, if Lumumba had been head of the provincial administration and Tshombe himself the Prime Minister of the Congo? And then Lumumba, prevented by the influence of the principal Western states at the United Nations from enforcing the reintegration of the Congo, committed the ultimate crime of inviting communist assistance. Such an interpretation of independence was impermissible, and only his own removal from rule could lead to a Western accommodation with Congolese unity.

The Congo crisis, of course, has been only one instance among many of the close correlation between the extent of Western influence and the

<hr>

[1] December 9th, 1964.   [2] The *Observer*, December 6th, 1964.

degree of Western support or hostility. The Nkrumah government in Ghana was widely abused in the West for detaining political opponents without trial. Yet no such criticism attached to Nigeria, where Regional authorities imprisoned political dissent without trial, or with a mere travesty of one. But then Nkrumah had committed Ghana to socialism and international non-alignment, while Nigeria – until the sudden military coup of January 1966, a 'progressive democracy' – was Western in allegiance and securely, indeed flamboyantly, capitalist in commitment. The military regime of Nasser in Egypt has long been assailed for its authoritarianism, though it is the first government in Egyptian history dedicated to improving the condition of the peasant masses. The regime of the seven generals in the neighbouring Sudan, which was not only authoritarian but showed itself unable or unwilling to undertake the necessary rural revolution, escaped serious censure, even when it set about suppressing, with considerable violence, Negro disaffection in the south. But then the seven generals were not nationalizing foreign companies, or threatening Western influence – and Western wealth – in the Middle East and North Africa. (Hostility to Israel is no criterion; Jordan is amongst the top recipients *per capita* of Western aid.) The one-party state in Tanzania comes in for increasing criticism from the West, while neighbouring Kenya, where the intimidation of dissidence is much more substantial, seems increasingly exempt from attack. But then Tanzania's Julius Nyerere, once the favourite African leader of the West for his supposed moderation and international dependability, is a passionate Pan-Africanist, seems to be taking non-alignment and socialism seriously, and even accepts money and technical assistance from China, while Kenya's Jomo Kenyatta, once a 'leader to darkness and death', seems to have learnt the value of moderation, free enterprise and Western friendship.

Decolonization has, on the whole, been directed at producing a sort of local autonomy, an independence formally acknowledged but ultimately subject to Western supervision. In one African territory after the other, the West has shown itself concerned not to promote a dynamic society, committed to the economic advance of all its citizens, and strong in its allegiance to a general freedom, but a frontier of influence, guarded by those loyal to Western standards and, above all, ready to serve Western interests. This is not merely or always because the main Western states have substantial economic investments to protect. There are new African nations rich only in their needs. Nor is it significantly because a Western state like Gaullist France cherishes clients, for the sense yet of imperial importance. Ultimately it is because the West as a whole (and, within it, especially the United States) seeks traditional stability, wishing to pre-serve Africa as a sphere of influence lest communist competitors – China even more now than the Soviet Union – should gain political and eco-nomic footholds there instead.

The evangelical anti-communism of John Foster Dulles may no longer be the established policy of the United States. International non-align-ment is no longer seen as evil now. But it is still seen as dangerous – on the assumption that power, like any other part of nature, abhors a vacuum. It is not, therefore, neutralism in itself that the West distrusts (France for one is prepared to allow her clients to play at non-alignment, provided that she maintains an effective suzerainty) as much as the opportunity it is seen to provide for the free rivalry of international power groups. Lumumba was blamed above all for importing the Cold War into Africa by inviting Soviet collaboration. That other African leaders, by pursuing a Western collaboration, were inevitably participating in the Cold War seems to have escaped the compass of such blame.

Alongside non-alignment stands socialism as a source of suspicion. This is not, of course, because the West still regards socialism as a pernicious doctrine. The nationalization of transport and crucial industries, graduated income tax, death duties, social security, all owe far more to the precepts of socialism than those of free enterprise. But socialism, like a free foreign policy, is not for export to Africa, where it encourages the nationalization of resources controlled and exploited by the West, promotes state agen-cies to compete with Western concerns, and tends to replace the tradi-tional Western direction of trade with a non-aligned search for the best bargain available. Barter agreements with the East, by which commodi-ties are exchanged for manufactures, industrial equipment and technical assistance, too often seem more profitable than do the markets of free enterprise, and such agreements lead inevitably to a warmer political relationship between the states involved. Socialism, in short, starts by fiddling with customary economic patterns and proceeds soon enough to a fiddling with foreign policy. And, in any event, socialist governments are not nearly so repelled by the prospect of establishing amicable asso-ciations with communist states as capitalist governments have been influenced properly to be.

The truth is that it is not neutralism or socialism that the West distrusts, as much as independence. And there is a peculiar anger displayed by the West when an African state flexes its independence. In part it is the anger of disappointment, of an affronted service. The West knows what is best for an Africa that it governed so long, bringing peace and law and order and the ceaseless productive demands of the modern world; to reject its standards, its institutions, its continuing supervision is not just stupidity, it is ingratitude. And this anger is no less real for being lodged in less than half the truth. It has, indeed, all the force of guilt. But the anger is an anger, too, of outrage, of affronted arrogance. The West needs African dependence – provided always that it does not cost too much, and proves on balance profitable – as an enduring sign of Western, and white, superiority. The rejection of such dependence is a challenge to the assumptions of the present no less than to the pride of the past.

Free enterprise; a privileged position for foreign capital; the trappings, if not the content, of democracy; an alignment with, and ultimate dependence on, the West; stability: these are the required characteristics of an African regime. The Nigerian seemed to have them all, and gathered its appropriate praise, till it revealed the absence of the most important one – stability. It was inevitable. For in Africa the very essence of the other characteristics required by the West is their instability.

The movement against imperial rule was an egalitarian one. There were, of course, rich blacks and poor blacks, intellectuals and illiterates, involved in it; but fundamentally all blacks saw themselves, alike, as deprived of power and the proper opportunity for advancement. Many nationalist leaders were themselves socialists, in rebellion against the system which subjected them; but whether personally committed to socialism or not, all projected a socialist appeal. The expulsion of foreign power would produce in itself if not the millennium, then at least the means of reaching it, by a co-ordinated effort in which all would work and receive their reward alike. Yet the reality of self-government has proved very different from the promise. The new states were poor, and the possession of their own flags and postage stamps has not suddenly made them rich. Some blacks have certainly prospered, by employing the system of free enterprise that their former rulers promoted; but they are few, and the many seem only the poorer to themselves in contrast. Moreover, the leaders who sustain the system have not produced the schools and jobs and hospitals and houses that they promised. This would be provoking enough, were they themselves as poor as the peasant and steadily swelling urban masses whose cause they were pledged to advance. But like the rich black planters and merchants and industrialists with whom they mix, they have showy homes and motor cars, and foreign liquor, and wives with splendid ornaments. Is this the meaning of the justice and equality which emblazoned the independence struggle? (The West cannot appreciate the resentment; for are there not conspicuously rich and poor in the West as well, without the menace of rebellion? But the poor of the West are not poor as the poor of Africa are poor, and they are not, above all, in the overwhelming majority. The inequalities of free enterprise are, in the world of today, supportable only within certain limits.)

The struggle for independence was materially directed at the ending of expatriate privilege. The very symbol of subjugation and denial was the alien, living so magnificently and in stubborn possession of the economic heights. Yet what has changed with the substitution of flags? Within most of the new African states, expatriates – of the old colour – continue to possess the economic heights, as planters, industrialists, traders, or the representatives of foreign mining and financial companies. The development and even maintenance of the economy, the education and welfare services, the administration itself, still depend upon the presence of highly paid expatriate technicians, whose living standards are no less strikingly superior to those of almost all indigenous citizens than they were before independence. Is this what the nationalist movement was all about? The more sophisticated discontent, measuring the extent of poverty and backwardness with the enormous costs of ending them, sees no reason why foreign enterprise, which has already done so well out of its investments, should continue to extract substantial profits from exploiting natural resources. The less sophisticated sees an enduring dominance by foreign power through its resident representatives.

Not all Africans, any more than all Westerners, are natural democrats; but tribal society has, in the main, promoted popular government. There have been autocratic chiefs, military despots, kings and emperors wielding a sacrosanct authority; but far more commonly, before European intervention, there were chiefs whose rule depended on the steady support of elders and the acquiescence of all, who were not sovereigns as much as spokesmen for a consensus. When Africans claim that their traditions, unlike those of the democratic West, have no room for the two-party system because they do not allow for periodic domination by a majority, they are not manufacturing excuses; tribal organization, especially at the village level, promoted decision by prolonged discussion to agreement. Such popular participation in government, however, could – and often did – exist alongside immense respect for the chief as the centre of ritual and symbol of unity. That such respect, and even awe, did not entail unchallengeable power should come, after all, as no surprise to the British, whose attitude to royalty today is little different.

Traditions of this sort tend to provoke a greater regard for the content than for the trappings of popular government. Western observers may be reassured by the existence of a parliament, imitating the procedure of the Commons in Britain or the French Chamber of Deputies. But the Africans themselves are more likely to consider the degree to which such institutions reflect popular pressures and opinions. The one-party state of Tanzania, so disparaged in the West, held elections in 1965 which unseated many sitting members of parliament and several important ministers. In the progressive democracy of Nigeria, so acclaimed by the West for preserving the formalities of two-party dispute, elections were increasingly marked by intimidation, force and fraud, till mass discontent, erupting in violence, provoked intervention – with the murder of the federal prime minister and of two regional premiers – by a section of the army. Not without significance, disaffection at the content of democracy was accompanied, in the declarations of the military rebels, by hostility to the prevalence of corruption, and the corruption meant, as the rebels themselves made clear, was not merely the widespread practice of bribery by businessmen but the mounting power of the business community.

The West is increasingly held responsible both for the system of economic inequality and the lack of popular participation in government. Who, after all, in the first place nourished the rise of indigenous capitalists and now, in societies of Western alignment, still sustains them? The easy relationship, commercial and social, between indigenous and expatriate businessmen; the prospering presence of the indigenous rich on the local boards of foreign companies; such obvious evidence of collaboration spreads the antagonism felt for foreign enterprise to indigenous capitalists, and the antagonism felt for indigenous capitalists, squandering money while the masses want, to foreign enterprise. (The Africans are more extrovert than the Indians, and their rich are in consequence less cautiously self-effacing. After all, as they would reasonably maintain, what is money for, if not to spend? The Nigerian federal finance minister, Chief Festus Okotie-Eboh, who was among the first singled out for killing in the military revolt, was a rich merchant and a byword far beyond the Nigerian borders for conspicuous consumption.) Furthermore, who promoted the form of parliamentary government that seems now to sacrifice the content of democracy for the procedures? Indeed, who taught the virtues of strong-arm rule so efficiently, under a variety of constitutional disguises, as did imperial government? The past is brought to confirm the suspicions of the present. Even where Western dominance is not apparent in Western alignment, it is supposed, as an invisible manipulation, through economic aid and technical assistance, of policy both domestic and foreign.

The supposition is, of course, generally – if not invariably – just. Western governments, either unilaterally or through such common instruments of credit as the World Bank, can and do exercise a control over policy, from the most precise supervision, as in France's relations with some of her former possessions, to an ultimate veto on drastic initiatives. Nor is a threat to cut off aid the most serious in the Western armoury. African states trade little with each other or, except for a few 'neutralists', with the communist bloc. Like the lines of communication, those of trade lead directly to Western Europe and especially to the former imperial powers. As Guinea discovered in 1958, when she chose independence from France and earned the Gaullist retribution, an African state that provokes too far can find itself immediately denied not only necessary supplies, like spare parts for industrial equipment, but the main – almost entire – established market for its exports. In a world where there is a steadily growing glut of Africa's major export commodities, the West carries a very big stick indeed. And even if barter agreements with the communist states can, in an emergency, be concluded with speed, the sudden economic disruption remains costly and intimidating. Yet the very extent of their vulnerability excites Africans to resistance. Is this, now that they have it at last, what their independence means?

When, at the end of his tour of ten African states in 1963–4, Chou En-lai, Prime Minister of China, spoke at Mogadishu of the excellent revolutionary prospects in Africa, his remarks were widely regarded in the West as a blunder, offensive to the governments whose support he was supposed to have been wooing. But Chou En-lai was not speaking to the governments; he was speaking to the restless Africa behind them. He was not, of course, claiming the continent for communism; still less – though there were those in the West silly enough to suppose so – was he heralding some apocalyptic conquest by China. He simply recognized that discontent had reached a pitch where revolution seemed unavoidable.

Was he wrong? Millions of peasants, as poor as they have ever been and resentful now at the unfulfilled promises of struggle, do not have the same awe or apathy before the heirs of imperial power as they may once have had before the original possessors. If the white men with their guns were forced in the end to go, why not their substitutes? In the towns and cities, the multitude of unemployed grows – the peasants attracted by jobs that do not exist, and more dangerous still, the output of the primary schools, articulate with ambition and finding neither further schools nor proper jobs to accommodate them. And increasing constantly, both in numbers and in resolute anger, are the intellectuals – some, students returned from abroad; most, students turned out by the shanty towns themselves and the experience of street politics – journalists, teachers, civil servants, trade unionists, even elements of the army. Who better than Chou En-lai might see in these the leadership of revolution? In China, too, it was the intellectuals who dreamt of a society without luxury and corruption alongside want, who felt most furiously the humiliation of their national past and the subservience of their present, and who harnessed the power of a desperate peasantry to revolution.

Yet it was not only the regimes of capitalist commitment, associated with the West, that provoked discontent and overthrow. In February 1966 the Ghanaian army, with the support of the police, deposed Nkrumah while he was on a visit to China and disbanded his Convention People's Party. The first African south of the Sahara to have led his country from imperial rule to independence, whose example had excited or encouraged struggle across the world of black abasement, and whose commitment to socialism, non-alignment and Pan-Africanism seemed the rising clamour of the continent, was toppled with ease. And it was not unexpected.

The traditionalists, many with a profitable investment in tribal authority and regional power, had been alienated first. And they had soon been followed by the bulk of the middle class with the onslaught upon free enterprise, through high taxation and the capture by the state of one after the other of its customary preserves. Yet nothing less could properly have been supposed from a resolve to eradicate vast differences in personal wealth and promote a popular sense of effort and achievement. Western capital within the country had been angered for the same reasons, and Western power outside additionally provoked by the Nkrumah regime's warming relationship, economic and political, with the communist states; its persistent criticism of Western policies; its continental cultivation of hostility to Western alignment and the survival of Western dominance; its constant calls for military action against the remaining African areas of white control.

In fact, as the West will doubtless in time have reason to recognize, Nkrumah was far more prudent, and indeed moderate, than either he himself or the extent of Western outrage pretended. When he nationalized foreign assets, such as a number of dying gold mines, he paid extremely high compensation, and his excursions into continental battle were much less damaging to Western interests than they might – had he, for instance, flung his resources behind the Stanleyville regime, or joined temporary hands with the Soviet Union, in the Congo crisis – very easily have been. None the less, he was the primary African object of Western distaste, and his detention of political opponents without trial, though borrowed from British and indeed general colonial practice, provided a ready occasion for selective clamour against his despotism in the Western press. This was dangerous enough, of course. The West was nurturing upheaval, by the pressures of its antagonism, if no more directly. There were still elements in Ghana, especially within the British-trained senior officer corps, who found Western hostility and contempt humiliating. But this, as well, was only to be expected. Other regimes had survived Western hostility and contempt, had indeed strengthened their popular support as a result.

What destroyed the Nkrumah regime was the almost total alienation of the intellectuals, and not merely the older, conservative members of the outlawed opposition, but the younger, radical recruits to change; the slow drift away from it of mass allegiance; and the promotion of the army as an independent source of power. Nkrumah himself drew steadily farther away from the Ghana of village and even city street, ruling in guarded seclusion among men who were more courtiers than colleagues in a popular and creative leadership. And the mounting threats of violence from the disaffected hastened the process, till he was less protected by isolation than immured in it. The single party withered at its roots, till it was held in place only from above, and the transformation of society became not a common enthusiasm but a series of alien directives. Government grew increasingly Byzantine; corruption was widespread, and decisions or appointments were made by flattery, favour or bribe no less than by the persuasions of policy. Dispute of any significant sort disappeared from the press, the radio, and the political meeting, and in this atmosphere the detention of political opponents and the manipulation of the courts nourished only conspiracy. The regime even lost its sense of the ridiculous, and the Nkrumah cult fell over reverence into derision. It is doubtful if Nkrumah himself realized the extent of the decay around him. His ultimate mistake was to confuse the associate with the parasite; once he had done so, the parasites did most of the rest themselves.

Yet this was in no sense the sterile terror commonly portrayed in the West. The savings of Ghana went into schools and hospitals and roads and industry, into the huge Volta River Dam and the new port at Tema, into Nkrumah's vision of an industrialized state from which poverty and ignorance and sickness and squalor would be finally expelled, far more than into the private enrichment of officials or the hollow prestige projects, mere genuflections to the grandeur of independence and the vision of African unity. The rot was more evident for consuming the excellence of the material. Had the country been rich, the regime might well have survived its political sickness; may even, indeed, have avoided it; and probably, in time, would have cured itself of it. But Ghana was poor, and caught in the customary trap of the poor. The more cocoa – her principal commodity – she exported, the lower fell the price, while the cost of machinery for her programme of industrialization rose steadily higher. Austerity produced massive discontent because the political isolation of the government made it seem aimless and alien, an imposition. Nkrumah's policies had dried up Western sources of aid, and the economy was tottering. When the army, whose power political isolation and Nkrumah's own fears had promoted, moved at last, the people in the main seemed to acquiesce.

The West, in marked contrast to the solemn discretion and even alarm with which it had greeted the Nigerian army *coup* shortly before, was jubilant.[1] While the new rulers of Ghana hastened to take those of the old ones they could find into protective custody, the hundreds of those detained by Nkrumah were released. But this was not the cause of Western pleasure. The defeat of Nkrumah was widely seen as a serious reverse for the African left, for militant Pan-Africanism, and for African nonalignment. The pleasure could scarcely have been more misplaced. Nkrumah had been toppled basically because a regime whose popular support had shrunk and twisted could not stand the strain of organized sacrifice. The political promise of the independence struggle had been broken in the disembodied bureaucracy of dogma and corruption. Indeed, the bribery, the waste, the squandering on the ostentations of power, were an inevitable accompaniment to the disembodiment, as was the self-destructive apparatus of intimidation.

Africans would not take the imposition of economic change from above any more than they would take the preservation of society as it was. Ghana did not discard Nkrumah because he offered her revolution; she discarded him because he denied it to her. The democratic content of institutions in Ghana was as empty as that of the institutions in Nigeria, and real economic revolution is not possible, is bound to produce the distortions of corruption and dogma, of force and fear, if it excludes, or

[1] The London Stock Exchange celebrated the event by marking up shares of Ashanti, Ghana's privately, mainly British-owned, major gold-mining company, from 6s. to 7s. 10½d., a rise of over 31 per cent, in one day. 'The fall of Nkrumah in Ghana gave rise to hopes of a new regime with a more lenient attitude to the profit motive.' *The Times*, February 25th, 1966.

cannot acquire, a popular commitment. The Nigerian regime fell because
it had, fundamentally, no purpose but the perpetuation of itself. The
Ghanaian regime fell because it separated purpose from power. It was not
the proclaimed objectives of the Nkrumah endeavour, the society of
equal standards, without privilege and want, independent from East and
West, and projected on a continental scale, that fell with Nkrumah himself, but the political methods employed to further them. And any suc-
ceeding regime that supposes otherwise is likely soon to find itself falling,
too. The founder of the nation is himself unlikely to remain idle, and may
perhaps examine his mistakes in his edifying exile.

How, then, is the desire of the African for change to be satisfied? In just
over two months, five African states – Dahomey (December 22nd, 1965),
the Central African Republic (January 1st, 1966), Upper Volta (January
4th, 1966), Nigeria (January 15th, 1966) and Ghana (February 24th,
1966) – succumbed to military rule, and beyond the special circumstances
of each coup, it was reasonable to wonder whether Africa had not entered into an era of aimless upheaval. For what stability is the army likely
to bring? As in Latin America, it is generally an élite. The very training of
its senior officers abroad, generally in the former imperial capitals, with
the higher and isolated living standards of most ranks from the mass of the
population, tends to produce a self-centred allegiance, and even, under the
leadership of the senior officers, a desire to contain discontent rather than
conduct it to a reshaping of society. Yet what can this accomplish, but the
certainty of civilian upheaval? The mere assumption of power by army
officers does not cure the social diseases of which administrative corruption
and public disaffection are the outward signs. The capture of the post
office, the radio station and the offices of government, with the dismissal
of the civilian rulers, does not produce food for the multiplying population, hospitals and doctors for the sick, schools for the children, work for
the idle, homes for the unsheltered. Indeed, by suppressing discontent for a
time in the name of order, military rule – where it is not, as it has been in
Egypt, to a significant degree itself revolutionary – makes the bursting of
the banks eventually all the more violent.

The harsh truth is that instability, even for some time apparent chaos,
seems inevitable in Africa – or rather, in the conditions of want and frustration that exist almost everywhere on the continent. Yet how is stability,
through the elimination of the conditions preventing it, to be acquired?
The West does not approve of socialist revolution. But what will it offer
instead? Will it provide the money and technicians, in enough time and
quantity, for the needed jobs and schools and homes, even for the needed

food? Will it, above all, promote a general sense of justice and equality and reason by encouraging – indeed, exciting – the eradication of glaring wealth, expatriate or indigenous, alongside the most debasing poverty? If it will not, it must expect socialist revolution, and should have the good sense, if not the decency, to accept it. Protracted chaos can only produce still more intense hostility to the West, as responsible by the depredations of the past and the sterility of its interventions in the present. Africa will have her revolutions. The West can turn them by its response into Vietnams and Chinas.

In a very few states the movement of nationalist struggle may succeed in maintaining and extending intellectual and mass allegiance for the era of revolutionary government, controlling the army by making it a militia, a real citizens' force, employed in part for economic construction and mirroring the mood not of an elite but of the whole society militant. In others the army or a section of it, in disgust at the irrelevance of civilian rule, and unwilling to endure a humiliation and helplessness which as Africans too, after all, its members necessarily share, may itself invite or conduct a revolution, discarding its isolation in the shaping of a mass movement. In most, probably, disorder and discontent will fortify each other till together at last they produce a revolutionary force, in the streets of the sprawling city slums, in the remote silence of the peasantry.

And Africa is in many important ways the most cohesive of the continents. The agitation of one area spreads quickly to another. Pan-Africanism at the moment seems to the outside world a unity of aimless upheaval. Yet the upheaval, if only negatively, has an aim – it is a rejection of conditions as they are. A unity of positive aim and effective method may take many years to develop, but develop it must.

The apparent obsession of Africans, especially the intellectuals, with foreign policy is a source of surprise, when not of a weary cynicism, in the West. Entrapped for so long in their own competitive nationalisms, Westerners wonder why so many otherwise evidently sensible Africans should worry so much not about the strength and security of their respective states, but about that will-o'-the-wisp, African unity, and the even more costly liberation of Southern Africa from settler rule. The reason, of course – as who should know better than the West itself? – is that, for the most part, the nation state exists in Africa at present as no more than an imperial imposition, tended by those who inherited power with independence. The frontiers generally correspond neither to language nor indigenous tradition, but to nineteenth-century European rivalries or mere subsequent administrative convenience; they bisect some tribes with a long history of antagonism. It is the tribe that largely held popular allegiance before, and if it has a rival now – one, indeed, of persistently mounting appeal – it is much less the nation than the race. And how should this not be so? Just as in the imperial era – and it is easy to forget how recent that was – the rulers were all white, so all the ruled were black, and the allegiance cultivated by struggle was a racial one. The word 'nationalist' is used, indeed, as shorthand for the rebel against alien rule, but very few of the rebels were – or ever thought of themselves as being – nationalists. France's former empire in black Africa may have disintegrated today into more than two handfuls of states, but the struggle against French power was itself an inter-territorial one, conducted in general by an inter-territorial leadership, through inter-territorial political and trade union movements, and with an important section of African opinion committed to only an inter-territorial form of independence. Though far less formally so, the struggle in British black Africa was also inter-territorial, whether through the merely personal contacts and co-ordination of the leaders on the west coast or the loose organization of PAFMECA (Pan-African Freedom Movement of East and Central Africa)[1] on the east. It was no accident that Nkrumah, first of the successful rebels, should have considered it as no more than a stage in the liberation and unification of the continent. (Sceptics should note that few of the new nation states in Africa possessed, or possess now, the cohesion and potential for individual development that Ghana does.) Indeed, the summoning at Accra in April 1958 of a Conference of Independent African States, and in the following December of an All African Peoples' Conference for African political movements from all over the continent, had a substantial impact on the speed of subsequent decolonization.

If Nkrumah seriously antagonized other African leaders by his often clumsy pressures and interventions, this does not mean – as far too many Westerners suppose – that he seriously damaged the aspiration for unity. One of his most vigorous critics was Tanzania's Julius Nyerere, whose allegiance to Pan-Africanism and personal militancy are not doubted. Nor does the failure to produce a real continental union so far mean that the impetus for it is not strong. Unions are made by governments, not peoples, and the present African governments differ widely in their basic character and objectives. But popular pressures, promoted by the intellectuals, have forced even the most cynical and self-centred nationalist regimes to pay lip-service to the Pan-Africanist ideal. And some progress,

[1] Subsequently expanded into PAFMECSA (Pan-African Freedom Movement of East, Central and Southern Africa).

after all, there has been. If the Ghana-Guinea-Mali Union speedily failed, and the long-projected East African Federation of Kenya, Uganda, Tanganyika and Zanzibar (the last two now united as Tanzania) never even got off the ground, thirty-two independent African states, representing all the conflicting blocs and bodies of opinion, did decide at Addis Ababa in May 1963 to establish the Organization of African Unity. The Charter followed the cautious thesis of Nigeria's late federal prime minister, Sir Abubakar Tafawa Balewa, that 'African unity must be based on the sovereignty of all African countries, whatever their size, population, and social level'; but the signatory states established a special fund for liberation movements, and 'invited' the 'allies of the colonial powers' to choose between their friendship for the African peoples and their support for those who oppressed them. If subsequently the Organization produced rather more dispute than concerted action, its very survival through conflicts of personality and purpose was an accumulating strength for the ideal of unity which produced it.

The African group at the United Nations, whose formal establishment had been urged at the founding conference of the O.A.U., has nourished a habit of diplomatic collaboration and a similarity of approach towards several major issues of African concern; the Security Council debate on the Congo rescue operation of November 1964 revealed a surprising alliance of moderate and militant, French- and English-speaking states. Such solidarity becomes increasingly legitimate, increasingly sustained by popular pressure, and increasingly dangerous for an African regime to disrupt, with time. Not the least of the reasons for the disaffection of intellectuals in Nigeria was the repeated readiness of their government to break African ranks and take a stand congenial to the West.

The Organization of African Unity may itself divide under the stress of difference between radicals and moderates, the disciples of socialist neutralism and free enterprise Western alignment. The coalitions of diplomacy may fall apart as the supporters and opponents of revolution develop their antagonisms. But it is difficult to believe that the momentum of closer association will diminish, even if it is deflected into the establishment of temporary rival blocs. And the establishment of rival blocs in itself is likely to advance the cause of the radicals whose Pan-Africanism is the deeper and more resolute.

A real continental association – with the substantial majority of states acceding to a common government of material authority – is for many Africans, indeed a growing number of them, essential policy. But whether or not such an association comes about in the graspable future, increasing collaboration is no less than a compulsion of the modern world. African states are generally so poor in population and resources that they can separately provide, even by the most strenuous endeavour, neither the investment nor the sustaining market for dynamic development. The cost of acquiring reasonably competitive industry constantly rises, while a domestic market measured not in thousands but in tens of millions of consumers is now necessary as a base. Even Nigeria, with by far the largest population in Africa, is scarcely the economic size for significant industrialization. How are the vast majority of states, with populations less than a fifth as large, to enter the industrial world? Which of them can afford a single fertilizer factory to make their main – often only – natural asset, land, more productive? Furthermore, the African states produce the same export commodities, increasing the world glut, competing with each other for markets, and driving down prices. Their separate independences succeed only in keeping them economically backward and so still dependent.

Yet collaboration on any significant scale is likely to be inseparable from revolution, for it is revolution that provides the ultimate impulse. The elimination of economic and political privilege; the elimination of mass poverty and want; the elimination of Western dominance; such is the triple cry not only of the African revolutionary but of the resolute Pan-Africanist. It is no accident that the leading radical African states, which have pursued social revolutions within and a policy of non-alignment without, are committed far more deeply to continental unity than are the moderates, which have shown themselves loyal to free enterprise and Western alignment. Radicals and moderates alike recognize the interaction of drastic internal change and a militant commitment to Pan-Africanism: each promotes the progress of the other; both require an end to effective Western dominance and carry the risk of a rupture with the West.

The circumstances of the clash are racial; the Africans are black and the Westerners are white. But the clash itself, on the example of the past, might be expected to escape being so. The struggle against imperial rule, though it certainly provoked racial awareness, provoked surprisingly little specifically racial hatred. Africans, even in areas like Kenya and Algeria where protracted warfare was waged, fought more against power than against the particular race possessing it. In Kenya, indeed, very few whites were killed, and the main black terrorist attack was directed less against the often vulnerable settlers than against blacks loyal to the imperial administration. In most instances, African rebellion achieved success with unexpected ease, and racial awareness stood still in the euphoria that followed the formal withdrawal of white power. What has since incalculably increased the danger of such racial awareness turning into racial hostility is the mounting frustration and rage produced by recognition of the West's still continuing dominion, and alongside it, the protective association of the white West with white oppression of blacks inside the continent.

The policy of permanent white rule pursued in the south is nakedly racial, and to expect Africans now to see it – in the same way that their leadership saw imperial rule – in broadly political and economic terms is to discount not merely the accumulating pressures of the past, but the declared dynamic of the surviving white regimes. The very existence of the white south is a challenge: to the control by Africans of their own continent and so to the security of the power they have already achieved; to African racial awareness and solidarity; to the recognition of the African's essential equality.

Pan-Africanism is a firm commitment to the emancipation of the whole continent from alien rule. (The right of settled whites – or Asians – to live as equal citizens in African states has, so far, been generally accepted and, under governments as notably militant as the Tanzanian, unequivocally secured. It is rule by a racial minority that is seen as alien.) Otherwise, what meaning must be attached to African unity? But the commitment is more than a principle of ideology; it is one, for many Africans, of survival. It serves no purpose that South Africa and Portugal, echoed by their Western apologists, proclaim their satisfaction with what they possess already and their pledge to stay within their present respective frontiers of power. Africans see white domination as essentially aggressive, driven to foreign interventions by its basic character as well as by desire to protect itself from attack by a buffer of influence on its border. And, after all, if such were indeed the policy of the white south, would it be any different from the policy pursued by all power, from the United States to China? But there is more than assumption; there is also evidence. From the outbreak of the First World War, white South Africa has sought a continental role, and its possession of South-west Africa still today is an undeniable spoil. J. G. Strijdom, Prime Minister at the time of the 'Mau Mau' rising in Kenya, offered Britain South African troops, and the Congo crisis provoked supplies of men and materials through, and directly from, white Africa. The African memory of white support for Katanga secession, from the pressures of the then Federal government in Salisbury to the mercenary camps in Angola, is still bitterly fresh. The help given to white Rhodesia by white South Africa and Portugal in the present is blatant. And there is – not unreasonably – a suspicion that the known instances of intervention by the white south constitute no more than the seventh on the surface of the sea.

The African sense of solidarity is no figment of propaganda. It is a natural product of the racial awareness which white imperial rule promoted. No one who talks to Africans elsewhere on the continent, from old traditionalist chiefs to young radical trade unionists, about South Africa or the Portuguese colonial war can reasonably doubt the strength of their identification with Africans still under white rule. The word 'apartheid', with its response of resentment, hatred and fear, has reached the most distant villages. It is idle for whites in the West to complain that Africans in Nigeria and South Africa are as different from each other as Swedes and Greeks. Swedes and Greeks may think of each other as they please. The fact is that Africans in Nigeria and South Africa think of themselves as ultimately one people, related inseparably by colour and the common experience that colour has produced.

The past is not merely a part of the present, it is an expanding part. If the slave trade and the imperial era provoked surprisingly little racial rage in Africa at the time – outbreaks of a racial character were far more common abroad in the plantation colonies, where slavery encompassed individuals from different tribes and regions in a racial consensus – a swell of rancour has risen in retrospect. Africans write today with a far greater consciousness of racial, in contrast to individual or tribal, wrong than they did generations ago in the first stirrings of resistance to alien rule. And it is not merely the consequence of a mounting racial awareness, with resentment at the riches and lingering dominance of the white West; it is a response to the reminder that white Africa represents. The suffering, the humiliation, the shame of the past exist starkly in the present of white Africa, in the yet open refusal to recognize the equality of blacks. African rage at the survival of white supremacy on their own continent is a rage at their subjection to racial arrogance now and for so long before. The mills of man, too, grind slowly; and they, too, may grind exceeding small.

Race war is already being waged on the continent: in the Congo, where white and black have fought, and fight still, against each other – in part for power pressures, in part for pay, but surely and increasingly in part for race; in the Portuguese colonies, where white and black bring to battle, like standards, the equipment of their racial alliances; at any moment in Rhodesia, with the fast-rising flow of racial passion between white and black within and everywhere around; above all, in South Africa, where racial violence could spill over to cover the continent and reach to the edges of the earth.

For South Africa is not a private obsession of Africa and the West. From India to Brazil colour sees in 'apartheid' the subjugations of the past and the still-subjugated present. South Africa is an expression on the face of the white world in history, and one which even yet the white world does not care to erase. For to erase the meaning of South Africa is more than merely to risk the West's considerable economic and political investments there; it is to alter a policy, and behind it a habit of thought, that grew with power itself. Yet the meaning of South Africa is no less to the world of colour, and all humanity may find it too costly a meaning to maintain.

3

The Coloured World of Southern America

The sudden multitude of countries south of the United States, mainly Spanish-speaking but with the largest of them all Portuguese-, and a few of them English-, French-, or Dutch-speaking, comprise that part of the earth's surface where racial antagonisms are conventionally supposed to have been resolved. Centuries of miscegenation have produced large coloured populations, and though there are still communities of Indians, Negroes, and even whites in a condition of approximate racial purity, discrimination has no formal identity and is devoutly denounced by tradition. Yet the area is one of substantial and mounting turbulence, and it would be strange if economic and political discontent did not assume racial form. For in most of the countries, power and wealth generally follow the contours of colour, with the lighter-skinned in command of palace, barracks and boardroom, while the darker-skinned constitute in the main the seething mass of city slum or the remote misery of the countryside. Of ultimately even greater significance, the peoples of the area are, whatever the difference in shadings, and despite the existence of self-declared white states like Argentina and Uruguay, overwhelmingly coloured, both in fact and in the view of the white world. They are also overwhelmingly poor. Their relationship with the rest of humanity is dominated by their relationship with the United States, which is both overwhelmingly white and rich. Any popular resistance to the political and economic power of the United States, therefore, could well rise in racial flood.

White contact with the indigenous peoples of Southern America[1] did not start propitiously. When Columbus reached the territory of present-day Haiti in the last days of 1492, he found the inhabitants – whom he called Indians, on the assumption that he had discovered the westward sea

[1] I have used this term because 'Latin America' seems to exclude the English-speaking countries like Jamaica; and 'South America', the countries in the Centre and even North like Mexico. 'Southern America' may better suggest America south of the United States, whose lower border represents, after all, the major racial, cultural and economic division. Where I have used the term 'Latin America', I have done so in the specific sense of the Spanish- and Portuguese-speaking bulk.

120

route to India – 'loyal and without greed', a set of 'most handsome men and women', with their attractions irresistibly encumbered by the casual gold ornaments that they wore. While he himself sailed back to Spain to report his triumph, forty-four of his seamen remained in the newly named La Isla Española (later Hispaniola) with orders to explore the island for gold but to abstain from cruelty and women. A year later, when Columbus returned with hundreds of prospective settlers, alongside horses and cattle, seeds and shoots of sugar cane, he found his forty-four pioneers dead; they had plundered the island of gold and women till the Indians had been driven beyond all fear and patience to attack them. Columbus tried to restore the former confidence, but his own men mutinied at any prospect of work, rounded up Indians to mine gold, and exerted themselves only in the panting pursuit of women. The Spanish Court was not satisfied by the trickle of gold, and Columbus acquired little credit by the dispatch of five hundred Indian slaves, most of whom died on the way or soon afterwards, while the conscience of Isabella the Queen was seriously disturbed.

In the years that followed, Spain spread itself over the Caribbean, steadily diminishing the Indian population of the islands by its labour exactions and suppression of inevitable revolts, but compensating in some measure by the ardour of its sexual demands. Unlike the Protestant peoples of the North, and especially the Anglo-Saxons, the Spaniards were not burdened by a crude contempt of colour or an obsessive sense of sin. Their experience of the Moors, whose blood had abundantly mingled with their own over the centuries, disabused them of any pretensions to the unchallengeable superiority of their colour, and their Catholicism had long considered promiscuity man's affair rather than God's. Their devotion demanded baptism, not chastity, and if they interrupted their efforts at conscripting labourers and concubines, it was to scatter the rewards of a formal conversion to the faith.

The Caribbean islands, soon to produce, with the necessary help of African slave labour, a rich return from sugar plantations, were immediately disappointing. Columbus had given Spain an empire but little gold, and he died in virtual disgrace; with their notable talent for deflecting any blame, the Spaniards later recorded on his tomb in the cathedral of Seville 'the ingratitude of America'. But the lure of gold was proof against such misfortunes, and Spanish enterprise soon switched to Mexico, an area which rumour was investing with limitless treasure.

The Indians of the islands – whether peaceful and settled farming Arawaks, or roving and aggressive Caribs – had produced no exceptional culture. In the region of present-day Guatemala and Honduras, however, the Maya had developed, from the early fourth century onwards, a civilization of substantial scientific and artistic accomplishment. They had built splendid cities, with tall pyramid temples and massive communal housing; had displayed a command of painting and sculpture both sweeping and intricate; had made paper from wood-pulp and kept records in a complex hieroglyphic; and had nourished not only poetry and mysticism, but mathematics and astronomy, predicting solar eclipses with precision and devising a calendar of 365 days that was closer to sidereal time than its contemporary Western equivalents. Then, overtaken probably by the exhaustion of the surrounding soil, they had, in the ninth century, abandoned their cities, moving northwards to Mexico and a protracted decay.

Their successors as the dominant force of the Central American mainland were the Aztecs, who ruled an empire of several millions from the capital at Tenoxtitlán, the site of the present-day Mexico City. With a scientific ability little, if at all, less remarkable than that of the Maya, they had a religion, reflected in ferocious art, of almost desperate terror. The gods were ranged against man in uniform malevolence, as earthquake, flood and drought consistently testified, and their appetite could only be appeased by human sacrifice. War was thus the solitary guarantee of survival, a way of providing sufficient victims for the altar without draining the blood and destroying the state of the Aztecs themselves. Having made themselves masters, therefore, of many peoples, from whom they exacted tribute to sustain their resplendent cities and court, they were at the height of their power when Hernán Cortés and his force of some five hundred men set out from Cuba in 1519 to extend the conquests of Spain.

By a combination of courage, treachery, doggedness and luck, along with aid from traditional enemies of the Aztecs, the enterprise succeeded. The Spaniards struck terror with their horses and guns – they seemed to be the invincible host which myth promised would one day come out of the East – and, once received in the capital, Cortés seized bold possession of Moctezuma, the emperor. Moctezuma himself, understandably uncertain of how to treat a stranger who might, after all, be the god-king of prophecy, was easily subdued; but his submission, with the devastation of the Spaniards who brought smallpox alongside their insatiable appetites, eventually turned his subjects against him, and he was stoned to death. The Aztecs then rallied behind a kinsman who had less regard for Spanish sanctity, but after fourteen months of resistance they were finally forced to succumb. In the process of pacification, Cortés destroyed the Aztec capital, building by building, the city which he himself called 'the most beautiful in the world'.

To the south still lay the greatest civilization of ancient America, the four-century-old empire of the Incas, stretching some three thousand miles from the present-day Colombia to northern Argentina and Chile.[1] From his capital at Cuzco, with its gold- and silver-embellished stone palaces, its paved streets linked by broad highways and fibre suspension bridges, to the ends of the empire, the Inca or emperor ruled a multitude of peoples, fixing their allegiance by enclosing them in a common culture and a ubiquitous paternalism. All citizens received an education, and the state cared for the old, the sick and the widowed as well as providing help to those in need at times of emergency; but in return the government exacted absolute obedience, choosing suitable careers for its subjects and gearing their education accordingly, shifting whole populations for political or economic reasons, regulating dress and diet, even ordaining mates when citizens remained single for too long. It was a society of monolithic benevolence, both more efficient and, for the vast bulk of its citizens, more congenial than any contemporary European order seems to have been. In many of its methods and objectives, it anticipated not merely Western imperialism at its proudest – with techniques of control from colonization to indirect rule, and the dispatch of colonial protégés to the capital for indoctrination and training in responsibility – but also the modern communist state, with its attempt to eradicate poverty by regimentation.

Astonishingly, the Inca empire knew neither writing – reports and orders were sent by couriers carrying knotted cords of different colours (*quepus*) – nor the wheel. But its religion, based on worship of the Sun God and his descendant representative, the Inca, was without ferocity and encouraged the conversion of subject peoples. Inca pottery, weaving and jewellery were unrivalled on the continent, and Inca architecture had a power lavish enough to have survived centuries of conquest and pillage. It was an empire of skill, order and general contentment; yet it collapsed to the assaults of a few Spanish fortune-hunters. In part this was because the *conquistadores* arrived just as the empire had emerged from its first civil war – between two contenders for the Inca throne – which had seriously depleted the imperial élite. In part the strangeness of the Spaniards, their colour and guns and horses – many Indians thought that man

[1] The estimated number of its inhabitants ranges from 3 to 33 million. See *A History of Latin America*, by Hubert Herring (Jonathan Cape, 1955), p. 47.

and beast were one, and were appropriately dismayed – gave them a military advantage worth an army of thousands at their back. But, above all, the very centralization and efficiency of the empire made it vulnerable. Once the Spaniards took possession of the Inca and his court, the millions of leaderless and astounded subjects were an easy prey.

In 1532 Francisco Pizarro, the illiterate bastard son of a poor Spanish gentleman, set out with a force of 62 horsemen and 106 infantry to strike at the heart of the empire. Ambushing the Inca with 5,000 of his warriors, the Spaniards captured him, and after solemnly promising to free him in return for an enormous quantity of gold and silver, tried and executed him for treason. Pizarro then appointed a puppet Inca and directed himself to plunder. Cuzco, the capital, was stripped; its palaces, temples and tombs were looted, and its citizens tortured to reveal any hidden treasure. The spoliation by Spain became insupportable, and at last the puppet Inca rallied the Indians to resistance. 'You Christians', he cried, 'have made us slaves … You took our wives and daughters for concubines, you stole our property, burning us and tearing us with dogs.' For some eight years until his death in 1545, Indian guerillas raided Spanish settlements from the mountains; but it was the last convulsion of the Inca empire.

In the years following, Spain spread its power everywhere in Southern America but the eastern bulge, which a Papal Bull soon after the first voyage of Columbus had given to Portugal. In 1500 Pedro Cabral raised the Portuguese flag in Brazil – named after the dyewood, red as a *braza* or live coal, found in its jungles – but for the next three decades the Portuguese themselves were too involved in the profitable spice and silk trade with the Far East for any real effort at exploiting their American possession. No precious metal had been discovered, and the Indians of the area had raised no rich civilization to rob. But the interest of other European powers in American empire, the decline in Eastern trade with the glut of spices, and the mounting European demand for sugar turned Portuguese attention to Brazil. Africa could provide a steady supply of slave labour for the plantations, to supplement the less robust Indians, and the costs of administration could be carried by the planters themselves. By 1580 Brazil had a capital city in Bahia; sixty sugar mills; some 20,000 Portuguese, 18,000 'civilized' Indians, and 14,000 Negro slaves. There were a few Portuguese officials, and municipal councils with wide administrative powers; but a country of one million people like Portugal could not afford to provide an extensive bureaucracy, and the real rulers of the colony were the *fazendeiros*, the plantation owners, with their vast tracts of land and the limitless authority that they enjoyed over their labourers.

The new Brazilian nation was formed from the relationship between the *casa grande* or great house and the *senzala* or slave-quarters.

The Portuguese, with their larger infusion of Moorish blood and their smaller numbers available for colonial settlement, were even less disdainful of sexual mingling with Indian and Negro than the Spaniards showed themselves to be. Miscegenation was not merely a natural response to the absence of sufficient white women, but a policy of state promoted for the most obvious economic and political reasons. The proudest of the planters took concubines from among their slaves, or wives from among the increasing numbers of coloured, almost always acknowledging their bastards and including them in the education and nourishment of their other children. If Portugal did not have the manpower necessary for imperial exploitation, she had to procreate it.

> The family and not the individual, much less the State or any commercial company, was from the sixteenth century the great colonizing factor in Brazil, the productive unit, the capital that cleared the land, founded plantations, purchased slaves, oxen, implements; and in politics it was the social force that set itself up as the most powerful colonial aristocracy in the Americas. Over it the King of Portugal may be said, practically, to have reigned without ruling.[1]

This is not, of course, to suggest that miscegenation promoted political and, far less, economic equality. Quite the contrary; colour-blind sex enabled an aristocracy to flourish and spread under circumstances that militated against its very survival. The sons of Portuguese and Indian parents, indeed, formed the body of the *bandeirantes*, the slave-hunters of seventeenth-century Brazil who penetrated the interior in their search for Indian captives, establishing settlements, building roads and advancing the frontier of plantation economics. In North America, it was the free farmer with the small homestead who pioneered the westward expansion and gave it its democratic character; in Brazil, the pioneer was the product and scout of the *casa grande*.

In Spanish America land and labour were regulated by the *encomienda* system, by which the Crown 'entrusted' specified numbers of Indians to deserving Spaniards, who could exploit them for work in field or mine but were required in return to serve their physical and spiritual well-being. Inevitably the exploitation took precedence over the service, and protests from the Church, even commandments from the Crown, were

[1] *The Masters and the Slaves*, by Gilberto Freyre (Alfred A. Knopf, New York, 1963), pp. 26–7.

ignored. When finally the system was outlawed at the end of the nine-teenth century, most of the best land was concentrated in the hands of the *hacendados* or plantation owners and of the Church, while the Indians outside of the most remote villages had been reduced to servitude. The Spanish Crown exercised a closer imperial control than the Portuguese one was ever able to do; but distance and feudal tradition encouraged the colonial aristocracy of Spanish, as of Portuguese, America to obey only such orders as it found amenable. The viceroys governing vast stretches of territory – the whole of Central America was encompassed by the single viceroyalty of New Spain – represented the King, and though their power was commensurately great and their state splendid, they were subject to the trade winds of court and so to the busy intrigues of the colonial aristo-crats. Effective administration reposed mainly in the *cabildos* or city councils, Spanish practice being to establish a city first and then promote rural settlement around it to meet its needs. The members of the councils were generally appointed by the King, but increasingly at a price – which was then recovered, with interest, by plundering the public treasury. They accordingly represented the colonial rich and influential, mostly natives of Spain eager to increase their fortunes, but with a scattering of the more powerful *criollos* or Spaniards born in America. The ultimate sanction of the Crown was its power, and this, alongside its prestige, steadily declined.

It was, paradoxically, the outcry of powerful Churchmen against Spanish treatment of the Indians – no doubt, alongside the reputation of the Negro as a labourer less subject than the Indian to sickness and melancholy – that led to the mounting introduction of African slaves for mine and plantation. By 1810 there were more than 750,000 of these in Spanish America, and the Church itself was a prominent purchaser and owner. They too, though far less than the Indians, attracted the sexual notice of the Spaniards, and helped to swell the population of mixed blood. By 1823, indeed, the year in which Spain lost her principal colonies, there were some 17,000,000 people in Spanish America, of whom 44·5 per cent were Indian; 19·4 per cent white; 4·6 per cent Negro; and 31·5 per cent, or almost a third, of mixed blood.[1]

In the viceroyalty of La Plata, the region of present-day Argentina and Uruguay, the Indians had been virtually exterminated. Africans were few, and those of mixed blood comprised, with the less successful whites, the main labour supply. But elsewhere in the empire, as in Brazil, the whole

---

[1] *Latin American Civilization*, by Bailey W. Diffie (Stackpole Sons, Harrisburg), quoted in H. Herring, op. cit., p. 192.

economy was based on Negro slavery or an Indian serfdom that was slavery in all but name. Those of mixed blood constituted the one element of mobility, with a few of them being absorbed by the colonial aristocracy, and most remaining close to the degradation of Negro or Indian. Time and ordered government promoted the snobberies of civilization. The lighter his complexion and so the further in appearance from the slave, the easier did the coloured find social acceptance and economic advance. Not surprisingly, therefore, the lighter looked down on the darker, and the darker on the black. By its very mobility the mixed population developed distinctions.

The Africans did not take easily to enslavement. They rose in desperate rejection at the African ports, flung themselves from the side of the slave ships, starved themselves to death, or plotted on the American plantations. In Brazil they gathered themselves into well-organized rebel groups called *quilombos*, and in the seventeenth century several of these joined to form in the north-east the Republic of Palmares, which survived for nearly seventy years. But it was in French, not in Spanish or Portuguese, America that racial rebellion defeated colonial rule and expelled the whites.

Hispaniola had soon lost its Indians, 'so lovable, so tractable, so peaceable', to the exactions of the Spanish settlers, and Spain herself, having taken what gold she could, had lost interest in the island where her empire had begun. In 1679 the French wrested the western portion from her, and a century later Saint Domingue, with its 30,000 whites, 30,000 mulattos and 500,000 Negro slaves, its sugar, indigo and other crops, had become the richest colony in the world. In 1789 Britain's total export trade was worth £27 million; her colonial trade, only £5 million. France's export trade was worth £17 million, of which nearly £11 million came from Saint Domingue.[1] But 1789 was, too, the year of the French Revolution. In the name of liberty, the white planters demanded self-government, fearful that the fervour of the Paris streets might enfranchise their slaves, while the Negroes, driven beyond endurance by their treatment and the promise of the revolution, rose in revolt. Led brilliantly by a former slave, Toussaint L'Ouverture, and supported by the mulattos whom white arrogance had alienated, the Negro insurgents registered astonishing successes. But the accord between Negro and mulatto did not last. Many of the mulattos were slave owners themselves, and the course of the revolution – the French government abolished slavery in 1794 – drove them into alliance with the whites in defence of property. Disaffection and conspiracy tugged at the Negro struggle. Yet

[1] *The Black Jacobins,* by C. L. R. James (Secker & Warburg, 1938), p. 37

by 1798, and despite British and Spanish intervention, L'Ouverture was recognized master of the colony. It was not a spectacle that Napoleon, aspiring to expand, let alone assure, the empire, approved. He restored slavery in the colonies and sent an army of 30,000 to enforce his will in Saint Domingue. Toussaint L'Ouverture was seized and taken to France, where he died in prison soon afterwards. But the Negro forces, now under another former slave, Jean Jacques Dessaline, and once again joined by mulattos in flight from white arrogance, gathered to fight – this time not merely for reform, but independence. Those French troops who escaped Negro bullets and knives were overtaken by yellow fever, and on New Year's Day, 1804, western Hispaniola, once Indian, then Spanish, then French, became an independent, overwhelmingly Negro republic, under its old Indian name of Haiti ('the place of mountains'). Those whites who did not flee were massacred in the following year, but this did not end racial turbulence. The legacy of division between mulatto and black survives to this day.

The Indians of Spanish America were no more cowed than the Africans showed themselves to be, and persistently rebelled against their treatment. Between 1770 and 1800, there were four major peasant risings in the Ecuadorian Sierra alone; many whites lost their lives and much property was destroyed before Indian resistance was crushed. In 1781 some 80,000 Indian men and women laid five-month siege to the city of La Paz in present-day Bolivia. But the independence struggle of Spanish America in general – the exception was Mexico, where Indian insurrection played an important role – was conducted by the largely white *criollo* ruling class which wanted to escape from Spanish control for its own economic and political purposes.

Spain, like the rest of Europe, espoused 'mercantilism', the gospel of colonial monopoly by which raw materials were drawn from tied overseas possessions, and manufactures sent in return, to the supposed ultimate profit of metropolitan and colonist alike. But the very extent of American treasure corrupted the system. As gold and silver flooded into Spain, agriculture and industry there, never efficient, helplessly deteriorated. The Crown squandered money on European wars and fell ever further into debt, while inflation pushed the price of key commodities to ruinous levels. But the more effort and investment the Spanish economy required, the less it obtained. Easy money had come in the past; why should it not come again? By the early seventeenth century, the industrialized states of northern Europe were providing five-sixths of the manufactures consumed by Spain herself and nine-tenths of those that she was shipping to America.

The easy-money fever of Spain was endemic to the colonies, too, where the prospect of gold, silver and precious stones had stimulated conquest and then drawn settlers across desert and jungle into the distant interior. The rewards of discovery were phenomenal; by the close of the colonial period, some $5,000 million in value had come from the mines of Spanish America. But such pillage was more productive in the colonies than it proved to be in Spain. Where rich mines were sunk, cities rose, and farms spread round them to feed their swelling populations. Small industries developed and trade increased. A new class elbowed its way between the imperious land-owning few and the subjugated landless many – a widening file of professionals, merchants, manufacturers and those of fresh enterprise in farming or ranching. To such men, and that portion of the creole aristocracy they influenced, the Spanish hold seemed increasingly insupportable. Why should American sugar, cotton, hides, tobacco and cocoa be sold cheaply to Spain, and textiles, agricultural and mining implements, a whole host of needed manufactures and machines, be bought expensively there, when England or France or Holland would pay far more for American products and, discarding the profit of the Spanish middlemen, charge far less for their own? The cry for free trade rose from the colonies, and with its persistent denial, discontent at Spanish government grew.

If economics fed nationalism, so did geography. The mountains, rivers, jungle and desert of Spanish America cultivated regional allegiances, with the prospects of regional power once the imperial panoply was removed. The control of the *peninsulares*, the native Spaniards, over most offices of state was both affronting and inefficient. Had the Spanish monarchy presented a less ignominious spectacle, its subjects might have hesitated to rebel. But it had sovereignty without strength, and pride without purpose; its corruption outstripped its resources, and its pretensions, its prestige. British colonies in the north had defeated a far more formidable power and were enjoying a prosperous independence. By the early years of the nineteenth century, Spanish America was ready to reject Spain. But the rejection was not to be a rising of the serf and slave. When Negroes and mulattos in Venezuela, stirred by news of the French Revolution, had rebelled in 1795, to proclaim 'the law of the French' with the freeing of slaves, they had been easily suppressed and savagely punished, without lighting fires in powerful colonial hearts. The strength of the nationalist cause in Spanish America lay in the frustrations of the free, who shouted the slogans of the French Revolution, but only as these applied to themselves. The North American colonists never supposed, in issuing their demand, that 'life, liberty and the pursuit of happiness' were to be given to the Negro slave or the Red Indian. The *criollos* shouting outside the town hall of Buenos Aires on May 25th, 1810, 'El pueblo quiere saber de qué se trata' (the people want to know what is going on), did not encompass Indians or Negroes in their definition of 'people'. Indeed, many Indians, Negroes and those of mixed blood did not want independence at all, since Spain was at least a devil that they knew, while *criollo* government might prove even more ruthless and exacting than the Spanish court had shown itself willing or able to be.

The struggle was prolonged and, since the various regions had few links with each other outside the overall authority of Spain, involved not only a whole series of liberation wars, but the dissolution of Spain's various viceregal areas themselves into different states. In 1810 the *criollos* of the Rio de la Plata viceroyalty rose in revolt; by 1813 the Paraguayans had declared their independence not only of Spain but also of Buenos Aires, and a movement for the separate sovereignty of the Banda Oriental, modern Uruguay, had begun. Then, in 1816, the *criollos* of Buenos Aires and the bulk of the viceroyalty proclaimed the independence of what would be called Argentina, and adopted a democratic constitution which promised popular suffrage, individual freedom, the inviolability of the home, the political neutrality of the armed forces and the abolition of slavery. The intentions were admirable, and some of them remain, a century and a half later, admirable intentions still.

It was a native Argentinian, José de San Martín, the son of a Spanish officer and himself a former soldier in the Spanish army, who carried revolution northwards. Realizing that there could be no secure independence for Argentina herself while Spanish power survived intact on the other side of the Andes, he raised an army, defeated the Spaniards in Chile and proceeded to Peru, where he augmented his forces with slaves. Simón Bolívar, the son of wealthy *criollos* in Caracas, who was carrying the revolution southwards, was less selective in his dedication to liberty. After the failure of insurrection in Venezuela, he had taken refuge in Haiti, where the mulatto President, Alexandre Pétion, had provided him with arms, ammunition, ship and money, and extracted in return a promise that the independence movement would free the slaves. Bolívar kept his promise, and even had one of his *criollo* generals court-martialled and shot for attempting to stir up antagonism between white and coloured.

By 1822, when Bolívar, President of Colombia, and San Martín, Protector of Peru, met at Guayaquíl, in present-day Ecuador, most of Spanish America had proclaimed its independence and was straining apart.

In Peru, Spanish forces held the highlands still, but dissension rent the republican leaders. The two liberators themselves could not agree on how to proceed. San Martín resigned his office and left for a quarter-century of exile and death in Europe. 'The presence of a fortunate soldier,' he proclaimed, with an insight that the future would consistently confirm, 'however disinterested he may be, is dangerous to newly constituted states.'[1] Bolívar effectively completed the defeat of Spanish power in 1824, and planned a Spanish-American League of Nations with its centre in Panama; but his efforts crashed against the force of regional allegiances and individual rivalries. 'I am convinced to the very marrow of my bones', he wrote in 1826, 'that our America can only be ruled through an able despotism.'[2] There was certainly no lack of candidates. Bolivia, the region of Upper Peru to which he had given his name, turned against the general he had left there as President. Peru invaded both Bolivia and Colombia, and Colombia itself, the centre-piece of Bolívar's proposed confederation, fell apart, with Venezuela and Ecuador establishing their separate sovereignties. Shortly before he died in 1830, on his way to exile in Europe, he cried with bitterness: 'America is ungovernable. Those who have served the revolution have ploughed the sea.'[3]

The new republics of Spanish America, like the Boer republics in South Africa a half-century later, were in the hands of aggressive individualists, resenting any authority but their own, and united only in a determination to secure their freedom and independence from the claims of those who had neither. That there were such claims, the Mexican war of independence had made uncomfortably clear. In 1810 a priest in the poor village of Dolores, Miguel Hidalgo y Costilla, rallied the Indians of the parish with the cry from the pulpit: 'My children, this day comes to us a new dispensation. Are you ready to receive it? Will you be free? Will you make the effort to recover from the hated Spaniards the lands stolen from your forefathers three hundred years ago?' Armed with a variety of weapons, his recruits multiplied rapidly to 50,000 Indians and *mestizos*,[4] who then attacked and pillaged the provincial capital of Guanajuato, leaving thousands of dead Spaniards and *criollos* in their wake. Hidalgo himself was captured by trickery, tried by a military court and shot ten months after his '*grito de Dolores*', the first call to Indian rebellion. But the rebellion could not so easily be crushed.

[1] *The New Cambridge Modern History*, Vol. IX (C.U.P., 1965), pp. 626–7.
[2] Ibid., p. 628.
[3] H. Herring, op. cit., p. 286.
[4] Of mixed white and Indian parentage.

José María Morelos, a *mestizo* priest who had early attached himself to Hidalgo's cause, now fired Indian aspirations throughout southern Mexico, where he convened a congress in 1813, proclaimed Mexico's independence and promulgated a constitution. He, too, was captured, tried, convicted and shot in December 1815. But the rebellion persisted, with guerilla bands roaming the countryside. The *criollos*, liberal and conservative alike, now united to demand independence of a more manageable nature, and a force was raised by Agustín de Iturbide, who had himself fought in the Spanish army against both Hidalgo and Morelos. The new battle-cry, which promised support for the Church and the equality of Spaniard and *criollo* in an independent Mexico, offered nothing to the Indians and the mass of the *mestizos*; rallied many of the royalist generals; and in 1821 yielded the country to Iturbide. As Emperor Agustin I, Iturbide reigned for less than a year and was then forced to abdicate by other contenders for power and his own incompetence. A republic was proclaimed, and a president inaugurated, together with an era of turmoil, corruption and violence. Almost at once the old Captaincy-General of Guatemala broke away to form the United Provinces of Central America, and this disintegrated in 1838 to establish the independent republics of Guatemala, El Salvador, Honduras, Nicaragua and Costa Rica.

Nowhere was the oligarchic character of the Latin American revolutions more apparent than in Brazil, where the independence movement was led from within the royal family. In 1807 the Braganzas fled from Napoleon's armies to their American colony, and when in 1821 King John VI at last returned home, his son Dom Pedro, whom he had left as Regent, refused to comply with the reactionary instructions from Lisbon. In September 1822 he raised the cry of independence and, enthusiastically applauded by the planters and merchants who hoped for much by free trade, was soon afterwards proclaimed Pedro I, Emperor of Brazil. A 'liberal constitution' was promulgated in 1824, but it would take another sixty-four years before slavery itself was abolished on the eve of establishing republican government.

With the retreat of Spanish and Portuguese power, other countries, especially Britain and the United States, moved to promote their own advantage. Britain recognized the independence of the new states long before Spain showed herself prepared to do so; invested money in mines, plantations, trade and industry (more than £20 million by 1825)[1]; and negotiated a series of agreements which were to give her a substantial

[1] *Latin America* by Gilbert Phelps (British Broadcasting Corporation, 1965), p. 70.

share in such profitable enterprises as meat-packing and the railways. Inevitably the United States, which had dispatched commercial agents to parts of Latin America even before the wars of independence had commenced, regarded such new European intrusions with alarm. In December 1823 President Monroe sent to Congress a message which propounded four main principles of policy: that the United States would not intervene in European affairs; would respect Europe's surviving possessions in the Americas; but would not allow the new republics to be regarded as 'subjects for future colonization by any European power'; and would consider any attempt by any European power to interfere in the affairs of the new republics 'for the purpose of oppressing them or controlling their industry' as evidence of 'an unfriendly disposition towards the United States'. It was a declaration without immediate menace, because the United States was not strong enough to enforce her will against European – especially British – sea power, or attempt the patrolling of her hemisphere on land; but as her strength increased, so did her ambition, and the Monroe Doctrine became a claim to continental suzerainty. By the middle of the twentieth century, European power had all but disappeared from the Americas, and the United States, with an overwhelming superiority of military strength in the West and an investment by her citizens and corporations of nearly $9,000 million in Latin America,[1] was in all but absolute control of her hemisphere.

Not the least of the reasons for this was the fundamental weakness of the new American states themselves. The *criollo* class which had seized power with independence had long possessed the 'El Dorado' mentality of colonial conquest. Riches were not to be made, let alone shared; they were to be found and splendidly enjoyed. And if they could not be found in new mines, new plantations, new trade, they could be found in extracting a share of the profits from foreign endeavour. But European and United States investment went less into industry, which promised slow returns and worse, competition, than into quick and easy extractive enterprises like mining and plantation agriculture, with the communications necessary to serve them. And so the economy of Central and South America remained colonial; it was just the nationality of the colonizers, and the character of the colonizing process, that had changed.

The 'El Dorado' spirit inevitably permeated politics as well. Power itself was a fortune to be won, suddenly by personal exploit, rather than an obligation to be reluctantly wrested from the popular will. Had it not

[1] *Arms and Politics in Latin America*, by Edwin Lieuwen (Frederick A. Praeger, New York, 1960), p. 3.

been so from the beginning? The mass of the ignorant and poor, so different still in culture and in colour, had always been conquered and ruled by the strong – by the heroic *conquistadores* themselves; by the King and his arrogant officials; by the feudal *criollos* on their vast intransigent estates. *Caudillismo*, the cult of the *caudillo* or boss, was more than an aggressive individualism, the longing for the personal triumph of pride and courage that the Iberian past, in the struggle for sustenance from a grudging earth, in the wars of a stark Catholicism against an Islam bland and urbane, in the single-minded seizing of empire and enrichment, had nourished; it was a contempt for people.

The rich and powerful *criollo* did not even bother with politics, provided that those who did served his interests as well as their own. Independence had stopped the flow of wealth to the imperial court and the intervention of imperial officials in his affairs, while opening up new areas of trade; that was sufficient. The Church, for all the efforts of its idiosyncratic reformers, was itself now the richest and most powerful of the *criollos*, satisfied to leave politics to others for as long as change represented no more than a replacement of one administrator by another. It was the ambitious among the poorer *criollos* who sought the power of government, with its opportunities for selling concessions to foreign enterprise, pillaging the public treasury, and breaking into the upper reaches of wealth and social prestige. For them there was only one instrument available – the army.

Between independence and the first world war, the republics of Spanish-speaking America experienced one hundred and fifteen successful revolts and many times that number of unsuccessful ones.[1] The procedure was all but invariable. An influential officer proclaimed his desire for necessary reforms, or his hostility to projected ones; rallied the disaffected to his cause; and organized the *cuartelazo* or barracks revolt. If he succeeded in capturing the presidential office, where power under the constitution resided, he busily enriched himself, his family and main supporters till the next successful revolt.

Over this struggle for personal plunder, a cloak of principle was customarily cast. Two issues distracted the attention of the politically articulate: the dispute between the landowner-and-Church-supported Conservatives and the mainly middle-class-supported Liberals; and the dispute between centralists, who wanted a strong national government, and the federalists, who wanted a large measure of autonomy for the constituent provinces or states. The *caudillo*, whether a civilian manipulator of votes or, more usually, a military commander, placed himself at the head of the

[1] E. Lieuwen, op. cit., p. 21.

Conservative cause when the Liberals were in power, or the Liberal cause when the Conservatives ruled; fought for federalism when he controlled a part of the country, and for centralism when he controlled the whole. The Liberals were seldom powerful or radical enough to threaten the interests of the Conservatives, and the Conservatives generally found the Liberals more useful than dangerous. If either group grew excessive in its demands, the other could subsidize a new *caudillo* to promote moderation. It was a profitable arrangement for all but the mass of the people, whose sporadic rebellions were ruthlessly crushed or shrewdly exploited to change one *caudillo* for another.

Such societies were less concerned with expansionism than with the internal melodrama of rule. (One terrible exception was Paraguay in the 1860s, where the dictator, Francisco Solano López, waged simultaneous war against Argentina, Brazil and Uruguay for six years, till his country's population had been more than halved to less than a quarter of a million, and only 29,000 males survived.) With their fundamentally static structures, on which the rivals for government performed as on a stage; with their ruling classes complacently in ultimate control, their Church concerned above all for stability, their *caudillos* permitted corruption as a safe and essential indulgence, their peasants generally sunk in sullen subjugation: they offered an easy prey to the sense of 'manifest destiny' in the United States.

Within a few years of achieving its independence, Mexico fell into the clutch of Antonio López de Santa Anna, a soldier of rich *criollo* stock who had fought in the wars against the Indian insurgents. From 1828 he was the dominant force in Mexican politics, placing and displacing presidents when he was not president himself; backing now the Liberals, now the Conservatives, always to his personal aggrandisement. He soon became embroiled with the United States over Texas, a Mexican possession into which some 25,000 citizens of the United States had filtered by 1830. In 1836 the two countries went to war, which Santa Anna's spectacular rashness and corrupt army contractors helped him to lose, and in 1837 Texas became independent under United States protection. Mexico refused to accept the loss, and the United States was not yet satisfied. In 1845 the United States formally annexed Texas and by the following year had engineered a war with Mexico over the adjacent territories. United States troops entered Mexico City, and the rich, fearing a general upheaval that would destroy their property and power, led the cry to rid the nation of these new *conquistadores* at almost any price. The price was high. By the Treaty of Guadalupe, Mexico gained $15 million and gave formal assent to the annexation of Texas together with the territory that is now California, New Mexico, Arizona, Nevada, Utah and part of Colorado – about half her total area. A later President of the United States, Ulysses S. Grant, described the war as 'the most unjust ever waged by a stronger against a weaker nation'.[1] Yet it was not the end of humiliation for Mexico. In 1853, two years before his final retreat into exile, Santa Anna, heavily in debt and dependent on his patronage and pageantry to survive, sold 45,000 square miles of the north to the United States for $10 million.

During the next few decades the United States contented herself with attempting – in the main, successfully – to block European, especially British, incursions into the hemisphere. Then, in the middle of the 1890s, a new mood of exultation and expansionism gripped the country. 'Today', Secretary of State Richard Olney proclaimed, 'the United States is practically sovereign on this continent, and its fiat is law upon the subjects to which it confines its interposition.' Industry was searching for new markets, and capital for new investment; the clamour was for empire. 'This country needs a war,' Theodore Roosevelt wrote in 1895, and it soon enough made one. Cuba had remained a remnant of Spanish empire in the Americas, its guerilla war for liberation from 1868 to 1878 crushed at the cost of 200,000 lives. Then in 1895 guerilla warfare broke out again, with money, guns and recruits gathered in the United States. Spanish forces seemed about to crush all resistance once more, when the United States herself intervened in 1898, annexing Hawaii as a naval station in the Pacific and expelling Spain from Cuba, Puerto Rico and the Philippines. She had publicly pledged herself to Cuban independence, but she intended it to be of a tractable kind. Her troops stayed on the island, helping to repair the economy and administration, and they left only in 1902, when a constitutional assembly had accepted, alongside the grant of naval bases and other limitations on sovereignty, a provision (the so-called Platt Amendment) that read: 'Cuba consents that the United States may exercise the right to intervene for the preservation of Cuban independence, the maintenance of a government adequate for the protection of life, property and individual liberty.' The island had become a United States protectorate, and in the years that followed United States power would repeatedly, by diplomatic menaces or the dispatch of marines, ensure a congenial administration.

In 1901 Theodore Roosevelt, an uninhibited imperialist, took office as President. On November 3rd, 1903, a tiny revolt broke out in Panama City against Colombian rule, and United States forces were opportunely

[1] H. Herring, op. cit., p. 324.

there to prevent the landing of Colombian troops. Then, on November 6th, the United States formally recognized the independent Republic of Panama, and on November 18th signed a treaty with the new government for the construction of a canal from the Atlantic to the Pacific. She was granted perpetual possession of a strip ten miles wide across the Isthmus 'as if it were sovereign', with the right to appropriate other land and water for the proper functioning of the Canal and to intervene when necessary for the Canal's protection. In return she paid a lump sum ($10 million) and annuity ($250,000), and undertook to maintain the 'independence of the Republic'.

United States investors were increasingly involved in exploiting the natural resources of Latin America, wedding economic to political interest. Large corporations commanded the exploitation of sugar, fruit, coffee, asphalt, petroleum, and from 1900 to 1919 trade with the Caribbean states alone increased from $195 million to more than $1,000 million.[1] Trade followed the flag, and the flag followed trade. In December 1904, after a clash between the United States and three European powers, whose warships blockaded Venezuela to enforce the repayment of debts, Roosevelt informed Congress: 'Chronic wrongdoing ... may in America, as elsewhere, ultimately require intervention by some civilized nation, and in the Western Hemisphere, the adherence of the United States to the Monroe Doctrine may force the United States, however reluctantly ... to the exercise of an international police power.' The United States was assuming the right to ensure amenable regimes throughout the continent.

The Dominican Republic was heavily in debt to European bondholders, and from 1905 the United States took increasing control over its finances and general administration. United States representatives supervised the elections of 1913, and three years later marines intervened to subdue a rebellion. The intervention soon turned into military occupation, and the occupation did not end – despite repeated Dominican protests – till 1924, after the republic's government had agreed to ratify all the acts of the military regime and enlarge the powers of the United States appointed General-Receiver of the Customs.

In 1915 United States marines seized the chief towns in the adjoining Republic of Haiti after a revolutionary outbreak there and compelled the acceptance of a treaty which turned the state into a virtual protectorate. The Haitian parliament was not altogether submissive, and the speech of

[1] *Political and Social History of the United States 1829–1925* by Arthur M. Schlesinger (Macmillan, New York, 1925), p. 491.

Dr Raymond Cabèche, one of the deputies, was re-echoed in the sentiments of most articulate Latin Americans. 'I do not favour a closed
republic. I do not think that isolationism is an instrument of progress for a
nation. I do not believe that the principles of patriotism lie in hatred of
foreigners and in refusals to accept foreign aid even when it is sincerely
offered. But I do not believe either that it can be honourable to sacrifice
the dignity of one's country, whether under compulsion or not. To sacrifice it for what? Order at the cost of shame? Prosperity in golden chains?
Prosperity we may get – chains we most certainly will have.'[1] Haiti had
been the first country of coloured population and Latin rule to wage a
successful war of independence; it had given not only refuge but material
help to Simón Bolívar, the hero of Latin American struggle. The humiliation of Haiti had symbolic implications for all those who lived within
reach of United States power.

The chains were unquestionably gilded. The occupying forces provided
an efficient administration, hospitals and medicines, sewage systems and
electricity. But their mastery was blatant and basically racist. At first,
indeed, the United States government sent marines from the Deep South,
on the assumption that they would best know how to handle Negroes,
and even when this policy was recognized as a blunder and changed, individual marines continued to display the same sure sense of racial superiority. Moreover, the administration favoured the light-skinned élite over
the dark, and arranged elections which deprived the Negro majority of
any real part in government. Deep resentment followed the revival in
1917–18 of the *corvée* forced labour system for building roads, and guerilla
rebellions in the north were crushed with gratuitous violence. All in all,
the rule of a long independent black republic by white troops and
officials, for almost twenty years, stirred racial sentiment throughout the
hemisphere.

The spreading suzerainty of the United States was a capitalist one,
directed at securing and promoting the trade and investment of private
enterprise. It concerned itself less with freedom than with stability, less
with popular betterment than with the protection of property, and it
promised therefore increasingly to collide with attempts by the peasant
masses to alter their condition. Mexico, nearest of all the Southern
American nations to the United States, was the first, by several decades,
to produce a peasant revolution of economic purpose, and inevitably this
became embroiled with the interests of United States investment.

[1] Quoted in *Latin America: The Balance of Race Redressed*, by J. Halcro Ferguson (O.U.P.,
1961), p. 73.

After a five-year period of foreign, mainly French, intervention – during which the country acquired and killed an emperor – and a few years of souring reform, before and afterwards, the government fell into the firm hands of Porfirio Díaz, a *mestizo* of little education who became the most efficient of the generals and seized power in 1876, to rule for thirty-four years. The army he kept faithful by allowing the senior officers a generous salary for display – with ample opportunity for amassing a fortune by starving their conscripts – while constantly shifting them from one regiment and region to another. The Church he consoled by ignoring the measures of reform introduced in 1857 by the Indian President, Juárez, and permitting it to increase the number of its clergy, dignities and landholdings. The politicians he conciliated by observing the letter of the constitution, while effectively naming all 'elected' officials himself. And the *hacendados* or land barons he delighted by giving them security, with his ruthless rural police; markets for their produce, with the construction of railways; and encouragement to extend still further their estates. Thousands of Indian villages were dispossessed of their communal land, and more than 180 million acres, almost a third of the national area, sold to the old and new *hacendados*. By 1910, nearly all the occupied land in the country was in the hands of the land barons, with the overwhelming mass of the population – some 98 per cent – altogether landless. The peon, with a wage that had not changed for a century, was a slave in all but name, forced to work at his master's command and devote his womenfolk to his master's pleasure, flogged for the slightest disobedience and shot at the first sign of rebellion.

Foreign, especially United States, enterprise found the regime amenably profitable and protective. Díaz himself had little respect for the Indian or *mestizo* and surrounded himself with *criollo* advisers, who considered that Mexico's future lay in the dominion of the white man, with the coloured mass useful only through its servitude. The laws of Spanish tradition were changed to grant possession of all subsoil wealth to the owner of the surface, and risk capital, mostly from the United States, rapidly revived the mining industry. Oil was discovered, and concessions granted to United States and British companies. Textile mills, retail stores, transport and power companies were established by European and North American investment, while more and more of the best land was bought up by foreign, especially United States, citizens. The rich grew steadily richer, and the poor, their wages eroded by inflation, increasingly restless.

In 1910 revolution broke out, fired by the liberal Francisco Madero but with the independent participation of peasant leaders like Emiliano

Zapata, who conducted guerilla warfare against the land barons and the police. Mobs surged through the capital in May 1911, Díaz fled to Europe, and Madero succeeded to the presidency. But peasant insurgency persisted; the right rallied round the head of the armed forces, Victoriano Huerta, with the encouragement of the United States ambassador; and in 1913 Madero was murdered. Huerta's regime received recognition from Britain and the other main European powers, but the new President of the United States, Woodrow Wilson, saw no future in opposing peasant rebellion with mere reaction, and backed Venustiano Carranza, a rich opportunist who had been a senator in the days of Díaz and associated himself with the aspirations of the middle class. Turmoil ensued as rivals led their armies in pillage across the country, and though United States intervention in 1914 toppled Huerta's regime – marines seized the city of Veracruz and proclaimed martial law – this infuriated even Huerta's enemies. Carranza secured the presidency only by publicly accepting the programme of agrarian reform demanded by Zapata and the Indian insurgents.

The constitution of 1917, climax of the revolution, contained a radical code for the protection and organization of labour; severely curtailed the wealth, power and activities of the Church; authorized a drastic redistribution of land, with the return of all communal village holdings alienated since 1854; and declared all land and natural resources to be national property, with private ownership and exploitation, especially by foreigners, subject to close control and even cancellation. Though it would long remain a constitution more of illusion than reality, it roused as much enthusiasm among radicals in Southern America as execration among investors and their governments abroad. 'Godless and socialistic Mexico' was stridently assailed, not least by the Church which had found godliness so profitable.

Carranza himself took the constitution less seriously, and despite the capture and murder of Zapata, could not crush the peasant unrest. By 1920 his hold was slipping fast, and deserted by Alvaro Obregón, the general who had sustained him, he plundered the treasury, set out for exile, and was murdered on the way. The next fourteen years did little to alleviate the lot of the Mexican masses. The United States raged against the provisions of the constitution affecting private ownership and exploitation; but assured by Obregón that they would not be made retro-active, the American government recognized his regime in 1923. When two years later the new boss of Mexican politics, Plutarco Calles, ordered the oil companies to exchange their holdings for fifty-year concessions, a clamour for armed intervention arose in the United States. Calles collapsed to the pressure and even agreed that the redistribution of land, hardly begun in earnest, had gone far enough. The labour movement grew steadily in influence, but though it achieved some improvement in wages, working conditions and security for the industrial force, it succeeded more spectacularly in advancing the personal fortunes of its own *caudillos*. Only in the struggle against the Church did the fervour of the revolution not flag. By 1926 all the priests had withdrawn from their altars in protest at government policy, and bands of believers under the name of *cristeros* were burning state schools and murdering state teachers, while Calles forced recalcitrant clergy into exile. After three years of this, and under United States pressure, the Mexican government recognized the supremacy of the Church in spiritual matters and permitted religious instruction within church walls; the priests returned to their altars and the *cristeros* to their prayers.

It was the election to the presidency of a peasant-born administrator, Lázaro Cárdenas, in 1934 during the depression, that gave some meaning at last to the long Mexican revolution. Cárdenas stripped the generals of their influence and the army of its traditional dominance; reorganized the nominal party of the revolution on a peasant and worker base; and initiated a major rural reform, transferring forty-five million acres of cropland to communal village ownership. Foreign enterprise stirred in alarm, and with reason. When the oil companies refused to devote more of their huge profits to raising wages, he decreed the expropriation of their properties. The Mexican masses were jubilant, but the companies hit back, boycotting sales of Mexican oil on the world market, blocking the purchase of essential machinery, and frightening off tourist traffic by their propaganda. Oil revenues fell disastrously; but Franklin D. Roosevelt was in the White House, war in Europe was looming, the oil companies in the end accepted compensation that they regarded as scathingly inadequate, and an open break between Mexico and the United States was averted.

The Mexican revolution was more than an economic and political upheaval. The assault on the land barons destroyed much of the urbane, consciously derivative European culture which their wealth and tastes had supported, and in its place a new dominant culture developed, consciously indigenous, drawing on Indian traditions, but contemporary and rich in original achievement. The arts flourished as never since before the coming of the *conquistadores*, and not as a mere embellishment of leisure, but as a deep concern with the purpose and direction of society. This reflected far more than the displacement of a class; it was the displacement of a race.

Though the Indian peasantry was – and is – not yet emancipated from the slavery of its past, Mexico ceased to be a white man's country. In its deepest cultural identification, it became a coloured one, a fusion of its white and Indian elements, with results that no part of the hemisphere could for ever escape.

Mexico was not alone in changing, though nowhere else did change reach so deep. In the years before the outbreak of the first world war, the population of Southern America rapidly increased – from 30 to 80 million between 1875 and 1914 – with immigrants from Europe, especially Spain and Italy, streaming to the promise of prosperity. Argentina became the world's leading exporter of wheat and beef; Brazil, of coffee; and Chile, of nitrate: while Bolivia became a major source of tin; and the small Caribbean and Central American republics, of sugar, coffee and bananas. But only in Uruguay, where an exceptional leader, José Batlle y Ordóñez, guided the country from the clutch of the land barons to a Swiss-type democracy based on the middle class, did mild social reform spill over to the masses. Costa Rica, acclaimed for its early and persevering dedication to democracy, was all but owned by the United Fruit Company, a United States corporation whose prosperity was not unconnected with the pitiless wages it paid to its plantation labourers. Elsewhere, the traditional oligarchy of land barons, higher clergy and military élite remained firmly in command, with foreign enterprise in contented alliance. In Brazil, a republic had been established in 1889 by an army revolt – with the support of the *fazendeiros* or land barons, whom the abolition of slavery had offended; the clergy, who feared the liberalism of the King; and the liberals, who thought the King too conservative. A period of turbulence, promoted by rabid regional rivalries and the disposition of the military élite to intervene at every opportunity, was brought under temporary control only by an understanding that the *caudillos* of the two major states, coffee-rich São Paulo and mineral-rich Minas Gerais, would alternate in possession of overall power. It was a bargain that suited the *fazendeiros* well enough, since the ordered plunder of office provided them with a stable and protective administration.

The first world war, by cutting manufactures and immigrants from Europe, encouraged industrialization and a drift to the cities from the countryside for the new jobs available. In Argentina and Chile, the Radicals, representing the interests of the middle class, took temporary power, and elsewhere the middle class increased its pressure for a sizeable share in the control and distribution of wealth. But in the main the Southern America of the post-war boom (excluding, of course, the remaining colonies of Britain, France and Holland) was commanded by the *caudillos*, who governed from one military intervention to the next for the greater good of the traditional oligarchy. Cheap loans – some $2,000 million worth of them – streamed from the New York banks to the independent governments, whose occupants commonly pocketed a suitable commission, and spent most of the rest on public works, more ornamental than productive; on the provision of a large bureaucracy; and on the conciliation of the military by supplies of money and the latest fashion in armaments. With the crash on Wall Street in 1929, New York suddenly stopped supplying loans, and as trade shrivelled in the deepening world depression, dismissed public servants, unpaid soldiers and the industrial unemployed rioted around the presidential palaces.

Echoes of the Russian revolution had soon reached Southern America. In 1918 a Communist Party was founded in Argentina, and mineworkers in neighbouring Chile were quick to adopt the new doctrines. European immigrants brought their long experience of economic struggle in their luggage, and the steady development of industry and the urban working force during the 'twenties nourished recruitment. But communism as a cry of industrial workers and a few venturesome intellectuals did not seriously challenge the traditional order on a continent still overwhelmingly rural. As the Mexican revolution was revealing, only the aroused peasants possessed the potential to change the basic social structure.

In 1924 a young army officer, Luiz Carlos Prestes, led an unsuccessful revolt against the government in Brazil and, taking flight with the remnants of his following, led a long march – almost as spectacular as that of the Red Army in China a few years later – through some of the most formidable terrain on earth, negotiating treaties with Indian tribes, establishing areas of insurgency, and fighting over fifty battles with federal troops. At last, after three years, Prestes and the other survivors entered Bolivia, leaving behind them the memory of rural endeavour and a powerful legend. Prestes himself then spent a few years in Moscow, where his ardour assumed doctrinal shape, and in 1934 founded the National Liberation Alliance, to advance the Brazilian revolution. But Brazil had already acquired a different sort of saviour, the dictator with his promise of disciplined reform, and it was this model – the old *caudillo* in demagogic dress – which Southern America would increasingly produce to answer the challenge of popular unrest.

The elections of 1930 were no more fraudulent than usual, but by placing a *paulista* to succeed a *paulista* in the presidency, they broke the long agreement by which the political bosses of São Paulo alternated with those of Minas Gerais in access to the spoils of office. The *mineiros* had supported the candidate of a third state, Getulio Vargas, and a military revolt now seated him in the presidency. Vargas ruled Brazil for fifteen years, using a revolt in 1935 as the occasion to arrest thousands of Communists and other left-wing opponents of his regime – Prestes, who had returned to Brazil, was among the first imprisoned– and then crushing in 1938 an insurrection by his former supporters, the green-shirted fascist *Integralistas*. In 1938 he dissolved Congress altogether and promulgated a new constitution which made him dictator for as long as he chose; he described the system as 'a disciplined democracy', and – with an eye on Salazar's despotism in Portugal – named it the *Novo Estado*, or New State. On the whole, however, he conducted himself more like the flamboyant Mussolini, even draining the marshes near the capital. He assumed close control of the trade unions and the whole economy, encouraging industrialization and national command of new projects like steel production; governed by decree and persecuted opponents, whether individuals or newspapers, but generally avoided any open display of brutality and padded the strong arm with sloppiness; and cajoled the urban multitudes not only with nationalism – he dismantled the barricades that the bosses had raised between state and state – but also with better housing, higher wages and medical care. The United States gave him $300 million in loans and grants, while private capital approved of the stability that his regime provided and leapt to take advantage of the new industrial opportunities he offered. The value of industrial production rose from $153 million in 1920 to $1,300 million in 1940; but the lot of the peasant altered little, if at all, and the city slums swelled with fugitives from the countryside. In 1945, when a military revolt unseated Vargas and elections were held, the Communists polled 10 per cent of the votes, placing Prestes in the Senate, and when two years later they increased their congressional strength, the party was declared illegal, and its representatives were expelled from office. Vargas was returned to the presidency in the 1950 elections, but the fall in commodity prices, languishing industry, and rampant inflation fortified the hostility of Congress, Press and the army; he committed suicide in 1954, leaving subsequent administrations to juggle with the problems of the country in the shadow of his demagogic appeal.

The other important new-style *caudillo*, Juan Domingo Perón, made himself the master of Argentina for years and remains still an enormous influence. The middle-class Radical government of the 'twenties did not long survive the coming of the slump; the army intervened, and a series of

Conservative administrations, representing the interests of the land-owning aristocracy, ruled the country till the next intervention of the army, in 1943. Then, from the military junta, one dominant figure emerged, Perón, who concentrated on building up a powerful trade union allegiance, among rural as well as urban workers, with the help of his brilliant mistress (soon to be his wife), Maria Eva (Evita) Duarte. In the elections of 1946, with the support of the Catholic hierarchy which feared the liberalism of his rivals, he gained the presidency, and he set out to rule as the saviour of the *descamisados* or 'shirtless ones', the labourers on the feudal estates, the badly paid industrial workers and, hardly better off, the lower ranks of the middle class. He reduced working hours and raised wages, initiated cheap housing projects, and promised land to the landless; but he kept the trade unions on a tight rein, avoided such rural reform as would provoke the land barons too far, and imprisoned the leaders of the left who continued to oppose him. Like Vargas, he exercised close control of the radio, Press and schools; like Vargas, he conciliated the armed forces with costly equipment and high pay; like Vargas, he encouraged industrialization as a nationalist objective; and, far more than Vargas, he rallied popular enthusiasm in a campaign against foreign, especially United States, power in Latin America. Helped by the hunger of post-war Britain for beef, he nationalized the British-owned railways, for the grudgingly accepted compensation of £150 million. Despite a soothing loan of $125 million from the United States in 1950, he set himself up as the protector of Latin, especially Spanish-speaking, America against United States imperialism; his emissaries recalled the intervention by United States marines in Haiti, Panama, the Dominican Republic, Nica-ragua and Columbia, and they busily denounced United States control of Cuban sugar, Bolivian tin, Chilean copper, Central American coffee and bananas. Perón even promised loans and a customs union to Argentina's poorer neighbours, as a defence against United States economic pressure; but the United States had far more money to spare, and raised the bids beyond Argentina's capacity.

Perón himself pretended to offer 'a middle way' between communism and capitalism; but despite his play for mass allegiance, he was essentially a paternalist *caudillo*, of the new demagogic right. He showed persistent admiration of Franco, exercised himself to have Spain admitted to the United Nations, and extended substantial credits to her for the purchase of Argentine meat and grain. Within Latin America itself, his agents worked to undermine the influence of the socialist trade unions and substitute ones of a *peronista* complexion, while military coups in Cuba, Peru and Venezuela, and the arrival of rigid right-wing regimes in Colombia and Chile, owed something to his hand. Then, in July 1952, Evita died to a tumult of popular mourning, and Perón gradually lost command of the country. Evita, herself born among the *descamisados*, had been able to measure and mould the mood of the streets, without dangerously antagonizing the landed aristocracy, the Church, or even the business community. Now alone, Perón provoked all three power groups too far, and faced by the opposition of the army as well, fled in 1955 to exile. But he left behind him an aroused industrial and rural working population, part of which remained strongly *peronista*, and a fresh resentment – which his agents had spread far beyond Argentina's borders – at the economic and political suzerainty of the United States over Latin America.

A different arousal was meanwhile developing northwards, echoing the Mexican experience in its racial quality. Venezuela, Colombia, Ecuador, Peru and Bolivia all displayed in varying degrees the domination of an Indian and *mestizo* population by a small white minority. In Peru, where 10 per cent of the people were white, 35–40 per cent *mestizo* and 50–55 per cent Indian, white command of economic and political power had long been blatant, and articulate disaffection early assumed racial as well as revolutionary tones. José Carlos Mariátequi, a dedicated Marxist, denounced the feudal landlords and proclaimed the communal justice of the Inca era, influencing many young intellectuals in the 'twenties not only to adopt communism but identify themselves with their Indian heritage. One young intellectual of Spanish ancestry, Haya de la Torre, repudiated such dogmas as the dictatorship of the proletariat and so earned the enmity of Mariátequi's Communists; but he absorbed much Marxist theory, drew inspiration from the rural revolution in Mexico, and sought a popular base for struggle in Indian and *mestizo* aspiration. In 1924, from exile in Mexico, he announced the formation of an international movement, the *Alianza Popular Revolucionaria Americana* or A.P.R.A., which was directed to nationalization of land and industry, the collaboration of workers and intellectuals, and the unification of Indo-America, as Haya wished Latin America to be called, against the imperial power of the United States. The *apristas* made small material headway elsewhere in Latin America, but rapidly extended their influence in Peru and forced a presidential election in 1931. Though Haya de la Torre appears to have won massive support, he did not control the ballot boxes; the current *caudillo* declared himself elected, and imprisoned or exiled the *aprista* leaders. The economy remained basically colonial, with the United States controlling 80 per cent of the country's oil production, close to 100 per cent of the mineral output,

and substantial sugar and textile interests,[1] while the Peruvian rich contented themselves with a share of sugar, wool and cotton production,
alongside their cut from the profits of foreign enterprise. The *aprista*
movement flowed underground and then, in 1945, burst to the surface
with the election of Bustamante, an indecisive liberal, to the presidency.
For three years the *apristas* dominated the Congress and cabinet, drafting
measures of social reform; but the oligarchy of planters, generals and high
clergy blocked all effective progress, and by now the *apristas* themselves
were far more cautious than they had been in their youth. The movement
had captured much of the middle-class and intellectual elements, but had
failed to organize a militant peasantry. In 1948 Bustamante, having denounced the *apristas*, was himself unseated by a military putsch; the leading
apristas were exiled or imprisoned, and the country returned to the close
clutch of its traditional rulers.

Yet the ideas propagated by the A.P.R.A. helped, alongside so disparate
a pressure as Perón's right-wing campaign against United States suzerainty, to produce during the 'fifties in neighbouring Bolivia the first significant revolution since the Mexican one. With some 90 per cent of the
population Indian or dark *mestizo*, the 10 per cent that was white or
'whitish' dominated the society, while a small group of land barons, treating their Indian labourers as serfs, and above all the three great tin companies, ruled through *caudillos* contending only for personal power. While
Indians in the forests and valleys starved, the capital threw up some sixty
irrelevant revolutions in little more than a century, placing and displacing
a multitude of similar presidents. Then in 1932, with the economy battered by the blast of the world slump, Bolivia went to war with Paraguay
over an area to which neither state had clear title and which rumours of oil
made suddenly desirable. Bolivia, possessing more than three times the
population of her enemy and flashy weapons bought with United States
loans, had high hopes of a rapid victory; but her army consisted mainly of
conscripted Indians, sometimes sent to the front-line in chains, and by 1935
the fighting was virtually over, with some 60,000 Bolivians – and almost
as many Paraguayans – killed, and the Bolivian economy near ruin. The
war led to little expansion of territory, but to the first real stirrings of
popular unrest; returning Indian soldiers brought their bitterness home,
and labour leaders began organizing resistance in mine and on farm. In
1936 an army coup placed in power a young officer who reflected popular
hostility to the role of United States investment by expropriating the

[1] *Inside Latin America*, by John Gunther (Hamish Hamilton, 1942), p. 170. Figures quoted
from article in *Fortune*, January 1938.

properties of Standard Oil; but when he then set out to impose higher taxes on the tin companies, he was overthrown. By 1940 the old guard was once again in undisguised control, and its *caudillo* in the presidential palace showed his zeal for the interests of the tin companies by shooting scores of strikers at the mines in 1942. The regime compensated Standard Oil for its expropriated properties, and in return received loans for public works.

Discontent was by now too widespread, however, for such rule to last. The left-wing P.I.R. (*Partido Izquierdista Revolucionario*) joined with the largely middle-class M.N.R. (*Movimiento Nacional Revolucionario*), an alliance of right-wing nationalists, even fascists, and radicals, in an assault on the regime of tin barons and foreign capitalists. In December 1943 a new military *caudillo*, Major Gualberto Villarroel, took power, granted concessions to labour, and attempted to rally middle-class support by taking several M.N.R. leaders, including the economist Paz Estenssoro, into his cabinet. The United States, fearing Axis and Argentine influence, refused to recognize the regime. Villarroel expelled the M.N.R. representatives from his cabinet, forced Estenssoro into exile, and took strenuous measures against P.I.R. leaders and labour agitators. The United States recognized his regime. Then, suddenly, in July 1946, a mob stormed the presidential palace and hanged Villarroel, with other members of his cabinet, on lamp-posts. This popular outburst soon spent itself, partly in astonishment at its own passion, and traditional authority yet again took command. But a break with the past had been made, and when the army refused to accept the victory of Estenssoro at the polls, the country erupted into violence. The miners blew up railways and military depots, while in the capital mobs raged through the streets, attacking public buildings. The ranks of the army, with many of the junior officers, supported the insurrection; the military *caudillos* lost control; and Estenssoro returned from his refuge in Argentina to assume the presidency.

The twelve-year regime of Estenssoro was one of substantial reform. It extended the vote to illiterates, and so at last started the process of integrating the Indian peasants into formal politics. It initiated a serious campaign against illiteracy. It expropriated the swollen estates of the land barons for distribution among peasants and then, alarmed by the proliferation of *minifundia*, or subsistence smallholdings, encouraged the establishment of co-operatives. It nationalized the tin mines and the British-owned railways.

The United States government, after some initial shock, chose to support the Estenssoro programme of reform, as the seemingly sole effective answer to communism, and provided a higher *per capita* amount in aid and loans to Bolivia than to any other state in Latin America.[1] Estenssoro himself was not a figure of the alarming left, and could reasonably be relied upon to refrain from any embarrassing international initiatives or flirtation with the communist bloc. Without him and his spreading influence among the peasants, the revolutionary elements, so strong among the miners and the urban labour force, might produce a more drastic upheaval. As it was, however, the Estenssoro regime neither satisfied nor stilled unrest in the mines and the slums of the capital. The country remained ultimately dependent on tin, which rising labour costs and the exhaustion of the richest deposits made diminishingly profitable. (There were cynics enough to claim that this diminishing profitability had helped accommodate the United States to nationalization and the Estenssoro regime.) Gradually Estenssoro lost control of the situation, and though elected to a third term as president in May 1964, riots six months later persuaded him to flee the country, and a military junta took over the government. The new regime immediately arrested the political leader of the miners, Juan Lechín Oquendo, and deported him to Paraguay; the striking miners were joined by factory workers in La Paz, and widespread violence ensued. The military junta bombed striker strongholds, the army took possession of the mines, and labour leaders were imprisoned or deported. But any lasting return to traditional *caudillo* rule seemed unlikely. A militant proletariat and an awakened peasantry promised to be dangerous passengers on a journey to the past.

If the United States government behaved with some prudence over the Bolivian reformist regime in 1952, it resorted two years later in Guatemala to the crude interventionist tactics of the Theodore Roosevelt era. The Guatemalans – of whom there are some four million today, 60 per cent Indian and the rest *mestizo* – had long been ruled by an alliance of the army, the few feudal landowners, and foreign enterprise. A mere 2 per cent of the population owned more than 70 per cent of the land; schooling of any sort existed for less than half the children; labour unions, like all basic civil liberties, had been proscribed; and foreign firms enjoyed monopolistic privileges. Dominating the whole economy was the United Fruit Company of Boston, Massachusetts, with its hundreds of square miles and thousands of peons, its $50–60 million investment in banana and coffee plantations, and its control of the country's communications through the $50 million International Railways of Central America. Then, in 1944, popular unrest persuaded the current *caudillo* to leave the country,

[1] *The Revolutions of Latin America*, by J. Halcro Ferguson (Thames & Hudson, 1963), p. 99.

and elections in the following year placed Dr Juan José Arévalo, a liberal of the left, in the presidency. The new government produced a constitution on the Mexican model of 1917, guaranteeing the basic rights of labour and free institutions, and authorizing land reform; but Arévalo was cautious and refrained from measures likely to provoke the serious displeasure of the United Fruit Company. His successor, elected in 1950 with his backing, was Jacobo Arbenz Guzmán, a former army officer rather farther to the left and under much stronger left-wing pressure. All the evidence available suggests that Arbenz himself was not a Communist, and that the Communists, though by now some of them held positions of public influence, numbered no more than a few hundred. But the new regime was without doubt revolutionary, committed to improving the condition of the Indian labourer and drastically changing the feudal pattern of land ownership.

The Agrarian Law of July 1952 was, none the less, a moderate measure, aimed at distributing uncultivated land among peasant smallholders. Only holdings of over 666 acres were involved; owners were to be compensated by thirty-year 3 per cent bonds; and purchasers were required to repay the government in small instalments. But foreign firms, especially the United Fruit Company, which held large tracts of uncultivated land in reserve, regarded the new law as little better than communist confiscation. The government inevitably directed itself to the holdings of the Company, expropriated several hundred thousand acres, and allotted some $600,000 as compensation instead of the $4 million at which the company valued the land. The Eisenhower administration in the United States, pressed by the Company, and itself concerned at reports of mounting communist activity in Guatemala, decided to intervene.[1] The Central Intelligence Agency, entrusted with the task, arranged the appointment of a reliable diplomat as United States ambassador to Guatemala and settled on Colonel Carlos Castillo Armas, a Guatemalan officer who had fled to Honduras after an unsuccessful revolt in 1950, as leader of an invasion force. Tiburcio Carías, the dictator of Honduras, and Anastasio Somoza, the dictator of Nicaragua, were both party to the plot and provided training facilities for the army of invasion, while the C.I.A. itself contributed not only money and overall direction, but its own pilots and aeroplanes. On June 18th, 1954, Armas with his small 'Army of Liberation' crossed the Honduran frontier into Guatemala, and C.I.A. planes bombed

[1] For a closely documented account of United States intervention, and particularly the role of the Central Intelligence Agency, see *The Invisible Government*, by David Wise and Thomas B. Ross (Jonathan Cape, 1965), pp. 165-83.

San José, Guatemala's major port on the Pacific coast. The invasion force then settled down six miles within Guatemalan territory and waited for the government to collapse as the C.I.A. air force extended its attacks to the capital, and the United States ambassador there intrigued with senior Guatemalan officers. Accused by Guatemala of responsibility for the air raids, the United States government, through its ambassador to the United Nations, declared: 'The situation does not involve aggression, but is a revolt of Guatemalans against Guatemalans.' It was not a contention that carried much weight with predominant European, let alone Latin American, opinion. On June 25th, Arbenz Guzman announced his resignation, and Colonel Armas took charge of the country at the head of a military junta.

As its first act, the new regime abolished the right of all illiterates to vote and so excluded some 70 per cent of the population – almost all Indians – from any even superficial role in the political life of the country. The junta appointed Armas as president, and he suspended all constitutional liberties, achieving his formal election in a referendum not notable for the secrecy of the vote. The government then seized several hundred thousand acres from peasant ownership, returned the land expropriated from the United Fruit Company, repealed legislation guaranteeing rights to workers and trade unions, and arrested thousands of citizens on suspicion of communist activity. Ten years and two *caudillos* later, the lot of the Guatemalan peasantry was as miserable as ever, with the land barons and especially the United Fruit Company in prosperous command. Former President Eisenhower himself, in June 1963, admitted the role of his administration in the overthrow of the Arbenz regime. 'There was one time when we had a very desperate situation, or we thought it was at least, in Central America, and we had to get rid of a communist government ... '

Observers of the Latin American scene themselves friendly to the United States, subsequently declared that the Guatemalan intervention had probably done more to alienate Latin Americans and further the cause of communism in the area than any other single action that a United States government had ever undertaken. In the Congress of Costa Rica – a predominantly 'white' country – one representative implied that the issues posed by United States policy in Latin America were racial as well as political and economic.

Honourable members, I am a Communist created by the White House. Juan José Arévalo [former President of Guatemala], who is not and never has been a Communist of the first kind, but certainly of the second, declares that there exists 'Communism with a C and Kommunism with a K: Communism with a C is the international current represented by the Communist Party whose seat is in Moscow; Kommunism with a K is every political and social democratic current which tries to defend the interests of the working masses, of the humble, of the exploited throughout the world, or those who speak of sovereignty, or nationalism, or those who dare to criticize the United States.'

I, honourable members, am a Kommunist with a K because I am openly against the foreign policy of the United States. Because this policy has done great harm to me and all my Latin American brothers. *Because due to this policy thousands of Indians, Negroes and Mulattos have died of hunger. Hunger of the stomach, hunger of the conscience, hunger for liberty, hunger for work and hunger for a little culture ... This has been the policy of the United States towards us, the Latin American peoples.*[1] For this reason, we in Latin America have known only one real dictator – the foreign policy of the United States.[2]

This United States confusion of Communism with Kommunism, the inevitable plethora of stupidities and mistakes it provokes, alongside the economic, political, cultural and, indeed, racial resentment that it has long produced, was now to make Cuba the first state in Latin America to ally itself openly with the Soviet Union and the communist world. Certainly, nowhere else in independent Latin America was United States economic domination more evident than in Cuba before the Castro revolution. The island had a classically colonial economy: the United States bought almost all its one important cash crop, sugar, and sold to it almost all the manufactures – as well as 70 per cent of the food – it consumed, registering a constant surplus on the two-way trade. Moreover, United States citizens directly controlled half of all Cuban sugar production, owning 67 – generally the largest – of the 174 mills, and a quarter of the cultivated land.[3] The extent of United States financial involvement was measured by John Gunther in 1942 as near to $1,000 million – the 'largest American investment in any country in the hemisphere, Canada excepted'.[4]

[1] Author's italics.
[2] Enrique Obregón Valverde, in a speech to the Costa Rican Congress, June 8th, 1959. Quoted in *Latin America*, by J. Halcro Ferguson, p. 66.
[3] H. Herring, op. cit., p. 411.
[4] J. Gunther, op. cit., p. 368.

United States capital controlled more than 90 per cent of the island's electricity and telephones, and about half the railways.[1]

The distribution of land on the island reflected the vast discrepancy between the few rich and the multitude of peasants. Of the 22,500,000 acres of farmland, 70 per cent belonged to 8 per cent of the individual holdings, and 25 per cent to a mere 0·6 per cent. Some 500,000 of Cuba's 6 million people worked in the sugar fields or mills, but only 12 per cent had year-round employment; the rest worked seasonally, for four months or less each year, earning from $100 to $400 each for themselves and their families.[2] The sugar-cane cutters, the *peons* on the cattle ranches, the tobacco workers and the thousands of unemployed or casually employed in the capital of Havana itself, formed a forgotten layer of the deprived and discontented beneath the display of luxury tourist hotels and foreign-owned enterprise. Almost two-thirds of Cuban children had no schooling at all, and of those who were fortunate enough to reach the elementary classes, only a tiny fraction survived into secondary education.[3]

The latest *caudillo* was Fulgencio Batista, a one-time army sergeant who had first seized power in 1933; ruled Cuba directly or through puppets for thirteen years; retired with his millions to Florida for an eight-year civilian interlude; and taken dictatorship control through a military coup in 1952. Increasingly since then, Cuba had been ruled by a regime of corruption and terror, with Batista himself and his exorbitant entourage amassing immense fortunes from bribery and intimidation, from official manipulation of credit, and from organized gambling and prostitution. The United States government may well have disapproved; but, if so, it assiduously refrained from allowing principle to embarrass expediency. It courted Batista with decorations and military equipment for supposed hemispheric defence, while within Cuba itself the Batista regime increasingly alienated not only the suppressed peasantry but most of the middle class and the intellectuals. Peasant distress, middle-class disaffection and intellectual disgust did not commonly in Latin America, however, lead to anything but a new *caudillo*. It was the accomplishment of Fidel Castro that Cuba was to constitute an exception.

Castro was an intellectual of middle-class background – his father owned a sugar estate in the east of the island – who had been educated first at Jesuit schools and then at the University of Havana. Somewhere along the way he had acquired not merely a hatred for the Batista regime but a

[1] *Castro's Cuba*, by C. Wright Mills (Secker & Warburg, 1960), p. 25.
[2] H. Herring, op. cit., p. 411.
[3] C. Wright Mills, op. cit., p. 45.

resolve to do something about it, and on July 26th, 1953, he led 170 men and two women – most of them students – in an attack on the army garrison of Moncada. It was, initially, a fiasco. Some of the attackers were killed by Batista's 1,000 soldiers on the spot, some subsequently by Batista's police. A few, including Castro himself, were put on trial. But Castro used his trial as an occasion to denounce the regime, and his speech – 'History Will Absolve Me' – was smuggled out of the courtroom and clandestinely distributed. The attack of July 26th became the symbol of resistance to Batista. Castro, after influential intercession, was not executed but imprisoned and then, in 1955, released under a general amnesty. He went into exile, and at a ranch in Mexico organized a group of guerillas for an assault on the Cuban government.

In December 1956, with 81 other men, he landed from a yacht on the coast of Oriente, the province where his family lived, to launch what he called the 26th of July Movement in memory of the attack on the Moncada garrison. It was again, initially, a fiasco. The insurgents got lost in a swamp, failed to meet up with the group awaiting them on the island, and fell an easy prey to the alerted troops of Batista. Only twelve of the original force survived. Yet these concealed themselves successfully in the mountains, gathering supporters and training them in guerilla warfare. The leaders were, like Castro himself, intellectuals; but more and more of the recruits were *campesinos*, peasants, whose families and friends provided concealment and information. This was no traditional Latin American revolt, plotted and promoted by the military élite; this was a rural insurrection. The guerillas burned sugar estates, starting symbolically with the one owned by Castro's family; blew up power stations, bridges and railway lines; sniped from trees. Batista sent 12,000 men, with tanks and planes, to crush the guerillas. But the pilots did not know where to strike, while the tanks were destroyed by petrol traps. Castro's men even captured a military transmitter and code book, and bamboozled the Batista force into bombing its own positions and parachuting supplies to the guerillas. More and more of Batista's soldiers crossed over with their equipment to Castro, whose cause was still further advanced by money, arms and volunteers from other parts of Latin America. At last, on January 1st, 1959, the guerillas entered Havana, a conquering army created by the activity and acquiescence of the Cuban countryside.

It was a revolution in which the Communist Party itself had taken no part. The classic left in Cuba had long collaborated with *caudillismo* in return for control of the Cuban trade union movement, and when in 1952 Batista had outlawed it in deference to United States policy, it had set out,

a doctrinaire banker, to husband its proletarian reserves. And so, as previously in China, the orthodox communist policy of seizing power in the
cities and only then consolidating the countryside was outflanked by rural
revolution. But where in China the rural revolution had still been communist-led and controlled, in Cuba the victorious leadership – despite the
influential participation of passionate Marxists like Dr Ernesto 'Ché'
Guevara and Fidel's own younger brother, Raúl Castro – was committed
to little more than the promotion of a liberal democracy with the emphasis on sweeping rural reform. It was the obtuseness and arrogance of
United States policy, its 'Guatemalan' rather than 'Bolivian' response, that
combined with a new communist flexibility to change so far the character
of the Castro revolution.

   At first the United States government and press welcomed the new
regime, acclaiming its steps to eliminate official corruption and organized
vice. *Fortune* itself, an important periodical of the United States business
community, praised the Cuban Finance Minister for picking businessmen
as his assistants and running his department 'like General Motors'.[1] But the
trial and execution of former Batista supporters, mainly soldiers and
police, excited noisy protests from that section of United States opinion
already viewing Castro's more radical colleagues with distrust. An
agrarian reform law was promulgated, gradually expropriating holdings
in excess of 1,000 acres and offering compensation by 20-year $4\frac{1}{2}$ per cent
bonds, while other measures lowered the price of development land, reduced rents by as much as half, and abolished real-estate speculation.
Cuban and United States property interests on the island responded by
instituting an investment boycott; private enterprise building virtually
ceased; foreign capital investment began seriously to decline; and a sharp
decline in the sugar price added to the new regime's financial difficulties.
To conserve Cuba's foreign exchange, the regime then placed high
import surcharges on a range of imported goods, especially luxuries, and
this antagonized not only merchants dealing in such goods, but the
United States, the island's principal supplier. Disaffected Cubans of the
landowner and business class began organizing to reverse the revolution,
while the United States government insisted on 'prompt and effective'
compensation for any expropriated property of United States citizens.[2]
Fortune carried an article some ten months after the revolution which was
far from its earlier appreciation. Castro, the author declared, had alienated

[1] *Fortune*, March 1959, p. 76.
[2] 'Social Revolution in Latin America – The Role of United States Policy', by Robert Freeman Smith, in *International Affairs*, London, October 1965, p. 641.

private capital and was now faced with only three choices: to reverse the revolution and return to orthodox economics; be overthrown by a counter-revolution; or plunge into 'out-and-out communism'.[1]

The Castro regime moved steadily leftwards, while relations between the United States and Cuban governments steadily deteriorated. For this the new policy of the Communist Party, which for the first time in Latin American history merged itself in a popular movement without possessing any immediate prospect of dominating it, was in significant measure responsible. It was a profitable policy, though not one welcomed by the more rigid party doctrinaires. By associating themselves completely with the Castro regime and unquestioningly accepting Castro's personal leadership, the Communists accomplished three important objectives: within Cuba itself, they now became part of a successful revolutionary force which they had previously done nothing to advance; in doing so, they acquired an effective weapon against the contention that theirs was a purely alien ideology, propagated in the interests of an alien power; and since *Fidelismo* – the developing revolutionary principles and programmes of Castro – was having a popular appeal far beyond Cuba, the Communists could hitch a ride on it to influence among the submerged and restless poor throughout Southern America.

Events tumbled over each other in 1960. The Soviet Union held a trade fair in Havana, and in March, when a French ship carrying munitions for the Cuban Army exploded in Havana harbour, the Cuban government blamed the United States. The United States House of Representatives discussed a Bill to cut the Cuban sugar quota, and the Cuban government turned the retail stores of a United States company into *tiendas del pueblo* or people's shops. In May the government of Guatemala, which Castro complained was entertaining an invasion force, broke off diplomatic relations with Cuba, and Cuba established formal diplomatic relations with the Soviet Union. The foreign, mainly United States owned oil refineries on the island refused to handle cheap Soviet oil, and Castro expropriated them. In July the United States banned all further imports of Cuban sugar; the Soviet Union offered to take the sugar instead, and in August Cuba nationalized United States owned electricity, telephone and oil companies, together with 36 sugar factories. Reports mounted that Cuban exiles were receiving military training near Miami; in September Castro took over United States rubber companies and banks, cancelled bilateral military aid agreements with the United States, and recognized the

[1] 'What has Happened to Cuban Business?' by Freeman Lincoln, in *Fortune*, September 1959, pp. 110–11.

People's Republic of China. In October the United States proclaimed an embargo on all trade with Cuba, and at the end of the year, severed all diplomatic relations.[1]

Meanwhile, under the direction of the United States Central Intelligence Agency, an invasion force of anti-Castro exiles was being mounted, though the United States government self-righteously denied all Cuban accusations and even arraigned Cuba before the Organization of American States on a charge of increasing tension in the Caribbean by 'resorting to lies and slander'. Already on March 17th, 1960, President Eisenhower had authorized the secret training and arming of Cuban exiles, and in April the C.I.A. had arranged for launching sites in Guatemala. An air strip had been specially constructed at Retalhuleu, and Cuban exiles transported there from Florida. For the next few months planes dropped equipment to guerilla bands already operating in Cuba; but most of the equipment fell into Castro's hands, the rebel underground appeared ineffectual, and the C.I.A. decided that an invasion in strength was necessary. Suddenly United States plans received a jolt. In November a section of the Guatemalan army rebelled against the current *caudillo*, and the C.I.A., fearing that a new regime might be less co-operative, sent its own planes to bombard the rebel stronghold. The rebellion collapsed, and the C.I.A. breathed confidently again.

By April 1961 its preparations were complete. On the 15th C.I.A. planes bombed strategic targets in Cuba, and on the following day Cuban exiles landed at the Bay of Pigs, on the south coast of Cuba. Subsequently, as Cuban exile pilots were shot down or retired because of exhaustion, United States pilots took their place in the C.I.A. planes. At the United Nations, the United States ambassador categorically denied any involvement by his government, and the Secretary of State announced: 'The American people are entitled to know whether we are intervening in Cuba or intend to do so in the future. The answer to that question is no. What happens in Cuba is for the Cuban people themselves to decide.' The air raids on Cuba were explained as attacks by defecting Cuban pilots. On the 19th the Soviet Union threatened to give the Cuban government 'all necessary assistance' unless the United States stopped the invasion. But victory was already Castro's. Despite frantic appeals from exile leaders, the Cuban people did not sabotage strategic installations or take to guerilla warfare, but rallied instead to the government. Moreover, the C.I.A. bomber raids had not destroyed all Cuban planes, and the invaders had to face substantial air attack. On the 20th Castro announced that his

[1] Details from *The Revolutions of Latin America*, by J. Halcro Ferguson, pp. 141–4.

forces had captured hundreds of prisoners and much valuable equipment. The United States government could retrieve the loss of its cause only by mounting a direct invasion, and this seemed likely to produce Soviet retaliation. It had no reasonable choice but to accept defeat, with the resultant plummeting of its prestige. For Castro himself it was a triumph. He had shown all Southern America that his revolution and his regime commanded the clear allegiance of the Cuban people, and that in consequence not even the power of the United States could safely overthrow him. His own forces were sufficient to deal with exile thrusts, and the support of the Soviet Union prevented direct intervention. In Southern America, the United States would never be feared in quite the same way again.

Castro was increasingly regarded as a continental revolutionary leader, whose success encouraged – as his material aid sometimes advanced – movements of dissent and rebellion. *Fidelismo* was an influence from Brazil, among the Peasant Leagues, to recently-British Jamaica, where the 'back to Africa' Ras Tafari sect regarded Castro with open admiration. In all this race played a far from insignificant part. When Castro had visited the United Nations in October 1960, he had stayed at the Hotel Theresa in the heart of Harlem, to the delight of the Negroes and the discomfiture of the United States government. Cuban propaganda emphasized the racial integration of the revolutionary island, and the contrast with previous regimes, under which Negroes had been effectively excluded from the smarter tourist regions – except, of course, for entertainers or servants – so as not to upset white visitors from the United States. Negro newspapers in the United States noted and approved, while throughout the Americas, leaders of the dark-skinned poor relayed the message. The proclamation of the Cuban government on April 16th, 1961, during the Bay of Pigs invasion, was directed at the coloured no less outside than inside Cuba.

> Onwards, Cuban people! Let us answer with iron and fire the barbarians who despise us and want us to go back to slavery. They come to take away the land that the Revolution has given to the peasants and the co-operativists. They come to take away from the people their factories, sugar mills and mines ... They come to take away from our sons, our peasant girls, the schools that the Revolution has opened for them everywhere ... They come to take away from the Negroes, men and women, the dignity that the Revolution has given back to them ... they come to destroy our country, and we fight for our country.[1]

[1] Quoted by J. Halcro Ferguson, op. cit., pp. 145–6.

A month before its Bay of Pigs adventure, the Kennedy administration had launched the Alliance of Progress, a ten-year plan which offered aid and protection to Latin American states in the cause of promoting and securing democracy. The attack on Cuba, so soon afterwards, confirmed the hostility of those who saw the scheme as United States imperialism in a new dress, while friendly critics wondered how democracy was going to be served by economic and military assistance to authoritarian regimes. Certainly the United States government began by assuming a radically new role. It pressed for drastic reform and severely criticized the cruder despotisms like that of Trujillo in the Dominican Republic. When the army seized control of Peru in July 1962, the United States government immediately stopped all aid. But it soon persuaded itself of the necessity to recognize the regime and start giving aid again under the Alliance for Progress.

When elections in March 1962 returned *peronista* majorities in ten of the sixteen Argentina provinces and an army take-over seemed imminent, the United States government declared that aid might be withheld from a military regime. The warning had no effect, the army deposed the constitutionally elected president, and the United States government accommodated itself with a shrug to the seemingly inevitable. John Moors Cabot, former United States Assistant Secretary of State for Inter-American Affairs, declared in November 1963: 'Whereas our policy seeks to promote reform and social justice in Latin America, the need to protect our large economic stake inevitably injects a conservative note into our policies.' In April 1964, the army overthrew the constitutionally elected government of Brazil. Seven months later, the army in Bolivia seized power, and the reformist regime of Estenssoro – an obvious rival to *Fidelismo* as a channel of necessary change – was no more. Less than four years after the Alliance for Progress had been launched, far more of Latin America was under military rule than before, and the cause of democratic reform had retreated rather than advanced.

Alongside the crumbling of the ideological façade to the Alliance for Progress was a public draining of prestige and independent purpose from the Organization of American States. The United States dominated attempts at Pan-American co-operation from the first International Conference of American States in 1889-90. In 1910 the Pan-American Union was established, with its seat in Washington, and such was the control exercised by United States officials – the United States Secretary of State automatically served as chairman of the ruling board – that some Latin American leaders openly scorned the organization as the 'American Ministry of

Colonies'.[1] Appearances had to be improved. At Montevideo in 1933 the
United States at last accepted the principle of non-intervention; in 1938 at
Lima all countries agreed to maintain their solidarity against foreign
intervention, with consultation at the first signs of a threat; and in 1945,
at Mexico City, in a measure provoked by Uruguay's fear of Perón's
Argentina, the states provided for joint defence in the event of aggression
against any one of them. Then, in 1948, the Pan-American Union gave
way to the Organization of American States, with its officials to be appointed from all the participating countries and the chairmanship to
revolve among their representatives. Yet the United States soon showed
what importance she attached in practice to the solemn agreements of two
decades. At Caracas in March 1954, against the opposition of Guatemala,
the abstention of Argentina and Mexico, and the very reluctant
acquiescence of many other states, who resented and feared what they
saw as her demand to intervene in the internal affairs of other nations, she
forced through the O.A.S. a resolution on communism.

That the domination or control of the political institutions of any
American State by the international communist movement, extending to this hemisphere the political system of an extracontinental
power, would constitute a threat to the sovereignty and political
independence of the American States, endangering the peace of
America, and would call for a meeting of consultation to consider the
adoption of appropriate action in accordance with existing treaties.

Who was to decide when and how and to what degree the political
institutions of any American state had fallen under the control of the
international communist movement? The answer came three months
later, with the United States prepared and equipped invasion of Guatemala. No emergency O.A.S. meeting of consultation had been called, and
no joint action mounted, while the repeated United States assurances
against unilateral intervention had been breached. In April 1961 came the
Bay of Pigs attack on Cuba, again without O.A.S. consultation, let alone
agreement. Then, in October 1962, President Kennedy suddenly announced that Soviet missiles had been placed on Cuba, that this constituted
a threat to Latin American countries as well as to the United States, and
that the United States Navy would accordingly blockade the island.
Neither the United Nations nor the O.A.S. had been consulted. A meeting of the O.A.S. was then called to give retrospective approval and did

[1] H. Herring, op. cit., p. 770.

so in the absence of Cuban representatives, with Bolivia and Uruguay withholding their consent. The decision was meaningless, where it did not flout its whole purpose. The United States had already acted without such approval and would doubtless do so again should the occasion arise. Moreover, the clear majority of governments in the O.A.S. had only a repressive relationship with their peoples. The Bolivian and Uruguayan were two of the notable and widely acclaimed exceptions, and neither had found it possible, despite the pressure put on them, to support the United States. A free plebiscite throughout Latin America would have produced an entirely different verdict, and since everyone in and outside the O.A.S. knew this, the divorce between most Latin American governments and their peoples, with the dependence of these governments on United States money and arms, was made all the more patent.

The fundamental failure of the Alliance for Progress, the determination of the United States to secure safe and submissive regimes throughout Southern America – whatever the cost to democracy or social and economic reform – and the hollow function of the O.A.S. were soon starkly to be emphasized by events in the Dominican Republic. After rule by United States Marines for eight years (1916–24) and an interval of disintegrating democracy, the unhappy republic fell in 1930 into the clutch of Rafael Trujillo, whom the Marines had left as head of the army and whose Caligulan conceit and ferocity were matched only by his efficient guidance of the economy for his own enrichment. For thirty-one years Trujillo ruled the state like a personal possession, renaming the capital of Santo Domingo, the oldest European city in the Americas, Ciudad Trujillo, and dating his proclamations by the year of the Trujillo era as well as the more widely accepted calendar. Hailed as 'Benefactor of the Fatherland' by an abject Congress – one vice-president placed a neon sign on his home reading *Dios y Trujillo* – the dictator shot, jailed or exiled all political opponents. His regime gave the country modern public buildings and power plants, hospitals and schools, roads and factories and housing estates. It also gave himself and his family an enormous share of the spoils. His personal holdings – over 150 relatives were on the national payroll or in businesses allied to the government – included the two newspapers in the capital, one-fifth of the sugar industry, the radio and television monopoly, the national aviation company and arms factory, an insurance concern from which all employees had to buy liability policies, and a whole host of factories producing anything from cement to shoes for the army.

It might reasonably have been supposed that the United States, if anxious to intervene against any Latin American regime, would have chosen the Dominican rather than the Guatemalan. But Trujillo, for all his posturings and personal rapacity, was patently a passionate apostle of capitalism and a shrewd host to foreign enterprise as well. He gave missile-tracking facilities to the United States, and was acclaimed as a dependable ally. The political condition of his three million subjects, with the general economic and social condition of the 60 per cent who were mulatto and the 12 per cent who were Negro, seemed of rather less relevance. The end of the 'fifties, however, brought a more turbulent climate. An exile invasion from Castro's Cuba failed, but the very attempt could scarcely leave Washington unmoved. Even the Catholic Church within the republic, for long complacent, began to criticize a regime which seemed to confuse Trujillo with God. The Kennedy Administration, busily scanning new frontiers, found the old ones round regimes like the Dominican Republic's an increasing embarrassment. And within the republic itself, the population was growing rebellious. At last, in May 1961, Trujillo was assassinated. The army attempted to keep control in its hands, but citizens began demonstrating in the streets, political parties surfaced, and early in 1963 Juan Bosch took office as president after receiving the votes of 64 per cent of the electorate.

Bosch did not promote a mass movement to sustain his reforms; he did not even attempt to dismantle the traditional power structure. He was a liberal who wished to carry the whole society with him in the changes that he saw as so long overdue. If the Alliance for Progress required an up-to-date showcase for its objectives, and a reasonable competitor with Castro's revolutionary Cuba, such seemed likely to come from the Dominican Republic. But business and property interests soon displayed their hostility to even the most cautious measures. Land reform, mainly involving the distribution of Trujillo's former property; more equitable taxation, and a law empowering the government to search out and confiscate Trujillo's hidden assets in business; the constitutional separation of Church and state, all led to an outcry from conservatives that the Bosch regime was flirting with communism. In September, the senior army officers, with the general support of business, the landed aristocracy and the Church, deposed Bosch from the presidency.

By late 1964, military control had antagonized even many former opponents of Bosch by its corruption and economic meddling. Donald Reid Cabral, head of the ruling junta, had no public support, as the United States Central Intelligence Agency itself discovered by opinion polls;[1] but Thomas Mann, overlord of Latin American affairs at the State Depart-

[1] *The Times*, November 16th, 1965.

ment, described him as 'the first honest President for a long time', and the United States government gave $61 million in economic and $2 million in military aid to his regime, while the C.I.A. constantly reported to him on plans for rebellion and trained his 8,000-strong special police force. Then, in April 1965, a section of the army itself, led by a young colonel, Francisco Caamaño Deño, rebelled, with the object of deposing the senior right-wing officers, restoring the 1963 democratic constitution, and opening the way for the return of Bosch to the presidency. The junta, with support from most of the air force, showed itself too strong, however; the rebelling officers decided to extend the struggle from the confines of the military by distributing arms to the angry population; and the whole movement assumed a revolutionary character. The United States government, without consulting the O.A.S., dispatched more than 20,000 marines and paratroops on the pretext of protecting the lives of United States and other foreign citizens. But the real reason was not slow in emerging. 'The American nations cannot, must not and will not permit the establishment of another communist government in the western hemisphere,' declared President Johnson, four days after the first landing of marines.

The United States government claimed that fifty-five listed 'foreign-trained Communists' were gaining control of the revolutionary forces, though it did not explain why a substantial section of the army and most of the civilians in Santo Domingo should be ready to lay down their lives for the sake of a few intruders. The truth was that the United States had now resolved to suppress all popular revolution in Latin America, as a probable threat to her interests. One influential British weekly[1] put it baldly enough: ' ... in the western hemisphere at least, the United States has reclaimed the old privilege of hitting first and seeing afterwards who precisely got hit'.

In the event, the increasingly civilian character of the revolution, with the battlefield in the streets of Santo Domingo, entailed United States military action against women and children if the capital was to be captured. The United States forces, therefore, limited themselves to shooting at stray revolutionaries and sealing off the insurgent-held areas, mainly the Santo Domingo slums, while diplomatic initiatives sought to produce some compromise settlement. The United States government summoned a session of the O.A.S., but found its allies less tractable than usual; five major republics – Mexico, Uruguay, Argentina, Chile and Venezuela – refused to condone the intervention by agreeing to the provision of a joint

[1] *The Economist*, May 8th, 1965, p. 617.

force in the Dominican Republic, and subsequently refused to sign a message to the United Nations Security Council affirming their attachment to the O.A.S. The countries which did provide troops to supplement the United States forces and give the intervention a Pan-American appearance, were, with the exception of Costa Rica, army-propped despotisms (Brazil, Honduras, Nicaragua and Paraguay).

At last, in September 1965, five months after the insurrection had broken out, the two Dominican sides accepted a provisional government under a compromise figure, with elections pledged for the middle of the following year. It was likely that a popular revolution of one sort or another had only been postponed – though for how long rested not with the Dominicans themselves, but with the United States government. The O.A.S. was in strident disarray, with the United States no longer paying even lip-service to its principles. Article 15 of its charter laid down categorically: 'No state or group of states has the right to intervene directly or indirectly, for any reason whatever, in the internal or external affairs of any other state.' On September 20th the United States House of Representatives passed a resolution, by 312 votes to 52, declaring communist subversion or the threat of it to be a violation of the Monroe Doctrine. Any Latin American country or countries might take steps, including the use of armed force, collectively or individually, 'to forestall or combat intervention, domination, control and colonization in whatever form by the subversive forces known as international communism and its agencies in the western hemisphere'. The State Department had apparently been consulted on the resolution and had raised no objections; the President himself had made no effort to intervene. In effect, therefore, the United States was proclaiming her intention to police Latin America – leaving her European allies, presumably, meanwhile to police their own small spheres of influence in the area – crushing revolts and overthrowing regimes, however popular they might be, whenever she alone saw fit. And if the timing of the resolution meant anything, the United States would in fact see fit to intervene against any popular rising, since only in this way could she hope to 'forestall' what she loosely described as communist subversion, whether 500, 50, 5, or no Communists at all were involved.

Yet popular revolution is inevitable, as the only answer to feudal landowners, predatory capitalism and military dictatorship. The United States, in opposing such revolution, is proclaiming the permanence of poverty, illiteracy, hunger and disease. She is also proclaiming her rule over Latin America, with a crudeness that is likely in itself to promote revolution as a nationalist protest. Such a policy will do far more to nourish than to starve communism. It is also, short of nuclear intimidation – with all its unpredictable consequences – finally unworkable. Dominican intervention required 1,600 marines in 1916, and over 20,000 in 1965. If intervention all over Latin America should be required, in countries far larger than the Dominican Republic, where are the means to be found? The policing of other continents is already absorbing much United States manpower and money, and its demands are unlikely to decrease.

Latin America is, of course, still far from being swept by popular revolution. The centres of radical disaffection are in the cities, where the power of the modern state can most easily be employed to crush an uprising; in the countryside, where guerilla warfare against the newest military equipment is made feasible by Latin America's tumultuous terrain, the peasantry blames God rather than government for its condition. Yet slowly the continent is gathering itself for upheaval. The young middle-class intelligentsia, from which the leadership of the Cuban revolution emerged, more and more rejects the objective of a merely constitutional democracy which is overthrown whenever it seeks to reshape the basic social structure and survives at the army's pleasure. At the University of Caracas, for instance, the extreme left, which favours the principle of armed struggle for the conquest of political power, has consistently increased its student support; in June 1964 it polled 5,426 votes, to 993 for *Accion Democratica*, the governing party of Venezuela, and 3,083 for the generally right-wing Christian Democratic Party.[1] From the universities and the cities stream ideas and men and material to arouse the countryside, and it is from the countryside, with the connivance if not at first the participation of the peasantry, that the assault on the state can be mounted.

The lessons taught and learnt are those of the Cuban revolution – that a group of professional revolutionaries, by establishing and extending a *foco* or insurrectionary centre, can excite and conduct to success a mass struggle for power; and that once having defeated the organized might of the state, a revolutionary leadership, sustained by popular aspiration, can depose the traditional ruling class and recast the whole society. 'We consider', wrote Ché Guevara[2] in the preface to his *Guerilla Warfare*, 'that the Cuban revolution has made three fundamental contributions to revolutionary strategy in Latin America: 1. The popular forces can win *a war*

[1] 'Latin America: The Long March', by Régis Debray, in *New Left Review*, London, No. 33, Sept.–Oct., 1965, p. 33.
[2] Castro's Argentine colleague in the revolutionary struggle and first years of government.

against the army; 2. It is not always necessary to wait until all the conditions for revolution are fulfilled – the insurrectionary centre can create them; 3. In under-developed America the terrain of armed struggle must basically be the countryside.'

Attempts to imitate the Cuban model have failed more often than they have succeeded. In Argentina, Brazil, Colombia, Ecuador, Paraguay, Peru and Venezuela, guerilla centres have been crushed by government troops. But the revolutionary movement has profited from its mistakes, and guerillas – more efficient and circumspect, less impatient and unready – seem to be taking the place of those now in prison or graves. In Venezuela, the states of Falcon and Lara were 'liberated' in 1963 – they have revolutionary political and social regimes, though military struggle has not ceased – and two new guerilla fronts were opened in the middle of 1964, to the east in Bachiller and to the west in the Andes. In Colombia, where civil war raged from 1948 to 1958 between Liberals and Conservatives, some peasant groups did not disband or disarm with the reconciliation of the two political parties, but organized themselves for autonomous survival under peasant leaders from the central committee of the Columbian Communist Party. One such zone of peasant insurgency, commonly called an independent republic – Marquetalia – was attacked in strength by government forces in 1964, but the guerilla leader, Marulandia, simply withdrew with his peasant army from the inhabited area, sealing the government troops inside and subjecting them to constant attack. In Peru, where the average Indian has a life-expectancy less than a half, and an income less than a tenth, of the average white's, peasant terrorism in the Andes, blamed by the government on the radio campaigns of the Soviet Union, China and Cuba, became serious in 1965. The terrorists were reported to be distributing food and supplies seized from the huge estates, and raising recruits for the struggle to create 'socialist government with equality for everybody'.[1] In Bolivia, the 26,000 tin miners enrolled in the F.S.T.M.B., Trade Union Federation of Bolivian Mineworkers, have made of their region a revolutionary centre. Organized into militia on each mine, with few arms but a terrible skill in the use of dynamite, and with the Indian peasants around as armed allies, they offer the most manifest possibility of exciting a proletarian revolution on the Bolshevik model.[2]

The guerilla movements are by no means all communist, or even

[1] *The Times*, July 6th, 1965.
[2] R. Debray, 'Latin America: The Long March', op. cit., pp. 23–6. Such information, of course, is no sooner gathered than it is out of date. But beyond the successes or reversals immediately encountered by particular initiatives, the underlying trend is an extension of peasant rebellion and guerilla strategy.

communist-led. Several Latin American Communist Parties – in Argentina, Brazil, Chile, Colombia and Peru – are still hostile to armed struggle, though sections (as in Colombia) have chosen guerilla warfare. In Bolivia substantial guerilla forces of the right-wing but fervently nationalist and anti-United States Phalangist Party operate in the tropical north-east on the Brazilian border. In Venezuela, where guerilla strength is greatest, the F.A.L.N., or revolutionary front, merged the Communist Party and M.I.R. (Revolutionary Left Movement) with independent nationalists and army rebels. Certainly, the more openly the United States dominates Latin America, propping up military despotisms with money and material, and intervening directly against popular rebellion, the closer will nationalists draw to the revolutionary left.

For most of Latin America, China as well as Cuba offers the pattern of peasant progress to power. Outside of largely urban societies like Argentina, Chile and Uruguay, the region remains fundamentally rural, and its structure of authority feudal. Even in countries with significant capitalist sectors, the relationship between factory and estate is close. In Colombia profits from industry are invested in land, and the families of big business are the families of the landed aristocracy; in Brazil, the sugar industry of the north-east and the coffee industry of São Paulo are organically linked to feudal land ownership. Rural reform, therefore, does not follow industrialization, even though, by expanding the internal market, it could promote the growth of the capitalist sector. The peasantry receives little if any relief from the sporadic emergence of democratic regimes representing the middle classes, and is forced to seek significant change in a revolutionary movement dedicated to dismantling the whole traditional economic structure. Yet the peasantry is cautious and unaware, and – as in China – the revolutionary leadership must exhibit the rewards of struggle in the midst of struggle itself. The confiscation of estates in guerilla areas and the distribution of land to the peasantry shift the visible horizon of peasant aspiration. And the Chinese revolution presents a further provocation. Chiang Kai-shek and the Kuomintang were swept from power not only because they neglected essential rural reform, but because they were unable to defeat foreign intervention. Students, civil servants, even sections of the middle class turned to the Communist Party as the only force apparently determined to end the humiliation of a long-proud people at foreign hands. The parallel with revolutionary Latin America is clear, and the Chinese, in public propaganda and private discussion, are busying themselves to make it even clearer.

In March 1963 the Spanish edition of the *Peking Review* appeared in

different parts of Latin America; it was soon transformed from a fortnightly to a weekly and supplemented by a Spanish edition of the illustrated *China Reconstructs*. Spanish broadcasts from Peking were totalling
ten hours a day by October 1964, and Portuguese ones – for Brazil – some
six hours. The outbreak of guerilla terrorism in Peru was accompanied by
broadcasts from Peking in Qechua, the Indian language of the central
Andes, and there have since been reports that young Marxists have been
trained by the Chinese not only in guerilla tactics but in the languages of
the Indian peasantry. Merely radical as well as communist politicians and
intellectuals have been invited to China, and have found themselves
stimulated and impressed by what they saw there.[1] Trade unionists,
students and cultural delegations, shrewdly selected for their potential
influence, have returned from Peking, their luggage crammed with the
Chinese view of the world. And China has received unsolicited advertisements. When the army took control of Brazil in March 1964, one of its first
acts was to arrest nine Chinese trade delegates on charges of subversion.

Cuba, of course, has her own radio centre for revolutionary propaganda, broadcasting not only in Spanish and Portuguese, but for six hours
a week in 'Creole' and an hour in the widely spoken Indian languages of
Guarani and Aymara. She has paid special attention to the insurrection in
Venezuela, and has not only broadcast news and encouragement to the
guerillas, but has carried interviews with their leaders and information on
their activities over wide areas of Latin America.[2]

The Sino-Soviet dispute, far from dimming the prospect of revolutionary leadership throughout Southern America by discrediting the
whole communist movement, has significantly brightened it. The traditional communist leadership, now overwhelmingly loyal to the Soviet
line, has long discouraged adventurous militancy, eschewed violence with
especial vigour, and cultivated a garden of relative respectability in the
labour unions. In countries like Chile and Uruguay, where the parties are
legal, the leadership has gone to considerable lengths to avoid banning.
Now the existence of an alternative source of doctrine, encouragement
and aid in Peking has enabled the more militant, usually the younger,
members to desert and denounce the cautious traditional leaders – the
'stone-bottomed bureaucrats' as they are called, after Molotov's nick-
name, in Santiago[3] – without feeling that they will be isolated as a result.
Increasingly such new revolutionaries see the old Communist Parties as

[1] *The Economist*, October 10th, 1964.
[2] *The Times*, January 27th, 1965.
[3] *The Times*, January 5th, 1966.

part of the corrupt and cruel system that they plan by their endeavours to defeat. Moreover, the Chinese are shrewdly pragmatic, despite their claims to doctrinal purity. As in Africa, they seek out and offer support to those whose revolutionary ardour is apparent and likely to be serviceable, whether they are Communists or not. What China wants among the Indians of the Andes, as elsewhere in Southern America, is violent insurrection, far more than a mere mimicry of her doctrinal views, and this suits the militants themselves, who want fundamental change far more than the assurance of orthodoxy, and some of whom are by no means persuaded that communism supplies all the answers.

Inevitably, too, the rivalry of the Chinese and their Southern American converts has provoked the Soviet Union and her Southern American loyalists to a show of greater militancy. The peaceful road to socialism, by way of infiltration, oratory and intrigue, has not been abandoned; but the violent road has been less strenuously denounced. Soviet influence was dominant in the organization of the Tri-Continental Conference at Havana in December 1965 and January 1966; but the very initiative of the conference, its association of Southern America with the areas of more obvious struggle in Africa and Asia, and the emphasis in debate and resolution on opposition to the United States as the principal enemy, must fortify the Chinese case for violent upheaval whatever the immediate cost. Indeed, the delegates designated specific areas of Southern America – notably Colombia and Venezuela – as ripe for widespread guerilla warfare, and appointed a committee to promote assistance.

The Chinese themselves have, of course, not refrained from underscoring the racial phrases in Southern American struggle and even those Communists who retain an allegiance to the Soviet leadership or find Chinese conduct all too arrogant and aggressive, see none the less the relevance of this Chinese view to their conditions. Throughout Southern America, the Indian, the Negro, the darker-skinned *mestizo* and mulatto constitute the poorest elements of society, whether as virtual serfs on vast plantations or as workless refugees in the suppurating city slums. The proclaimed racial indifference of Southern America is largely a myth. Miscegenation has, certainly, produced substantial – sometimes majority – sectors of mixed blood in the population; no Southern American state promotes or permits formal race discrimination in public relationships (though informal discrimination, of course, exists – especially, as in Panama, where a substantial foreign white community resides); and the very darkest citizens have reached the highest offices and incomes. But the basic pattern of society – even in Mexico, where the long revolution

attached almost a cultural snobbery to Indian blood – has remained one of
white, or relatively white, superiority. In essence this has resulted from the
inflexibility of economic power. The white conquerors and colonists
seized the land, and their descendants secured possession, fortifying their
control with the opportunities of industry and commerce. It was these
criollos who in the main took political command with independence, and
who have naturally used that command to protect their economic
dominion. Countries like Ecuador, Guatemala, Honduras and Nicaragua
are as rurally feudal today as they were a century ago, and if others, like
Bolivia, Colombia, Peru, Venezuela and the largest of all, Brazil, have
experienced some significant change with industry and urbanization, the
crude racial design of economic power has changed scarcely at all. Except
for the relatively 'white' states of Argentina, Chile, Costa Rica and Uruguay, the remote villages, the landed estates and the cities themselves
display a largely white economic ruling class and an overwhelmingly
coloured peasantry and proletariat, with the upper regions of the middle
class lighter in complexion than the lower ones.

The massive immigration from Europe in the last century has done little
to change this design. However poor and uneducated many of the immigrants were, they possessed an acquaintance with the urban world and an
individual enterprise – the very act of immigration required much
personal initiative – that fitted them far more than the sunken peasantry
for economic struggle. They generally settled in the cities, where social
and economic mobility was much greater than in the countryside. And
they were, inevitably, accepted with greater speed and ease by the dominant 'whites' than were coloured emigrants from the countryside. The
native whites who would deny most passionately any taint of racial arrogance, pointing complacently to their own heritage of mixed blood, displayed a cultural conceit which amounted ultimately to the same thing.
And the immigrant whites themselves quickly assumed an even grosser
consciousness of colour, as the promise and guarantee of their acceptance.
It is the middle-class immigrant of the first, second and third generation in
Latin America today who resists most strenuously the advance of the
peasantry and urban proletariat, as a threat to his own social and economic
position, and when the threatening peasantry and proletariat are coloured,
the resistance is increased by cultural and even overtly racial considerations. The military regimes that repress mass discontent serve in the main
the interests of the landed and industrial oligarchy; but they draw their
recruits and necessary public sustenance from the insecure and frightened
middle class.

'This correspondence between colour and poverty is, of course, not limited to Spanish- and Portuguese-speaking Southern America. The English- and French-speaking islands of the Caribbean have similar myths of racial indifference and similarly different realities. It is almost invariably the white or light-skinned mulatto who speaks most movingly in Jamaica or Martinique of the racial harmony that centuries have developed. The darker-skinned and black, who constitute the poorer classes, are not heard as often; but, when they are, their bitterness is plain.'It is no accident that the leading poet apostle of Négritude – along with Léopold Sédar Senghor, present President of Senegal – is Aimé Césaire, who won election to the French National Assembly from Martinique against all the candidates of the established political parties in 1957. Césaire writes not only of Martinique and the present, but of America and the past, the slave ships and plantations, and – above all – of Africa, which is for him more than the place of his 'Bambara ancestors', but the promise of a new strength and intelligence and beauty. For him the independence of Southern America from Europe is hollow, because the people of Southern America are still culturally, indeed racially, captive.

Think of the race struggles in Central America or Latin America, and you will observe that it is a question there of an inheritance or a survival of the colonial system in countries which have, nevertheless, achieved independence for the last hundred and fifty years ... we must make ourselves realize one thing: that the combat against colonialism is not over as soon as one thinks and *because imperialism has been conquered in the military sense*.

In short there can be no question for us of displacing colonialism or making servitude an internal affair. What we must do is to destroy it, to ... tear up its roots, and that is why *true* decolonization will be revolutionary or nothing.[1]

In his early poem, 'Cahier d'un Retour au Pays Natal', Césaire saw Martinique as 'this death which limps from pettiness to pettiness; little greeds heaped on top of the *conquistador*; little flunkeys heaped on top to the great savage; little souls shovelled on top of the three-souled Caribbean.'[2]

[1] 'The Man of Culture and his Responsibilities', paper delivered to the Second Congress of Negro Writers and Artists at Rome, March 26th–April 1st, 1959, in a Special Issue of *Présence Africaine*, No. 24–5, Feb.–May, 1959, p. 128.
[2] Translation by John Berger in *The Success and Failure of Picasso* (Penguin Books, 1965), p. 139.

But his was not only rejection, it was also acceptance and resistance.

> And here are those who do not console themselves for
>   being made *not* in the image of God but of the devil,
> those who consider that being a Negro is like being a
>   second-class official:
> waiting for better and with the possibility of rising higher,
> those who capitulate to themselves,
> those who live in a little cellar of themselves,
> those who flaunt their proud pseudomorphosis,
> those who say to Europe: See, I know like you how to
>   make courtesies,
> how to present my respects, in short, I am no different
>   from you; pay no attention to my black skin, it is
>   the sun that has burned me.
> And there is the informer Negro, the askari Negro, and
>   all these zebras shake themselves in their own way to
>   make their stripes fall off in a dew of fresh milk.
> And in the midst of all that I say Hurrah! my grandfather
>   is dying,
> I say Hurrah!
> The old negritude is gradually becoming a corpse.[1]

All over the Americas, more and more Negroes, and in their similar and different ways, Indians and *mestizos* and mulattos, have been crying 'Hurrah!' Old English planters in Jamaica will say with tremulous sincerity that there is no racial tension on the island, that a new mingling of men is taking place in tenderness and understanding. But one can almost always – there are the inevitable exceptions – place the economic and social status of a Jamaican by the mere colour of his complexion. And the dark slums of Kingston seethe with African cults – religious, political, frankly racist like the thousands of Ras Tafarians who see their homeland in Africa and their saviour symbol in the Emperor of Ethiopia. There, in the shanty streets, is the unease, where programmes for birth control are met with cries that the whites only want to diminish the black population.

The Ras Tafarian choice of the Emperor of Ethiopia as a symbol of longing and self-assertion is not casual. Ethiopia has been in modern times – except for the relatively short Mussolini interlude – the only black

[1]Cahier d'un Retour au Pays Natal, quoted in *Muntu* by Janheinz Jahn (Faber & Faber, 1958) p. 206.

African state to remain independent of white imperial control. For the Negro in the Americas the era of slavery and conquest, his racial past, was a humiliation, a shame that often kept him silent. But the Africa of presidents and ambassadors and newspaper headlines is speedily expelling the shame to leave room for assertion. Defeat feeds on itself, but so does conquest. The Africa that has conquered its own freedom carries the demand of Negroes everywhere in its wake. And in a world where the coloured races are everywhere asserting themselves, the Indians, too, must find provocations in the present no less than in the half-remembered splendours of their past.

Revolution in Southern America, therefore, is likely to be racial because it will be not only political and economic, but psychological. Whether it will be racist as well must depend largely on the response it receives from white oligarchies and especially the continental oligarchy of the white United States.

> ... my heart, preserve me from all hatred,
> do not make of me the man of hate for whom I have
>   but hate ...
> you know that it is not through hate of other races
> that I make myself a digger ... [1]

So Césaire wrote in his poem on Martinique in 1939. Twenty-two years later, in 1961, another native of Martinique, Frantz Fanon, who had associated himself with the Algerian struggle against France, gave a cry, just before his death, that was like – and unlike – the earlier cries of Césaire.

> We must leave our dreams and abandon our old beliefs and friendships of the time before life began. Let us waste no time in sterile litanies and nauseating mimicry. Leave this Europe where they are never done talking of Man, yet murder men everywhere they find them, at the corner of every one of their own streets, in all the corners of the globe. For centuries they have stifled almost the whole of humanity in the name of a so-called spiritual experience. Look at them today swaying between atomic and spiritual disintegration ...
> Europe undertook the leadership of the world with ardour, cynicism and violence. Look at how the shadow of her palaces stretches out ever further! Every one of her movements has burst the bounds of space and thought ...

[1] From J. Jahn, op. cit., p. 236.

She has only shown herself parsimonious and niggardly where men are concerned; it is only men that she has killed and devoured ...

Two centuries ago, a former European colony decided to catch up with Europe. It succeeded so well that the United States of America became a monster, in which the taints, the sickness and the inhumanity of Europe have grown to appalling dimensions ...

No, we do not want to catch up with anyone. What we want to do is to go forward all the time, night and day, in the company of Man, in the company of all men. The caravan should not be stretched out, for in that case each line will hardly see those who precede it; and men who no longer recognize each other meet less and less together, and talk to each other less and less.

It is a question of the Third World starting a new history of Man, a history which will have regard to the sometimes prodigious theses which Europe has put forward, but which will also not forget Europe's crimes, of which the most horrible was committed in the heart of man, and consisted of the pathological tearing apart of his functions and the crumbling away of his unity ...

For Europe, for ourselves and for humanity, comrades, we must turn over a new leaf, we must work out new concepts, and try to set afoot a new man.[1]

The new concepts, the new man that Fanon wanted to see, are wanted, with rising impatience, by the submerged peoples of Southern America. If there are leaders who lack a following, the following will be found; and if a following exists without leadership, the leadership will be made. One certainty exists: that whether excited by want or hatred, aspiration or despair, the coloured of Southern America will increasingly rebel against the cruelty of their condition, They will rebel in the first instance against the oligarchies that hold them captive; and if the United States continues to sustain the oligarchies, because she considers stability safer than change, and repression more profitable than revolution, then they will rebel against the United States inevitably as well. They will rebel, in the same way that the Cubans rebelled, as nationalists and reformers; they will be driven to revolution because only revolution can provide the reforms that they demand; and they will attach themselves to communism if only communism can promote and secure their revolution.

Their rebellion must be racial, because they are coloured and their

[1] *The Wretched of the Earth*, by Frantz Fanon. Translated from the French by Constance Farrington (MacGibbon & Kee, 1965), pp. 252–5.

masters are white, whether immediately in indigenous oligarchies or ultimately in the United States. And the more the United States tries to
prevent revolution, the more blatantly she is forced to employ her power
in response, the wider the allegiance of colour will become, and the more
consciously racial the character of war. For colour itself, or race, is relative. Indian and Negro blood is in the stream of most Argentines, let alone
Chileans or Uruguayans. Not least in the view of the white United States,
Southern America is coloured country. The arrogance with which the
United States treats the Latin American republics is seen by some of their
whitest citizens as a sense of racial superiority. Theodore Roosevelt, gaining the presidency in the mid-morning of United States expansionism,
proclaimed that he would 'show those Dagos that they will have to behave
decently'. The whiter Puerto Ricans, now citizens of the United States, no
less than the darker Mexicans, migrant labourers on the farms and ranches
of the West, find today a generally similar disparagement of Latin
Americans by the 'Yankees'. Paradoxically, therefore, the white Latin
Americans, in the very conceit of their complexions, may ally themselves
as coloured against the white suzerainty of the United States. The slum-
dwellers of Buenos Aires are as ready for revolution as the slum-
dwellers of Lima or Caracas, and as ready to blame the United States for
their condition. The middle class is less aware of squalor and want, but
even more aware perhaps of weakness and frustration. Nationalism has
accommodated together the most improbable allies before. Racism is
likely to prove no less potent.

Where then must Césaire's 'unique people' go? There is enough reality
in the myth of American mingling to see at least some slight possibility
of racelessness, the new world human conscious only of his humanity,
developing there. The American is an Indian, a Negro, an Asian, a
European, a *mestizo* and a mulatto – but somehow still separately so, in
the way of the old world. The revolutions of Southern America can combine all Americans into an American, an ultimate man, heir to and bearer
of several cultures and enrichments; or they can separate further, perhaps
only between two races – white and coloured, but then finally, unbridge-
ably, with a violence against all humanity. The burden of choice is a
white one.

4

The White World of the United States

The major cities of the United States are sick with racial violence and alarm. The exact extent of gratuitous violence in crime and of racial responsibility for this is, of course, impossible to measure. But what can be reasonably established is that a substantial proportion of crimes, significantly larger than the proportion in other cities of the Western world, consists in acts of seemingly motiveless violence, where theft is – if an accompaniment at all – merely an excuse; that far more crimes than population statistics would connect with some law of averages are committed by whites against blacks or blacks against whites; and that many of the crimes committed by whites against whites and by blacks against blacks owe much to the peculiar character of each racial environment and to the increasing antagonism between them.

Far more potent than the violence itself, however, is the alarm which it has increasingly helped to promote. When secretaries at the United Nations in New York refuse to work after dark unless they are given the cost of their taxi-fare home, because they are genuinely afraid to walk through the streets or use public transport, they react to incidents, which they themselves consider racial, experienced by their acquaintances or lavishly reported in the press. (Even newspapers of serious standing like the *New York Times* sporadically use race in the headlines to their crime stories.) Nor are international civil servants especially sensitive. White parents in middle-class down-town Manhattan will seldom let their children travel by subway at night, if at any time, and reply to expressions of surprise with lurid accounts of racial violence, while anyone proposing to walk through Central Park after sunset is looked upon as debauched or hopelessly tired of life. And any suggestion by a stranger that he should stroll through Harlem or Chicago's South Side in the middle of the day is greeted by urgent admonitions and, if these fail, by compassionate denials of any personal responsibility.

Of course the seats of subway cars are not littered with the victims of rape and assault; whites have been known to wander alone through Harlem unharmed, just as there are Negroes alive in Harlem today who have never been attacked by white police. The incidence of racial violence, however large, is a tiny fraction of the incidence believed to exist. Yet the alarm is general and feeds increasingly on fact. Since the riots of the 1964 summer in several cities, and especially since the explosion of violence and explicit race hatred in the Negro ghetto of Los Angeles the year after, many Americans have come to see their streets as battlefields, in a mounting guerilla warfare of race. What has long been happening in the South of the United States is now happening in the North – a development of racial stress to the degree where it threatens society itself with a nervous breakdown. And in both regions the clash is based upon fear and centred round power.

* * *

Since the prosperous mid-morning of slavery, the white South has regarded the numbers of its black subjects with disquiet and has sought to be and, even more, to feel secure. It was not so in the early hours. When a Dutch warship brought its cargo of twenty 'negars' to Virginia in 1619, land-holders in the colony put them to work on tobacco plantations alongside the far more numerous white servants. The supply was for many years small – by 1649, thirty years after the first arrivals, there were only three hundred black labourers in all Virginia – but as plantation owners came to assess the economic advantages of slavery, and as English, together with homespun American, merchants entered the trade on a substantial scale, the level rapidly rose. Some half a million Negroes were brought to the South legally before 1808, and thousands more, illegally, afterwards, so that with natural increase the Southern slave population topped a million by 1810.[1] Moreover, the appetite for profit was stronger than the stirrings of prudence, and swiftly the ratio between white and black inhabitants of the Southern colonies changed; by the outbreak of the American Revolution in 1774, Virginia had as many blacks as whites, while in South Carolina the blacks outnumbered whites by two to one.

The existence of a large and increasing slave population demanded moral excuse – for white Christians were not supposed to be concerned, at least exclusively, with profits this side of the grave – as well as measures to preserve the privileges it conferred from assault or corrosion. And so there sprouted a series of myths and laws to comfort conscience and fear while still satisfying greed. Slavery belonged to civilization, as the splendours of ancient Greece and Rome might be brought to witness. Indeed it was a charity, since its victims were prisoners-of-war who would

[1] *The Peculiar Institution*, by Kenneth M. Stampp (Eyre & Spottiswoode, 1964), p. 35.

probably otherwise have been put to death. Furthermore, the Negro was a natural inferior, seized from the darkness of savagery and paganism for his own ultimate benefit; the plantations on which he laboured were schools of Christianity and culture, providing an essential step in his moral and mental development. Certainly he required the closest control, for though amiable enough most of the time, with an inherent light-hearted-ness, he was unstable and suddenly given to displaying the cruelties of his primitive condition. Negroes, proclaimed the preamble to South Carolina's code of 1712, were 'of barbarous, wild, savage natures, and ... wholly unqualified to be governed by the laws, customs and prac-tices of this province'; they needed such special statutes 'as may restrain the disorders, rapines and inhumanity to which they are naturally prone ... and may also tend to the safety and security of the people of this province and their estates'. What the Negro did have in admirably more abundance than the white was physical strength, a compensation for his mental back-wardness, which the wisdom of Providence had set suitably to labour in the difficult but so-close-to-the-African climate of the South.

Gradually the law promoted the distinctions between white servants and black. In the 1660s, statutes provided that Negroes should be slaves for life, that the child inherited the condition of his mother – an early comment on the pursuits of Southern white manhood – and that conver-sion to Christianity made no difference to the status of a slave. Yet greed and fear were merely further aroused by the feeding, and in the years that followed slaves were legally defined as property, their movements placed under strict public control, and their standing in courts of law made ap-propriately helpless (they were prohibited from testifying under oath or instituting suit), while their masters were entrusted with powers of coer-cion and punishment. Finally the overt purity of the white race had to be secured, by statute if not by appetite, and inter-racial marriage was forbidden.

American slavery was profoundly different and more vicious in its effects than its counterpart elsewhere in ancient or contemporary times.[1]

> The slave could not, by law, be taught to read or write; he could not practise any religion without the permission of his master, and could never meet with his fellows, for religious or any other purposes, except in the presence of a white; and finally, if a master wished to

[1] A conclusion increasingly emerging to public recognition from under the disguise of popu-lar Southern fiction like *Gone With the Wind*. See, for instance, the view of United States Assistant Secretary of Labor, Daniel Moynihan, in his recent report on *The Negro Family* (Office of Policy Planning and Research, U.S. Department of Labor, March 1965).

free him, every legal obstacle was used to thwart such action. This
was not what slavery meant in the ancient world, in medieval and
early modern Europe, or in Brazil and the West Indies.[1]

At first Negroes and whites in similar service had laboured together in
the fields, taken their leisure in each other's company, and with or without
marriage begun to blur the colour contrasts of the South. But the white
poor were soon provided by myth and law with an easy consolation; if
they did not own slaves or plantations themselves, they shared at least in
the superiority of white over black. Their colour became a refuge from
failure and want, and the privilege it bestowed was all the more ruthlessly
to be defended for being unique. Then, as now, it was the rich Southern
whites who might occasionally afford the luxury of moderation, of an
eccentric charity; their colour was only one of many possessions, and
their possessions were secured by the partition of the poor.

The rich badly needed the prejudices of colour, for of all the Southern
myths none was more extravagant than the dependence of all white
society on the slave. By 1860 there were only 385,000 slave-owners in the
South among 1,516,000 free families, while of the slave-owners themselves,
88 per cent held less than twenty slaves each – the mark of the planter
class – and 50 per cent, less than five.[2] The very rich planter families,
owning more than one hundred slaves each, numbered less than 3,000, a
very small proportion of the white South; yet it was from them, with their
commercial and professional associates, that the dominant political and
economic outlook of the society emerged.

The typical white Southerner before the Civil War was neither the poor
white nor the rich planter, but the independent yeoman farmer who
tilled his own fields with help only from his wife and children. In raising
and selling cash crops, he faced inevitable competition from the more
efficient of the planters, with their more economic tracts of land and a
large labour force that cost no more than the requirements of mere survival. Seldom able, in consequence, to accumulate capital for expansion or
even reserves for sudden emergency, he was increasingly driven to subsistence farming or even the loss of his land and degeneration into tenancy
or share-cropping. Yet his allegiance to the system from which he
suffered could be – and was – ensured by his need to preserve the privilege
and power of his race; if hardship proposed an alliance with the slave

[1] Nathan Glazer in his Introduction to *Slavery* by Stanley M. Elkins (Grosset & Dunlap,
New York, 1963).
[2] K. Stampp, op. cit., p. 39.

against the planter, fear enforced an alliance with the planter against the slave.

And fear was rampant, hideous with individual imaginings – fear of losing status, with all its heady attributes; fear of rivalry from free Negroes for land and labour and sex; fear of violence and a retribution all the greater for being so repressively postponed. From the very first the slaves rebelled against their condition, with many flinging themselves overboard or starving themselves to death during the ocean passage. Within America itself, countless slave conspiracies were mounted, and the cruelty with which the sporadic risings were crushed did not dissuade fresh instigators from seeking success.

In 1741 a slave plot led to the firing of many buildings in New York City, and two Negroes were chained to stakes before a howling mob, confessed to a part in the plot, and were burned alive, followed by the execution of twenty-nine others and four whites, including two women. During the summer of 1800 several thousand Negroes, led by a six-foot-two-inch-tall, twenty-four-year-old slave called Gabriel, were involved in a conspiracy to kill their masters in Virginia, seize Richmond, and 'if the white people agreed to their freedom ... then hoist a white flag';[1] but betrayal, together with storm floods that made massing impossible, led to the easy arrest and subsequent execution of thirty-six Negro rebels. Gabriel himself, when questioned by the one-time revolutionary leader James Monroe, then Governor of Virginia, 'seemed to have made up his mind to die, and to have resolved to say but little on the subject of the conspiracy'.

Whites, it appears, were occasionally involved in these hopeless bids for freedom, but even when caught did not always, as in the New York City plot, suffer the same punishment as Negroes. In 1822 one of the most extensive slave conspiracies in American history was mounted under the leadership of Denmark Vesey, a Negro in Charleston, South Carolina, enlisting thousands of slaves in the city itself and surroundings to a distance of eighty miles. But again betrayal sped the arrest of the ringleaders before any rising took place; thirty-seven Negroes were hanged and four whites, convicted of sympathy with the rebels, were fined and jailed. Vesey himself, like Gabriel earlier, died silent, but one of his associates, named Rolla, a slave of the Governor, described before being executed a meeting which Vesey had addressed. '[He] said that we were to take the Guard-House and Magazine to get arms; that we ought to rise up and fight against the

[1] *A Documentary History of the Negro People in the United States*, edited by Herbert Aptheker (The Citadel Press, New York, 1963), p. 45.

whites for our liberties; he was the first to rise up and speak, and he read to us from the Bible, how the Children of Israel were delivered out of Egypt from bondage.'[1]

The Bible might be plundered by the masters for proofs of their right to rule, but it was open to plunder for very different purposes by the slaves, and despite the rigorous promotion of ignorance and illiteracy, the seditious message of the Scriptures could not be suppressed. The most celebrated of all slave rebellions broke out, after three years of widespread slave unrest in the South, on August 21st, 1831, in Southampton County, Virginia, under the leadership of a thirty-one-year-old Negro called Nat Turner. In childhood, according to a statement he made when in prison, he had been visited by visions, and his religious family had measured in him the makings of a prophet.

'I had a vision – and I saw white spirits and black spirits engaged in battle, and the sun was darkened – the thunder rolled in the heavens, and blood flowed in streams – and I heard a voice saying, "Such is your luck, such you are called to see; and let it come rough or smooth, you must surely bear it" ...'

In the uprising itself some sixty whites were killed, while at least a hundred Negroes died in the retribution that followed. Thirteen slaves and three free Negroes were arrested immediately, tried and hanged, but Nat Turner was captured only on October 30th, when he was 'loaded with chains', to be executed twelve days later.

The resort of the American Negro to armed revolt was, however, a necessarily rare explosion of despair. The whites then – though in proportionately far lesser a degree than now – had the power of arms and numbers, and both the few free and the many enslaved Negroes tried to better their condition by appeal to conscience and consistency. It was the Revolutionary War which itself provided the Negro with his first important weapon, a weapon which would acquire, with time and the development of the judiciary, a deep-cutting edge. The sheer absurdity of two and a half million white Americans shouting 'Liberty or Death' while enslaving three-quarters of a million black ones was not lost on the black ones themselves, who attended to the Declaration of Independence and wondered – increasingly aloud – why its terms should not apply to them. In 1777 a number of Negro slaves petitioned the Massachusetts House of Representatives for their freedom and were careful to point the moral of the recent war, using the very arguments and phrases which had inspired the revolutionary leaders.

[1] H. Aptheker, op. cit., p. 76.

... Your Petitioners apprehend that they have in Common with all other men a Natural and Unaliable Right to that freedom which the Grat Parent of the Unavers hath Bestowed equalley on all menkind and which they have Never forfeited by any Compact or agreement whatever ... they Cannot but express their Astonishment that It have Never Bin Consirdered that Every Principle from which Amarica has Acted in the Cours of their unhappy Dificultes with Great Briton Pleads Stronger than A thousand arguments in favours of your petioners ...[1]

The Massachusetts rebels of yesterday, however, were the satisfied governors of today, and once having felt themselves the Children of Israel in bondage, now as Pharaohs resolutely hardened their hearts.

What the Revolution did allow was the emancipation of some Negroes for individual initiative, because they had fled from their Tory masters or had given service in the war. Many of the five thousand or so Negroes who had fought in the rebel army were slaves, and those who petitioned their respective state governments for freedom afterwards frequently received it as a reward. Furthermore, if most revolutionary slogans lost their force when those who mouthed them were black, one at least appears to have stirred a sympathetic response. In 1780 seven free Negroes in Dartmouth, Massachusetts, petitioned the revolutionary legislature of their state for 'no taxation without representation', and three years later, by court decision, all Negroes subject to tax were declared entitled to vote.

Amongst those who signed the Dartmouth petition was Paul Cuffe, who subsequently became a successful ship's captain and merchant and who in 1815 pioneered the colonization of West Africa by American Negroes, transporting thirty-eight of them at his own expense. The return to Africa was to be a recurrent dream of those Negroes who saw in it the only real escape from racial servitude, but it never became a popular aspiration. It was clearly impractical for all but a few, whose skills and vision might be put to greater profit in assisting the struggle of their people in America, while most Negroes in any event refused to consider changing the only home they knew for one which promised a multitude of strange tribulations. White propaganda had excused black slavery by portraying Africa as a savage wilderness, and for many years to come American Negroes would accept this portrayal at its face value. Indeed, the more militant and articulate Negroes generally regarded proposals for the repatriation of their people as attempts to weaken the struggle for

[1] H. Aptheker, op. cit., p. 10.

racial emancipation within America itself, and their contention was not without testimony.

The first organized effort at substantial emigration was made by the American Colonization Society, founded in December 1816 by whites, with several prominent slaveholders amongst them, to repatriate free Negroes on the grounds that they were incapable of leading useful lives in the United States and would, by their removal, make the institution of slavery more secure. Negro groups were quick to oppose the Society and its objectives, and one meeting at Philadelphia in January 1817, registering its strong protest at the description of free Negroes as 'a dangerous and useless part of the community', resolved:

'That we never will separate ourselves voluntarily from the slave population of this country; they are our brethren by the ties of consanguinity, of suffering, and of wrong; and we feel that there is more virtue in suffering privations with them, than fancied advantages for a season.'[1]

The Philadelphia meeting had fittingly been convened 'at Bethel church', for organized Christianity among Negroes was already beginning to serve much more than a religious purpose alone. During the Revolution the establishment of separate Negro churches had begun, among Virginia Baptists in 1776 and Georgia Baptists three years later; but these had remained under the jurisdiction of all-white bodies until legal separation, with full control over property, was achieved by the African Methodist Episcopal Church (to which Philadelphia's Bethel church belonged) in January 1816.

The Negro Church quickly became the most effective organized Negro institution in the United States, with the richer and more numerous congregations erecting monumental buildings and endowing their ministers with wide influence as well as wealth. It was the minister indeed who provided the first real communal leadership, while the church itself gave the community a social cohesion and resilience, providing welfare for its poorer members, establishing and running schools, encouraging insurance societies. Before their own congregations Negro ministers could freely denounce the injustices of white America and recruit popular participation in campaigns of appeal and protest; it is no accident that so many leaders of the civil rights movement in the United States today are or were once Negro preachers. Moreover, the Church enabled the Negro, if only for a few hours once a week, to escape the constant reminders of white

[1] *Thoughts on African Colonization: or an impartial exhibition of the Doctrines, Principles & Purposes of the American Colonization Society. Together with the Resolutions, Addresses & Remonstrances of the Free People of Color*, by William Lloyd Garrison (Boston, 1832), Part II, pp. 9–10.

authority, to feel himself strong and capable in the united presence of his
people. The Church restored pride to the Negroes. It nourished their art
and all America's, producing in the gospel choir and the spiritual a new
music and a new poetry. By financing foreign missions to Africa and by
retaining the word 'African' in the title of many large denominations, it
promoted the Negro's identification with a force in the past and in the
present world outside, diminishing his sense of loss and isolation, the
psychological impact of white myths and black abasement. It achieved for
the Negro, by the simple fact of its separation, increasing independence
from white control and the dominion of white values.

In time, of course, the Church would lose some of its communal
leadership to secular organizations, founded specifically to project the
Negro struggle for political and economic advance, while its prestige
would dwindle as it came under attack by militants as over-cautious and
corrupt. The rich harvests gathered by the more successful ministers would
make them wary of an open clash with white authority; possessions encouraged prudence. Besides, emancipation of the slaves and the subsequent
– if slow and erratic – progress of constitutional reform would make the
Negro's degradation less obvious, his advance less urgent, his struggle
more complex and strangely more radical, entailing a perilous and sometimes solitary initiative. In the revolution of the 1960s, the Negro clergy
would in the main be far more moved than moving, associating themselves
with the provocations of sit-in and boycott, picket-line and march, only
when driven to do so by the pressure of their communities or the indiscriminate assaults of white antagonism. Yet the contribution of the Negro
Church to the civil rights movement, especially in the nineteenth century,
cannot easily be exaggerated, and the secular Negro leadership today owes
much to the tradition which developed in the pulpit.

Just as the religious segregation of Negroes – they had been made to
worship at different times from the whites, or at the same time in special
seats – led to the establishment of a separate Negro Church, so the denial
to Negroes of membership in white charitable and other social institutions
led to the organization of separate Negro fraternal societies. The first
Negro lodge, the Masons, received its charter in 1787, and in the same
year the Philadelphia Free African Society was founded to provide for its
members – 'without regard to religious tenets' – support in sickness and
assistance to 'widows and fatherless children'. Similar societies were
formed soon afterwards in Boston, New York and many other centres of
the free Negro population in the North, and these maintained a steady
correspondence with each other, their members exchanging visits and

conveying news. The welfare work of the Philadelphia society – each member agreed to advance one shilling in silver every month for the relief of the needy – served as the beginning of a major modern Negro business enterprise, the insurance companies, while its secular pattern pointed to communal effort outside the Church.

Prince Hall, the founder and first Master of the Negro lodge, took the lead, too, in an endeavour that would culminate, more than a century and a half later, in a crucial ruling against segregation by the United States Supreme Court. In October 1787, together with other free Negroes in Massachusetts, he petitioned the state legislature for the enjoyment of equal educational facilities by all free citizens. The petition was rejected, and Prince Hall started a school for Negro children at his own home in 1798.

The Negroes were beginning to organize themselves for corporate constitutional action, but it was only in 1827 that the first Negro-owned and edited newspaper, *Freedom's Journal*, appeared. Published in New York City, it flung itself into the fight against slavery and racial discrimination from its first editorial, and only five months from its founding could bitterly issue the first press report of a lynching; in Perry County, Alabama, a Negro accused of murder had been burnt to death, 'even against the remonstrances of several gentlemen who were present', by a raging white mob. In 1831 the white Abolitionist William Lloyd Garrison founded the *Liberator*, which was to become the flagship of the Puritan conscience in the propaganda war against slavery, and it was the Negro support it received that kept it afloat: in its first year of publication, 400 out of its 450 subscribers were Negro; and three years later, 1,700 out of 2,300. The Negro reading public would increasingly influence the development of the Press, both within the Negro community and outside.

Beyond the South, white opposition to slavery gathered force, and the Northern states, starting with Vermont in 1777 and ending in 1804 with New Jersey, either abolished slavery all at once or adopted measures to effect its phased elimination within their boundaries. But emancipation in the North only sharpened the issue of slavery in the nation at large. Northern slave-owners, faced with the gradual freeing of their slaves, sold them to the ever-hungry Southern markets; the Abolitionists demanded federal action to free the slaves throughout the country; both North and South became, with growing bitterness, embroiled in a dispute over whether slavery should be outlawed in the new territories; and the freedom of Negroes in the North enticed an irresistible flow there of slave fugitives from the South.

The Louisiana Purchase of 1803 opened a vast area – from New Orleans to the Canadian border – to American settlement and the struggle over slavery. And in this struggle it was the free-soil West, home of Lincoln, which was to ensure the final victory for emancipation. The lands beyond the Mississippi were coveted by exploiters from North and South alike, and the small farmers already staking out homesteads there were not slow to see that their whole economic future would be endangered if Congress yielded to the demands of the slave state lobby. It was no passionate humanitarianism that made the free-soiler in the West send the first strong contingent of anti-slavery representatives to Washington. Racially and economically the white West was hostile to the Negro, slave or free; indeed, the Topeka constitution adopted by the Kansas free-soilers barred Negroes altogether from the new state. But the free labour settling on the new lands wanted no rivalry from plantation ownership; though the moral argument against slavery was doubtless fundamental to some, it was to most no more than a handy weapon against economic attack.

The state of Louisiana, in the extreme south of the Purchase area, joined the Union as a slave state in 1812, but when Missouri attempted to do the same a few years later, a swelling protest spread through the North and West, to carry most of the Congressmen from these sections of the country with it. The Missouri Compromise of 1820 admitted the new slave state to the Union but drew a line across the Purchase area, corresponding to the southern boundary of Missouri, north of which slavery would in the future be for ever outlawed and south of which, it was generally understood, new slave states could be established. It was no more than a holding operation, and sentiment on either side of the slave border steadily hardened.

Within the South itself, the invention of the saw-gin had made the cultivation of cotton prodigiously profitable – cotton exports leapt from less than 200,000 lbs in 1791 to 42,000,000 in 1804 – and the powerful planters intensified their devotion to the slave system commensurately. And since the whole basis of the system lay in the laws of the individual states, the governing class in the South took its stand on the issue of state sovereignty rather than on the morally treacherous terrain of human enslavement.

The admission of California to the Union as a free state in 1850 was allowed by Southern strength in Congress only as a return for certain concessions, among them the passing of the Fugitive Slave Law, which stirred the Abolitionist movement to fresh energy and rage. It was an attempt to crush, with the help of federal power, the work of the Underground Railroad and other efforts by which the flow of slaves to freedom in the North was being encouraged. The Negro claimed as a fugitive – by a master's affidavit presented before a federal commissioner – was to be given no jury trial; the official's fee would be ten dollars if he found the Negro to be a fugitive, and only five dollars if he did not; and all citizens were required to prevent the rescue or escape of any fugitive condemned. Harriet Beecher Stowe's novel *Uncle Tom's Cabin*, a fierce attack on the new law, was published in 1852 and achieved a swift and massive success, while prominent Abolitionists declared aloud their intention of protecting fugitive slaves from the injustice of the law. The whole character of the Union and the principles on which its Constitution was based were now generally seen to be at stake. Frederick Douglass, the outstanding Negro leader of the time, spoke for all Negro and much white opinion at Rochester in 1852.

What to the American slave is your Fourth of July? I answer: a day that reveals to him, more than all other days of the year, the gross injustice and cruelty to which he is the constant victim. To him your celebration is a sham; your boasted liberty, an unholy licence; your national greatness, swelling vanity; your sounds of rejoicing are empty and heartless; your denunciation of tyrants, brass-fronted impudence; your shouts of liberty and equality, hollow mockery; your prayers and hymns, your sermons and thanksgivings, with all your religious parade and solemnity, are, to him, mere bombast, fraud, deception, impiety and hypocrisy – a thin veil to cover up crimes which would disgrace a nation of savages.[1]

It was in this atmosphere of passion, made daily more explosive by the ruthless enforcement of the Fugitive Slave Law, that Congress, under a Democratic regime straining to retain the South, committed an extravagant blunder. It organized the two new Territories of Kansas and Nebraska, and (by the Kansas-Nebraska Act of 1854) left both to decide whether to be slave or free. All at once a vast stretch of the new America, settled by the Missouri Compromise of 1820 as for ever free, was snatched from the settlement to become a prize for the contending forces of free and slave labour. Protest in the North and West produced a fresh Congressional grouping, which called itself the Republican Party, and in 1856 for the first time the two major political parties of modern America faced each other.

[1] H. Aptheker, op. cit., p. 334.

Nebraska was largely desolate, and so Kansas became the immediate field of battle. In the North and West emigrant associations were formed to send Abolitionist settlers to the territory, while Missouri, backed by the South, sent proponents of slavery or forcibly blocked the path of free state settlers. The Civil War had begun, though seven more years would pass before the secession of the South and the first military collision.

At no other time in American history have so many whites – and whites of such public prominence – been so militantly involved in a movement for Negro advance. Some even lost their lives, like Elijah Lovejoy, a young Abolitionist from Maine who had moved to St Louis, Missouri, and published there a religious newspaper, called *The Observer*, dedicated to the struggle against slavery. Threats of mob violence had forced him to shift his press across the Mississippi, to Alton in Illinois, but even there his machinery had several times been destroyed by mobs, and on the night of November 7th, 1837, when a mob had again attacked his press, he himself had been killed. Lovejoy was a manifest martyr, and the news of his death had much strengthened Abolitionist sentiment in the North. Some twenty-two years later, slavery would claim another significant white sacrifice, even more costly to its cause if also more controversial.

John Brown, a bankrupt businessman and farmer whose early financial dealings bear little sympathetic scrutiny, became a passionate Abolitionist and in 1855 moved from New York to Kansas, where the violent settler conflict over slavery had begun to rage. In 1856 he took a major part in the 'Pottawatomie massacre', when five supporters of slavery were murdered in retaliation for the killing of five opponents, and in 1858–9 he established a stronghold in the mountains of Virginia for fugitive slaves. Then, on the night of October 16th, 1859, with eighteen men – five of them Negroes – he attacked the Federal arsenal at Harper's Ferry, capturing it and taking sixty leading citizens of the town as hostages. Two days later a small force of marines recaptured the arsenal, killing ten of Brown's associates and arresting Brown himself, who was soon afterwards convicted of treason, conspiracy and murder, and hanged on December 2nd.

It is difficult to see what Brown could reasonably have expected to achieve by his assault on Harper's Ferry. His capture of the arsenal provided him with enough weapons to sustain a massive slave rising in the South, but there were no slaves ready to make use of them; though there were plans to promote such a rising, preparation seems to have been largely a matter of hope. If, however, it was no more than immediate martyrdom, with the most profound agitation of public opinion, that he sought, he consummately found it. 'John Brown may be a lunatic', proclaimed the

Boston *Post*; but, if so, 'then one-fourth of the people of Massachusetts are madmen.' 'Harper's Ferry was insane,' declared the New York *Independent*, but 'the controlling motive of this demonstration was sublime'. Thoreau, on the day after Brown's capture, pronounced Harper's Ferry 'the best news that America ever had' and Brown himself 'the bravest and humanest man in all the country', while Emerson described Brown as 'the saint, whose fate yet hangs in suspense, but whose martyrdom, if it shall be perfected, will make the gallows as glorious as the cross'. With New England's paramount moralists and thinkers on his side, Brown became the intellectual passion of the hour, provoking a new commitment to militant means for ending slavery. And the response of the North was widely echoed in the West. If Lincoln himself deplored Brown, Lincoln's law partner, Billy Herndon, considered him a hero and a saint. Citizens of Oberlin erected a monument to the three Negroes who had lost their lives in Brown's raid, while Joshua Giddings, influential Ohio Republican, wrote: 'I find the hatred of slavery greatly intensified by the fate of Brown and men are ready to march to Virginia and dispose of her despotism at once.' On the day that Brown was hanged, church bells tolled in mourning all over New England, in Ohio and in Illinois.

The whole Brown episode, especially the extent of public sympathy expressed for Brown himself in the North and West, deeply stirred the South. Forced inexorably on to the defensive by the discrediting of slavery throughout the civilized world and the steady expansion of free state power in the United States, Southern whites felt themselves besieged, menaced from within by slave unrest and from without by forces speedily growing strong enough to seize control of the federal government. In reaction they withdrew increasingly into themselves and their own myths.

> Convinced that the South was honeycombed with subversives, Southerners tended to see an abolitionist behind every bush and a slave insurrection brewing in the arrival of any stranger. Victims of vigilante and mob action ranged from aged eccentrics and itinerant piano-tuners to substantial citizens of long residence. The mob spirit was no respecter of person or class. A sixty-year-old minister in Texas, who was a believer in the Biblical sanction of slavery and a Democrat of Kentucky birth, made the mistake of criticizing the treatment of slaves in a sermon and was given seventy lashes on his back ... Not only Northerners but associates of Northerners were subject to persecution, for guilt by association was an accepted principle in the crisis.[1]

[1] 'John Brown's Private War', in *The Burden of Southern History*, by C. Vann Woodward, a Vintage Book published by Random House, New York, 1960, pp. 64–5.

To deal with the dangers of subversion, books critical of slavery – even if written by Southerners – were publicly burnt, while newspapers were seized and suppressed. Extremists even organized economic boycotts, publishing blacklists of Northern firms with suspected abolitionist tendencies, and the Richmond *Enquirer* advocated a law 'that will keep out of our borders every article of Northern manufacture or importation'. On December 8th, 1859, thirty-two agents of firms in New York and Boston arrived in Washington from the South, reporting 'indignation so great against Northerners that they were compelled to return and abandon their business'.

Before the white poor of the South loomed the menace of slave rebellion with all the morbid visions of race retribution, and many became more frenzied secessionists than the planters. By 1860 the South was tossed by a series of wild rumours – slave plans to fire buildings and poison wells – fed by and feeding the general paranoia. The Southern whites were ready for an act as mad as Brown's, and when at last they committed it, it was, one feels, with a glad sense of relief, as though anything, even war, was preferable to the prolonging of their uncertainty.

When the Democratic convention met at Charleston in 1860, the Southern delegates demanded a declaration that Congress should protect slavery in the Territories; but the Northern delegates, only too aware that this would spell their political suicide, voted down the proposal, and the Southerners withdrew to meet separately at Richmond. With the Democratic Party split and its sections nominating different candidates, the Republicans won the elections of that year, and Lincoln became President. It was the signal for secession. A state convention in South Carolina on December 20th formally dissolved the union with other states, repealing the various acts by which South Carolina had ratified the United States Constitution, and its example was followed early in 1861 by Mississippi, Florida, Alabama, Georgia, Louisiana and Texas. Delegates appointed by the seven state conventions then met together at Montgomery the capital of Alabama; adopted on February 8th a provisional constitution for the 'Confederate States'; chose a provisional President (Jefferson Davis); and established an army, treasury, and other executive departments.

For the next few months peace manoeuvres were busily promoted by representatives of the border states; but these all came to nothing, and war awaited only an occasion. It arrived in the middle of April 1861, when the dispatch of a federal force to provision Fort Sumter in Charleston Harbour brought on an attack by Confederate batteries and the surrender of the fort. Lincoln called for 75,000 volunteers, and four border states – North Carolina, Arkansas, Virginia and Tennessee – upholding the doctrine of state sovereignty, joined the Confederacy.

The two sides were unequally matched from the start. The North and West, which retained the border states of Delaware, Maryland, Kentucky and Missouri as well as a substantial part of Virginia itself (the western portion broke away and joined the Union in 1863 as the new state of West Virginia), possessed the clear superiority in manpower, land area, natural resources, industry and popular allegiance. Its enormous potential enabled it to borrow by bond issues for the payment of the war, while its industrial capacity allowed it to divert labour from the land into the army by increasing the supply of agricultural machinery. The South, on the other hand, could raise no mortgage on its future, and its present wealth in cotton was sealed off from sale by the Northern naval blockade; Southern bonds were virtually unsalable, and a torrent of paper issues produced runaway inflation (by May 1864 shoes in the Richmond market cost $125 a pair, and flour, $275 a barrel). Since it had no real industry of its own, the destruction of a railway line or rolling stock was a serious setback, and any keeping pace with the North's supply of armaments a sheer impossibility. Moreover, while the North could securely send all its fighting men to the front, the ever-present danger of slave insurrection in the South kept a substantial portion of fighting manpower at home. Conditions of service in the Southern Army steadily deteriorated, and the ruthless methods of recruitment employed by an increasingly despotic executive – towards the end of the war every man between the ages of 17 and 55 was legally liable to serve – led to popular discontent and mass desertions; when fighting ended, there were barely 200,000 men in the Confederate Armies, while the men in Unionist colours numbered over a million.

Though personally a strong opponent of slavery, Lincoln believed in the rights of local democracies (however racially limited) and recognized property interests in the slave. A cautious liberal, devoted to the Constitution, he was willing to yield a great deal if by doing so he could save the Union. But as the hope of compromise with the South retreated before the contending armies and the forces of Abolitionism swept public opinion in the North and West, he moved towards the eradication of slavery throughout the United States. On April 16th, 1862, slavery was prohibited in the District of Columbia, and on June 19th in the Territories. Then, on September 17th, Lincoln called on the rebellious states to return to their allegiance before the next year or face the freeing of their slaves; none of the Confederate States submitted, and so, on January 1st, 1863, Lincoln proclaimed the emancipation of the slaves throughout the country. It was an act – and Lincoln himself was shrewd enough to see this – that crushed any real hope of a Southern victory. The blockade of Southern cotton had deprived the textile industry in Britain and France of its chief raw material supplies, and the Confederate States firmly believed that the two great powers would be forced to intervene on their side; but the conversion of the Civil War into a crusade against slavery swung international opinion decisively against the South and made any alliance with it impossible.

Opposition in the North and West to slavery was one thing, however, and the grant of equal rights to Negroes quite another. At the outbreak of the Civil War, Negroes in their thousands offered to serve as soldiers; but it took more than a year, with swelling casualties and public agitation, before the enlistment of Negroes in the Unionist forces began. Even then the conditions of service for Negroes were made inferior – in July 1863 the War Department ruled that all Negro troops were to be classed for purposes of pay with hired fugitive slaves, receiving $10 a month (with three dollars of this deducted for clothing) rather than the $13 paid to white troops – and it took another year, with repeated representations by Negroes both inside and outside the Army, before Congress finally equalized the pay of white and black soldiers. In the end some 200,000 Negro men joined the Unionist Army and 30,000 the Navy, while a further 250,000 Negro men and women served as teamsters, cooks, builders and in other non-combatant capacities.

Most white Americans may, for a variety of motives, have wanted the Negro free, but the free Negro himself they regarded as an alien. Even Lincoln directed his attention to proposals for repatriation, though deploring any hint of compulsion – the very law emancipating slaves in the District of Columbia provided $100,000 for colonization – and only the resolute protests of the Negroes themselves effectively shelved the issue. All over the North discrimination against Negroes was practised, and the Civil War period is full of appeals and protests by Negroes – against taxation without representation in Connecticut, against segregation on the city cars of Philadelphia, against lack of the vote in Washington itself, the nation's capital, against exclusion (by order of the City Council) from Lincoln's funeral procession. Some representations were successful – a telegram from the Assistant Secretary of War allowed the presence of 2,000 Negro mourners at the end of the long procession behind Lincoln's coffin – but most were not. There were even riots against Negroes in

Northern cities; in the first of them, at Detroit in March 1863, one of the rioters was heard to say, 'If we are got to be killed up for Negroes, then we will kill every one in this town!'[1]

It is small wonder, then, that even at the height of a war against the slave South there were Negroes, however few, who turned their backs on the whole struggle. Frederick Douglass, attacking them in his Rochester newspaper on March 2nd, 1863, advertised their existence and arguments.

There are weak and cowardly men in all nations. We have them amongst us. They tell you this is the 'white man's war'; that you will be no 'better off after than before the war'; that the getting of you into the army is to 'sacrifice you on the first opportunity'. Believe them not; cowards themselves, they do not wish to have their cowardice shamed by your brave example. Leave them to their timidity, or to whatever motive may hold them back.

By the time of the Second World War and, still more evidently, the Korean War a few years later, the contraction out of white America and its struggles would be more widespread – and intellectually respectable – among Negroes, in response to the many decades of disappointment.

The Civil War ended effectively on April 9th, 1865, with the surrender of the main Confederate army under General Robert E. Lee to General Grant at Appomattox, Virginia. Six days later Lincoln was assassinated, and Andrew Johnson, a Southern Unionist from the poor white mountain region of Tennessee, succeeded to the presidency and the task of reconstructing a shattered South. He had, however, none of Lincoln's flexibility or imagination, and his hostility to the Southern white planter class – he exempted from amnesty all those whose taxable property was valued at over $20,000, as well as those who had held high posts in the Confederacy – was more an outcrop of poor white rancour against the rich than of any resolution radically to change race relations in the South. Inevitably, therefore, he clashed with a Congress which, dominated now by Northern Republicans, saw no reason to trust the mass of Southern whites and feared the return of unreconstructed Southern influence to its midst.

There was much justification for the suspicions of Congress. The new state governments of the South, chosen by those who had been qualified

---

[1] *A Thrilling Narrative from the Lips of the Sufferers of the Late Detroit Riot* ... by Thomas Buckner. Published by the author, Detroit, 1863; reprinted by The Book Farm, Hattiesburg, Mississippi, 1945.

to vote before secession and who now took an oath to support the constitution together with the laws and proclamations emancipating the slaves, were less aristocratic in complexion than the old ones had been, but hardly less racist. They formed bodies of white militia for protection against the possibility of Negro attack, and passed various 'black codes' or 'peonage laws', aimed at treating the former slaves as a separate and still dependent class; Mississippi prohibited Negroes from owning land or even renting it outside of incorporated towns, while South Carolina limited them to farm or domestic service unless specially licensed. But humanitarianism was far from being the sole concern of the North.

Indeed, the Northern Republicans, radical and moderate alike, were in the main less interested in the justice of granting the franchise to the former slaves than in the danger of withholding it from them. The great Abolitionist, William Lloyd Garrison of the *Liberator*, himself wrote in 1864:

> When was it ever known that liberation from bondage was accompanied by a recognition of political equality? Chattels personal may be instantly translated from the auction-block into freemen; but when were they ever taken at the same time to the ballot-box, and invested with all political rights and immunities? According to the laws of development and progress, it is not practicable.

Only five states in the North, each with a negligible Negro population, provided for the coloured franchise. In 1865 Wisconsin, Minnesota and Connecticut defeated proposals for Negro suffrage; the Nebraska constitution of 1866 limited the vote to whites; New Jersey and Ohio in 1867, and Michigan and Pennsylvania in 1868, rejected demands for an extension of the franchise to Negroes.

What did move many Northern Republicans was fear of the returning Southern Democratic vote to Congress, with the threat that this would pose not only to Republican power but to the whole economic order that had been established during the period of secession. The manufacturing interests in the North trembled for protective tariff legislation, government grants and subsidies to business, the whole machinery for financing industrial expansion, and flung their support to a policy of radical Reconstruction. Thaddeus Stevens, champion of the freedmen and master of the Republican majority in the House of Representatives, was frank. In proclaiming the need for military rule in the South, the disfranchisement of many whites, and the immediate extension of suffrage to the former slaves, he declared that it would ensure the ascendancy of the Republican Party.

> For I believe, on my conscience, that on the continued ascendancy of that party depends the safety of this great nation. If impartial suffrage is excluded in the rebel states, then every one of them is sure to send a solid rebel [Democratic] representation to Congress, and cast a solid rebel electoral vote. They, with their kindred Copperheads [Democrats] of the North, would always elect the President and control Congress.

The radicals in the Republican Party decided to seize the initiative from the President. By the Thirteenth Amendment to the Constitution, Congress had already abolished slavery throughout the Union, so placing the emancipation proclaimed by Lincoln beyond legal dispute or the power of any state to dismiss. Now, in March 1866, it resolved not to admit any reconstructed state until Congress itself declared the state entitled to recognition, so asserting ultimate control over the whole reconstruction policy. Then, in the following month, it passed, over the President's veto, a Civil Rights Bill which declared the freed slaves to be citizens of the United States with the same civil rights as whites and the same title to the protection of the federal government. Furthermore, to secure this measure against attack in the courts or alteration by a change in party control, Congress in June produced the Fourteenth Amendment, guaranteeing equal citizenship rights to the freedmen, and made ratification a prerequisite for restoration of the Southern states to Congress. Every state which had been party to secession but Tennessee, which submitted and so received admission in 1866, rejected the Amendment, and Congress turned to coercion.

The Reconstruction Acts of March 1867 – passed over the veto of President Johnson – declared that no legal governments or adequate protection for life and property existed in the former Confederate states (except for Tennessee); divided them into five military districts, each under a general; declared the existing civil administrations provisional and subject to modification or abolition by the federal government; provided for the summoning of state constitutional conventions elected by general suffrage; and disfranchised many whites for military or civil service in the Confederacy.

The new Southern electorate, produced under military supervision in 1867–8, had just over 700,000 Negro voters and 625,000 white ones; the

disfranchisement of whites was substantial, and though only two states had
a popular coloured majority, five had more Negroes than whites on the
electoral rolls. The white South was, for the most part, outraged. It
dubbed the Northern political managers 'carpet-baggers' and those whites
involved in the new regime 'scalawags', while extremist groups like the
'Ku Klux Klan' and the 'Knights of the White Camelia' arose to intimidate or forcibly restrain the Negro voters. Yet constitutional conventions
were duly elected; the Fourteenth Amendment was ratified and the
states were restored to the Union; state legislatures and Congressional
representatives were chosen; and a short period of inter-racial rule was
begun.

It was an interlude in Southern history that would sustain white myths
for decades; it sustains them still. It became, indeed, a new white myth on
its own, piously tended not only by mint julep novelists but even by sober
historians. Through the eyes of a bitter and fearful tradition, Reconstruction emerged as a sort of flickering night orgy, with Negro legislators
squandering their responsibilities in a riot of extravagance, corruption,
arrogance and sin.

Of course there was graft and misuse of public funds. It was not an age
of generally upright government. But there is no evidence to show that
the extent of such corruption was any greater in the Reconstructed South
than elsewhere in the Union at that time, while the evidence there is
suggests a more profuse gathering of illicit Reconstruction rewards by
the whites in power than by the Negroes. In the main the new citizens
were remarkably reticent and never held office in proportion to their
numbers; indeed, no state in the South had at any stage a Negro-domi-
nated administration. Their success varied, naturally, from state to state;
but if the example of Mississippi is to be cited – a state today pre-eminent
in the exercise of white supremacy and the corruption of officialdom
– their record was illustrious. The three Negroes who represented the state
in Congress were unexceptionable, while those in the state legislature –
they constituted only two-sevenths of the House and even less of the
Senate membership – sought no particular advantages for their race and
in one of their very first acts petitioned Congress to remove all political
disabilities from whites. Under the joint control of Negro and white
Republicans, the state government vastly expanded its functions, and at a
relatively lower cost than in most other states of the Union.

As one distinguished American historian of Southern background has
described it,[1] 'a sort of historical colour bar' operates in the customary

[1] C. Vann Woodward, 'The Political Legacy of Reconstruction', op. cit.

account of Negro suffrage during Reconstruction. More than twelve million white immigrants – all but a few of them without experience of any participation in democratic government – acquired American citizenship in the fifty years from 1880 onwards, and their initial encounter with American institutions was marked by the sway of corruption, the small political bribe and the big political boss. They had many prejudices to face and many obstacles to surmount, but the prejudices and obstacles in their way were trivial compared with those surrounding the newly freed Negroes of the South.

The white immigrants did not have to register their votes under the protection of federal rifles; they did not receive their right to vote at the same time as the members of the traditional ruling class lost theirs; their political leaders were not considered puppets of a hostile government, and their civil rights a deliberate humiliation inflicted upon their fellow citizens; they may have lacked self-assurance or education or experience in public affairs, but they had not endured years of that absolute privation which is slavery.

As the new Negro voters went to the polls, in the very rags of their former condition, and as their representatives took their new seats of authority, they might well have promised a degenerate – even a disastrous – result. That on the whole they did so well, that they produced so many competent and honest public servants, that the twisted figures of myth were the exception rather than the rule, must be considered one of the greatest collective triumphs – short as it was – of the Negro in America. And this is being increasingly recognized, increasingly proclaimed by articulate American Negroes today. They see in the traditional portrayal of their Reconstruction past a concerted effort to belittle their capacities and so excuse their present degradation. For them there is a race war being fought no less around the history book, the recording and the interpretation of facts, than the ballot-box and the school, the factory and the home.

The Republican Party convention of 1868 chose General Grant, a strong Reconstructionist, as its presidential candidate and declared its intention to entrench the profitable Negro vote in the South; but on the embarrassing issue of the Negro vote in the North, it was blandly evasive. 'The guarantee by Congress of equal suffrage to all loyal men at the South was demanded by every consideration of public safety, of gratitude and of justice, and must be maintained; while the question of suffrage in all the loyal states properly belongs to the people of those states.' Such inconsistency could not last long. Grant won a decisive victory in the elections of that year, in consequence mainly of the Negro vote in the

Reconstructed South, and shortly after it assembled Congress produced the Fifteenth Amendment – ratified in March 1870 – which proclaimed that 'the right of citizens of the United States to vote shall not be denied or abridged by the United States or by any state on account of race, colour or previous condition of servitude'.

The Fifteenth Amendment, with the enforcement legislation of 1870–72, marked the culmination of Northern white concern for Negro rights. Public opinion now shifted its attention to corruption in government, disputes over currency and tariffs, the assimilation of immigrants from Europe, and reconciliation with the white South; within a few years the Negro in the South would be effectively deprived of his vote, and the Negro throughout the nation subjected to multiplying forms of discrimination. The last decade of the nineteenth century and the early decades of the twentieth seem in retrospect to have constituted an era of undeclared civil race war, in which every engagement further increased the Negro's enforced inferiority.

In 1875 President Grant refused an appeal by the 'carpet-bagger' Governor Ames of Mississippi for troops; the Governor resigned, and substantial intimidation of Negro voters in the state ensued. The 1876 election proved so close that its result was disputed, and the Republican candidate, Governor Hayes of Ohio, took office as President with the co-operation of leading Democrats on the understanding that he would withdraw federal troops from Louisiana and other parts of the South where they were still sustaining Republican regimes. This bargain – the Compromise of 1877 – spelt the end of Reconstruction and the arrival of what the white South subsequently named Redemption; in the Congressional elections of 1878, the former slave states sent 101 Democrats to the House of Representatives and only four Republicans.

The 1877 Compromise, accepted as it was by Northern liberals, signalled the beginning, not the end, of a general retreat on the race issue. It shut federal eyes to infringements of the Fourteenth and Fifteenth Amendments, and established the practice – by no means abandoned today – of leaving legal authority in the Southern states to treat Negroes as it pleased. Northern business needed Southern white support to bolster the new capitalist expansion, while Northern liberalism, identifying graft in government with the demagogues of radicalism, and seeing the Negro as the symbol of civil strife, denounced any further agitation for Negro advance, in the cause of reconciling North and South. Former campaniles of liberal and even strong Abolitionist sentiment in the press and pulpit increasingly pealed out sympathy for the view of Southern whites.

Then, in 1898, under the leadership of the Republican Party, the United States flung her power into the Caribbean and the Pacific, extending her sway over some eight million coloured people – 'a varied assortment of inferior races', according to the *Nation*, 'which, of course, could not be allowed to vote'. Both North and South saw and accepted the implications. What was sauce for the Philippines, for Hawaii and Cuba, was sauce for the Southern Negro. 'If the stronger and cleverer race is free to impose its will upon "new-caught, sullen peoples" on the other side of the globe, why not in South Carolina and Mississippi?' asked the *Atlantic Monthly*. 'No Republican leader', proclaimed Senator Tillman of South Carolina, ' … will now dare to wave the bloody shirt and preach a crusade against the South's treatment of the Negro. The North has a bloody shirt of its own. Many thousands of them have been made into shrouds for murdered Filipinos, done to death because they were fighting for liberty.' Throughout the United States doctrines of racial superiority received the assent of influential politicians and noted academics. The very rationalizations that had eased the conscience of the slave trade now provided the sanction for imperial expansion.

The South, however, did not hurl itself headlong into racial hysteria as soon as Reconstruction collapsed, and there seemed some slight chance, with the former ruling class re-enfranchised and the visible signs of Northern conquest removed, that whites would work with Negroes in promoting now a slow integration. Slavery may have reduced the Negro in the South to a unique debasement, but it had allowed, indeed necessitated, the development of personal relationships between white and black. The Negro was considered an essential, if subservient, part of Southern society, not as in the North an increasingly resented intrusion.

In 1878 Colonel Thomas Higginson, a militant Abolitionist who had conspired with John Brown before the Harper's Ferry raid, visited Virginia, South Carolina and Florida, and reported his findings in the *Atlantic Monthly*. Noting the easy acceptance by whites of the Negro on trains and streetcars, at the polls, in the courts and legislature, in the police force and militia, he decided that the South came off rather better than his native New England in any comparison. 'How can we ask more of the States formerly in rebellion than that they should be abreast of New England in granting rights and privileges to the coloured race?' And six years later, in reviewing conditions, he found no reason to change his mind. In 1885, eight years after the end of Reconstruction, a Negro radical and correspondent of the New York *Freeman*, T. McCants Stewart, travelled through the South and reported with astonishment the general absence of segregation in trains and restaurants, the lack of social restraint between the races. 'I think the whites of the South are really less afraid to [have] contact with coloured people than the whites of the North.' In contrast with the opinions of the Southern press in later years, the Richmond *Dispatch* of October 13th, 1886, declared: 'We repeat that nobody here objects to sitting in political conventions with Negroes. No lawyer objects to practising law in court where Negro lawyers practice ... Coloured men are allowed to introduce Bills into the Virginia Legislature; and in both branches of this body Negroes are allowed to sit, as they have a right to sit.'

Personal relations were frequently close and even embarrassing to strangers.

A frequent topic of comment by Northern visitors during the period was the intimacy of contact between the races in the South, an intimacy sometimes admitted to be distasteful to the visitor. Standard topics were the sight of white babies suckled at black breasts, white and coloured children playing together, the casual proximity of white and Negro homes in the cities, the camaraderie of maidservant and mistress, employer and employee, customer and clerk, and the usual stories of cohabitation of white men and Negro women. The same sights and stories had once been favourite topics of comment for the carpet-baggers and before them of the abolitionists, both of whom also expressed puzzlement and sometimes revulsion.[1]

Of course there was still much exploitation, as there were strident apostles of white supremacy. But the general mood of the white South was easy; the changes already experienced had contradicted the extravagant fears of the slave days – the dark myths of Reconstruction had not yet sprouted – and social closeness made integration much less strange a prospect than opinion in the North allowed. George Washington Cable, a distinguished white citizen of Louisiana who had fought for the Confederacy and felt himself belonging 'peculiarly to the South', declared that there could be neither free nor honest government without equal rights for all citizens, and he personally fought discrimination in employment and the administration of justice as well as in politics. Had public pressures in the North supported such a stand, the subsequent history of the South might have been very different; as it was, the new Northern reaction reinforced the recalcitrance of the racists and so ensured a national drift to repression.

[1] *The Strange Career of Jim Crow*, by C. Vann Woodward (O.U.P., 1955), pp. 24-5.

The Democratic Conservatives who inherited power with the 1877 Compromise were in the main members of the old governing classes, paternalists who at first deplored racial fanaticism as dangerous and vulgar, and wanted instead a gentle suzerainty. 'The Negro race is under us. He is in our power. We are his custodians,' proclaimed the Conservative Governor Jones of Alabama in the 'nineties. And he added with a perceptiveness which events would prove only too accurate: 'If we do not lift them up, they will drag us down.' These Conservatives, far from desiring Negro disfranchisement, made full use of the Negro vote against the rural poor whites, who opposed the alliance between Northern big business and the Southern rich. Even in states with a high concentration of former slaves and white prejudice like Mississippi and South Carolina, Democratic Governors solicited the Negro vote and appointed Negroes to minor administrative office. But Negroes did not flock to a party that they associated with the old days of slavery or to a leadership that regarded them with little more than a benevolent contempt, and as the Republican Party became more and more racist in its search for the popular white vote, more and more of them withdrew from the conventional two-party contest.

The Conservatives, with their backing for and from Northern business interests, could be overthrown – and racial conflict ultimately averted – only by an alliance of the poor Negro with the poor white, and this, despite the traditional racism of the poor white, the Populists tried to promote. As Tom Watson, the leader of Southern Populism, told the two races: 'You are made to hate each other because upon that hatred is rested the keystone of the arch of financial despotism which enslaves you both.' In the new party Negroes served alongside whites as members of state, district and county committees, as delegates to national conventions, as campaigners from the same platform before racially mixed audiences. Inevitably they gave of their hopes and their energies as they had given to nothing but the struggle against slavery before, and throughout the South there grew – and flourished for a time – an understanding between white and black, a shared aspiration, greater than any known before or since.

Embarrassed by financial scandals – in the 'eighties the treasurers of seven Redeemed states absconded or were charged with misappropriating funds – and faced by a severe agricultural depression which only strengthened the Populist appeal, the Conservatives fought back frantically. Raising the cry of Negro domination, they rallied the racists, and meanwhile exercised their dominance in the 'Black Belt' to buy and intimidate Negro voters or simply cast ballots on their behalf. When in 1896 they carried only a fifth of the parishes with a white majority in Louisiana but won the state, the New Orleans *Times-Democrat* shrewdly noted that white supremacy had once again been 'saved by Negro votes'. The Populist wave, which had threatened to overwhelm the South, broke on the reef of prejudice and fraud. The Negroes, dismayed, turned from political activity altogether, while the white Populists bitterly joined in the race to strip the Negro of his rights. By 1906 Tom Watson had become the political boss of Georgia on a campaign for Negro disfranchisement.

The first onslaught, of course, was on the Negro vote, and in this the triumphant racists in the Democratic Party were helped by the United States Supreme Court which, pursuing the change in public opinion, had hacked away in a series of vital decisions at federal responsibility for protecting civil rights and at the automatic assumption of the franchise. Allowed a reasonable criterion for granting the vote, the Southern states, led by Mississippi, introduced the poll tax, the 'general understanding' or 'good character' test, and the white primary. The success was almost total. There were over 130,000 registered Negro voters in the state of Louisiana in 1896; by 1904 there were less than 1,350.

To reassure the poor white that the new franchise qualifications would not be directed against him, the leading Democrats engaged in a campaign of frenzied racist propaganda, while the press gave prominence to stories of Negro violence, crime and insolence. Inevitably whites were incited to outbursts of fury, and mobs sporadically seized the initiative in teaching the Negro his place. After the white supremacy election of 1898 in North Carolina, whites attacked the Negro district of Wilmington, setting fire to buildings, killing and wounding many Negroes; the white supremacy election of 1906 in Georgia was followed by four days of mob rule in Atlanta, with widespread lynching and looting; two years after the disfranchisement of Negroes in Louisiana, mobs took over New Orleans for three days, robbing and assaulting Negroes. From 1890 to 1920 some four thousand Negroes were put to death in the South without pretence at a trial. This was race war, in a supposedly peaceful society, with a vengeance.

From the late 1890s, the Southern states adopted in quick succession statutes to segregate Negro from white, on passenger trains and streetcars and steamboats, in factories and theatres and parks, prescribing separate seating and work-space, toilets and water fountains, waiting-rooms and ticket windows, entrances and exits. Thirteen Southern and border states required the racial separation of patients in mental hospitals; ten specified segregation in prisons; and a multitude of laws effected segregation in homes for the aged, the orphaned, the poor, the deaf, the dumb, and the blind. Cities introduced compulsory residential separation, by block or district, while a few small towns prohibited Negro residents altogether. North Carolina and Florida required the segregation of textbooks used in the public schools by children of different races, and a New Orleans ordinance placed white and Negro prostitutes in separate districts. Jim Crow took command throughout the South.

Books reflected the racial fanaticism of the time, and popular Southern contributions – like *The Clansman: An Historical Romance of the Ku Klux Klan* by Thomas Dixon (1905); *The Negro a Beast or the Image of God* by Charles Carroll (1900); *The Negro, A Menace to American Civilization* by Robert W. Shufeldt (1907) – joined the 'Yellow Peril' school of the West and the obsession with white superiority throughout the country.

*   *   *

The Negro, though constituting the major enemy of the racist white, was, of course, neither the only one nor the first. When European explorers first encountered the American continent, there were some 850,000 Indians, living in tribes, scattered across what is now the United States, with the greatest concentration in the west, and as white settlement spread along the eastern seaboard, the Indians retreated westwards before it. There was little prejudice at the outset – the two races traded and treated respectfully with each other – and if intermarriage was not common, it did take place, and without any public censure. But a struggle for land soon enough developed, and with it the racial hatred that was partly a result and partly the excuse.

The American government that emerged from the Revolutionary War treated with the various Indian tribes at first as with national entities, so assuring legal title to any lands gained in this way against the claims of rival powers. But it took no steps to halt the constant drift of white settlement westwards, and it was along the lawless shifting frontier that Indian rights were most blatantly ignored and the competition for land exploded into racial war. In 1820 President Jackson announced his intention to dispense with the 'farce' of regarding Indian tribes as sovereign powers, and in May 1830 the Cherokees were simply ejected from their lands at the news of gold discoveries in Georgia. Inexorably the Indians were pushed westwards, till the discovery of gold in California (1848), Colorado (1859) and Montana (1861) made even the far west an immediate target of mass white migration.

The faster the frontier moved, and the smaller the area left free for Indian occupation became, the fiercer grew the racial conflict and the hotter the hatred. Beeson, an early settler in Oregon, wrote in his journal: ' ... it was customary [for the settlers] to speak of the Indian man as a buck; of the woman as a squaw; until, at length, in the general acceptance of the terms, they ceased to recognize the rights of humanity in those to whom they were so applied. By a very natural and easy transition, from being spoken of as brutes, they came to be thought of as game to be shot, or as vermin to be destroyed.' One of the first debates in the Colorado legislature was over a measure to offer bounties for the 'destruction of Indians and Skunks'.

The Indians, isolated geographically and kept insulated politically from the Negro, never even enjoyed the temporary support of a considerable public opinion, such as the Negro slave had achieved in the Abolitionist era, but, driven from the most productive land and diminished in numbers by war, the white man's drink and a host of new diseases, were popularly abandoned to extinction. Military conquest, interrupted by the Civil War, was virtually complete by 1880, and white America could pride itself on its unparalleled plunder; yet sufficient land remained in Indian possession to allure the frontiersman still, and at last, in an alliance of greed and muddled reformism, Congress resolved to protect the now sub-jugated enemy.

Since Indian society itself was doomed to disappear, with cultural assimilation seeming to provide the only prospect of individual survival, the American government mounted an assault to hasten the process. The potency of white values had, after all, been more than adequately proved. Of course, the Indians were still to be kept in special reservations – estab-lished, after conquest, to facilitate surveillance, and then promoted as an efficient form of segregation; cultural assimilation might be desirable, but never as an accompaniment to integration of the races.

By the General Allotment Act of 1887, every Indian was given a plot of reservation land with full property rights, and Senator Henry L. Dawes, one of the Act's sponsors, expected this to instil that spirit of 'selfishness' which was the mainspring of white civilization. Since the Indians were a dying race, however, no provision needed to be made for future genera-tions, and once the allotment was completed, surplus reservation land was to be bought by the government at $1·25 an acre and thrown open to white settlement. Furthermore, no provision was made for the capital, equipment and technical guidance that the new farmers needed, and though the Act originally prohibited any alienation of allotments for a period of twenty-five years, a series of subsequent amendments soon nullified this safeguard. The result was predictably disastrous. The best reservation land was sold as 'surplus', and many individual allotments were acquired for white possession by fraud as well as purchase; of the 138 million acres owned by Indians at the time the Act was passed, only 52 million were left in 1933, and half of these were desert or semi-desert.

> The cultural consequences of the allotment policy were, however, more disastrous than the economic ... In weakening Indian social organization, the allotment policy nearly destroyed the only foundation upon which a transformed Indian society might have been built. Far from making a go-getter of the Indian, it destroyed his initiative and self-confidence ... It was the culminating humiliation of a century of defeat and reversals.[1]

The programme of cultural assimilation did not stop with the robbery of land apportionment and the consequent erosion of traditional authority. Indian children were seized from their parents and placed in special schools, where the Indian languages were ignored, the Indian religious ceremonies, arts and crafts systematically discouraged, and conversions to Christianity forcibly acquired. Sapped by poverty, sickness and a final apathy, the Indian population of the United States declined from the pre-Columbian estimate of 850,000 to some 220,000 in 1923. The white American seemed to be demanding of the red not merely defeat, but obliteration.

*   *   *

The flow of white racism did more than sweep over Negro and Indian; by promoting a new attitude to Asians, it carried domestic discrimination on to the international scene. With the spread of white settlement to the west coast, the United States acquired another ocean frontier, and it soon became apparent that the second was to be very differently regarded from the first. From Europe millions of immigrants were welcomed and with surprising speed absorbed by American democracy; from Asia immigrants came in small numbers, were greeted with increasing prejudice, and were then prohibited altogether. If the Atlantic was a bridge, the Pacific became a chasm.

In the beginning the racists met considerable resistance. From 1860 onwards, California's legal attempts to discriminate against Chinese settlers were declared unconstitutional by federal courts, dismissed as violations of treaty provisions, the Fourteenth Amendment or the various

[1] *Brothers Under the Skin*, by Carey McWilliams (Little, Brown & Co., Boston, 1964), p. 75.

civil rights statutes. Indeed, it was the Chinese in California, with their capacity to raise the substantial sums of money that were needed, who rather than the Negroes first tested in the courts the national validity and scope of Civil War reformist legislation. Moreover, after work had begun on a trans-continental railway in 1863 and an American steamship service across the Pacific had been established in 1867, the United States government showed itself anxious to encourage trade with China. The Burlingame Treaty of 1868 between the two countries asserted the broad principles of free migration and commerce, and Article VII conferred upon American citizens in China 'most favoured nation' privileges, immunities and exemptions, in return for similar treatment towards Chinese citizens in the United States. The concord was to have a short life.

White California decided to shift its struggle from the state to the national level and was soon helped by the change in public opinion on civil rights. With the end of Reconstruction, Congress acquired a powerful block of Southern Democratic votes, and these were readily available for any measure to advance white supremacy. Accordingly, in 1882, Western and Southern pressures forced legislation – over the Presidential veto – that suspended all Chinese immigration for ten years and expressly prohibited the naturalization of Chinese residents. In the debate on the measure, Senator Hawley had pleaded: 'Make the conditions what you please for immigration and for attaining citizenship; but make them such that a man may overcome them; do not base them on the accidents of humanity.' In dismissing his appeal, Congress not only made a formal break with traditional American foreign policy, but committed itself inevitably to involvement in international racism.

As in the South, the statute book signalled the streets. Three years after the passage of the Chinese Exclusion Act, a riot at Rock Springs in Wyoming led to the death of twenty-eight Chinese and the widespread destruction of property; shortly afterwards, whites in Tacoma, Washington, burnt down the Chinese quarter, and only prompt official intervention prevented similar action in Seattle and in Portland, Oregon. In California itself a fury of law and violence swept Chinese residents from their homes and left whole districts no more than morgues of rubble.

China was outraged and negotiated an amendment to her treaty with the United States which provided indemnity for the loss of Chinese lives and property. But if Congress accepted the amendment out of embarrassment or shame, it rapidly recovered its normal mood. By the Scott Act of 1888, it prohibited re-entry to some twenty thousand Chinese who had temporarily left the United States, and it followed up this malignant measure with the Geary Act of 1892, which suspended all Chinese immigration for a further ten years, denied bail to Chinese residents in *habeas corpus* proceedings, and provided for the deportation of all Chinese not in possession of special residence certificates. The Chinese government dispatched protest after protest to the State Department, but its representations were ignored. The United States proceeded to forbid all Chinese immigration to her new possessions of Hawaii and the Philippine Islands; in 1902 indefinitely extended the ban on Chinese immigration to America and the denial of naturalization to Chinese residents; and by the Immigration Act of 1924 made it impossible for the few American citizens of Chinese origin to bring their alien wives to the country.

What was good enough for the Chinese, however, was by no means good enough for the Americans; the Pacific was not closed to traffic, but simply turned into a one-way street. In its Open Door policy, first expressed by Secretary of State Hay in 1899, the United States government insisted upon free entry to Chinese markets; it did not take the lead in seizing Chinese territory itself, but by the pursuit of what has aptly been called 'hitchhiking imperialism',[1] it demanded and received unrestricted access to what other nations seized.

It was an odd sense of justice that prohibited any free Chinese participation in American life but insisted upon a free field in China for American trade and enterprise. From the days of the first Exclusion Act to the communist revolution and the barring of China's legitimate government from the United Nations, the policy of the United States towards China has been marked by an arrogance and stupidity of clear racist ancestry. If contemporary China has placed the United States in the forefront of her enemies and increasingly projected her own role in international affairs as the leading coloured power in a struggle against the predatory whites, American conduct in the past bears not an insignificant responsibility.

* * *

From its citadels in the South and the Far West, white racism had taken all but complete possession of the United States by the early years of the twentieth century. Even Woodrow Wilson, soon to achieve final renown as the archangel of international democracy, reached the White House by a path paved with enthusiastic Southern votes and once in residence extended segregation in federal employment, curtly dismissing

[1] *The Making of Modern China*, by Owen and Eleanor Lattimore (George Allen & Unwin Ltd, 1945), p. 121.

the protests of Negro leaders. And the First World War, promoted as a democratic crusade, was fast followed by the ugliest period of racial rioting in American history.

The war itself, even before the United States joined in the fighting, set off a massive change in the racial pattern of the country. By cutting off white immigration from Europe at the same time as it excited the expansion of American industry, it produced a huge demand for labour in the cities of the North. And meanwhile, in the industrially stagnant South, the natural population increase, combined with the relative westward shift of cotton cultivation, was forcing whites into traditionally Negro jobs and so further impoverishing the Negro community. Lured by the promise of ready employment, better equipped and more accessible schools, the glamour of big city life, and the promise – if mostly hollow, yet none the less potent – of greater freedom, Negroes from 1915 onwards began streaming to the North. Encouraging letters from relatives and friends already there, the spread of Negro newspapers which not only published advertisements for particular jobs but promoted migration in editorials and news coverage, the dispatch of agents by Northern firms to recruit Southern labourers on the spot, all turned the flow into a flood. Southern whites, in the very throes of their passion for racial purity, tried to stop labour recruitment by law and personal intimidation – for the attraction of white supremacy diminishes with the number of blacks over whom it can be exercised – but with small success. In 1910, of all the Negroes in the country only one in ten lived outside the states of the old Confederacy; by 1940 the ratio would change to one in four, and by 1960 there would be more Negroes outside the South than in it.

This great migration had a swift and substantial impact. For many Negroes the very act of leaving the South marked a break with the acquiescence of the past, and in the swelling ghettoes of the North there throbbed a new strength and pain. The ideological commitments of the war – more than 360,000 Negroes did military service, and many of these went overseas – combined with the prosperity of war production to raise among Negroes hope of a rapid betterment with the coming of peace and a growing resolve to achieve eventual equality. But the slogans of war were not serviceable to their wielders in peace. Democracy abroad was one thing, and democracy at home quite another. As though to erase the lessons of patriotic propaganda before they could be properly learnt, white America acted to crush black aspiration.

Twenty-six serious race riots took place in the Red Summer of 1919, and though some occurred in the South, in Texas and Arkansas and

Tennessee, most were in the North, with the worst of all in Chicago. White mobs seized control of whole cities for days on end, shooting and burning, assaulting and looting, and when Negroes displayed a sudden determination to defend themselves, the fury increased. During the first year following the war, over seventy Negroes – some of them still in uniform – were lynched.

White labour in the North, reacting strongly to Negro encroachments on the city slums and industrial plants, barred Negro workers from the unions and agitated for their dismissal from the more desirable jobs that the labour shortage of the war years had allowed them. Negro postmen and police vanished from the streets, and even crafts – like the barber's – which had once been regarded as naturally the Negro's, were taken over by whites. The Ku Klux Klan, revived in 1915, spread out of Georgia across the country and reached an allegiance of five million in the mid-twenties, with more members outside of the South than within it. At least two state governments, those of Texas and Oklahoma, were for a time under the domination of the Klan, and the influence of such organized racism was everywhere evident in the elaboration of the Jim Crow code.

The shift in ruling white attitudes since the end of the Civil War was not, of course, without its effect on thought within the Negro community. The first leader of significance to emerge after the collapse of Reconstruction was Booker T. Washington, who had been born on a Virginia plantation in 1859 and had risen by his own efforts to become in 1881 head of a new Negro college at Tuskegee in Alabama. Coming to terms with the reality of power in the South, Washington turned his back on the political struggle and concentrated instead on economic progress, in the belief that once Negroes had produced industrious workers and successful businessmen, the whites would no longer be hostile to Negro suffrage. Furthermore, convinced that Southern whites would not support Negro education unless persuaded that a docile and efficient supply of labour would result, he dedicated himself to vocational training and assailed academic education as useless and even dangerous. It was a profitable blend of innocence and calculation. White America was delighted at this gospel of accommodation and heaped money with honours upon Washington's mission; only three years after the opening of the Tuskegee Institute, the Alabama legislature voted it an annual appropriation, and Northern philanthropists like Andrew Carnegie gave it large and frequent sums.

Inevitably, however, Washington raised a host of Negro critics, who saw in him a shrewd appetite for personal power and in his policy an acceptance of indefinite racial subjection. The Boston Radicals, as the first of them were called – they came from various New England colleges and had as their principal organ the Boston *Guardian* – were enthusiastic for battle, but enthusiasm alone did not promise success; they needed a leader of stature like Washington himself, and this they found at last in William Edward Burghardt Du Bois, a distinguished sociologist who had been born three years after the end of the Civil War and was now teaching at Atlanta University.

In 1903 Du Bois published his *Souls of Black Folk*, a book which alienated him completely from the Tuskegean school and became for the more militant Negroes the testament of their revolt. Accusing Washington of having sealed an economic bargain with the white South, and of having accelerated with his doctrines the stripping of civil rights from the Negro, Du Bois himself rejected as virtual slavery the price of reconciliation. His own way would be different, and in the summer of 1905 he founded the Niagara Movement to wage all-out war against the policy of gradualism.

In a pamphlet on its objects, the new organization struck a note of defiance. 'We believe in taking what we can get, but we don't believe in being satisfied with it and in permitting anybody for a moment to imagine we're satisfied.' The bark, however, was more impressive than the bite. A movement of intellectuals, aimed – in the words of Du Bois himself – at a 'thoughtful' and 'dignified' membership, it concentrated on fighting racist laws in the courts, and lacking both mass support and white liberal subsidy, fell an easy victim to the powerful Washingtonians with their access to political patronage and the press, their ability and readiness to use economic weapons of intimidation.

In the process of dying, however, the Niagara Movement produced a vigorous heir. At the end of May 1909, a group of influential whites and Negroes met in New York and formed the National Negro Committee with the aim of promoting racial equality; Booker T. Washington considered it inadvisable to attend, and Du Bois, with other Niagara Radicals, became increasingly prominent in the new organization. The Committee stressed the need for a free and complete Negro education and accepted the argument of Du Bois that the right to vote ultimately determined the condition of the Negro; it was a decision for political struggle – if only along cautious constitutional lines – and the Washingtonians prepared themselves for another successful assault. But this time the militants had the backing of liberal whites with prestige and money, and the Washington programme had begun to lose favour with the new thrusting Negro middle class. The Committee flourished and at its 1910 conference formally changed its name to the National Association for the Advancement of Coloured People (N.A.A.C.P.); Du Bois himself became Director of Publications and Research, with all the other elected officers white.

From his studentship days Du Bois had regarded the race problem as an international one and taken pride in his own ancestral relationship with Africa, whose colonial degradation he deplored. It was with great eagerness, therefore, that he attended the Universal Races Congress at London in the summer of 1911, together with distinguished scientists from many countries who urged 'the vital importance ... of discountenancing race prejudice, as tending to inflict on humanity incalculable harm, and as based on generalizations unworthy of an enlightened and progressive age'. But the discussions were carefully genteel, and political issues were ignored; in the end, while providing impressive authority for the race egalitarians, the conference produced nothing concrete and held no subsequent meetings. The idea of international action against racism, however, was to remain with Du Bois and gain constantly in force.

In November 1910 Du Bois started *Crisis* as a monthly publication of the N.A.A.C.P., and by 1913 its circulation had topped 30,000, with three-quarters of the copies sold to Negroes. Using the magazine openly as a vehicle for his own ideas, despite the sporadic embarrassment and even protest of influential N.A.A.C.P. executive officers, he accused white Christian Churches of being 'the strongest seat of racial and colour prejudice', and even clashed with the powerful Negro preachers, attacking them for their hypocrisy, pretentiousness and political timidity.

The First World War was initially seen by Du Bois as a falling out of imperialist pirates over their spoils, 'the real soul of white culture' laid bare. American society itself was no more than 'the daughter of a dying Europe', and the best in civilization was a product of the coloured races – 'the iron and trade of black Africa; the religion and empire building of yellow Asia ... ' The hands of the Negro race were clean, and in the pages of *Crisis* – already dedicated to exciting interest in African art and history and encouraging the development of Negro music, painting and literature – Du Bois called on American Negroes to return to 'old ideals ... old standards of beauty ... not the blue-eyed, white-skinned types which are set before us in school and literature but rich, brown and black men and women with glowing dark eyes and crinkling hair ... the heritage of Africa and the tropics.'[1]

With America's entry into the war, however, Du Bois flung himself into patriotic fervour and even called for a moratorium on protest. 'Let us,

[1] *Crisis*, No. XII (1916), pp. 216–17.

while this war lasts, forget our special grievances and close ranks shoulder to shoulder with our own fellow citizens and the allied nations that are fighting for democracy ... If this is OUR country, then this is OUR war.'[1] Such views – he was actually supporting the establishment of a segregated training school for Negro officers, to show whites the capacity of Negroes for leadership – were bitterly attacked by more militant leaders who saw him now as a cautious conservative, tied to the rich white backers of the N.A.A.C.P. The new left-wing Negro paper, the *Messenger*, founded in 1917 under the editorship of Chandler Owen and A. Philip Randolph (who would play a crucial role in the development of Negro trade unionism and father the civil disobedience movement) denounced his 'superlative sureness' that racism would retreat before the Negro's military and industrial contributions to the war effort.

The dilemma of Du Bois was endemic to the American Negro, a dilemma of allegiance which to this day has not been communally resolved. What was the aspiration of the Negro to be: political, economic and social integration with the whites, even to the extent of eventual assimilation, or some form of separate development associated with the liberation and progress of the whole black world?

Du Bois himself constantly wavered between the two aims and loyalties, and though he must be counted among the most important figures in the history of the integration movement, with his early clear demands for the grant of equal citizenship to Negroes, he was a periodic propagandist for the development of a self-sufficient and socialist Negro community (it was over the issue of his support for voluntary segregation that he finally resigned from the editorship of *Crisis* in 1934), an apostle of the American Negro's commitment to the black world, and the first significant exponent of Pan-Africanism.

The four Pan-African Congresses which he organized – at Paris in 1919; at London, Brussels and Paris in 1921; at London in 1923; and at New York City in 1927 – were apparent failures, for the African delegates were either men of little influence or those like Blaise Diagne, a deputy for Senegal in the French parliament, who were reluctant to excite the hostility of European governments, while American Negro interest never extended beyond a small group of intellectuals. Not clear in his own mind about methods or immediate objectives, Du Bois seemed at the time to be doing emotional exercises before an audience of intransigent whites and indifferent blacks. But his ideas were to ferment long after his particular initiatives collapsed, and men who would later help to shape modern

[1] *Crisis*, No. XVI (1918), pp. 111, 164.

Africa, like Nkrumah and Azikiwe (both of whom attended his important Fifth Pan-African Congress at Manchester in 1945), owe no less to his endeavours than does the whole radical internationalist strain in the current civil rights struggle of the American Negro.

One vision which Du Bois seems to have had constantly before him and which he intermittently recorded was the possibility of world-wide racial conflict. As far back as 1905, encouraged by the success of an Asian people against a Caucasian one in the Russo-Japanese War, he predicted that there would one day be a joint awakening of the black, brown and yellow peoples, and that unless the whites changed their conduct and attitudes, there would be a general race war. Eleven years later he wrote in *Crisis* that he hoped armed conflict between the races would not be necessary, since 'war is Hell', but 'there are things worse than Hell, as every Negro knows.'[1] In 1917 he wrote that the 'dark world' – Japan, China, India, Africa and the Negroes in the Americas – might wage war upon the 'white world',[2] and in 1930 he proclaimed again the possibility that American Negroes would join Asians and Africans in a 'world movement of freedom for coloured races'. One biographer suggests that Du Bois in his frustration threatened race war 'as an ego-defence mechanism', that 'he was trying to bluff the whites'.[3] Such may indeed have been the case – then; but it would be silly and dangerous now, in the middle of the nineteen-sixties, to scoff any longer at such predictions.

With many of the ideas that Du Bois had already propounded, and with several very different ones of his own, it was a Jamaican, Marcus Garvey, who in the racist fury following the First World War managed what Du Bois himself failed always to do – awaken the Negro mass. Born in 1887, Garvey early in his life identified the subservient condition of Negroes in the Americas with the colonial subjugation of Africa, and from then onwards maintained that until Africa itself was free, black people everywhere would remain oppressed. Having travelled widely in Latin America, he went in 1912 to London, where he met Africans from different parts of the British Empire, and in 1914 returned to Jamaica with the object of 'uniting all the Negro peoples of the world into one great body to establish a country and government absolutely their own'. At the beginning of August he founded the Universal Negro Improvement Association (U.N.I.A.) with the motto 'One God! One Aim! One

[1] *Crisis*, No. XII (1916), pp. 166–7.
[2] 'Of the Culture of White Folk', in *Journal of Race Development*, No. VII (April 1917), pp. 440–45.
[3] *W. E. B. Du Bois – A Study in Minority Leadership*, by Elliott M. Rudwick (O.U.P., 1960), p. 234.

Destiny!', and in 1917 established its first branch in the United States at Harlem.

By 1922 the movement, with its own anthem and its own flag – black for the Negro's skin, green for his hopes, and red for his blood – had a following estimated at somewhere between one and six million, and membership in the United States, where Garvey set up his headquarters, included 30,000 in New York City, 9,000 in Chicago, 6,000 in Philadelphia and 4,000 in Detroit. Garvey himself was a supreme showman, and in August 1920 he organized in New York City an International Convention of the Negro People of the World, which elected him provisional president of Africa, as well as President-General of the U.N.I.A. with an annual salary of $22,000; he then formed a provisional government, and decorated its members with peerages and knighthoods. The movement itself established a Black Star Steamship Company (a name later taken by Ghana's national shipping line) to unite the different parts of the black world, an African Orthodox Church, the Universal African Legion, and the Universal Black Cross Nurses, among much else, while a weekly newspaper, edited by Garvey himself and called *The Negro World*, became its propaganda organ. Recognizing the latent power of the Negro vote, Garvey then founded, in 1924, the Negro Political Union and issued a list of approved candidates for the elections of that year; in New York and Chicago the canvassing efforts of Garveyite teams had a marked effect on the results from Negro districts.

For Garvey the dilemma of aim and allegiance did not exist, as it existed for Du Bois. He came out unequivocally for race purity – 'Race amalgamation must cease; any member of this organization who marries a white woman is summarily expelled' – world-wide black solidarity, and an eventual return of Negroes in the West to a liberated Africa. His call was high.

Two hundred and fifty years we have been a race of slaves; for fifty years we have been a race of parasites. Now we propose to end all that. No more fear, no more cringing, no more sycophantic begging and pleading; the Negro must strike straight from the shoulder for manhood rights and for full liberty. Destiny leads us to ... that freedom, that liberty, that will see us men among men, that will make us a great and powerful people.[1]

[1] Quoted in *Black Nationalism*, by E. U. Essien-Udom (Dell Publishing Co. Inc. New York, 1964), p. 385.

Towards Du Bois and his work Garvey was unrelentingly hostile, castigating *Crisis* as a reactionary paper published from an 'aristocratic Fifth Avenue' office, and the N.A.A.C.P. as 'the National Association for the Advancement of (Certain) Coloured People'. Du Bois himself, with his light skin, was mocked as 'more of a white man than a Negro', the 'associate of an alien race' who ignored the masses and led a 'caste aristocracy' of mulattoes towards the objective of race amalgamation. *The Negro World*, predicting a race war, proclaimed that the traditional leaders were not properly preparing for it.

The Black Star Steamship Company soon fell apart under its debts, and Garvey himself was imprisoned in 1925 for having used the United States mails to defraud. After his deportation to Jamaica in 1927, he ceased to be a great personal force, and he died in London in 1940 with his once vast following reduced to a few loyalists in the United States and the West Indies. But his achievement was lasting. It was he more than any other man who gave the mass of Negroes in the Americas and especially the United States a sense of race pride, a new strength in the association with Africa, a release from the despair of the post-war period. He saw, as Du Bois did not, the force of the silent conflict between dark- and light-skinned within the Negro community, and by his attacks on the arrogant mulatto middle class not only raised the standing of the black poor in their own eyes, but began the corrosion of white values, the lure of mere racial imitation, inside Negro America. To black people everywhere, no less in Africa itself than in the white world, his message was a discovery that would be a fresh source of striving.

The 'twenties produced a vigorous Negro artistic awakening, with poems and novels, paintings and songs testifying to the heightened racial awareness and spirit of protest. Negro newspapers multiplied, and Negro participation in movements of struggle increased; there was a rebellious stirring among students, and a new mood in the ghettoes which Garveyism had partly excited, partly revealed. Yet white America was confident of its place in the world and undismayed by the prospect of having to contain black discontent by force. Besides, there was still a substantial buffer zone between threat and reality. The Negro middle class was in the main comfortably concerned with its relative superiority and its pursuit of the white image in hair-straightening and skin-lightening applications; those within it who took to political protest kept to the intricate processes of constitutional reform, fighting costly law suits for rulings against discrimination that then remained wrapped in the records. The mass was growing uneasy, but there seemed little danger in its

parades and rallies, and it was likely to be kept busy enough by the
struggle to survive in the slums of free enterprise. The Negro was not in
general, despite the efforts of men like Du Bois and Garvey, even making
proper use of his vote. With the two major parties proclaiming policies
that were alike in ignoring Negro claims, and with minor parties promising almost everything but the faintest prospect of success, most Negroes,
where able to vote, retained their customary allegiance to the Republican
Party of Lincoln or did not vote at all. Yet in the deeps a current was
already stirring that would, slowly gathering force, bring racial tumult
to America.

The first break in established Negro voting patterns came with the
Depression, when hundreds of thousands across the country deserted to
the Democratic Party of Franklin D. Roosevelt. At last an alternative to
the hollow rivalries of the past had appeared; but it was an alternative, it
soon became clear, with very little substance. The New Deal, like so much
else in the United States, was black only at the edges. Young Negroes,
jobless in the streets, turned their backs on the lobbying and litigation of
their leaders and took to picket-lines, boycotts and sudden demonstrations. A riot swept Harlem in 1935, a sign of despair that promised more
than broken glass in the future. Books like *Native Son* by Richard Wright,
published in 1940, reflected the hatred and violence swelling within black
America.

The Negro middle class woke up to its final frustrations, and the
N.A.A.C.P., with its local chapters increasing from fifty to more than
five hundred between the two wars, could claim a membership of half a
million and a place of influence in national politics by the 'forties. In
June 1941, A. Philip Randolph, founder and president of the Brotherhood
of Sleeping-Car Porters, threatened a march of 100,000 Negroes on
Washington to protest against racial discrimination in defence industry
employment. The Negro mood had so changed that not only could a
responsible leader make such a threat, but his ability to carry it out could
be widely accepted. Before the march took place, President Roosevelt
issued an Executive Order 'to encourage full participation in the national
defence programme by all citizens of the United States, regardless of
race ... ', and to enforce this policy appointed a Commission on Fair
Employment Practices. Racial discrimination persisted in war plants all
over the country, but the gesture postponed an internationally embarrassing clash between white and black.

With America's entry into the Second World War, the Negro protest
movement quickened further. No leader of stature called, as Du Bois had

done in the First World War, for a shelving of grievances, and such Negro following as the American Communist Party had acquired in the 'thirties dwindled rapidly with the communist cry that the war was, with the involvement of the Soviet Union, a people's war and should be supported. So strong and widespread was Negro alienation from white America that – as one moderate Negro leader in the N.A.A.C.P. subsequently put it[1] – 'had the Japanese arrived in Louisiana and torn down the Jim Crow signs, they would have been welcomed by cheering Negro crowds.' War novels like *And Then We Heard the Thunder* by John Killens[2] testify to the reluctance with which many Negro soldiers served and the ingenuity exercised by some to escape the draft.

∗   ∗   ∗

The war into which the Americans had suddenly been thrust by the Japanese bombardment of Pearl Harbour was not altogether unconnected with the long ill-treatment of Japanese immigrants to the United States. These had begun arriving in the late 1880s, and though their numbers were small – there were only 72,000 of them in the country by 1910 – they became from the first the focus of racist agitation, especially in California where most of them settled.

'The forces that had accomplished the exclusion of the Chinese had developed legends, techniques and arguments which with little editing could be turned against the Japanese. Politicians and pressure groups had served their apprenticeship in the anti-Chinese crusade. By the turn of the century these veterans were ready to launch a new offensive.'[3]

The first mass meeting against Japanese immigration was held at San Francisco in May 1900, and by 1905, after a series of hotly hostile articles on the immigrants in the *San Francisco Chronicle*, both houses of the California legislature had unanimously called for the complete exclusion of the Japanese. Japan herself was fast becoming a great power and had just emerged victorious from her war with Russia. But this merely increased white American resentment and fear, encouraging cries of the 'Yellow Peril' and predictions of an inevitable conflict between Japan and the United States. In the autumn of 1906 the San Francisco city administration, controlled by the party of organized labour, set out to

[1] Interview with author.
[2] Jonathan Cape, 1964.
[3] *Wartime Exile: The Exclusion of the Japanese-Americans from the West Coast*, by Ruth E. McKee for U.S. Department of Interior, p. 10.

segregate the 93 Japanese schoolchildren from the 25,000 of other stock. The white South was delighted, but Japan lodged furious notes of protest in Washington, and by the 'Gentleman's Agreement' of 1907, the President persuaded the city to reverse its decision in return for attempts to limit Japanese immigration.

It was not that the Japanese were difficult to assimilate; on the contrary, they pursued cultural imitation and the commandments of economic success with equally alarming earnestness. They wore American clothes, took to American cooking and furniture in their indistinguishably American homes, and even adopted Christianity in large numbers. They were enterprising, industrious, adaptable, and thrifty. Despite their exclusion from trade unions, they organized themselves efficiently for collective bargaining and won higher wages; then, with their savings they bought farmland, and began competing with white agriculture. This was too much; in 1913 the California legislature adopted an Alien Land Act, which effectively forbade all but those Japanese born in America and so entitled to citizenship from owning agricultural land anywhere in the state. There were widespread public protests in Japan, and the Japanese government again made angry representations to Washington.

Japan was becoming increasingly bitter at the racial arrogance of the white West, especially the United States, and at the Paris peace conference of 1919 her representatives proposed that the League of Nations should adopt the principle of racial equality, with all member states agreeing to treat each other's nationals justly and equally in law and in fact. They explained that their proposed clause did not require the immediate realization of racial equality and left methods of applying the principle to individual governments; they even modified its wording to meet objections. But the proposal obtained only 11 votes out of 17, and since unanimity was ruled to be essential, suffered defeat.

A further Alien Land Act in 1920, aimed at eliminating evasions – immigrants were putting land in the names of their citizen children or operating companies with white façades – finally forced the Japanese off the established farmlands of the West Coast and into contract gardening or the cultivation of wasteland and leased plots, unwanted by whites, on the fringe of urban communities. The immigrants pioneered new crops, and were soon supplying nearly all the specialty produce required by the local markets. White agitation increased, and in 1924 the Exclusionary Immigration Act barred all further Japanese arrivals. Coming as this did when Japan was still suffering the consequences of the Tokyo earthquake and fire, the Act was regarded 'as a piece of warlike provocation', and was 'deeply and enduringly resented'.[1] Japanese militarists were quick to exploit it. American treatment of Asian immigrants combined with America's spreading presence in the Pacific to produce an impression of racial imperiousness, which both excited and assisted further Japanese expansionism.

Denied citizenship through naturalization (which itself closed many areas of effort to them), most forms of urban employment by the hostility of the trade unions, agricultural expansion by restrictive laws, and access to most white-owned hotels, restaurants and barbers' shops by general prejudice, the Japanese were forced to retreat into ghettoes or 'Little Tokyos', where they provided goods and services for those of their number who operated a narrow range of enterprises outside the walls. The white policy of 'containment' was successful. Despite their early economic gains and irrepressible vigour, the Japanese Americans had an average income per head in 1941 of $671, compared to $982 for all Californians. Gradually, with the ban on all new arrivals and the departure of some settlers in despair, their numbers declined: in 1930, there were about 139,000 in the whole United States, 50·2 per cent of them foreign-born; in 1940 there were about 127,000, of whom the foreign-born represented only 37·3 per cent.

For this small, still passionately American community, Pearl Harbour was a disaster. Incited by organized farming interests in California, who resented the remaining hold of the immigrants on the local produce markets, and by patriotic groups of predictable hysteria like the American Legion, a campaign for the removal of the Japanese from the West Coast altogether excited the support of powerful lobbies like the Los Angeles Chamber of Commerce and politicians panting after public opinion. Acting under the authority granted to him by President Roosevelt's Executive Order No. 9066, General J. L. De Witt commanded the evacuation of all Japanese Americans from the three West Coast states. And during the spring and summer of 1942, some 110,000 men, women and children, two-thirds of them American citizens, were moved from their homes and businesses to internment. No act of sabotage had taken place, or was reasonably expected. There had been no sabotage at all in Hawaii, where 35 per cent of the population or some 160,000 were of Japanese descent, and where only 980 of these were interned. The general's explanation was simple. 'A Jap is a Jap ... It makes no difference whether he is an American citizen or not, he is still a Japanese ... The Japanese race is an enemy race, and while many second- and third-generation Japanese born

[1] C. McWilliams, op. cit., pp. 146-7.

on United States soil, possessed of United States citizenship, have become "Americanized", the racial strains are undiluted.'

*   *   *

Internationally and nationally alike, the war shattered seemingly age-less patterns. In the world at large, white nations – with the United States foremost amongst them – suffered serious defeats at the hands of a coloured one, heralding, it seemed, an end to the white expansionism of five centuries. And within the United States itself, the migration of Negroes to the cities, especially from the rural areas of the South, increased with the call of wartime industrial boom, swelling the already vast Negro ghettoes across the country, especially in the North. The ratio of Negroes in urban and rural areas, almost equal in 1940, shifted decisively during the next ten years.

Year	Urban (in millions)	Rural (in millions)
1910	2·7	7·1
1920	3·5	6·9
1930	5·2	6·7
1940	6·2	6·6
1950	9·4	5·6

This population upheaval would persist through the 'fifties, and by 1960 the Negro urban community would reach 13·8 millions, with the rural one reduced to almost a third the size, at 5·1 millions. One consequence was an increase of Negro political power in the closely contested in-dustrial states with their large electoral vote, and presidential candidates, as well as congressional and mayoral ones, began to court Negro support. But between Negro demands and the careful promises of the politicians stood the party machines, busily assimilating both into the long indiffer-ence of white America. The other consequences had sharper edges. The migrants all but overwhelmed the crumbling tenements and schools in the existing ghettoes, spread beyond to submerge street after street in segregated squalor, and added ceaselessly to the numbers of unemployed and underpaid nourishing little more than the spirit of revolt. The protest movement grew.

In 1942 the Congress of Racial Equality (CORE) was established in Chicago to conduct non-violent direct action and staged its first sit-in, while elsewhere in America's blind cities Negroes picketed stores and gathered at mass meetings to pray or sing or shout their impatience. But white America remained in the main unmoved. At the moment when delegates at San Francisco were adopting the United Nations Charter and proclaiming freedom for all the peoples of the world 'without distinction as to race', Southern Democrats were in alliance with Republicans at Washington to kill the Fair Employment Practices Commission by filibuster. On February 25th, 1946, the first major post-war race riot broke out, at Columbia in Tennessee, and in July, a few days after the triumph of racist former Governor Talmadge in the Georgia 'white primary', five Negroes were lynched in the state; riots struck Philadelphia in September, and the first in a series of public housing riots occurred at Chicago three months later. It seemed as though the era of racial repression that followed the First World War was now to be repeated – in March the Ku Klux Klan had announced its revival at a meeting in Atlanta – but the changing relationship between white and black both in the United States and in the world at large made any such retreat into the past too dangerous. The war against Nazi Germany had been sold in significant measure as a war against racism, and a strong body of public opinion held on to its new idealism despite victory. Besides, the alliance with the Soviet Union which fighting had forged was now fast crumbling into open struggle, with the uncommitted peoples of the coloured world as the prize.

The Supreme Court in April 1944 had declared the Southern 'white primary' unconstitutional, and Negro ex-servicemen returning to their homes in the South during 1946 were in a mood to test their rights. White Mississippi, however, had no intention of acquiescing, and in the Democratic primary of June 1946 Senator Bilbo proclaimed the right of white men to use 'any means at their command' to keep Negroes from the polls. The means used provoked a public outcry, and in the subsequent Senate investigations almost 150 Negroes in the state demanded to be heard. Mississippi was no more amazed than the rest of America. 'For the first time since Reconstruction', reported the *New York Herald Tribune*, 'Mississippi Negroes stood up as a group to fight their enemy.'

In December 1946 President Truman issued an Executive Order establishing a Committee on Civil Rights, and ten months later the Committee issued its report, calling for a 'new charter of human freedom', with the outlawing of state restrictions on the franchise, a federal law against lynching, an end to housing segregation in the cities, and a denial of federal aid to individual states which did not renounce racial discrimination. In February 1948 Truman asked Congress to adopt some of the proposed measures, and when it refused he made a civil rights programme one of his main campaign issues for the presidential elections of that year. In rebellion, thirty-five Southern delegates, most of them from Alabama and Mississippi, walked out of the Democratic convention, and two days later, at Birmingham, launched the States' Rights party – popularly known as the 'Dixiecrats' – to oppose the growth in federal power and maintain racial segregation against federal assault. Once again, as in the last years of the nineteenth century, the rich whites of the South set out to hold the poor ones in line by flourishing the menace of Negro equality. 'The civil rights programme endangered the privileged status of planters, landlords, bankers and those manufacturers whose profits depended upon cheap labour. To win the votes of the masses, these economic interests were translated into states' rights on the racist level.'[1]

The Dixiecrats, however, failed in their aim of holding the electoral balance of power in a close contest. They carried only four states – South Carolina (whose governor was their presidential candidate), Alabama, Mississippi and Louisiana, with 37 electoral votes and little more than one million popular votes in all – largely on the returns from 'black' counties, where a few white planters and tenants voted on behalf of a large Negro population, while Truman carried nine Southern states, including such traditionally racist ones as Texas, Georgia, Florida and Arkansas. Moreover, in winning an election from which the Republicans had generally been expected to emerge not only victorious but triumphant, Truman owed much to the Negro vote, which gave him several important industrial states in the North as well as the edge over the Dixiecrats in the South. Yet the immediate consequences for civil rights were slight. The white South maintained its Democratic representation in Congress and in collaboration with the right-wing Republicans killed the civil rights programme. As so often in the past – and in the future – a clear mandate for Negro advance stumbled and fell over Congressional manoeuvres.

All the same, the 1948 elections had revealed the force of the Negro vote, and this force would grow, especially in the South, during the next few years; between 1948 and 1952 the percentage of eligible Negroes registered to vote in the South increased from 12 to over 25, raising the number of Negro voters to more than 100,000 each in Texas, Georgia, Florida, North Carolina and even Louisiana (where there had been some 1,600 in 1948). Moreover, the international scene was assisting the Negro struggle. In October 1947 the N.A.A.C.P., with the energetic participa-

[1] *The South in American History*, by W. B. Hesseltine and D. L. Smiley (Prentice-Hall Inc., New Jersey, 1960), p. 553.

tion of Du Bois, filed formal charges of racial discrimination in the United States with the United Nations, and though the Commission on Human Rights voted down a Soviet proposal to investigate, Washington was seriously embarrassed. Attorney-General Tom C. Clark declared: 'No act of accidental injustice, let alone those of calculation, will go unobserved by our enemies. Lip-service to our ideals will be seen for the mockery that it is.' In July 1948 President Truman ordered the full desegregation of the armed forces, and though the measure was then opposed publicly by Chief-of-Staff General Eisenhower, it was largely put into effect by President Eisenhower under the battlefield necessities of the Korean War. Indeed, with the Korean War, pressure on the United States to change her racial image immeasurably mounted, while Chinese military successes made many white Americans feel much less sure of themselves.[1] And as white self-confidence drooped, so Negro self-confidence lifted. Ghana was already on the apparent path to independence, and soon one black African state after the other would raise its flag at the United Nations.

Just as the United States Supreme Court had reflected the racist temper of the country in its rulings during the last quarter of the nineteenth century, so now it increasingly reflected general support for Negro civil rights. In 1946 it had declared segregation in inter-state travel unconstitutional, and in a series of judgments during the early 'fifties it struck at segregated education. The Southern states responded by sending enormous sums to equalize their schools and so maintain segregation under the 'separate but equal' criterion laid down in the Plessy v. Ferguson judgment of 1896. But the Court was not satisfied, and at last, on May 17th, 1954, it ruled against the very principle of segregation in the public schools. Basing its judgment on the psychological and sociological evidence produced by the Negro plaintiffs, it found that school segregation denied minority groups the equal protection of the laws guaranteed by the Fourteenth Amendment. 'To separate [children] from others of similar age and qualifications solely because of their race generates a feeling of inferiority as to their status in the community that may affect their hearts and minds in a way unlikely ever to be undone ... Separate educational facilities are inherently unequal.'

It had taken the Court almost ninety years to apply the force of the

---

[1] See, for instance, *The New World of Negro Americans*, by Harold R. Isaacs (Phoenix House, 1964), p. 53, where a young Negro writer describes 'a certain feeling of panic' among whites at the time, an insecurity and bafflement, with 'a wry kind of disenchantment' among Negroes.

Fourteenth Amendment to the schools; it was now to take the federal government several years more to apply the force of the Court ruling. While Washington did nothing, White Citizens' Councils to preserve segregation spread across the South, their largely middle-class membership waging economic war on those who furthered the fight for integrated schools. In January 1956 the governors of Georgia, Mississippi, South Carolina and Virginia proclaimed at Richmond the slave-day Southern doctrine of 'interposition' by the state authority to protect its citizens from federal encroachment, and in March Congressmen from eleven states, in a 'Southern Manifesto', threatened all legal means to reverse the Supreme Court decision. State governments resorted to a mass of legal subterfuges, from decentralizing school administration, so that costly cases had to be fought for court orders in countless districts, to the turning over of public schools to private management.

In the end the courts discarded the evasions for what they were, but the lack of federal initiative, or even adequate surveillance, had serious long-term effects. The moderates were swept aside in several Southern states, and extremists, especially in Mississippi and Alabama, took unquestioned control. The Negro community, disappointed so often in the past by the failure of practice to follow legal or administrative command, turned further away from the private engagements of white America to a new-found source of power in mass action.

On Thursday, December 1st, 1955, Mrs Rosa Parks, a Negress in Montgomery, Alabama, refused to give up her seat on the bus for a white man. She was a politically alert woman, had once even been an official of the local N.A.A.C.P., but she had not planned her revolt. She had just suddenly had enough; and so, it soon became clear, had the other Negroes in Montgomery. The news that Mrs Parks had been arrested swept through the community, and prodded by a group of angry women, the local Negro leaders gathered on Friday evening and decided to call a boycott of the city buses from Monday morning. That Sunday the Negro clergymen rallied their congregations, and on Monday some 17,000 Negroes, three-quarters of the city's total bus-using population, rode in cars or, far more commonly, walked to work and home again. In the evening hundreds packed into one of the churches to establish an organization that would direct the boycott, and a young Baptist minister, Dr Martin Luther King, Jr, mounted the pulpit. His opening remarks, with the responses of his audience, told much about the past and much about the future.

'There comes a time when people get tired.'

'Yes, Lord.'

'We are here this evening to say to those who have mistreated us for so long that we are tired – '

'Help him, Jesus!'

' – we are tired of being segregated and humiliated.'

'Amen.'

' – *tired!* ... did you hear me when I said "*tired*"?'

'Yes, Lord!'[1]

The meeting formed the Montgomery Improvement Association, with King as President, and the Association formulated the Negro demands: courteous treatment of Negroes on the buses; the seating of all passengers on a first-come first-served basis, with Negroes starting from the back of the bus and whites from the front; and the hiring of Negro drivers for predominantly Negro routes. The demands were so mild that the N.A.A.C.P. refused to associate itself officially with them; but they were still far too harsh for the whites of Montgomery. The bus company refused to consider them; white gangs used increasing violence against individual Negroes; and the boycott leaders, including King, were jailed on one of the ever-available technicalities. The Negroes of Montgomery responded by insisting now on an end to all segregated seating; the N.A.A.C.P., with its substantial resources, joined the boycott organization and steered its claim through the courts; and on June 4th, six months after Mrs Parks had sat unyielding in her seat, the Federal District Court ordered an end to segregation on the buses.

The Montgomery movement had an immense effect on Negro opinion throughout the country, and if it led to no immediate initiatives, it reached deep and there worked to produce the mass militancy of the 'sixties. (Martin Luther King himself would, with clergymen from other Southern cities, form in 1957 the Southern Christian Leadership Conference, to mobilize and co-ordinate local organizations in the struggle against segregation.) That thousands of Negroes with no tried leadership or record of coherent endeavour, Negroes belonging to the supposedly cowed and ignorant black mass of the South, should so readily unite and for several months successfully conduct – despite official persecution and multiplying acts of white hooliganism – a boycott of the only available bus services, stirred pride and determination among Negroes everywhere.

[1] *The Negro Revolt*, by Louis E. Lomax (a Signet Book, published by The New American Library, New York, 1964), pp. 101-2.

For television had carried events in Montgomery to the minds of millions with a vividness unrivalled by the radio and press. Americans, black and white alike, had watched and listened as Negroes in Montgomery sang and prayed their resolve together in church or walked in their thousands to work, had seen the set faces of white authority and heard the shrill hatred of the traditionally genial and delicately romantic Old South. Americans, black and white alike, had learnt something about themselves, as well as about each other, on the television screens.

The pictures that flashed into American homes flashed also on to the television screens and newspaper front pages of other countries, and the course of the Negro challenge assumed a new importance for America's relations with the outside world. In 1957 Negroes at Little Rock, the capital of Arkansas, won a court order for the admission of Negro children to the city's all-white Central High School; but Orval Faubus, governor of the state, commanded National Guardsmen to surround the school and prevent the entry of any Negro applicants. Ordered by a federal court to end his defiance, Faubus then withdrew the Guardsmen, but at the same time virtually invited whites in the city to do the defying instead; on the morning after his statement, September 23rd, a white mob gathered at the school and attacked several pressmen, most of them Negroes. Pictures sped round the country and the world, and Eisenhower, roused by the State Department, dispatched paratroops on September 24th to enforce the court orders. In a television and radio message to the nation, he made clear the international implications of the crisis.

> At a time when we face grave situations abroad because of the hatred that communism bears toward a system of government based on human rights, it would be difficult to exaggerate the harm that is being done to the prestige and influence and indeed to the safety of our nation and the world. Our enemies are gloating over this incident and using it everywhere to misrepresent our whole nation. We are portrayed as a violator of those standards of conduct which the peoples of the world united to proclaim in the Charter of the United Nations.

Under the protection of federal forces, nine Negro children entered the school, and in May 1958 the troops were withdrawn. But the battle was not over. In the autumn Faubus closed all the high schools in Little Rock and leased the properties to a private corporation. The Supreme Court immediately pronounced the act unconstitutional, and school officials began televising courses. Then, one year later, in May 1959, school board elections, called to eliminate the pressure of moderates, resulted instead in a defeat for Faubus and his supporters; faced with a choice between integrated schools and no schools at all, the white parents of the city had decisively chosen schools. A federal court in June ordered the schools to be opened, and in the autumn of 1959, some two years after the first attempt by Negroes to enter Central High, Little Rock surrendered its schools to integrated classes.

It was in this period of mounting Negro frustration that the Black Muslim movement registered its most dramatic growth. The Nation of Islam, as it calls itself, was founded in 1930 at Detroit by W. D. Fard, a light-skinned coloured whose early life remains a mystery and who claimed to have been born in Mecca of the Prophet Mohammad's tribe. Fard assumed several names, including 'God, Allah', and while peddling silks and raincoats through Paradise Valley, the Negro ghetto of Detroit, spread his message of freedom for the Negro from the 'Caucasian devil'. He undoubtedly had considerable talent and energy, for from the many black nationalist groups of the time which Garveyism had helped to nourish, his own speedily prospered; by 1934 it claimed 8,000 adherents in Detroit, and the first Temple of the movement there was not only a place of Muslim prayer, but also the home of several subsidiary organizations, including a University of Islam for the training of Negroes in the 'knowledge of our own'. Then, some time in 1933, Fard himself disappeared as mysteriously as he had come, leaving an assistant minister of his to continue and vastly to embellish his work.

Robert Poole – now known as Elijah Muhammad – was born, the son of a Baptist minister, in 1897 on a tenant farm in Georgia, and migrated with his family to Detroit in 1923. There he involved himself in the Muslim cult of Fard and by 1933 seems to have exercised control. Seeking to establish parochial schools for the movement, he was arrested by the Detroit police in April 1934 for refusing to send one of his children to the public schools; he moved to Chicago and there established a second Temple which became his headquarters. The movement itself, having lost most of those members recruited in the first flush of Fard's propaganda, now stagnated; the Negro mass, where not reduced to sullen apathy by the dark days of the Depression, was still hopeful of eventual advance within one American community. Then, in 1942, Muhammad was arrested in Washington, D.C., for inciting his followers to resist military conscription, and sentenced to five years' imprisonment; it was a profitable persecution, and he was released in 1946 with his leadership much enhanced. In 1945, despite the establishment of two new Temples – in Milwaukee and Washington, D.C. – the active membership had totalled less than one thousand; by 1955 there were fifteen Temples, and four years later twice as many. Figures for membership varied widely, but reasonable estimates suggest that by the end of the 'fifties there were some 10,000 registered 'followers', at least 50,000 'believers', and a vast if vague number of the influenced.

In Black Muslim teaching, as expounded by Elijah Muhammad, God or Allah visited the world in the person of W. D. Fard, and Elijah is his prophet or representative, 'The Messenger of Allah'. Mankind itself began with the black race, which brought civilization to the earth; the white race was no more than a degenerate offshoot, given 6,000 years of devilish dominion by God so as to test its capacity to rule with justice and try the courage, strength and faith of the Black Nation. That dominion is now drawing to its close, and on the Day of Judgment the white devils will be destroyed, together with their religion, Christianity, leaving the righteous blacks to inherit power over the whole world and produce a civilization beyond all previous splendours.

The ultimate impetus of this doctrine is, of course, hatred of the whites, a rejection of their religion, values, conduct and declared objectives, to-gether with their whole 'modern Babylon' of the United States, which – it is predicted – will suffer the fury of God first of all. The Black Muslim not only discards integration, but passionately opposes it, as a trick of the whites to bewilder and so further to subjugate the Negro. His only salva-tion lies in maintaining his identity, in knowing and cherishing and cultivating – eventually by geographical, meanwhile by social and eco-nomic separation – his culture and character.

In the beginning, and till late in the 'fifties, the emotional direction of the movement was towards the Arabs and the Asians, with a correspond-ing dissociation from black Africa in its colonial abasement; but with the retreat of white political control and the emergence of so many in-dependent black African states, the movement has increasingly stressed its black African connections. The Black Muslims now publish their own his-tory books, highlighting the glories of the African past, and reject the term 'Negro' altogether as derogatory, using instead 'Afro-American'; they even discard their surnames, as brands of the past – it was the custom in the days of slavery for slaves to assume the surnames of their owners – and substitute 'X', the symbol of their new nationality.

Until the coming of the scriptural redemption, Elijah Muhammad advocates the establishment of an independent black republic within the present borders of the United States, or a return to Africa, where Zion is among the black Muslim states. 'Separation of the so-called Negroes from their slave-masters' children ... is the only solution to our problem. It was the only solution, according to the Bible, for Israel and the Egyptians, and it will prove to be the only solution for America and her slaves, whom she mockingly calls her citizens, without granting her citizenship.'[1] Meanwhile, Black Muslims must separate themselves from white Americans as much as possible, attending their own schools, establishing and patronizing their own businesses, ignoring national politics as white-controlled and evil.

On its own followers – recruited mainly from the working class – the movement imposes a severe discipline, prohibiting adultery, pork, gambling, alcohol, drugs and gossip, amongst much else. Members are required to be industrious, responsible for helping their community as well as themselves, thrifty, clean, restrained in appearance (women are forbidden to use conspicuous cosmetics, like lipstick, or expose their legs and arms), formal in manners, and scrupulously correct in all their dealings. Emphasis on the importance of the man assails the matriarchal pattern of many Negro families and has undoubtedly led to a new discipline in Black Muslim homes (modern Negro writing deals abundantly with the damage done to children by the father's lack of prestige and authority in a world of white power and black poverty). The whole concept of a voluntary and dynamic racial separation places a premium on self-improvement, and the movement has had extraordinary success with Negro criminals, one of whom, the late Malcolm X – drug-addict and peddler, gambler, tout and thief – emerged from conversion in jail to leadership and a wide influence.

The swift spread of the movement had effects far beyond the members it enlisted, however. Negroes with no interest in the Muslim faith, who found most of Elijah Muhammad's doctrines absurd and suspected the integrity of his leadership, were encouraged by the movement's open hatred of whites to express their own, and were confirmed in their sense of futility by the movement's assault on the myth of integration. Young Negroes in Harlem or on Chicago's South Side rejected the Black Muslim acceptance of segregated advance, but accepted the Black Muslim rejection of the white world, and their resultant despair was a recipe for riot. Less destructively, within the Negro community at large, the movement spread the earlier appeals of Garvey and Du Bois to promote the recognition of links with the coloured and especially the African world, raising

[1] Quoted in E. U. Essien-Udom, op. cit., pp. 284–5.

expectation with the growth of coloured power and encouraging a pride in colour itself. If Negroes in the American ghetto go less to wig shops now – recently, indeed, rioters have taken to attacking them – and if glossy magazines of the Negro middle class like *Ebony* show model Negro couples on their advertisement pages much darker than they were ever once allowed to be, the Black Muslims are not without responsibility.

Nor has the movement left white America unaffected. In the middle of 1959 a television documentary called 'The Hate That Hate Produced' brought the Black Muslims to sudden national attention, and articles in mass-circulation magazines like *Time* and *Reader's Digest* further provoked white concern. That a significant section of the Negro community should not only hate whites but wish to withdraw altogether from any association with them, that thousands of American citizens should proclaim their allegiance to colour rather than country, combined with an awareness of change in the world outside to stir and even frighten many white Americans. What had happened to the once irresistible magic of the American dream? And what would happen if the hatred preached by the Black Muslims took hold of the whole Negro population? Could the United States survive in a world of powerful enemies if one in nine of her own citizens looked eagerly for her destruction? If such anxieties led to no real efforts at exciting integration, they did promote two reformist tendencies: a widening impatience with the rigid racism of the South, which was seen smugly and mistakenly elsewhere in white America as the sole cause of Negro extremism; and a desire to fortify the influence of moderate Negro leaders by openly soliciting, if not too often following, their advice.

Inevitably progress was painful and slow where it took place at all, trailing ever further behind the mood of the Negroes themselves. In 1957 the first Civil Rights Act since the days of Reconstruction was passed by Congress, but only after a Southern filibuster in the Senate had produced the provision of jury trials for criminal contempt in cases involving civil rights. As Eisenhower himself observed, this amendment made 'largely ineffective the aim of the measure to protect the voting rights of Negroes in the South'. At the end of the 'fifties, indeed, Negroes were still denied the right to vote in hundreds of communities throughout the South, and all but completely segregated in transport and other public amenities, while right across the country there were restaurants and hotels, housing estates and whole areas of employment barred to them. Behind the newspaper headlines of finally falling barriers, the condition of the Negro remained much the same and in some important respects even deteriorated. The aggressions of automation reduced the demand for unskilled labour in industry at the same time as Negro migration from the rural areas increased in momentum. Most integration was merely token in character – the appointment of a Negro to a senior post in the Administration or in industry; the admission of a few neat Negro middle-class families to a new housing project – while the ghettoes grew virtually unchecked and federal-aided building did little more than substitute a concrete for a brick segregation. As whites fled from areas of Negro infiltration, schools there lost such of their integrated character as they had gradually gained and crumbled into racial slum. The deepening discontent of black America was displaying one of its faces in the total rejection advanced by the Muslim movement; it would now display another – already revealed on the buses of Montgomery a few years before – in massive assertion.

On February 1st, 1960, four Negro college students in Greensboro, North Carolina, sat down at the traditionally all-white lunch counter in the local Woolworth's store and, unsuspectingly, set off a vast revolt. As the news reached television screens, radio sets and newspapers, students at dozens of distant colleges decided to adopt a similar defiance, and within a fortnight 'sit-ins' had spread to fifteen cities in five Southern states. But that was still only a beginning. Sit-ins at lunch counters became stand-ins at cinema box-offices, kneel-ins at churches, wade-ins at beaches, a host of new techniques in challenging the practices of racism across the whole country.

Within 1961 alone, more than 50,000 people – most of them Negroes, but some of them white – would participate in civil rights demonstrations, and over 3,600 of them would serve sentences in jail. In 1963 there would be more than 2,000 separate demonstrations, involving hundreds of thousands, and over 10,000 people would be arrested.

Montgomery had killed one cherished myth of white supremacy – that ordinary Southern Negroes were contented with their condition. Greensboro killed another, sturdy since the days of Booker T. Washington – that the educated Negro could be indefinitely conciliated by according him special, if still segregated, treatment. For it was from the relatively favoured Negro colleges, with their cautious staff and long-placid student bodies, that the shock troops for the battle in the South were increasingly coming. And the contrast that these troops made with the upholders of white supremacy was not altogether lost, even on a newspaper like the *Richmond News Leader*, which had supported 'massive resistance' to school desegregation in Virginia.

Many a Virginian must have felt a tinge of wry regret at the state of things as they are, in reading of Saturday's 'sit-downs' by Negro students in Richmond stores. Here were the coloured students, in coats, white shirts, ties, and one of them was reading Goethe and one was taking notes from a biology text. And here, on the sidewalk outside, was a gang of white boys come to heckle, a ragtail rabble, slack-jawed, black-jacketed, grinning fit to kill ... Eheu! It gives one pause.[1]

The demonstrations were disciplined, peaceful in intent and operation, and in many parts of the country – notably the Border South – produced a sudden lowering of barriers; but elsewhere, especially in the Deep South, they led to the customary response of white racists confident in the protection or, at the very least, indifference of authority – assault, arson, bombings and careful police brutality. The students were, however, only fortified in their resolve by the violence they encountered, and when their leaders first met together at Raleigh, North Carolina, over Easter, there were representatives from fifty-eight Southern communities in twelve states. Helped by a grant of money and encouragement from Martin Luther King and his Southern Christian Leadership Conference, the new militants established the Student Nonviolent Coordinating Committee[2] (S.N.C.C.) or SNICK as it was to become popularly known, and it was this organization, loose in structure but tight in the dedication of its membership, that would with its initiatives henceforward galvanize the whole civil rights movement.

Growing Negro political power had been largely concealed by the status of Eisenhower as a folk-hero of white America. Though almost 80 per cent of Negro voters had supported Adlai Stevenson in 1952, and some 60 per cent had done so again four years later – the Supreme Court judgment against segregated schooling in 1954 had bathed the Eisenhower Administration in some of its glow – he had lost substantially in both presidential elections. The Negroes were a substantial minority, but they were still a minority and could not materially affect the result when one candidate had overwhelming support within the rest of the nation. When the presidential candidates were reasonably matched, however, the Negro vote was now crucial, and recognizing this, both major parties set out to capture it with promises in the 1960 campaign. It is possible

[1] Editorial, February 22nd, 1960.
[2] For an excellent history of the S.N.C.C., see *The New Abolitionists*, by Howard Zinn (Beacon Press, Boston, 1964).

that in any event Kennedy would have sold himself as the more sympathetic of the two candidates to civil rights; but, as it was, he found an
unrivalled opportunity for displaying his political flair. During the last
stretch of the campaign, Martin Luther King was arrested in Atlanta and
sentenced to four months' hard labour for leading a sit-in demonstration;
while Nixon did nothing, Kennedy at once telephoned Mrs King to
express his concern, and his brother Robert appealed to the judge with
such effect that on the following day King was freed. Certainly one
experienced political observer[1] believed this intervention to have been
vital and pointed out that in Illinois, carried by a margin of only 9,000
votes, 250,000 Negroes are estimated to have voted for Kennedy; that
in Michigan the Democratic margin was only 67,000, and some 250,000
Negroes voted for Kennedy. Without the overwhelming Negro support
that he achieved, Kennedy, it is unquestionable, would never have won
so close an election.

His assassination three years later in the racist stronghold of Dallas
has obscured his personality and achievements with a cloud of sentiment,
and his protracted failure to provide effective impetus for Negro advance
has been largely forgotten, together with the impatience and anger it
produced among militant Negroes. The promise was certainly immense,
but even had it been modest, the performance would have fallen behind it.

Racist judges sitting in federal courts had long blocked or at least
substantially delayed applications for the enforcement of civil rights, and
it was generally supposed that, as vacancies occurred on the federal bench
in the South, Kennedy would use his constitutional power to appoint
judges of liberal commitment. But in Georgia, Alabama, Mississippi and
Louisiana he made appointments that could reasonably be explained only
as steps in the conciliation – for some political return unrelated to civil
rights – of the powerful Southern Democrats in Congress. One such new
judge, Harold Cox in Mississippi, would use his position in the federal
court persistently to oppose any advance in civil rights for Negroes, calling
them 'niggers' with open contempt from the bench.

Again and again during Kennedy's period of office, the federal government stood by idly while law and its own declarations of policy were
flouted by state administrations in the Deep South. That Kennedy had the
power to intervene he made clear himself when, soon after becoming
President, he declared that there was no need for yet another civil rights
bill, since executive orders could accomplish whatever was necessary.
Yet he himself delayed for almost two years before signing a cautious

[1] Theodore H. White in *The Making of the President* (Jonathan Cape, 1964), pp. 321–3.

order against discrimination in federally aided housing, till the *New York Times* suggested that he was accepting 'the doctrine of government by Gallup Poll' and declared that this marked 'a weakening in the concept of strong moral leadership by the President, about which the President spoke so movingly during the campaign'. Indeed, it required the widespread violence at Birmingham in the spring of 1963 for Kennedy to address himself publicly to the moral issues involved in the Negro struggle, and even then he took no sweeping executive action but off-loaded the responsibility on to Congress with a new civil rights bill.

Early in 1961 James Farmer, Programme Director of the N.A.A.C.P., resigned to become National Director of CORE, and in this switch of an established leader from the organization of constitutional struggle to one of direct action was mirrored the new mood of impatience spreading through the older Negro ranks. A recent decision of the Supreme Court had outlawed segregation in bus terminals; but, like so many other court rulings, this one was being assiduously disregarded throughout the South, and CORE decided, under Farmer's fresh leadership, to do something about it. On May 4th, 1961, seven Negroes and six whites boarded buses in Washington, D.C., and there followed one of the most dramatic series of events in the history of the modern civil rights movement – the Freedom Rides. At Rock Hill, South Carolina, the first group of riders was attacked by white hooligans; at Anniston, Alabama, one of the buses was burnt to its iron bones by a mob; and at Birmingham, the riders were met at the terminal by young whites with metal bars who assaulted them in the shrill absence of any police. No bus driver would take the freedom riders any farther, and they flew on to New Orleans where a mass rally was to be held.

Hearing of their decision, a group of SNICK students at Nashville, Tennessee, at once decided to continue the ride, and after being turned back on their first attempt, arrived at Birmingham by bus on May 19th. By now much of the nation had been aroused by the rides, and both the President and his brother, Robert Kennedy, the Attorney-General, conferred with representatives of the Alabama state government to ensure adequate protection for the students. Yet when the SNICK bus reached the Montgomery terminal on May 20th, a mob of some 300 whites was there waiting without a single policeman present. Newspapermen and the riders themselves were attacked with clubs and beaten to the ground while women screamed encouragement, and the President's personal emissary, Justice Department Attorney John Siegenthaler, was knocked unconscious. Police arrived only twenty minutes after the violence had begun, and though ambulances were summoned, none came. The President declared the situation 'a source of the deepest concern', but apart from dispatching a small contingent of U.S. marshals to protect the riders from any further mob violence in Montgomery, the federal government did nothing, calling instead – in a statement by Robert Kennedy directed more at the organizers of the Freedom Rides than at the state of Alabama – for a 'cooling-off period'.

While the riders waited in Montgomery, more students arrived to join them, and on May 24th they left in the company of National Guardsmen and press correspondents for Jackson, Mississippi, where they were arrested at the bus terminal on the usual technicalities – breach of the peace and refusal to obey an officer. All through the summer, despite Robert Kennedy's plea and Dr Martin Luther King's promise of a 'temporary lull', students streamed into Alabama and Mississippi – and not only students, for now clergymen, both Negro and white, were joining the Freedom Rides – to be arrested as they walked through racial barriers at the terminals. Refusing to pay their fines, they went to jail, despite the police cruelty that they expected and almost invariably experienced there, and though by the autumn they had not yet succeeded in desegregating the terminals of the Deep South, they had succeeded in much else. They had revealed Southern segregation as a crude defiance of the law, secured by mob violence, state protection, and federal indifference or timidity. They had shaken the self-assurance of the white South and excited the more civilized white Southerners into a sudden self-examination. Twenty-six white students from Auburn University in Alabama spoke for many when they wrote to the *Montgomery Advertiser*: 'Governor Patterson referred to the freedom riders as "rabble rousers". He is entitled to his opinion, but is Alabama to glory in the fact that it furnishes sufficient rabble to be roused?' Finally, the activists of SNICK and CORE had discovered a group courage and endurance, and so a new determination and discipline, in the experience of defiance, arrest and imprisonment.

Meeting in the autumn, the leaders of SNICK decided to extend their campaign against segregated facilities to an assault on the all but entirely white voters' rolls in the Deep South, for – as they saw – the very basis of white supremacy there was the effective disfranchisement of the Negro. In Mississippi, for instance – where all those wishing to vote were required to complete a twenty-one-question form and interpret, to the relevant county registrar's satisfaction, any one of the two hundred and eighty-five sections in the state constitution – only 3 per cent of the eligible Negroes were registered to vote, in contrast to 50 per cent of the eligible whites. Not surprisingly, therefore, though Negroes constituted 43 per cent of the state's total population, they held no political offices at all, lived for the most part in shacks with no running water, and possessed an average income only a third of that enjoyed by the average white.

In early August 1961 SNICK established the first voter registration school – in Pike County, Mississippi, just north of the Louisiana border – and to this and other such schools in southern Mississippi there came students from all over the country, to explain the voting requirements to Negroes, help applicants prepare for their tests, encourage them to visit the court-house and attempt to register, and alongside this activity conduct sit-ins at segregated restaurants and terminals. Few Negroes, however, got past the registrars on to the voters' rolls, demonstrators were attacked by white citizens – or police – and arrested, and one local Negro farmer suspected of assisting the SNICK campaign was murdered. Yet federal ears remained blocked to urgent appeals for intervention to protect civil rights workers, and all over Mississippi white violence increased, stirring the anger of black America with acts like the murder at his Jackson home in June 1963 of Medgar Evers, leading N.A.A.C.P. official in the state.

Despite their fear of losing their jobs and even their lives, Negroes continued to queue at the court-houses for their sterile interviews with the local registrars. In their persistence, despite arrests, assaults and sporadic assassinations, was reflected the whole surge of Southern Negro discontent. This popular recruitment to struggle, spontaneous as in the Montgomery bus boycott, or aroused by the arrival of student shock troops as in Mississippi, was a force that the nation could not long afford to ignore.

In the town of Albany, capital of south-west Georgia's one-time flourishing slave-plantation society, Negroes comprised an economically depressed, politically voiceless and socially segregated 40 per cent of the 56,000 inhabitants, a long-cowed and quiet mass which was just beginning to stir when SNICK workers opened a ramshackle office there in October 1961. On November 1st these students, together with volunteers from the Albany State College for Negroes, sat down in the white waiting-room of the local bus terminal and were ordered out by the police; the police action, a flagrant flouting of the law, was immediately reported to the federal Department of Justice, but the Department did not choose to intervene and Albany's Negroes took matters into their own hands. The various Negro church and social groups in the town met and joined with SNICK to form the Albany Movement, and a series of popular demonstrations against segregated facilities followed; by the middle of December over 730 people had been imprisoned. The struggle continued, into 1962 and then into 1963 and 1964, and slowly it registered its successes: a boycott of the municipal buses forced the responsible company out of business; hundreds of new Negro voters were registered; the public library was desegregated by court order; token school integration began in 1964; and at last the town removed all legal basis for segregation from its statutes.

Yet during these years of battle and sacrifice in Albany, the federal government confined itself to occasional law suits, taking no action against police who beat demonstrators in the broad daylight of the streets or released them with broken bodies from the jails. Indeed, when the Department of Justice at last took decisive and effective action, it did so, with the help of thirty agents from the Federal Bureau of Investigation (F.B.I.) – more than had ever been present at any of Albany's mass protests and arrests – against nine civil rights workers. A Negro had brought civil suit against a sheriff for having shot him in the neck while holding him in custody, and after an all-white federal jury had dismissed the case, members of the Albany Movement had picketed the shop of a juryman. The federal government speedily instituted prosecutions against those it held responsible for the picketing, and all but one were sentenced, to various jail terms and fines, in late 1963.

The militancy of SNICK was meanwhile encouraging other elements in the civil rights movement to take vigorous initiatives, and throughout the second half of 1962 and the early months of 1963 Martin Luther King's Southern Christian Leadership Conference prepared for a massive demonstration of protest in one of the centres of American racism, Birmingham, the chief city of Alabama. By the spring, the Negro organizations there were ready for action, and when the city's white leaders refused to negotiate desegregation, King and his colleagues led their non-violent troops into the streets. From April 12th, for more than four weeks, Birmingham Negroes paraded in disciplined ranks, to be bitten by police dogs, beaten with clubs, assailed by powerful water hoses or jabbed with electric cattle prods, and arrested in their thousands. Theophilus Eugene (Bull) Connor, the city's Commissioner of Public Safety, might have been leading a battle against Asian Communists thousands of miles away for all the concern that Washington displayed to prevent him. And then, on May 11th–12th, after white racists had launched a bombing counter-attack, the city's Negro community exploded into riot, burning the stores of white businessmen, and fighting with police and state troopers. The President had already been alerted by sympathy rallies and marches in other cities; 100,000 people had gathered in San Francisco, and even more in Detroit, to express their support for the Negro struggle in Birmingham and protest against federal inaction. The fury of black Birmingham itself, which threatened to fire the Northern ghettoes, forced him at last to act, and he dispatched his demand for new civil rights legislation to Congress.

Negro leaders throughout America decided that it was time to show the force of their feelings and set out to organize a mammoth march on Washington. America plainly did not want the march – a Gallup Poll on August 26th showed 63 per cent hostile, 22 per cent sympathetic and 15 per cent undecided – but a march America got, with well over 200,000 in its ranks. The temper was generally mild in the August heat, but there was a notable exception. One of the speakers was John Lewis, Chairman of the Student Nonviolent Coordinating Committee, and he delivered an attack on the Kennedy Administration that remained angry and bitter although cuts had been made in his prepared speech at the insistence of some distinguished participants in the march. One such cut had been a sharp question: 'I want to know; which side is the federal government on?'

In the autumn of 1963 SNICK, with help of varying kinds from the other main civil rights organizations, expanded the purpose of its voter registration campaign to challenge the very legitimacy of government in the Deep South by holding an unofficial election in Mississippi. Aaron Henry, N.A.A.C.P. leader in the state, was nominated as Governor, and Edwin King, Mississippi-born white clergyman, as Lieutenant-Governor; hundreds of students, some of them white, went canvassing through the state, ignoring threats and sustaining the usual arrests and assaults; ballot boxes were placed in churches and other assembly points, and when they were cleared, some 80,000 Negroes, or four times the number registered as official voters in Mississippi, were found to have taken part in the Freedom Ballot. The new campaign was a clear success; it showed that Negroes would vote in large numbers, even in the face of widespread intimidation, if given the opportunity to do so, and that the elected representatives of the Deep South, in Congress and the state administrations alike, held office not because so many citizens supported them, but because so many who opposed them were denied the right to vote at all. The Freedom Ballot was a challenge not only to the basis of authority in a portion of the United States, but to the democratic pretensions, at home and abroad, of the whole country.

A hardening of temper within both racial groups was now evident.

Many whites in the North and West, suddenly aware that Negro advance had deep implications for them as well as for the benighted Southerners, set out to protect themselves. Parents in New York launched boycotts of integrated schools; real-estate dealers in California agitated for the right to maintain segregated residential areas; working-class whites in Illinois and Wisconsin opposed the entry of Negroes into skilled jobs. Governor George Wallace of Alabama entered three Democratic primaries outside of the Deep South in April and May 1964, and in a flamboyant racist campaign won 30 per cent of the vote in Indiana, 34 per cent in Wisconsin and 43 per cent in Maryland. By the middle of July, when the Republican convention met in San Francisco, Senator Barry Goldwater of Arizona, campaigning on a general right-wing policy that included impatience with the force of the civil rights struggle – he voted against Kennedy's civil rights bill in the Senate – had won sufficient support to achieve nomination on the first ballot, by 883 votes to 214, as his party's presidential candidate. And that racism was a significant element in his selection was made abundantly clear with the defeat – by 897 votes to 409 – of an Eastern liberal motion to strengthen the civil rights plank in the party's election platform; delegates gave liberal spokesmen like Rockefeller a rough reception and wildly cheered Goldwater's own assertions of reaction.

A poll undertaken by the magazine *Newsweek* in mid-1963 revealed a surprisingly large proportion of Negroes – 26 per cent – accepting, for various reasons, the need for violence,[1] while half of all those questioned expressed willingness to participate in direct action.[2] (See table page 240.)

Mass Negro anger flared higher when a bomb exploded during a Sunday School class at a Birmingham church in September 1963 and four Negro children were killed, while the assassination of President Kennedy in November – Malcolm X called it another instance of 'chickens coming home to roost' – promoted the general drift to violence. Demonstrations grew more aggressive and less concerned with cajoling white public opinion; Negroes lay down in the streets to stop traffic, threw themselves in front of trucks and machinery to stop work at construction sites, sat blocking the entrances to schools and boards of education, even – in Berkeley, California – took perishable food from the cold shelves of supermarkets and left it to spoil in shopping carts. Furthermore there was a notable increase in the involvement of the poorest Negro class, with rent

[1] *The Negro Revolution in America*, by William Brink and Louis Harris (Simon & Schuster Inc., New York, 1963), pp. 206–7.
[2] Op. cit., p. 203.

NEGRO WILLINGNESS TO PARTICIPATE IN DIRECT ACTION

NON-SOUTH

IF ASKED WOULD:	Total rank and file %	Total Non-South %	Low Income %	Lower Middle Income %	Middle and Upper Income %
March in a Demonstration	51	60	63	59	67
Take part in a Sit-in	49	59	63	59	58
Go to Jail	47	52	56	51	63
Picket a Store	46	54	44	54	58

SOUTH

IF ASKED WOULD:	Total South %	Urban %	Non-Urban %	Middle and Upper Income %	Leaders %
March in a Demonstration	44	43	43	53	57
Take part in a Sit-in	42	41	44	45	57
Go to Jail	43	44	41	47	58
Picket a Store	40	38	39	51	57

strikes in New York City and Washington, D.C., and hunger marches in Chicago. The press, American and foreign alike, registered fears of widespread violence in the summer.

Responding to such pressures, the Senate passed the new civil rights bill – by 73 votes to 27 – in June, 1964, just one year after President Kennedy had asked Congress urgently to consider it. The measure, signed by President Johnson soon afterwards, attacked discrimination in voting and employment, but its main – and most contentious – provisions were those outlawing discrimination in public places, even where privately owned, like hotels, restaurants, shops, cinemas and petrol stations. Within a few weeks, Negro and white were together using beaches and cafés where the presence of a Negro before – outside the capacity of a servant, of course – would have excited a riot, and the world had, after all, not come to an end; with federal agents making a few well-publicized arrests for violations of the new law, Southern businessmen in the main found it prudent – and profitable – to obey.

Yet the tide of violence continued to flow. White terrorism was still increasing in Mississippi, with the burning of Negro churches, and at almost the same time as the Senate was passing the civil rights bill, three civil rights workers – two young whites from the North and a young Negro from Mississippi itself – were being murdered by a group of local whites that included county law officers. The summer wore on, and at the end of the third week in July riots struck New York City, with Negroes attacking police and white-owned shops in Harlem and Brooklyn for five days of racial fury. Then, as violence seemed at last to be ebbing within the city, rioting broke out at Rochester, in up-state New York, to rage for three days till the dispatch there by Governor Rockefeller of one thousand National Guardsmen. The storm that swept over New York City had been more than half expected; the storm in Rochester came as a national shock. For Rochester, its surface smoothed by the huge paternalism of the Eastman Kodak Company, had a prosperous and tidy reputation together with a city government of some – rather recent – enlightenment. Certainly the local Negro ghetto was smaller and a little less economically depressed than Negro ghettoes in several other cities. Yet the local Negro ghetto was, after all, a ghetto, and its nervous streets, its shabby schools and imprisoning tenements should have produced a proper expectancy. The 'shock' of Rochester was a measure of the complacency with which white America had come to regard all but the most tumultuous of Negro slums.

While the state of New York counted its loss in millions of dollars' worth of wrecked property, hundreds of injuries, more than 700 arrests and at least four deaths, cities with large Negro minorities elsewhere in America anxiously awaited their turn, and by the end of September five more had been struck by serious rioting. As the country considered the causes, extent and consequences of the violence, the predictable accusations of communist incitement and criminal leadership seemed more than usually irrelevant; for whoever may have fomented the riots – and the evidence for spontaneous eruption was a great deal stronger than that for conspiracy – the Negro mass was dangerously responsive. Certainly the established Negro leadership seemed to have lost its hold; even Bayard Rustin, organizer of the Washington march, a close associate of Martin Luther King's, and himself a prominent apostle of direct action, was roughly handled when he visited Harlem during the riots to try and restore order. Moreover, Negro violence seemed an expression of racial hatred as much as of frustration and despair; in Philadelphia, looters left their plunder in the streets, as though the mere act of looting white-owned shops supplied emotional satisfaction enough.

Strains were increasingly manifest within the civil rights movement itself between the moderates, who were anxious to consolidate the gains already made, and the militants, who believed that any loss in the momentum of struggle would lead – on the pattern of ninety years before – to retreat. The moderates were fearful of antagonizing white public opinion by too great an aggressiveness and pointed to the 'backlash' of the Wallace vote in the North and the Goldwater nomination; the militants maintained that white public opinion succumbed only to persistent pressure and that the fastnesses of discrimination – politically in the South, economically and socially across the country – remained uncaptured. The moderates, with the support of the major civil rights organizations, called for a moratorium on demonstrations during the presidential campaign; the militants, with the unsought backing of the ghetto rioters, ignored the call.

In Mississippi the organizers of the successful Freedom Ballot formed the Freedom Democratic Party to conduct future voting campaigns and send to the Democratic convention in August delegates who would challenge the all-white state representation. As the Democrats gathered in Atlantic City, the seating of the official Mississippi delegates seemed likely to split the convention wide open; but Johnson, who felt sure of the Negro vote against Goldwater and so saw no point in sacrificing Southern white support to buy what he had already, arranged that the decision should be kept from the convention floor and reserved to the careful handling of a credentials committee. In the end, the Freedom Democratic Party was permitted two representatives, as members of the convention at large, and the official Mississippi delegation was given its full 68 votes provided that it pledged itself to support the Johnson ticket in the elections; both groups rejected the compromise, with the official delegates walking out of the convention and the F.D.P. staging a sit-down in the Mississippi seats. As the press, radio and television carried reports of the contest, a chorus of public comment condemned the provocations of the Freedom Democratic Party, while admitting that its initiative had dramatized Mississippi's racial totalitarianism. The Freedom Democratic Party itself, which began spreading to other states, set out its reply in its first Freedom Primer for use in civil rights schools.

'Most people think that you have to give in at some point so that other people will not be mad. They think that you are supposed to accept what you are offered by powerful people because that is the way things are done in this country. That is the way things have been done in Mississippi, too, for a long time ... '

Not the least important aspect of the civil rights struggle in the South was its spreading radicalism. Increasingly the young militants of CORE and, especially, SNICK, in the process of challenging the political structure, were challenging the economic structure, too, not only in the South but throughout the whole country. Leaders from the ghettoes of the North influenced their Southern colleagues to a pervasive disaffection, which soon enough reached the rank and file. To visit the student teachers at their Freedom Schools was to engage in long discussions on African revolutionary movements, American foreign policy and the system of free enterprise, as well as on the immediate campaign in the South. While I was in Mississippi, I met some of those who had recently returned from a trip to Guinea. Their excited comments on what they had seen, and their view of the Negro revolution as involved in a vast endeavour, affected by and affecting developments across the world, seemed as natural a part of their environment as the teaching of the alphabet to adults, and the huge hole in an outside wall where a bomb had been thrown from a passing car a few nights before.

In the middle of October, China exploded her first nuclear device (initially discounted by American pundits as 'primitive', then suddenly upgraded to 'sophisticated'), and the psychological fall-out reached right across the United States. A rush of reports, on television and in the press, revealed a new regard for China's strength, and a growing recognition that her place in the United Nations could not much longer be denied her. I had just arrived in America and busily sought out reactions among Negroes of various backgrounds and political viewpoints: they included, for instance, a Southern university president of unimpeachable respectability (Negro Cautious); an important official of the N.A.A.C.P., and a senior journalist on a Chicago-based Negro 'glossy' (of the uncertain Centre); and a novelist directing a busy workshop of Negro writers in New York (Radical). All in their different ways confessed to a flush of pride that a coloured people had at last reached the front rank of technology and power; all led me to suppose that the growth in China's international influence was doing for Negro self-confidence something like what the proliferation of independent African states had done a few years before, despite the evident discrepancy between Negro emotional investment in Africa and in Asia. Even those Negroes who regarded themselves as ineradicably American and so inevitable enemies of America's enemies seemed to believe that Chinese strength would sap the racial arrogance of whites, making Negro advance much easier.

As election day approached, the civil rights organizations, fearful that the support for Goldwater among whites was greater than the public opinion polls suggested, and eager in any event to ensure as massive a rejection of Goldwater's policies as possible, gave increasing attention to the registration of Negro voters, not only in the South but over the rest of the country. In the end, Johnson won an unprecedented victory, registering the highest proportion of votes in American history (61 per cent) and by far the largest plurality (just under 16 million), while his majority of electoral votes (486 to 52) was surpassed only by Roosevelt's score (523 to 8) in 1936. His majority of popular votes in the Eastern industrial states was spectacular; he took 76·2 per cent of the votes in Massachusetts, 68·6 per cent in New York, and 65 per cent in Pennsylvania. He won the two rigidly Republican states which even Roosevelt had failed to take in 1936, Maine by 68·8 per cent and Vermont by 66·3 per cent. He defeated Goldwater decisively in Mid and Far Western states where the white backlash was supposedly substantial – Wisconsin by taking 62·1 per cent of the votes, Illinois by 59·5 per cent, and California by 59·2 per cent. He even won such Southern states as Texas (63·3 per cent), North Carolina (56·2 per cent), Virginia (53·5 per cent), and Florida (51·1 per cent). Goldwater took only his own state, Arizona (50·4 per cent), and the five Deep South states – Alabama, where Johnson was not even on the ballot, Mississippi (87·1 per cent), South Carolina (58·9 per cent), Louisiana (56·8 per cent), and Georgia (54·1 per cent).

That the Negro vote was of immense significance there can be no doubt. Negroes voted wherever they could and with near unanimity, producing or swelling the large Democratic margins outside the South and saving much inside it from Republican capture. Furthermore a Negro support which in some precincts reached 99 per cent secured crucial seats in Congress for the Democrats; in Texas the Democratic candidate for Senator won by some 287,000 votes, with an estimated 247,000 Negroes, or 95 per cent of the total Negro vote in the state, supporting him; in Ohio a Democrat was elected Senator by only 15,000 votes, with an estimated 96 per cent of the state's 400,000 Negro voters behind him; in states like Indiana, Kentucky, Ohio, Tennessee, and even Georgia, the solid Negro vote gave victory to the relatively liberal Democratic candidates in Congressional districts expected to go Republican.

Johnson's success would clearly have been much smaller had the Negroes voted differently; but the extent of their partisanship could not disguise the overwhelming support which Johnson obtained among the whites. Wall Street, a small but not unimportant fastness of the Republicans, deserted to Johnson, and whole stretches of traditional Republican territory, from New England to the farming West, went Democrat. Goldwater's rampaging right-wing individualism, with its often wild attacks on conventional policies, frightened millions of voters: big businessmen and small investors alike feared that cuts in federal spending would lead to a slump on the stock exchange and a general economic recession; the poor, the unemployed and the aged, all those dependent in some way on social security, feared that their allowances would be cut or altogether revoked; all levels of society feared the consequences of Goldwater's 'trigger-happy' posture, his threat to withdraw recognition from the Soviet Union, his repeated promises to be tough with communism, his suggestion that military commanders should be given control over tactical nuclear weapons. Some seven and a half million voters who had supported the Republican candidature of Nixon four years before fled from Goldwater, a defection equivalent to well over 10 per cent of the total American vote.

The Johnson landslide, therefore, was far from a popular acceptance of Negro demands; it was rather, in the words of the *New York Times*, a reaffirmation of 'the broad consensus that has dominated the American political scene since the New Deal days – a moderate approach in domestic and foreign areas with acceptance of the fact that some expansion of the role and powers of the Federal Government is inevitable.'[1] On closer examination, indeed, the whole election appeared to many Negroes less of a triumph than a threat. If 43 million Americans had voted for Johnson, 27 million had still voted for Goldwater – a clear minority perhaps, but clearly a substantial one. Nor, when the desertion of Republican fortresses like Maine and the middle class in the Mid-West was considered, could the Goldwater vote be comfortably dismissed with the old excuse that certain areas of American society will support the Republican candidate if a dead dog is nominated. The Goldwater vote disclosed the existence of a strong radical right, of which the new Republican recruitment in the Deep South was no more than a small part.

This radical right was by no means altogether composed of America's professional purveyors of race hatred and a frantic anti-communism; but there can be little doubt that such people and their organizations made the running in the Goldwater campaign. They produced a spate of 'smear' propaganda in films and pamphlets, press advertisements and paperbacks

[1] November 8th, 1964.

that played constantly on the old themes of widespread subversion and the need to preserve the traditional (white and unrestrictedly capitalist) American way of life. Only one customary note, indeed – anti-Semitism – was seldom sounded, for Goldwater freely acknowledged his Jewish ancestry; one prominent racist in the South resolved the dilemma in a short wry comment to me: 'He's an unregenerate Jew, but I hope to hell he wins.'

The 'hate' groups in the United States direct their attention – with varying degrees of emphasis and often simultaneously – to the Negroes, all non-whites, the Jews, the Catholics, and all recent immigrants. Since the Russian Revolution of 1917, moreover, the fear of communism in a fanatically 'free enterprise' society has excited the hunting down of subversives, and the 'hate' groups have commonly attempted to further their own peculiar objectives by associating themselves with a general persecution of the 'unAmerican'. Basically racist organizations like the Ku Klux Klan and the White Citizens' Councils have wielded anti-communism as a weapon against integration, and basically anti-communist organizations like the influential John Birch Society have found it profitable to employ racism in the search for recruits. The association, however, is more than one of mere convenience. The racist and the extreme anti-communist groups share several fundamental aims and characteristics; hostility to the spread of federal power; fear of 'foreign' influence; hatred of the liberal as the proponent of integration or the pre-cursor of communism; a rampant individualism that yearns for the simple rough problems and solutions of the frontier; a passion for personal liberty that does not interfere with the demand for authoritarian measures against anyone else; an easy indifference to the poverty or oppression of others (except those under communist or non-white rule); the strategy of argument by accusation and accusation by 'smear'; the exercise of pressure by infiltration and intimidation. Not surprisingly, therefore, leading racists will frequently be found to be members – sometimes important ones – of an extreme anti-communist organization, and financial backing for both racist and anti-communist groups comes not merely from the small contributions of individual sympathizers but from foundations and big, even very big business. It is estimated that something over $14,000,000 is spent annually by the far right on propaganda, and among contributors to one or other group have been corporations like United States Steel, Gulf Oil and Eversharp.[1]

[1] See *Danger on the Right*, by Arnold Forster and Benjamin R. Epstein (Random House, New York, 1964).

To the fanatics of the right, Goldwater, with his frontier attitudes, hard line on communism, and opposition to civil rights legislation, was a godsend. That Goldwater himself emerged from the election campaign as rather more stupid than malignant makes ultimately little difference; his candidature was carefully fostered by the extremist groups, and though he dissociated himself from several and denounced the more vicious propaganda ploys, he notably refused to repudiate the John Birch Society. The most dangerous feature of his campaign, however, was that he should have been nominated at all. Outside of the South, the organizations of the radical right had generally suffered from their reputation for crankiness; they had seemed to be threads of a lunatic fringe, with little prospect – despite Senator McCarthy's short individual sway – of serious popular influence. Goldwater's nomination as presidential candidate for one of the two major political parties made them and their ideas relatively respectable.

How and why Goldwater managed to capture the Republican Party will doubtless be the subject of conjecture and dispute for years to come. Certainly he mounted a campaign of Kennedy dimensions and diligence, while his more formidable moderate opponents were disunited and indecisive until it was too late; furthermore, the Republican Party had been out of power for so long, with the idiosyncratic exception of Eisenhower's eight years, that Goldwater's offer of 'a choice, not an echo' roused those so often disappointed in the use of the usual blandishments. Yet all this does not explain the massive popular support which Goldwater registered in important state Republican primaries and without which his nomination would have been impossible. Part of the answer would seem to lie in America's international frustrations, the shrinking of her real power to shape the world alongside the swelling of her economic and military strength, a process which the revolution in China, the effectively unwinnable Korean and Indo-Chinese wars, the spreading area of non-alignment and the traumatic revolution in Cuba made progressively evident. It was the resultant hysteria of helplessness among many who sought for simple drastic remedies that combined with the real white 'backlash' to produce a surge in the strength of the radical right.

The choice of Johnson and the Democratic Party at the polls was fundamentally a choice of the known and safe, a choice against change, by the American electorate. Yet change – of a kind very different from that projected by the Goldwater ticket – was precisely what the Negroes wanted. When one celebrated Negro night-club entertainer told me that he had gone fishing on election day, and a young Negro civil rights

worker proclaimed that he had wanted Goldwater to win because that
would have brought the Negro mass fighting into the streets, they were
not reflecting the behaviour of the Negro multitude at the polls, but they
were reflecting the unease, the underlying hostility with which that
multitude registered its support for Johnson. The 'moderate approach'
which the New York Times saw as the meaning of the Johnson avalanche
was a white objective; the millions of Negroes who formed part of that
avalanche voted not to put Johnson in power but to keep Goldwater out,
and a 'moderate approach' was anything but the 'broad consensus' of
their ballots.

Within weeks this would become only too obvious. Selma in Dallas
County is almost at the geographical centre of Alabama and exactly at
the ideological one; it was a slave market before the Civil War, a military
depot for the Confederacy, a lynch law town in the early years of this
century, and a cradle in the 'fifties for the White Citizens' Council movement of the state. In Dallas County itself, 64 per cent of the eligible whites
were at the 1964 elections registered to vote, but only 1 per cent of the
eligible Negroes. In Dallas and the four counties around it there lived
87,972 Negroes and 47,289 whites; on the voter registers there were
24,037 whites and 904 Negroes. In Lowndes County not a single Negro
out of the nearly 12,500 living there was entitled to vote; in Wilcox
County, among the nearly 14,500 Negroes who constituted 78 per cent
of the population, no Negro voter existed.[1]

In February 1963 the first SNICK workers arrived at Selma to conduct
a voter registration campaign, and the customary series of demonstrations,
assaults, arrests and mild federal remonstrances followed. If there was anything unpredictable about the incidents, it was the peculiar fervour of the
Sheriff, Jim Clark, who added several hundred ordinary white citizens to
his regular force of deputies and armed them with clubs and cattle prods.
By early October over 300 people, including John Lewis, had been
arrested in the town for civil rights activities, mass meetings had involved
thousands of local Negroes in the movement, and the voter registers were
as bleached as ever.

After the presidential election of November 1964, Martin Luther King –
his national prestige much enhanced by his acquisition of a Nobel Peace
Prize, but his leadership in the civil rights struggle under increasing
criticism from the militants – responded to the Negro mood by swinging
his Southern Christian Leadership Conference into action. Concentrating
on Selma, where SNICK workers were still engaged and mass Negro

[1] The Times, February 5th, 1965.

awareness already existed, he initiated a voter registration drive in the middle of January 1965. Within two weeks some 3,000 people, including King himself, had been arrested, and international attention began to focus on the town. Malcolm X – the former Black Muslim leader who had now established a militant movement of his own and would soon be assassinated in New York City – visited the area and announced: 'I think the people would do well to give King what he is asking for, before another group comes in and tries another way.' King called for a pause – under pressure, his Negro critics said, from Washington – but the demonstrations continued, and Sheriff Clark continued to use violence in disbanding them. On Sunday, March 7th, several hundred Negroes and white sympathizers started a march to the state capital of Montgomery fifty miles away, to protest against racial discrimination in registering voters, and state and county officers – apparently under orders from Governor Wallace – attacked them with clubs, whips and ropes behind a screen of tear gas. At least sixty-seven Negroes were injured, some seriously, among them SNICK Chairman, John Lewis.

Much of the nation was outraged, and several Congressmen demanded that federal marshals, even troops, be sent to the scene, but the Johnson administration stayed silent. King invited representatives of religious groups from all over the country to join him in a new march from Selma, in protest at the brutality of the Alabama authorities, and recruits streamed into the town. On the 9th marchers set out again but were soon stopped by Clark and his deputies, now reinforced by state troopers, and King called a retreat; that night three white clergymen were assaulted by local whites, and one of them, a Unitarian minister from Boston, subsequently died. A delegation from thousands of clergymen met the President to express anger at the events in Selma, and for the first time in history a sit-in was staged at the White House by civil rights demonstrators, while one thousand more marched singing with banners on the pavement outside.

At last, on March 17th, President Johnson submitted to Congress draft legislation which would make it possible for federal officials to register voters in states where special franchise tests were applied and where less than half of those eligible to do so had voted in the 1964 election. It was a frontal assault on franchise discrimination in six states of the Deep South. But as though to remind America that the Deep South was not the preserve of racism, white and Negro students on the following day fought in the streets of Cleveland, Ohio, with crowds of whites chanting: 'Two, four, six, eight; we do not want to integrate.'

On the 25th the marchers, who had set out four days earlier under federal court protection and whose numbers had swollen along the way to over 20,000, reached Montgomery, streamed to the state capitol singing 'We shall overcome' and shouting 'Freedom!', listened to speeches from their leaders and dispersed, their representatives and petition unreceived by Governor Wallace. That night, while driving back marchers to Selma, a white woman – Mrs Viola Liuzzo, mother of five children – was shot dead in Lowndes County. President Johnson announced the arrest of four Klansmen on charges of having conspired to deprive her of her civil rights – unlike murder, a federal crime – and in a strong attack on the Klan invited its investigation by Congress.

In his speech to Congress on March 17th, Johnson had measured the significance of the civil rights struggle. 'All Americans must have the right to vote. And we are going to give them that right. All Americans must have the privileges of citizenship regardless of race. And they are going to have those privileges. But to exercise that privilege takes more than legal right. It requires a trained mind and a healthy body. It requires a decent home, and a chance to find a job, and the opportunity to escape from poverty.'

Like Kennedy before him, Johnson publicly acknowledged the twin challenge of the racial struggle in the United States – that the status of the Negro denied the whole American presumption, and that this denial had economic roots. The American presumption – a closer description than 'dream', since the ideal is in general taken for the reality – is of a nation, finally indivisible, which is dedicated to the liberty and enterprise of the individual, rewarding talent and industry, eschewing prejudice and privilege, permitting the rise of any native citizen to the highest office. The condition of the Negro contradicts this image, because prejudice and privilege make of him a separate, and inferior, citizen, whose talent and industry cannot earn their natural rewards; whose enterprise and liberty are restricted by discrimination in housing, schools, employment and general amenities; whose vote, let alone access to the lowest political office, is over a large area of the country withheld. The Negro is thus the ultimate denial of America's ideological genesis; he is the colonial subjection from which the United States revolted, the oppression and poverty from which the European immigrants of the nineteenth century fled, the regimentation and restraint which the world of communism now represents to almost all Americans.

According to statistics cited by Whitney Young, Jr, Executive Director of the National Urban League, 20 per cent of all Negro workers are unemployed, compared to a figure for all workers in the country of 4–5 per cent, while average family income for Negroes is only 53 per cent of the average family income for whites. Of one million Americans under the age of twenty-one who are out of school and out of work, 50 per cent are Negro, or five times the number that the population ratio would properly allow. Negroes get some three and a half years less schooling than whites, and generally live seven years less. Moreover, the racial discrepancies are growing; the gap between average white and average Negro income is persistently widening, and while the low white infant mortality rate falls even further, the high Negro rate is actually rising.[1]

In the South, where 98 per cent of all Negro farmers live, federal aid to agriculture, dispensed in the main by white-controlled agencies, has swollen the differential in resources between white and black on the land. In 1950 the average white farm in the region was 175·3 acres in size; the average Negro farm, 47: by 1959, the average white farm had expanded to 249 acres; the average Negro farm, to only 52·3. During the 'fifties, therefore, the actual difference in land holding increased from 128·3 to 196·7 acres. Between 1949 and 1959 the average income of a Negro farming family fell from 52 per cent to 45 per cent of that received by an average white farming family. Between 1950 and 1960 the proportion of white farmhouses with hot and cold piped water increased from 20·4 per cent to 60 per cent; the proportion of Negro ones, from 2·3 per cent to 9·7 per cent.[2]

Despite the common assertions to the contrary, racial segregation in the crucial area of housing has increased and not diminished during the past few years. Analysing the United States census reports, Karl E. Taeuber, of the Population Research and Training Centre at the University of Chicago, established an index to measure the degree of segregation in an American city: 'O' denotes complete residential integration, and 'if each city block contains only whites, or only non-whites, and there are no blocks of mixed occupancy, then the distribution is as uneven as possible and the index will assume the value of 100.' Taking 109 cities, Mr Taeuber found that the segregation index for the whole country, which had been 85·2 in 1940, had risen to 86·1 in 1960, with the high figure for states in the North and Centre of 88·4. In eighteen Illinois cities, the index in 1960 was 90, and in Chicago itself the index rose to the formidable figure of 93 in 1963. In Mr Taeuber's overall assessment, 'there is no indication

---

[1] Quoted in 'The Negro Now', by Robert Penn Warren in *Look*, March 23rd, 1965.
[2] A Civil Rights Commission Report quoted in *The Times*, March 2nd, 1965.

that residential segregation and its accompanying problems will diminish over time without governmental intervention ... It seems likely that the degree of residential segregation between whites and non-whites has been increasing in both Northern and Southern cities during most of the century since the Civil War.'[1]

In 1965 an important report prepared by Daniel Moynihan, Assistant Secretary of Labour, and entitled *The Negro Family: The Case for National Action*, was – after several months of embarrassed postponement – finally released. It depicted a degree of decay in Negro society, of alienation from the standards of white America, so great as to make the prospect of mounting race violence seem only too probable.

The Negro family is steadily disintegrating. At any specific time, 36 per cent of Negro children are growing up in broken homes. Proportionately three times as many Negro married women as white ones live apart from their husbands (the urban rate is 22·9 per cent for non-whites and 7·9 per cent for whites). The Negro illegitimacy rate is more than seven times that for whites, having risen from 16·8 per cent in 1940 (when the white rate was 2 per cent) to 23·6 per cent in 1963 (when the rate for whites was 3·07 per cent). And the very structure of the family in black America is diverging farther and farther from the national norm. An already high and increasing number of Negro families are headed by females, with the rate more than double the steadily diminishing one for whites.

In large measure, this is a consequence of the past, when first slavery and then segregation humiliated and harassed particularly the Negro male, as traditional guardian of the home and source of discipline and prestige, promoting instead the predominance of the female. But the drift of population to the cities, proportionately even greater among Negroes than whites – 73·2 per cent of American Negroes, and 69·5 per cent of whites, were urbanized by 1960 – has continued the process, by thrusting the family into the corruption of the ghetto, where high unemployment and squalid housing have nourished the Negro male's appearance of failure and his search for compensations in drink, drugs, gambling, promiscuity, crime and the violence of despair. The female, more acceptable in white-collar jobs or domestic service, has increasingly assumed the role of stable breadwinner, so corroding still further the value and self-assurance of the male. Inevitably, this has had tremendous repercussions. In a country where, formally at least, the male is regarded as the head of the family, it has produced among Negroes a dangerous sense of exile from dominant white values, exciting a bitter hatred of

[1] Report in the *New York Times*, November 26th, 1964.

white America itself as responsible, and a readiness to see the remedy in racial insurrection.

As the Moynihan Report proclaims, the Negro is no longer satisfied with constitutional liberty; he demands equality, and equality not just of opportunity, but of results. The mere removal of barriers to free competition – for jobs, university places, posts and public offices of high salary and prestige – means little when the Negro himself is so heavily handicapped by centuries of oppression, psychological distortion, and neglect. For, despite all the recent advances in civil rights and employment opportunities, the relative condition of the Negro is actually deteriorating. Between 1960 and 1963, a period of general prosperity, the average Negro family income slipped from 55 per cent to 53 per cent of the average family income for whites.

In part the problem is that of the coloured world at large. Poverty promotes large families, and large families promote poverty; poverty produces low levels of education and training, and low levels of education and training perpetuate poverty. The Negro population increase in the United States is 2·4 per cent a year, compared with the national 1·7 per cent. (And this, of course, increases not only the relative size of the Negro community, but the challenge it presents. In 1950, the Negro was one in ten of all Americans; by the early 'seventies, he promises to be one in eight.) But the Negro population is also caught in the peculiar trap of a self-propagating psychological distortion. Poverty, unemployment and humiliation in a society devoted to individual enterprise and success produce a sense of failure and hopelessness that produce in their turn poverty, unemployment and humiliation. As Moynihan shows, there is a clear relationship between social class and I.Q., and an even more striking relationship between family disintegration and I.Q.

Social Class and School Grade	Father Present	Father Absent
Lowest social class level:		
Grade 1	95·2	87·8
Grade 5	92·7	85·7
Middle social class level:		
Grade 1	98·7	92·8
Grade 5	92·9	92·0

Eighth-grade children in the Negro ghetto of central Harlem, New York City, have an average I.Q. of 87·7, 'which means that perhaps a third of the children are scoring at levels perilously near to those of retardation'.[1] Fifty-six per cent of Negroes fail the Armed Forces Qualification Test, a rate almost four times that for whites, and this in turn has a substantial impact on employment, since the armed forces provide the largest single source of jobs in the country.

Poverty, unemployment, family disintegration and educational failure have had a predictable effect on the rate of crime and delinquency. 'It is probable that at present the majority of crimes against the person, such as rape, murder and aggravated assault, are committed by Negroes.'[2] To be sure, Negroes are arrested far more casually than whites, and the relationship between citizen and police in the ghettoes is increasingly like that between contending armies. But this cannot explain away the weight of statistics, which is confirmed, after all, by reasonable expectation.

NUMBER OF ARRESTS IN 1963	White	Negro
Offences charged total	31,988	38,549
Murder and nonnegligent manslaughter	2,288	2,948
Forcible rape	4,402	3,935
Aggravated assault	25,298	31,666

Source: *Crime in the United States* (Federal Bureau of Investigation, 1963), table 25, p. 111.

The truth is that the white and Negro worlds are moving farther and farther apart. Like Taeuber, Moynihan recognizes that the United States is growing more segregated, not less, and that the process is a self-perpetuating one. Even middle-class Negroes are largely confined to the over-crowded schools and street rot of the ghetto by the reluctance of whites to sell homes to them in the new suburbs, the high cost of escaping to accommodation outside the city, and the alternative of low-cost federal-aided housing projects for slum clearance. In New York City, during the school year 1957–8, there were 64 schools with a Negro or Puerto Rican student ratio of 90 per cent or over; six years later, there were 134. 'The present generation of Negro youth growing up in the urban ghetto has probably less personal contact with the white world than any generation in the history of the Negro American.'[3]

In the presence of such facts, the doctrine of pacific evolution displays less practical relevance for the Negro multitude than does the Second

[1] *Moynihan Report*, p. 36.   [2] Ibid., p. 38.   [3] Ibid., p. 44.

Coming. The Northern Negro has had the vote for a century. But how has his debasement changed? It is hardly surprising that so many of the activists in the civil rights struggle, especially the leaders of CORE and SNICK, should now be speaking of the need for revolution. Bayard Rustin, an influential strategist within the established Negro leadership, has explained: 'Subjectively, the Negro does not want a revolution; objectively, he sees that only revolution can get him what he wants.'[1] The word 'revolution' is a strong one, but it is not misapplied. For nothing less than a fundamental change in the whole pattern of American society can make a significantly single nation out of the separate citizenships of race.

North and South in the United States will each have to undergo an upheaval, and it is not altogether improbable that the South will do so more easily, in the end, than the North. For, as is increasingly acknowledged, the North recognizes the rights of the Negro but not the Negro himself, while the South recognizes the Negro but not his rights. The distance that each region has to travel is vast, but most Negroes I have asked seem to think that the Southern route is the shorter.

Like the Afrikaner in South Africa, the Southern white is so emotionally bound to the non-whites that life without them would seem utterly unnatural, ultimately unreal. Pleading affection for the Negro nurse of his childhood, a sweeper at the office or a farm labourer's family, he may be a robust, even sporadically brutal paternalist; but the pleading is not hollow, it is a painful display of his need. Certainly it is no accident that the Afrikaner and the white Southerner are so preoccupied with speculation on the sexual prowess and appetite of the black races, or that both have so much more to do sexually with the coloured than have their supposedly more liberal fellow whites; the law against physical relations between white and non-white in South Africa is far more frequently broken by Afrikaners than by whites of English culture, while Southern white manhood is traditionally tried on Negro women.

The strength of colour prejudice within both Afrikanerdom and the American South is its greatest weakness – the fear of surrender that is a deep recognition of the ease with which such surrender could be accomplished. There is no anti-Semite, some Jews say, quite like the one with Jewish blood in him, for his hatred is an ecstasy of disavowal. There is, equally, no more rabid racist than the poor white in the American South or the Afrikaner with a consciousness of coloured connection.

In late October 1964, a friend and I were driving through South Carolina and, catching sight of a small, solitary, sun-blistered café by the

[1] Said in a personal interview with the author.

road-side, we decided to stop there for lunch. On the closed front door was a shabby notice announcing the existence of a private club with admission restricted to members, and inside the juke-box shone in lonely cherished contrast to the flyblown tables and the grimy contraceptive machine in the men's lavatory. The woman in charge, with short curly black hair, a skin that seemed constantly in shadow, and a surly address, gathered that we were not law enforcement officers seeking out infringements of the Civil Rights Act, issued us with temporary membership cards, and having delivered chicken and chips from a dark interior, became garrulous. She told us of her troubles with the law – she was being prosecuted at the instance of local 'agitators' for refusing admission to Negroes – and as her animation grew, her expressed attitude to Negroes became steadily more morbid. Then abruptly she changed the subject, and after a while showed her friendliness by bringing out the photographs of her children. Her grown-up daughter was unquestionably pretty, and unquestionably dark – the sort of colour, as far as one could reasonably judge from a photograph, common to the more frantic white supremacists in the South African parliament. 'Of course,' she said suddenly, 'the light was very bad when the pictures were taken. You can see how dark it was.'

The upper and middle income groups have used the fear of these poor and more vulnerable whites to obtain political power and secure economic ascendancy for themselves. Rich plantation owners like Senator Eastland of Mississippi have employed racism to protect a virtually feudal hold at home and provide a place of influence over the affairs of the nation as a whole; bankers and industrialists have retained the benefits of cheap labour, from Negroes cowed into accepting any wage above the pittance paid on the plantations, and from whites made manageable by the menace of Negro competition; lawyers, doctors, engineers, journalists have profited from a market for their skills always twice the size of the supply, since half the population of the South is effectively excluded from such professions. With the Supreme Court judgment of 1954 against segregated schooling, therefore, this dominant class immediately set out to sustain its advantages against attack, organizing the White Citizens' Councils to spearhead resistance. The poorer whites were excited to display their hostility, and if acts of mob or hooligan violence were planned in railway workshops and bars, their initial encouragement issued from the speeches of politicians and the boardrooms of businessmen, as well as more crudely from the pages of *The Citizen*, propaganda instrument of the Councils. If state and county law enforcement officers behaved brutally to civil rights demonstrators, it was not only because they were themselves generally poor white in background and members of extremist organizations, but because they knew that the spokesmen of local economic and political power would connive at, if not noisily approve of, their conduct.

It soon became clear, however, that threats would not long intimidate a federal authority subject to other, stronger pressures, and that defiance of the law was likely to prove much more expensive in the end than a phased acquiescence. The withdrawal of federal aid for segregated schooling would force a refractory state to raise by new taxes or the introduction of fees the revenue needed to keep education alive – a course which the South early showed itself reluctant to take – while capital across the country shrank from investment in areas of civil discord. Few large national concerns were willing to antagonize the huge Negro purchasing public by openly moving into the belt of Southern intransigence, while the enticements of cheap labour did not cancel out the costs of protracted racial tension and turbulence. In states like Virginia and South Carolina, accordingly, and in cities like Atlanta, Georgia, demonstrations of resistance gave place to an ordered retreat, and the firm initiatives of the dominant class, through pressures by organized industry and commerce, and through close control by state, county and municipal authorities, reduced defiance to a widely unexpected and rapidly absorbed trickle. The state university of South Carolina, for instance, was integrated without incident, and after the passing of the Civil Rights Act formerly whites-only restaurants in Atlanta served Negro customers with little unease.

James Kilpatrick, editor of the *Richmond News Leader* and one of the crucial figures in the campaign of 'massive resistance' to school desegregation in Virginia, seemed not a little apologetic when I met him in October 1964. 'I expected blood to flow in the streets of the South,' he said. 'I never thought it would all be so smooth. It became a matter not of preserving segregation but of defying the law, and there weren't many prepared to do that. And then prosperity made integration much easier; the dollar beat a path where federal force alone would have found the going rough. In the end, I think, the South will integrate far further than the North shows any signs of doing.'

Precisely because the poorer whites of the South are so close, culturally and economically, to the Negro, integration in states like Virginia and the Carolinas is less 'token' in character than in states of the supposedly progressive North like Pennsylvania and Illinois. White and black have long mingled on the pavements of the South, visiting the same shops or simply idling past the same windows; even downtown Birmingham, Alabama, a citadel of white racism, has far more 'integrated' an appearance than downtown New York City or Chicago. Where class in the cities of the North is a high wall around racial ghettoes, class in the South is often a thoroughfare between them. And so the desegregation of a lunch counter at a Woolworth's store in Atlanta, Georgia, or Columbia, South Carolina, means more than a formal acceptance of Negro customers; Negroes have long shopped there together with whites and will now increasingly, together with whites, use the lunch counter as they would any other part of the store. After only two months of desegregation in Winston Salem, North Carolina, the manager of a large shop declared: 'You would think it had been going on for fifty years. I am tickled to death over the situation.'[1]

Where the dominant class has not acted with speed and resolution, however, or shown a fractured front; where demagogy has been permitted free sway in the state capitals; where violence, official and maverick, has been fed by the ambition or indifference of authority, society has become the cornered prey of hatred and terror. In rural Georgia and Louisiana, in nearly all of Alabama and Mississippi, a frantic racism elects mayors and sheriffs, rouses mobs, defies and ridicules the law, elevates assault and murder to patriotism. This is the putrefying South of Faulkner's novels, with its illiterate, often inbred and degenerate poor whites; its decayed plantation houses; its dark swamps, where the very vegetation seems to rot; its brooding on a heavy splendid past that never existed. This is the home of the burning cross and the bombed church; of the sullen narrow eyes and cramped faces of whites in the street; of old men gossiping half asleep on the court-house steps and young thick police continually fingering their badges and guns; of prohibition and moonshine and fundamentalist preachers; of near-naked Negro children spilling from twisted shacks, and shabby Negro women crooked with cotton picking; of, every now and then, among the trees or in the river, the suddenly discovered body of a Negro who unaccountably disappeared.

John Gunther has reported[2] how Eric Louw, for many years South Africa's Foreign Minister, used to answer, in a mixture of fury and self-righteousness, American attacks on the policy of 'apartheid' with the cry, 'We have no lynching here!' But then white South Africa is, in the main, too sure of itself to need the mob or the shot through the window. Farmers who beat their labourers to death are sometimes prosecuted and even fined, and when murder is considered necessary, of a movement

[1] Quoted in H. Zinn, op. cit., p. 28.
[2] *Inside Africa* (Harper & Brothers, New York, 1955), p. 479.

or an individual, it is done with the careful majesty of parliament and the courts. The non-white is not better placed, his rights are not more generous – as Mr Louw suggested – in South Africa than in the America of Mississippi; quite the contrary. The lawlessness and disorder of rural Louisiana are a response to the realization of impending defeat, a resistance to change that is part of the change in itself. The old violence, of election riots and public lynchings, was afraid, but it was also jubilant, a flexing of power, to preserve and not disrupt. The new violence, furtive, turned too against the traditional leadership, is the violence of panic (like the last thrashings of the O.A.S. in Algeria), to destroy rather than secure. The Deep South today is in a state of nervous breakdown, and this may well be the beginning of progress to a proper state of health.

At Natchez by the Mississippi, in September 1964, the mayor's home and store were bombed in broad daylight because he had criticized local extremism in an interview with a Chicago journalist. At McComb in the south of Mississippi, a city councillor in June spoke out for moderation at a meeting, and straight afterwards a bomb was thrown through the front window of his home. The local newspaper, the *Enterprise-Journal*, cautiously proposed obedience to the law; shots were fired at its windows, and a cross was burnt outside the house of its editor, Oliver Emmerich.

I went to see Mr Emmerich at his office in the centre of McComb, a mild-mannered man who spoke anxiously of the need for a newspaper to be responsible and effective at the same time. I am not sure that he meant to do so, but the picture he presented of the town's leading citizens was of badly shaken men and women just beginning to pick themselves up from among the broken pieces of their society. They had been careless or resentful of the changes in their way of life debated and decided at Washington, and they had taken no steps to ensure that the seemingly now unavoidable transition should be orderly. When, therefore, at the start of 1964, terrorism came to McComb – conducted by the Klan and by Americans for the Preservation of the White Race, with their main support among the poorer white railway workers – the dominant class was bewildered, helpless and afraid. Several Negro churches were bombed or fired, the local SNICK voter registration school was dynamited, and when a few whites expressed their disapproval, they were threatened with assassination, and their property was attacked. At last in September, with some encouragement from Emmerich himself I suspect, the Sheriff approached three prominent citizens with a proposal to raise a reward of $2,500 for the capture of those who had been destroying churches. A front-page editorial in the *Enterprise-Journal* that Friday appealed for the money, and by the following Monday $5,000 had been raised. It was as though everyone had been waiting for someone else to show that he felt the same way. The first arrests were made at the end of the month, and on October 23rd nine white men were given long, if suspended, prison sentences for the illegal use of explosives; moreover, the probations were subject to withdrawal 'if another wave of racial violence occurred', whether or not the nine were themselves involved. It was the sternest judgment from a Mississippi judge that anyone could reasonably have expected.

The sudden courage or despair – doubtless a blend of both – shown by a very few men made a breach at last in the conformity of intimidation sealing off McComb from civilized America. Other communities in the Deep South have equally, through the belated initiative of civic leaders, managed to emerge from what one Southern historian has called 'The Closed Society'.[1] In Monroe, Georgia, fifty miles from Atlanta, school desegregation came with relative ease because the mayor and council recognized the need to secure respect for the law and acted with vigour. In the spring of 1964 whites in Macon County, Alabama, home of the Tuskegee Institute, burned down a previously all-white school which admitted a few Negro pupils, and the local Klan group swore publicly to prevent integration for ever. But the white power structure remained firm: in September a crucial white school accepted twenty-two Negroes without difficulty; and whites from the town even began drifting to concerts and other public functions of the Tuskegee Institute, which itself admitted white students for the first time in 1964. When I visited Tuskegee in late 1964, there were Negro town councillors, and one Negro served on the student council of the Tuskegee Public School. Not irrelevantly, the Sheriff of Macon County had first been elected, in 1954, with the help of the Negro vote in a three-cornered contest, and had ever since swung his authority against manifestations of extremism.

It is in this context that the failure of the federal executive, under successive presidents, to act with adequate force and firmness displays its disastrous irresponsibility. Time and again, when compelled by the momentum of events and public opinion, Washington has at last taken effective action, to reveal in the very ease of the submission it has encountered the needlessness, the gratuitous damage of delay. No Southern governor, for all his show of defiance, has ever risked arrest by his actions; no Southern government has accommodated itself to change unless cause

[1] *Mississippi: The Closed Society*, by James W. Silver (Harcourt, Brace & World Inc., New York, 1964).

was clearly shown for a belief that resistance would be more costly than surrender.

In the spring of 1963, before the passing of the 1964 Civil Rights Act or the 1965 request by President Johnson for a new law to end voting discrimination in the Deep South, a group of distinguished lawyers and social scientists met at Notre Dame University to consider the racial struggle. The conclusions of the conference remain pressingly pertinent.

... The condition which requires federal attention is the lawlessness that exists in a relatively small number of outlaw communities of the Deep South. This condition does not pose an issue of federalism. Federalism is a system of divided power among governments, and governments are instruments whose whole purpose is to establish an order of law. In these outlaw communities where citizenship rights are flagrantly destroyed, there is no law to respect. We have here, in short, a problem of enforcement ... New and more refined legislative remedies are not required to reach this blatant disregard of rights. To contain and disarm lawlessness, a clear federal presence is required at the first outbreak.

It is not, after all, that the American government lacks the resources or readiness to enforce its will elsewhere. Provided that some manifestation of international communism can be projected, however distantly, as the menace, federal power has intervened – often on the pretext of preventing violence and disorder – without making strenuous efforts to cajole public opinion. Yet it has repeatedly shown itself unwilling to prevent violence and disorder in a little Southern town. A president who ignores calls for federal intervention to stop brutal assaults on American citizens in an American town by American police in open violation of the American Constitution, but who sends 20,000 marines to the Dominican Republic on the pretext of saving American lives, suffers from severe moral astigmatism. Certainly the seriousness of the complaint is lost neither on the peoples of Africa, Asia and Latin America, where such policing takes place, nor on the Negroes and a growing number of whites in the United States, where it does not.

Johnson's Voting Rights Act, passed in the summer of 1965, sent federal officials scurrying through the South to promote and, if necessary, themselves conduct the registration of Negro voters, and their evident resolve persuaded not a few local authorities to co-operate. But the struggle in the South is far from over. Wide wastelands of intransigence remain, and the federal government is going to require more than exhortation and example to plant civil rights there. Furthermore, the formal concession of suffrage is one thing; its exercise, another. The remembrance of Redemption, with its relentless intimidation of registered Negro voters from the polls, will now more and more prod white resistance. Violence may well increase rather than diminish, and neither the eloquence of presidential speech-writers nor a further Congressional Bill is likely to dispel it. Full civil rights exist – have long, through constitutional amendments, existed – in theory; their existence in practice will have to be enforced. Above all, however, the enjoyment and exercise of suffrage by the Southern Negro need not significantly alter his circumstances. The South itself is the poorest part of the country, and the Negro population is the poorest part of the South. Negroes constitute so large a proportion of Southerners that their accession to the local electorate in anything like the strength of their numbers must change the whole complexion of power in the South. Candidates for political office in areas of traditional racism that have recently acquired a multitude of new Negro voters are ceasing to campaign on programmes of specifically racial prejudice. And the new Negro voters themselves, made generally radical by the course of their political struggle, are already in open rebellion at their economic condition. But their poverty is so profound, their want is so pervasive, that an enormous investment of resources – far beyond the steadily shrinking capacity of state power to supply – is required to rescue them. Within the nation as a whole, the Negroes can at best comprise 12 per cent of the electorate, or less than a seventh the size of the white proportion. Is the black vote in the South, therefore, to accomplish as little as the black vote in the North, enjoyed for so long, has done? Is the political emancipation of the Southern Negro to be swallowed by the alienation and destruction of the Northern ghetto?

One does not have to accept the explanations and remedies offered by Barry Goldwater and other, more coherent apostles of an irretrievable past[1] to agree that American society is in a state of dangerous turbulence. Indeed the American city itself, as traditionally known, seems to be dying under the assaults of racial tension and a constant battery of fears. Negro ghettoes are advancing steadily towards the centre, while whites flee in panic to the suburbs; New York City, Chicago, Detroit, Philadelphia are increasingly assuming the design of archery targets, with a business bull's-eye overwhelmingly white, an inner congested ring of black slums, and an outer one of spacious white suburbs escaping ever farther into the

[1] See, for instance, *Suicide of the West*, by James Burnham (Jonathan Cape, 1965).

countryside.)(Whether, indeed, the business centre will itself survive, with the flight of commerce also to the suburbs in pursuit of the white purse, and the advance of Negro control over city government, is already a reasonable speculation. It is hideous but no longer fantastic to suppose a society of white swollen suburbs lavish with services, and cities sinking into abandoned black decay.)

(Inevitably, therefore, though the doctrine of integration enjoys general approval, economic and geographical distances produce general segregation in practice. Undeniably, more and more commercial concerns of importance are finding it prudent to decorate their board-rooms with a Negro executive, just as federal administrations now consider it advisable to dress their windows with a few Negro appointments. But the mass of Negroes remain unaffected by such strides in 'tokenism'. They go to the churches and schools, shops and bars and cinemas in their ghettoes, just as the mass of whites go to the churches and schools, shops and bars and cinemas in theirs) Only a few Negroes who can afford the price of theatre seats or luxury shopping stray into the centre of the cities, while the many whose work takes them there stay no longer than the stretch of their jobs.

(This physical separation of the races is hardly less substantial now than it would be if the government of the United States, like the government of South Africa, were formally committed to a policy of permanent segregation) Nor are the ghetto walls high only on the ground; they rise, unclimbable for all but a very few, in the mind itself. Whites in the United States, much like their English-speaking counterparts in South Africa, see the Negro not as a person but as a problem. The more liberal recognize an injustice pleading for remedy; the less, a threat requiring resistance; most recognize an anxious mixture of both, with the anxiety made the more manageable as the theme is made the more abstract. And this depersonalization, of course, enables them the more easily to segregate principle from personal involvement. Most whites say that they believe in the need for integration, and they believe what they say, but they will soon enough move their children from a school with a rising Negro attendance or themselves move to an all-white suburb from the encroachments of Negro neighbours.)

Naturally the depersonalization works, as it has long done, in reverse, and Negroes see whites not individually but collectively, as a close conspiracy aimed at perpetuating racial dominance. Inexorably, for each race, the stereotype of the other gathers truth: whites correspond more and more to 'the white' who domineers and deceives, promising but never conceding the substance of equality; Negroes correspond more and more to 'the Negro' who will not wait for the gradual processes of law, who is violent and rash and driven not by reasonable aspiration but by racial hatred. The attitude of whites to blacks and of blacks to whites is the exclusive attitude of one nation to another, with the issue between them increasingly that of peace or war.

Most whites reassure themselves with the power of their numbers and the propaganda of constitutional remedy; most Negroes, long persuaded that the American promise has little relevance for them, foster a rage that increasingly sends demonstrators into the streets, increasingly flares into riot and crime. There is a race war, every day more evident, in the sick streets of the cities, in the faces of black men on bar stools and black women standing suddenly still outside shops, in the faces of white taxi-drivers and policemen and white women reading the newspapers on the subway from work. For many of both races violence, direct or vicarious, has become a kind of comfort, a consolation: for the whites, an assertion of their power, a momentary release from anxiety and guilt that can only lead to a greater sense of constriction; for the blacks, some contact across the no man's land of indifference, a defence against total alienation, a flight, if only for a moment too, from the sense of futility and loss.

A sign of what race violence could mean to the American city significantly appeared at the same time that members of the government and senior leaders of the civil rights movement were celebrating the successful passage of Johnson's Voting Rights Act, with its promise to extend through the South the formal equality possessed by Negroes elsewhere in the nation. Suddenly in August 1965 Los Angeles, which had long congratulated itself on its excellent race relations, was swept by five days of Negro revolt that made the rioting of the previous summer in New York or Rochester or Philadelphia seem a mere skirmish in comparison. As usual, the apparent provocation was the arrest of a Negro by white police, and as usual the centre of insurrection was a ghetto, the slum suburb of Watts, 98 per cent Negro, with rotting houses and schools, and with the streets seething under the sullen surface of unemployment. Of the 600,000 Negroes in the city, some 30 per cent were workless,[1] most of them unskilled and many of them illiterate, while almost a third of those under the age of eighteen came from broken homes. The alienation felt by many of these, not only from the traditional Negro leadership of constitutional advance but from any community outside that of race, was increasingly predictable.

The command of rioting was held from the first by gangs of young

[1] *The Economist*, August 21st, 1965, p. 692.

Negroes, whose leaders met at the end of the first day in what they themselves called a 'war council' to distribute assignments and co-ordinate assaults. Their attacks were directed overwhelmingly at white property, and Negro shops, whose owners hastily scrawled 'Blood Brother' on the windows or walls, were generally safe. From street to street the devastation spread, reaching far beyond the ghetto to penetrate the city's commercial centre and, in the end, encompass more than forty square miles. Whites who entered Negro-held territory were commonly attacked, and even those in distant suburbs armed themselves for defence. It was less a riot than, indeed, guerilla warfare of race. The government moved troops into the city, restored a smouldering order, and Americans began assembling the statistics: 34 killed, most of them Negroes; over 800 treated at hospitals (and how many of the injured were not?); some 3,800 arrested; and damages assessed at $175,000,000. The impact on relations between white and black throughout the country was less easy to assess.

Such violence is not, and cannot be, contained within the rim of struggle between white and black Americans alone. It must affect the relations of white with white Americans and black with black, as well as the relations of each with the outside world. The growing violence of American thought, language and action, the mounting acceptance of apocalyptic possibilities, are in significant measure the outcome of racial tension and turbulence within America itself. The racial struggle is a disease of the American system, and the failure to treat it properly and in time may have overwhelming consequences for all humanity.

Certainly there can be no cure, no longer even much relief, in the patent medicines of civil rights laws and civic commissions. While America is economically two segregated races, it must be socially and politically so. And that is why America needs not another dose of reform, but a revolution. The traditional structure of American society, for all the neon signs of rewarded enterprise on its façade, confines Negroes to the basement, and the commandments of free competition keep them there. How many Negroes can reach the board-rooms, when one in five cannot even find unskilled work? How many Negroes are equipped in their decaying slum schools to satisfy the demands of an increasingly technical appetite? How fitted for effort and enterprise at all are those who grow up in rat-infested tenements, along streets of broken bottles and discarded lives, where the buildings cage the very air and the gutter seems the only escape?

If there is any prospect at all of a lasting racial peace in the United States, it rests in the recognition by Negroes and an ever-increasing number of whites, the more vigorous of them among the young, that American society needs reshaping at its roots. After the long grey conformity of the McCarthyite era and its pale aftermath, a surge of discovery and dissent is sweeping not only the whole civil rights movement, but the mainly white universities of America. SNICK and CORE have drawn their activists from white students and teachers as well as from Negro ones, and among the jailed in Mississippi towns or the assaulted in Alabama streets have been white lawyers and doctors, clergymen and housewives searching not just for a method of furthering Negro rights but for the outline of a new society. As Abolitionism a century ago was a movement of emancipation not from slavery alone, but, inevitably, if often unsuspectedly, from the clutch of plantation feudalism as well, so the civil rights struggle today is and must be concerned with an emancipation from poverty and the totalitarianism of wealth.

As has frequently been observed, the traditional American commitment is to liberty and not equality. Indeed, many of those who shout loudest for liberty are most passionate in their opposition to the demands of meaningful equality. For them, the American way of life is precisely the freedom to be or become unequal, to rise through individual talent and endeavour above those whom incapacity or indolence or indifference leaves in weakness and want. This frontier mentality seems increasingly out of place in a massive industrial democracy. After all, the majority of Americans, and so the majority of voters, do not rise to the ranks of the rich and powerful. They require some assurance against ruthless free enterprise, against unemployment and sickness and the terrifying vulnerability of old age. They demand and they get state education, subsidized housing, social security, and all the restraints on the rich, like graduated income tax and death duties, to pay for them. But they, too, have been seized by the traditional commitment, and see equality not as the prerequisite, but as the denial of liberty. They are not poor themselves and they hope that they or their children will enjoy the opportunity to become rich. They accept the struggle and insist only on mitigating the consequences of defeat. It is from among those who are already poor and who see how poverty, like wealth, propagates itself, that the cry comes for equality, as the essence of liberty. Just how many Americans are poor, so that they cannot eat and clothe and shelter themselves properly, or compete with any confidence in the struggle for success, is as much the subject of dispute as is the definition of what is proper. Most estimates vary between a fifth and third of the nation. But all estimates agree that poverty encompasses the vast majority of Negroes.

It is a crucial factor. The white poor are overwhelmingly unrebellious.

They have accepted the traditional commitment. They see their defeat as somehow their own fault. But the black poor are different. They have been segregated from the traditional commitment for so long that they see it as a white and not as a necessarily American – let alone, human – one. Furthermore, they do not see themselves, as do the white poor, a helpless minority, bound by natural allegiance to the dominant values of their race. Their own racial awareness, producing a sense of independent existence inside America and a sense of identity with a coloured world outside, gives them the rage and the self-assurance to rebel. They believe that they can safely be neither ignored nor denied any longer. And they press their claims not merely by a political cohesion that the two-party electoral system invests with disproportionate power, but by open violence, the pressure of the streets.

Yet the bulk of the American nation, still loyal to the traditional commitment, will not give them the equality they demand. It will try even further to mitigate the consequences of defeat, so as to keep the supply of votes flowing through the customary channels, and reduce recruitment to the violence of despair. No one can discourse more eloquently or blandly than can that representative of the national consensus, President Johnson, on the need for building a Great Society at home, with the elimination of poverty and ignorance, unemployment and the corruptions of want. Funds have been extracted from Congress for a multitude of new projects, from the Anti-Poverty Programme – mainly aimed, through the Office of Economic Opportunity, at vocational training of the young – to Urban Renewal, the rescuing of the American city, by expenditure on housing and public services, from its dangerous decay. But the provision is far too small and far too slow for the challenge that faces it. For every young Negro trained to an accessible job, many arrive untrained and jobless on the streets. And for every home snatched from the rats and the crumbling walls, many succumb helplessly to squalor. The very cures are questionably better than the diseases. The festering vivacity of tenements becomes the anonymous silence of the concrete apartment blocks. Instead of being spread on the ground, segregation is raised in the air; it brings the sense of an American community no nearer. Schools are rebuilt or provided with new equipment, for the teaching of segregated children more efficiently. White America sees that something is being done, and its concern dozes off, till the next mass outbreak of violence jerks it awake. Is it so surprising that welfare officials, bustling through the ghetto to dispense new benefits, are assaulted and robbed?

The Negro rejects the whole system of makeshift mitigation. If the past has made it difficult for him to achieve equality of results by liberty of struggle, then the present must compensate by providing him with privileged treatment or an end to the traditional struggle itself. Either way, what he demands is an upheaval in American values; not a Negro, but a national revolution. And if he does not get it, he intends, in the fury of his despair, to wreck American society. Unlike the beleaguered Southern white defiance, he feels the assurance of the world outside and the new power of his race; he works on the scale not of the small town, but of the country and the age. And where there is so much hatred, there is not much room for fear.

White America, however, has neither the will nor the available resources for the revolution he demands. And its lack of both is tightly connected with the view not only of itself but of its place and function in the world. It is no accident that the Negro rebellion is exciting, and itself becoming steadily more involved in, a reappraisal of American foreign policy. In the year 1965 the gross national product of the United States reached some $675,600 million, and the Federal Administrative Budget for the fiscal year June 30th, 1965, to July 1st, 1966, was some $106,400 million. Expenditure listed for Education, Health, Labour, Welfare, Housing and Community Development totalled $10,800 million, representing just over 10 per cent of the budget and something like 1·6 per cent of the 1965 gross national product. In contrast, National Defence took $56,600 million, over half the total budget, and over 8 per cent of the 1965 gross national product. The welfare allowance constituted a fifth of military expenditure, therefore, and little more than twice the money allocated for the Vietnam war alone ($4,700 million). And when the time came to vote funds for the financial year 1966–7, the promises of a large rise in allocation for building the Great Society fell over the demands of the mounting conflict in Vietnam. With the gross national product estimated to reach $722,000 million in 1966, and the budget allowing for an increase in expenditure to $112,800 million, the listed welfare items would absorb an additional $2,100 million (to $12,900 million), making the overall proportion of the budget some 11·4 per cent. Spending on National Defence, however, would mount $3,900 million, to $60,500 million, or over half the total budget again, with expenditure on the Vietnam war alone estimated at $10,300 million (or over three-quarters of the welfare allotments).[1]

[1] *The Budget of the U.S. Government for the Fiscal Year ending June 30th, 1967* (U.S. Government Printing Office, 1966). Estimate of gross national product from the Economic Report of the President transmitted to the Congress in January 1966.

The containment of revolution is an expensive business, and it cannot be conducted with any real prospect of success – if success is, indeed, ultimately possible at all, without satisfying the desires that make revolution so formidable – simultaneously at home and abroad. The Negro rebellion cannot effectively be defeated without an investment of national resources so vast that policing the world for the American commitment is out of the question. The rebellion in South Vietnam alone (and it is not likely long to remain the sole source of serious conflict) cannot be effectively defeated without an investment of American resources so vast that purchasing the allegiance of the Negro for the American commitment is out of the question. Yet which objective is to be pursued? The probability is both, however ruinous the cost, or neither. For the domestic and foreign commitments are inextricably intertwined in the present overwhelming consensus of white America. If the world is not made safe for American values, how safe can the values be within America? And if the values which have made America so great are surrendered at home, how secure can America be in the world at large?

The consensus, like the mass of white Americans it represents, wants a policy of moderation on both fronts: mitigation, not repression or eradication, of Negro discontent; the stalemate of limited warfare on the frontiers of revolution abroad. It assumes, still, a fundamental infallibility, a belief that no success is beyond the exertions of so rich and powerful a nation as the United States, and its leaders, in their repeated resolutions, confirm the confidence. But what will follow the inevitable encounter with failure? The refusal of the Negro to be satisfied with the formalities of constitutional advance is already moving some whites from the policy of mitigation to one of repression; an inability to contain the revolution in South Vietnam by local warfare has led the government – so far with the allegiance of most white Americans – to extend the fighting, with the bombardment of North Vietnam and a rising risk of conflict with China. The 'hawks' of international conduct are unlikely to leave the 'doves' of domestic policy undisturbed. Not the last victims of war are the appeal of moderation and the tolerance of dissent. And any increase in white hostility to Negro demands is likely to strengthen the pressures for a more aggressive posture to revolution abroad. The apostles of repression at home and the apostles of repression in the world at large are generally the same people. The force of one sentiment will rally support to the other.

But the inescapable failure of the one may also in the end promote the failure of the other. For on the other side of the present consensus is an agreement, too, between the apostles of fundamental change at home and the apostles of fundamental change abroad. Those who recognize the primary need to drain the swampland of poverty that is Negro America recognize too the agony and danger breeding in the swampland of poverty that is the non-white world. (They are not reassured by the workings of a system which displays stock exchange jitters at the rumour of peace talks over Vietnam and the possibility of diminishing defence expenditure.) Those who rebel against the violence used to crush pacific Negro demonstrations of dissent at home rebel too against the violence used to crush popular risings abroad, even when this is done in the sanctified cause of containing communism. Those especially concerned with making American foreign policy rational and democratic, support the new Negro movement, in the belief that a powerful Negro community inside the United States will ensure at last a real American commitment to the cause of the poor and denied everywhere. They see that a nation can promote equality so as to fortify, not weaken, liberty. Such, after all, is the only proper safeguard of the American dream. The choice is not either the totalitarianism of individual struggle or the totalitarianism of individual submission. The choice may be of a different, more meaningful democracy, a new economic Bill of Rights which a new adventurous America will revolt to produce, for all and not merely American humanity.

A large and significant portion of American public opinion is no longer docile, and perhaps no achievement of the Negro revolt in the last decade is greater than this. It was from among the civil rights workers in SNICK that the first important demonstrations against American policy in South Vietnam were mounted; it was students, in the main from universities where the civil rights movement had long been active, who led the massive protest rally of April 1965 in Washington against President Johnson's policy of escalating intervention in South-east Asia; it was the same universities which seethed with opposition in May to American intervention in the Dominican Republic. There can be little doubt that the increasing opposition of influential politicians and diplomats to the course of American foreign policy owes much to the public ferment which the new militants of the civil rights movement first raised. And this new international commitment was paralleled by the activities of the Negro leaders themselves. While powerful American newspapers and magazines were recounting black atrocities against whites in the Congo, to explain American participation in the Belgian paratroop drop over rebel territory, the heads of the Negro civil rights organizations jointly approached the President to reconsider America's support of Tshombe.

Increasingly Martin Luther King and other Negro leaders have promoted public pressure against America's economic links with, and ultimate diplomatic support for, the government of white supremacy in South Africa.

The increasing identification of coloured America with the coloured world has implications which neither white America nor the white world can reasonably expect to escape. The Moynihan Report acknowledged one aspect.

It was in no way a matter of chance that the nonviolent tactics and philosophy of the [Negro] movement, as it began in the South, were consciously adapted from the techniques by which the Congress Party undertook to free the Indian nation from British colonial rule. It was not a matter of chance that the Negro movement caught fire in America at just that moment when the nations of Africa were gaining their freedom. Nor is it merely incidental that the world should have fastened its attention on events in the United States at a time when the possibility that the nations of the world will divide along color lines seems suddenly not only possible, but even imminent.

(Such racist views have made progress within the Negro American community itself – which can hardly be expected to be immune to a virus that is endemic in the white community. The Black Muslim doctrines, based on total alienation from the white world, exert a powerful influence. On the far left, the attraction of Chinese Communism can no longer be ignored.)

It is clear that what happens in America is being taken as a sign of what can, or must, happen in the world at large. The course of world events will be profoundly affected by the success or failure of the Negro American revolution in seeking the peaceful assimilation of the races in the United States.[1]

It is also clear, however, that what happens in the world at large is being taken as a sign of what can, or must, happen in America. Negroes are less and less indifferent to the exercise of white suzerainty, whether American or not, over the coloured peoples of three continents. Harlem and Watts and the Black Belt of the South see the dispatch of American marines to the Dominican Republic and, above all, the American military effort in Vietnam rather differently on the whole from the way that the white

[1] P. 1.

suburbanites of Connecticut and Illinois do. It was not a matter of chance either that one of the eight Negroes recently elected to the lower house of the Georgia legislature publicly associated himself with an anti-war statement issued by the Student Nonviolent Coordinating Committee. The Georgia legislature in consequence denied him his seat, and African diplomats at the United Nations honoured him at a luncheon. This spreading deafness within the civil rights movement to the demands of pure patriotism has already alienated some whites who gave their support in the past to the struggle against racial segregation. The militant Negroes are quick to reply that such whites understand neither the content nor the purpose of the Negro revolt.

The protests and initiatives of this revolt are likely to grow in number and effect. The ghettoes of the North are being daily strengthened in the force of their disaffection by the rising political influence of the Negro millions still in the South. The Voting Rights Act has been adding to the electorate a new Negro multitude, whose leadership and temper have been made revolutionary by the long and violent intransigence of white authority. Any further intransigence, any display of timidity or caution or indifference by the federal government, will only increase the impatience of the black South for a different America. Any further advance in electoral power will increase the political pressures throughout the country for a different America. And the prospect of an alliance between the black poor and the white poor for the achievement of equality, if wildly improbable still in the North, has a Southern precedent at least in the populism of the last century. It is the one chance, if seemingly now a slight one, of extending the Negro revolution beyond the militants of race.

But alone or in some new alliance, the Negro revolution is unlikely to be deflected from its course. And the course involves a new commitment by America no less to the world at large than to itself. Certainly, the abandonment of the old standards becomes relentlessly more and more vital and urgent. The policy of white America towards the poor nonwhite peoples of the world is as purblind and clumsy as its policy towards the poor non-white population at home. There is racial violence in the fields of Africa and Asia as well as in the streets of America itself, and the struggle is as likely to be won by planes in the world beyond as by police in New York or Chicago. If white America as a whole does not see this, black America does. And so in the end, perhaps, the Negro may yet save white America from itself.

5

The White World of London and Moscow

The racism so marked in Britain today that it has become a major influence on the main political parties is recent only in its domestic application. No society but one with an assumption of racial superiority would have conducted and countenanced the slave trade so long, or have acquired and ruled so vast a coloured empire with such self-assurance. Indeed, this assumption developed into a vested interest: for the classes involved in the slave trade, through shipping, mercantile and plantation interests; simultaneously and long afterwards, for the classes, commercial and administrative, involved in empire.

The powerful lobby of West Indian planters worked through and on the British parliament to prevent any action against the slave trade, providing and paying pamphleteers to produce a constant stream of racist propaganda. And if in the end the lobby was defeated, this was at the very least as much through the efforts of the new industrialists, aggressively pursuing the morality of free trade, and the activity of slave-owning competitors, as through the awakened conscience of the Church and liberal opinion. The classes involved in colonial commerce and administration – including the new industrialists, whose dedication to free trade did not exclude captive sources of raw material and markets for manufactures – then constituted a powerful lobby for imperial consolidation, if not expansion, and steadily promoted the myths of racial superiority by rationalizing rule as a necessary service of civilization. The belief that Britain had everything to teach and nothing to learn was for many the same as the belief that the British were inherently superior to their subjects, a superiority which nature had circumspectly confirmed by providing the distinction of colour.

That there has generally been a group, if a relatively small one, of Christian and liberal leaders who have taken their principles seriously, cannot be denied. Missionaries and meddlesome philanthropists denounced the greed of charter companies and the cruelty of white settlers, but seldom the value, indeed the necessity, of British rule. Their belief, too, was that they had everything to teach – whether by the gospels or by science and sound government – and nothing to learn. If they did not believe in racial superiority themselves, they propagated a sense of cultural superiority that encouraged others to suppose a racist reason. They offered not the horizontal but the vertical, not the different but the better, and the generality transferred the scale to race.

It was this cultural assumption that certainly assisted in distinguishing the treatment of coloured colonial subject from white one. No Afrikaner, despite his antiquated religious enthusiasm, his rather coarse rural ways, and his eccentric dress and language, was regarded by the British with the same disparagement as the most sophisticated Hindu metaphysician. The Afrikaner was, for all his straying, a European, and European civilization was the highest attainment of the mind. The British allowed, both during and after the Boer War, a respect for the Afrikaner insistence on the right of self-government that they cheerfully denied the Asian, the Arab and the African.

Yet cultural prejudice was only a part of colour prejudice, reinforcing and in its turn being reinforced by it. The alien is unsettling: who is not, against all reason, wary in the presence of an albino or an epileptic? Reverence or contempt is a natural form of defence, a way of dealing with the mysterious, and it is power that frequently determines the choice. The American Indians received the *conquistadores* initially with awe; the *conquistadores* despised the American Indians for their very vulnerability. When Europe first encountered the Chinese empire, she was deferential; when she saw that she was stronger, she became contemptuous. The weak demanded disparagement for their weakness; the strong, respect for their strength. Yellow civilization was inferior because yellow power succumbed so easily to the white. Indeed, 2,000 years ago the Romans found the Britons inherently inferior, and Cicero advised his friend Atticus against buying any of them as slaves because 'they are so utterly stupid and incapable of learning.'[1]

Racial arrogance and aggression inevitably fed on themselves. The capture of Africans for slavery itself promoted the belief that Africans were meant for the slave trade. When the Portuguese first encountered the Kingdom of the Bakongo, they treated its citizens with the respect due to a people of untested strength; within a few years, they were classing them as property. The very possession of empire had a profound effect on the British. All those who visited the colonies at some time or other as soldiers or civil servants, traders or tourists – comprising with their

[1] Quoted in 'Race and Culture', by Michel Leiris, *The Race Question in Modern Science* (UNESCO, 1956), p. 111.

families an extensive area of the British population – experienced and sustained the contrasts of power: the firm, orderly, intelligible white government, and the sprawling, disorderly, unintelligible mass of coloured subjects. The very fortification of rule, by investing government with grandeur and infallibility, elevated the rulers as it debased the ruled. The segregated club, where whites could be humiliatingly human without being seen and so despised, became a symbol of specifically racial superiority; no coloured, whatever his culture or – for the British, more telling – his wealth, could attain to membership. The coloured had to be inferior, and made to appear inferior, or where was the excuse for his subjection?

To the support of the colour bar, and the doctrine of racial superiority, sex brought a feverish vigour. A traditional puritanism reinforced the worldly awareness that one thing generally led to another, and that the levelling processes of sex might soon enough produce the toppling of all distinctions. Indeed, since vice was supposed to be more enjoyable than virtue, and sexual prowess a sign of the more primitive mind, white men and women alike stressed the sexual superiority of the coloured races, so making miscegenation both a sin and a debasement by the very heralding of its attractions. While the French, the Portuguese and the Spanish in their varying degrees accommodated race rule to sexual democracy, at least for the male, the British, less self-assured perhaps, and more scrupulous of scriptural sin, made the sexual separation of races a central myth of their rule.

Imperialism was immensely rewarding – it would have been neither promoted nor defended otherwise – and psychologically so, no less than financially. To the rich and powerful already, it gave riches and power without precedent; to the adventurous in commerce and the skilful in the civil service, it offered ample opportunity for advancement, and eventual recruitment to the ranks of the ruling class; but perhaps its most considerable impact was on those – the vast majority – who were, and were likely to remain, the ruled of Britain. By moving to the colonies, an artisan or clerk became an aristocrat – by virtue of his race alone, the unquestioned superior of coloured wealth and culture. The son of a teacher, clergyman, minor army officer, with little prospect but that of a genteel poverty in Britain, could become a district commissioner in the colonies, with an all but absolute command over thousands of subjects. Even a soldier or policeman of the ranks entered into a new authority and splendour with colonial service. But empire conferred distinction equally on those at home. The lowliest Briton felt – and was encouraged to feel – himself the heir and upholder of racial achievement. If there were some who saw in their own condition a mirroring of colonial subjugation, there were many who took comfort from the belief that however poor and degraded they were, the coloured were poorer still and more degraded. The working class in Britain, as elsewhere in Europe, was not shaken by passion for colonial causes. If a Labour government in the exhausted aftermath of the Second World War put the Indian empire into liquidation – and a Conservative government would have found it impossible for long to act otherwise – it was also a Labour government that contained African disaffection with force and imprisoned or exiled recalcitrant colonial leaders. The basic bipartisanship of colonial policy was a common response first to the enjoyment of imperial power and then to the discovery of how prohibitive would be the cost of attempting to preserve it.

The surrender of empire was as much a trauma for the working and lower middle classes as for the long established wielders of authority and wealth. If anything, indeed, the traditional oligarchs escaped the greater sense of injury. The process of decolonization was in the main conciliatory enough to leave investments intact, and however reduced abroad, power survived at home. The working class, and the more socially restless and demanding lower middle class, had no such compensations. But most Britons suffered in varying degrees from bewilderment, and if few expressed their outrage, many felt a deep disappointment and even disbelief. It was the sheer disbelief, perhaps, that more than any other response led to the frantic adventure of Suez in 1956. Britain simply could not have lost the power to deal with a bumptious coloured people when her interests demanded it. (A snap plebiscite on the invasion, before its failure became inescapably clear, would probably have upheld the government with a massive majority, produced by working-class voters eager to teach the 'wogs' a lesson rather than by the morally distracted middle class.) But she had, humiliatingly, lost the power, and the realization led to a deep racial embitterment among many Britons.

Furthermore, while decolonization was proceeding abroad, the coloured population at home was rising with immigration from the Commonwealth, attracted by the jobs and higher wages available in Britain. The overwhelming majority came to settle, arriving with their families or sending for them as soon as they had saved sufficient for the fares, and inevitably the bulk of settlement took place in industrial areas, where housing shortages, hard-pressed social services, and economic insecurity already existed. The net inflow reflected the demand for labour: it rose from 42,700 in 1955 to 46,850 in 1956; then fell slightly to 42,400 in 1957; dropped to 29,850 and 21,600 in 1958 and 1959, years of recession; and then rose to 57,700 in the more prosperous 1960.[1] But many white workers saw only the threat of competition for jobs in lean times, and the deflection of housing, educational and medical facilities from themselves.

The British have, on the whole, always resented foreigners, in bland disregard of their own inclination to settle in other people's countries. From 1871 to 1931, a net outflow of well over 3,000,000 nourished the rest of the world, and especially the empire, with foreigners from Britain;[2] but that did not make foreigners arriving to nourish Britain herself any more welcome. The persecuted French Protestants of the seventeenth century in their thousands, and the famine-fleeing Irish of the nineteenth century in their hundreds of thousands, encountered immediate hostility, especially among those who felt their livelihood threatened by the influx.[3] But the politicians, who represented in large measure the commercial classes, and were presiding over Britain's industrial supremacy, supported the free movement of labour no less than of goods. It would not last. With industrial rivalry came demands for protection, and with the flight of Jews from persecution in Russia and Eastern Europe – some 120,000 came to Britain between 1875 and 1914 – there were politicians who decided that a shrewd investment in racism would produce electoral dividends.

One Conservative M.P., Major – soon to be Sir – Evans Gordon, spoke in 1902 for immediate immigration control with sentiments that would feel happily at home in the Smethwick of the 'sixties.

> Not a day passes but English families are ruthlessly turned out to make room for foreign invaders ... Rents are raised 50 to 100 per cent and a house which formerly contained a couple of families living in comparative decency is made to contain four or five families living under conditions which baffle description ... It is only a matter of time before the population becomes entirely foreign ... The rates are burdened with the education of thousands of children of foreign parents ... Among the thousands who come here there is a considerable proportion of bad characters, and the competition with home industries extends to burglary and other cognate crimes.

[1] The official figures include a small proportion of white Maltese.
[2] Royal Commission on Population, 1949.
[3] See chapters 5 and 6 on 'Politics and the Alien', in *Immigration and Race in British Politics*, by Paul Foot (Penguin Books, 1965).

By 1905, the Conservative government, wildly searching for an issue able to turn the Liberal tide, had rushed a Bill restricting immigration through parliament. Joseph Chamberlain, the Birmingham protectionist, revealed the objective in addressing himself to the working class: 'It is on the unskilled labourer that this immigrant produces the greatest mischief.' The Liberals won the 1906 election triumphantly none the less; but at least one prominent Conservative campaigner for immigration control increased his majority against the national trend, and the new Liberal government, while softening the effects of the new law, did not repeal it.

Then, in the hysteria produced by the imminence of war in 1914, parliament passed, without division, an emergency Aliens Restriction Act, which gave to the Home Secretary sweeping powers to prohibit immigrants and deport aliens. By early 1916, the Liberal government had repatriated some 21,000 people of German or Austrian birth, and interned 32,000. Hostility to aliens, encompassing a shrill anti-Semitism, made permanent the main provisions of the war-time restriction law. Only the Labour Party produced firm opposition in parliament; but, when given power, administered the law with little change.

Few immigrants entered Britain during the 'twenties, and only in 1935–40 did the overall figure rise to some 18,000 a year. But much to the consternation of British governments, and especially the Conservative apostles of empire, other countries began to follow Britain's example in the depression years, and recent British arrivals in Canada and Australia met with mounting antagonism. Some 500,000 British emigrants, indeed, returned home during the 'thirties, and parliament established an Empire Settlement Board to try and reverse so abnormal a flow.

Little by little even the long loudly proclaimed recognition of the right to political asylum gave ground before the agitation against aliens and dangerous revolutionaries. A Labour government in 1929 refused asylum to Trotsky and proudly announced that it had naturalized fewer Russians than its Conservative predecessor had done. The rising clamour of anti-Semitism in the 'thirties led to tight immigration control, and Labour members of parliament, always more compassionate in opposition, complained repeatedly that Jewish refugees were being sent back from the ports to persecution in Germany. Certainly some measure of responsibility for the casualties of the concentration camps must attach to a British government which all but sealed off one passage of escape.

Labour shortages after the Second World War led to the recruitment of Poles and other Europeans for British industry, and in 1951 there were 429,000 aliens in Britain compared with 239,000 in 1939. But Britain's burgeoning industry needed labour, and with her European competitors taking immigrant workers in their millions from the available reservoirs of Eastern Europe and Southern Italy, Britain at last turned to her empire. It was a reversal of policy, but not one requiring formal ratification. All subjects of British rule were supposed to be citizens of the empire and entitled to move freely within its confines. A Commonwealth country like Australia, committed to keeping its population white, could and did prohibit free immigration; but Britain herself, for so long an exporter of people, carefully sustained the right of unhindered movement between the 'mother country' and its Commonwealth associates or colonies. From 1948 West Indians began arriving in Britain, to be followed after 1954 by significant numbers of Indians and Pakistanis. For the first time, Britain was acquiring a substantial coloured community.

Labour-hungry employers welcomed the change, and it was among British workers that serious resentment first appeared. The entry of coloured labour into a particular occupation was seen as symbolizing its social decline, and some white workers who felt their status threatened, like busmen and railwaymen, agitated, and even called strikes, against coloured recruitment. (Others, fearful that coloured immigration would be used by employers to depress wages, were somewhat mollified by the drift of the immigrants themselves into organized trade unionism and careful propaganda against discrimination by the senior trade union leadership.) The social sensibilities of the upper working and lower middle classes were disturbed by the arrival in their residential areas of intruders from apparently so low a class who crowded into the available property and whose attitudes to dress, diet, and noise were disconcertingly different.

To the customary British distrust of strangers was added the traditional disparagement of colour. Sociologists investigating the character of prejudice against the new immigrants discovered a sediment of racial conceit among whites of all classes, produced by the relics of imperial myth in school textbook and story; the acquired arrogance of many who had served in the empire as soldiers, technicians or minor administrators; the derogatory – often comic – treatment of Negroes in earlier fiction and current American films; the commonly accepted standards of beauty and proper behaviour.[1] The accumulated image of the coloured, especially when possessed of Negroid features, was of someone culturally primitive, highly sexed and easily aroused to violence, generally lacking in

[1] See, for instance, *Dark Strangers*, by Sheila Patterson (Tavistock Publications, 1963), pp. 230–35; and Dr Michael Banton's 'Beware of Strangers' in the *Listener* (British Broadcasting Corporation, April 3rd, 1958).

self-control, lazy and irresponsible, though often with athletic or artistic talent and an appealing simplicity.

Hostile responses were nourished by local newspapers in areas with a high proportion of coloured immigrants. Crime or sexual incidents involving coloureds were reported with stress – not infrequently through headlines – on the colour of the participants. And if the national press seldom carried similar reports, its treatment of world events, and especially of the clash between white and black in Africa, contributed significantly to a contempt for black culture and conduct. Newspapers of the unregenerate right staunchly defended the interests of white settler communities, representing African rebellion against colonial rule in the most lurid light and proclaiming as soon as occasion allowed the incompetence and tyranny of African self-government. Atrocity accounts were in the overwhelming main racially selective. A reading of most British newspapers in the 'fifties would have led the otherwise uninformed to suppose a more violent and ubiquitous political police in Ghana than in Portugal, a more ferocious despotism in Nasser's Egypt than in French Algeria. And where the atrocious was not immediately available, the picturesque – in the mood of Technicolor adventure films – served to distinguish Africa as the home of noble wild animals and savage tribes.

The disfigurements of propaganda were not excited by racial solidarity alone. The newly independent Asian and African states not only opposed imperial rule and demanded swifter decolonization, but tended to assume a neutralist position between East and West. India was derided as hypocritical and ungrateful for assuming a freedom of manoeuvre in international affairs that aimed to increase her sources of aid and promote a lessening of cold war tension. The Ghanaian government was attacked less because of its preventive detention laws, which it had borrowed after all from British colonial practice, than because of its warming relationship with the communist world. The imprisonment of political opponents in pro-Western Pakistan or Jordan received scant attention from the British press. Inevitably, too, the growing representation and strength of Afro-Asian non-alignment in the United Nations led to a souring of British support, especially in the right-wing press and the Conservative Party, for the Organization. The part played by the U.N. in casting international opprobrium on the 1956 Suez adventure of Britain and France rankled deep, and since the United States and the Soviet Union were too powerful for offence, the hoses of anger and frustration were turned on the Afro-Asian rabble. As the ranks of the decolonized increased, so too did British discontent with the very basis of U.N. representation. Newspapers and commentators on radio and television wondered why a country of wealth, power and a population of fifty million like Britain should have equal representation with an African state of poverty, weakness and a million or so inhabitants. The memory of imperial grandeur had not faded so far as to provoke questions of why India, with a population eight times as great, should have the same single vote as Britain in the General Assembly, or why – if wealth and power were the major considerations – the United States and the Soviet Union should not have several votes each to Britain's one.

In this thickening dusk of racial propaganda and international disappointment, the British public took less and less kindly to the steadily swelling coloured community in its midst. Complaints multiplied that the coloured was not assimilating easily, but producing provocative ghettoes in the cities and promoting squalor and disease. The coloured was, of course, unable 'to profit from those devices of protective mimicry which enable immigrants from, say, Europe to conceal their strangeness at closer and closer range, and thus actually to lose it the more quickly.'[1] With their shrill visibility, the coloured immigrants were easy to identify, as the increase in their numbers was easy to mark.

Already in 1950 Cyril Osborne from the Conservative back benches in parliament was demanding 'separate figures for coloured immigration' from the government, and in 1952 he initiated his campaign for control of Commonwealth immigration. At first he was regarded as an embarrassing crank by the parliamentary leadership, but Conservative sentiment in the country responded to his persistence, and in 1955 the Central Council of the Conservative and Unionist Associations called, by a narrow majority, for the application to Commonwealth immigrants of the laws against aliens. In 1956 a nation-wide survey conducted by Michael Banton found that half those interviewed would consider it wrong for a landlady to reject a tenant on grounds of colour; but a survey by John Darragh in the same year, of 1,000 people in Birmingham, many of them living in 'immigrant areas', revealed that only 15 would accept a coloured in their homes as a lodger, while 985 would refuse. The closer that white and coloured approached each other in locality and class, the more intense was the assumed competition for housing, employment and social services; the more provocative did the contrast in customs appear; the nearer the prospect of social degradation seemed to draw; and the more rapidly prejudice spread. There were Conservatives ready to note this, and see

[1] 'A Sociological Report', by Judith Henderson in *Coloured Immigrants in Britain*. An investigation carried out by the Institute of Race Relations (O.U.P., 1960), p. 109.

an unprecedented opportunity to gather working-class votes. The recession of 1956-8 produced a sense of insecurity in the labour force, and though coloured workers were frequently the first dismissed as the most recently hired, their presence was now seen as a menace to white employment. The sight of coloureds queueing at labour exchanges in search of work excited substantial resentment, especially in areas of little local industry and generally high unemployment.

The far right of British politics, battered by the war and the disaster of Nazism, soon battened on to colour as a natural food for propaganda and recruitment. Sir Oswald Mosley's Union Movement, formed in 1948, with its periodical *Action*, concentrated on areas where the proportion of coloured immigrants was high, and where slum housing bred frustration and resentment. Its efforts were at last rewarded in 1958 at Nottingham and Notting Hill, London, where sporadic race rioting pock-marked the summer and autumn. Severe action by the courts – nine youths received prison sentences of four years each for having attacked coloureds in Notting Hill – helped to stop the violence; but only energetic efforts by the local authorities, as in Nottingham, crusted racist sentiment with the prospect of social relief. Few local authorities, however, bestirred themselves, and the government showed no sign of even considering steps to encourage integration.

Colour prejudice steadily increased. In March 1955, a Gallup Poll revealed that 79 per cent considered it wrong to refuse to work with coloureds, while 12 per cent considered it right, and 9 per cent replied 'Don't know'. Three years later, only 50 per cent of respondents in London agreed that coloureds from the Commonwealth should be allowed to compete for jobs in Britain 'on equal terms with people born here,' while 36 per cent said 'No', and 14 per cent, 'Don't know'. Despite vacancies, the bus companies in Bristol and Coventry refused to take coloured labour, in deference to the views of the local white transport workers. The recruitment of coloured busmen in Birmingham, West Bromwich, Wolverhampton, Nottingham and Newcastle-upon-Tyne led to widely publicized opposition from white workers, and in several instances to the establishment of an informal quota.

Cyril Osborne began gathering substantial support on the Conservative back benches for his campaign against coloured immigration, and in October 1958 Lord (later Sir Alec Douglas-) Home, Minister of State for Commonwealth Relations, announced that 'curbs will have to be put on the unrestricted flow of immigrants to Britain from the West Indies.' The Conservative Party Conference later that month called for control of

Commonwealth immigration, and when the leadership, concerned with international repercussions, took no action, the propaganda of the anti-colour lobby redoubled. The 1959 elections sent to parliament several new Conservative members, especially from the industrial Midlands, who immediately added their voices to the call for immigration control, and new organizations like the Birmingham Immigration Control Association, founded in October 1960, produced a constant stream of pressure on public opinion. Fears of legislation to bar them helped to excite more coloureds than ever before to enter Britain – 136,400 in 1961, compared with 57,700 in 1960 and 21,600 in 1959;[1] the organizations of the far right, joined in 1960 by the foundation of the fascist British National Party, intensified their efforts; and the election-time boom shrivelled into recession. Conservative candidates at by-elections began concentrating on the immigration issue, and at the end of October 1961 the Conservative government announced that 'legislation will be introduced to control the immigration to the United Kingdom of British subjects from other parts of the Commonwealth and to give powers for the expulsion of immigrants convicted of criminal offences.'

Race prejudice, however, was by no means restricted to the Conservative benches. The very first Commons debate on coloured immigration was instigated by a Labour member in 1954, who complained of the immigrant inflow and excused Sheffield dance hall proprietors for imposing a colour bar. While some members pressed the government for measures to ease integration, others insisted instead on the need for control. In April 1958 three Labour members provoked a debate on the control of Commonwealth immigration, and with the Notting Hill riots later in the year, others – including the member for the Notting Hill area – called for speedy legislation. But the Labour leadership, shaken by the race rioting and still unpersuaded by the arguments of mere electoral advantage, considered it imperative to oppose control, and in September the party declared: 'We are firmly convinced that any form of British legislation limiting Commonwealth immigration into this country would be disastrous to our status in the Commonwealth and to the confidence of Commonwealth peoples.'

The Immigration Bill of the Conservative government, published at the beginning of November 1961, effectively prohibited the entry of Commonwealth immigrants who did not have a Ministry of Labour voucher, and classified vouchers into three types: 'A' for those with a specific job promised by a specific employer; 'B' for those with certain

[1] The figures include a small number of Maltese.

special qualifications, like doctors, nurses and teachers; and 'C' for un-skilled workers without the assurance of specific employment. The grant of 'C' vouchers would vary, 'subject to any limit which the government from time to time consider necessary'. Courts could recommend the deportation of Commonwealth immigrants resident in Britain for less than five years who were found guilty of a crime punishable by imprison-ment; and the period necessary for registration as a British citizen was extended from one to five years. Symbolically, Cyril Osborne was knighted in the same year for his services.

The racist character of the Bill emerged clear through the thicket of equivocations. Only the Irish Republic, outside the Commonwealth but with her citizens granted unrestricted entry none the less, rivalled the coloured Commonwealth countries as a source of unskilled labour for Britain. The British economy, burdened by the steady growth in the numbers of the unproductive aged, by the long neglect of efficient modernization, and by a generally wasteful use of the available labour supply, needed immigrants from somewhere to meet the demands of industrial expansion. And so the government excluded from the new restrictions the whites from the Irish Republic, on the pretext that a policing of the frontier was impractical. The Bill also carefully dis-criminated between skilled and unskilled Commonwealth immigrants, for after years of relative indifference to the training and adequate reim-bursement of professionals and technicians, Britain was not merely failing to produce enough skills for her requirements, but was losing much of those she possessed in emigration. The National Health Service alone was increasingly dependent on doctors and nurses from the coloured Com-monwealth, and no government could face with equanimity an end to such supplies. Britain thus declared her intention of taking as many skilled coloureds from the Commonwealth as she could get, although skills were precisely what the coloured Commonwealth needed, along-side the opportunity to send unskilled workers to Britain (some hopefully for training and return one day, others at least for the subsidy of money orders to relatives). That Britain proposed to continue exploiting the coloured poor of her one-time empire was injury enough. That she should ceaselessly stress the need for the urgent economic development of the same coloured poor, and proclaim her petty programme of aid as signi-ficantly assisting, added sanctimonious insult.

Labour attacked the Bill as nakedly racist, and was joined not only by the Liberals but by a small group of Conservatives, most of whom still attached an imperial mystique to the Commonwealth. A move by 12

Labour M.P.s to press the party into supporting immigration control had been met by determined opposition from Hugh Gaitskell, the leader, who felt passionately about the injection of racism into British politics and law. He saw that immigration was closely related to the number of jobs available, and that the talk of a coloured flood ready to overwhelm Britain was a figment of prejudice. He gave force and direction to the whole parliamentary struggle against control, but he could not altogether arrest the racism and, more immediately dangerous, the concern with electoral expediency, developing within his own party. Several important Labour M.P.s, notably Patrick Gordon Walker, the future short-lived Foreign Secretary, and Sir Frank Soskice, the future Home Secretary, were absent from the final Commons vote on the Bill in February 1962. Gaitskell himself died in January 1963, and the leadership passed to Harold Wilson, whose own commitment to principle tended to follow the course of the public opinion polls.

In November he rose in a debate on the annual re-examination of the Immigrant Act to announce that his party did not contest the need for immigration control and even wanted more effective health checks as well as a tightening up of the provisions for deportation. Labour would support the Act if the government instigated Commonwealth discussion to stop immigration at its source, and when the Conservative Home Secretary announced that such discussion had proved useless, Wilson replied that a Labour government would try to obtain Commonwealth collaboration, keeping the Act meanwhile to prevent immigrants from 'jumping the gun'. The party manifesto for the 1964 general election was a model of 'realism' and brash *non sequiturs*.

> We believe that the Commonwealth has a vital part to play in grappling with the terrible inequalities which separate the developed and under-developed nations and the white and coloured races. That is why a Labour Government will legislate against racial discrimination and incitement in public places and give special help to local authorities in areas where immigrants have settled. Labour accepts that the number of immigrants entering the United Kingdom must be limited. Until a satisfactory agreement covering this can be negotiated with the Commonwealth, a Labour Government will retain immigration control.

The temper of the country at large was becoming increasingly racist. The massacre of Africans by white police at Sharpeville, South Africa, in

March 1960 stirred the British press and public to an expression of unprecedented outrage at the policy of 'apartheid', but the sins of white
supremacy were soon swallowed up by the apparent power of the South
African government to deal effectively with disaffection and the terrible
events that pursued the independence of the Congo from the beginning of
July. In the months and years to come, the Congo would return repeatedly
to the headlines, often in the stories of raped white nuns and mutilated
white missionaries, scarcely ever in the accounts of Africans murdered
and pillaged by white mercenaries. The allegiance of the right-wing press
to Katanga secession, and the energetic propaganda and influence of the
Katanga lobby – many of whose members possessed or represented
sizable financial interests in the Congo, the Northern Rhodesian (now
Zambian) Copperbelt, and South Africa – led to a rising clamour against
the United Nations itself, for promoting the expulsion of white mercenaries from Katanga and the enforced reunification of the Congo. With
Conservative leaders, notably Sir Alec Douglas-Home, sniping at the
irresponsibility and – *pace* Suez – double standards displayed by the
Afro-Asian group in the United Nations, and the press furiously reporting
atrocities by the United Nations forces in Katanga, not the least of the
Congo's victims was the respect among many in Britain for international
authority and opinion.

The hostility, even contempt with which Lumumba was treated by a
substantial section of the British press – sentiments not extended with
much enthusiasm to his murderers, who were after all more dependable
trustees of Western interests – rubbed off on African leadership itself.
The atrocities committed by Congolese soldiers and subsequently Congolese rebels; the cruelty, corruption and incompetence of Congolese
politicians; the support apparently given by Afro-Asian leaders to the
enemies of Western influence and order in the Congo – these excited a
widespread disparagement not of the Congolese alone, but of all Africans
and, indeed, of all coloureds. The forces of Congolese and militant
African nationalism seemed to lack even the long-regarded virtues of
strength and success. A few hundred white mercenaries defeated not only
the armies of the central government, but when at last attached to them,
the supposedly popular insurrection of Lumumbists encouraged and
equipped by African and communist intervention. Forgetting the long
rebellion waged in Kenya, and the victory of Algerian nationalism against
the armed power of France, a large section of British opinion concluded
that when it came to fighting, one white was worth a host of blacks.

The departure of South Africa from the Commonwealth in March

1961 increased British irritation at the Afro-Asian members who had precipitated this, as well as spreading doubt on the value of a Commonwealth so numerically dominated by coloured countries. Britain continued to provide South Africa not only with significant economic privileges in her home market, but with a defence at the United Nations against demands for effective intervention. The importance of South African trade for Britain, and of South Africa's strategic situation for the West, was increasingly stressed by the Conservative leadership and the bulk of the British press. Moreover, negotiations to join the European Economic Community further reduced the stature of the Commonwealth for British public opinion, which recognized the hollowness of dutiful references to the Commonwealth as an essential bridge between white and coloured in a multi-racial world. By the middle of the 'sixties, Britain was gazing fixedly at Europe as the motorway to enrichment and renewed power in the modern world, while paying the Commonwealth little more than the courtesy of a passing platitude. The degree to which racism had become a public force was to be starkly revealed in the general election of October 1964.

A county borough whose visible identity has long been lost in the sprawl of Birmingham, Smethwick contains some 4,000 coloured immigrants – mainly Asians – in a total population of 68,000. This proportion of one in seventeen, or 7 per cent, is substantially outstripped by the immigrant ratio in All Saints, Handsworth and Small Heath, among other Birmingham constituencies, as well as in the London constituencies of Brixton, Deptford and Southall; yet it was in Smethwick that colour prejudice emerged as a popular passion. It had not been so at the beginning. When a few coloured immigrants first settled there in 1953, drawn to the local engineering factories by the boom in the motor industry, they were greeted with no more than the customary reserve presented to strangers. They lived in squalid hostels or rooms let out by enterprising compatriots, and when employment contracted with the 1956 recession, many left for areas of surviving opportunity. But those who remained brought their wives and children from their homelands, and as prosperity returned to Smethwick in 1959, the immigrant population, more settled now, steadily grew, swamping the available accommodation. The Labour-controlled council, rebuffed in its appeal for help from the government, could do little, and did less, to relieve the situation; but overcrowding was even worse in other industrial areas of the country, and Smethwick had been losing population since 1931, to suffer a decline of nearly 20 per cent in the next thirty years. There was a higher proportion of immigrant children in the schools of neighbouring West Bromwich; health facilities were no harder pressed in Smethwick than in most other parts of the Midlands; and the immigrants were being received in the main by the whites of Smethwick, if not with enthusiasm, then without any significant display of hostility.

It was the achievement of a few people, exploiting racism for personal satisfaction or profit, that antagonism emerged from the shy silence of the mind into the clamour of the ballot box. It may reasonably be argued that no small group of men, however shrewd and energetic, could have raised such a public structure of prejudice unless the groundwork had already been laid in popular sentiment. The leaders of the Smethwick campaign against immigration did not so much create racism as make it articulate and acceptable. But equally, of course, it may be claimed that, without the efforts of such men, the sanctions of custom and propriety, however sanctimonious, the sheer fear of ridicule, in fact, would have continued to confine open racism to the cranks. In the end, perhaps, it is always a confluence, the meeting of a new public sentiment with the men ready to take advantage of it, till the resultant force bursts the traditional banks. Racism was already a flow in the country, but one still restrained by convention. In Smethwick it became a flood, raising the level dangerously everywhere.

The *Smethwick Telephone*, the local newspaper which reached into 95 per cent of the borough's homes, had occasionally published letters attacking the coloured immigrants, but it was only in 1959, before the general election, that it selected immigration as a major issue. Asking the candidates their views on questions of public concern, it placed immigration third on the list, and the Conservative, Peter Griffiths, replied: 'Immigration into this country should be limited to persons of sound health who have jobs and living accommodation arranged before they enter ... Immigrants should not be permitted to remain here without working, nor to overcrowd their housing accommodation.' The election itself was a quiet one, in this safe Labour seat, but in the following year, colour became a more serious issue; one Conservative candidate, who campaigned for the eviction of immigrants from overcrowded houses without council responsibility for providing alternative accommodation, almost won a safe Labour ward, and soon afterwards minor racial disturbances broke out on the border of Smethwick. Increasingly the *Smethwick Telephone* devoted space to court cases or sexual incidents involving coloureds, while its correspondence columns seethed with complaints against the immigrants, their habits and hygiene, their danger to health (they carried tuberculosis and leprosy) and the race (they were adulterating the blood), their parasitic dependence on the social services. One of the most violent of these correspondents was a planning engineer called Donald Finney, who was largely instrumental in establishing during the spring of 1961 the Smethwick branch of the Birmingham Immigration Control Association. The committee consisted almost entirely of working-class men and women who had voted Labour – as Finney himself had done until 1959 – all their lives; some three hundred people attended the clamorous inaugural meeting on April 25th, and within a week the branch had registered over five hundred members. Letters denouncing coloureds swamped the apparently unreluctant *Smethwick Telephone*, and in May Peter Griffiths led the Conservative councillors in supporting the demands of Harold Gurden, a Birmingham M.P., for immigration control.

Peter Griffiths, by now in command of the Conservatives on the council, was a fresh-faced schoolteacher with an easy smile and a sly intelligence. Adopted in March 1962 as Conservative parliamentary candidate again, he began to concentrate on the colour issue in the weekly political column which he wrote, along with the other party candidates or their agents, in the *Smethwick Telephone*. And in significant harmony Donald Finney, who had joined the Conservative Party and soon afterwards been adopted as the candidate for a Conservative-held ward, contributed his letters. In March he had disbanded the Smethwick branch of the Birmingham Immigration Control Association. It was no longer needed.[1]

In the 1962 local elections, the Conservatives won three Smethwick seats against a national swing to Labour, and Finney won his ward with the largest majority recorded there since the war. In the local elections of the following year, the Conservatives won yet another Smethwick seat. On reports that children in the borough had chanted 'If you want a nigger neighbour, vote Labour', Griffiths commented to a correspondent of *The Times*: 'I should think that is a manifestation of the popular feeling. I would not condemn anyone who said that. I would say that is how people see the situation in Smethwick. I fully understand the feelings of the people who say it. I would say it is exasperation, not fascism.'[2]

As the general election approached, Griffiths grew cruder and more confident. He warned of rioting if immigrants got council flats; he supported a national petition demanding a complete ban on immigration for five years; he accused the Labour Party – falsely – of having bestowed

[1] P. Foot, op. cit., pp. 9–62.   [2] *The Times*, March 9th, 1964.

the Commonwealth right of free entry to Britain, and – falsely now, too – of opposing immigration control. He protested at 'the plight of English children held back by the presence of non-English-speaking children in a class' and blamed 'the Socialists and their immigrant friends'. In the local elections of 1964, the Conservatives finally gained control of the council, and in the midst of rejoicing Griffiths paused to claim that in the poll 'a quarter of Labour's voters could not speak English', and to suggest that 'Smethwick people who stayed at home should ask themselves just whom they wish to decide Smethwick's future.'

The Labour M.P. for Smethwick, Patrick Gordon Walker, had little heart for such a fight. As Labour Commonwealth Secretary in 1950, he had banned Seretse Khama from Bechuanaland – 'a very disreputable transaction', as Churchill had described it – for having married a white woman; relations with neighbouring South Africa might have been endangered. In 1954, when the Labour Party opposed the Conservative government's constitution for the Federation of Rhodesia and Nyasaland, he had been one of its eleven members to abstain in the division, on the grounds that the safeguards for African interests were, in fact, adequate. As early as November 1954 he had hinted at the need for control of Commonwealth immigration, and his opposition to the Conservative Bill of 1961 had been less a matter of principle – he abstained in the final vote – than a show of loyalty to Gaitskell.

His proclaimed opposition to racial prejudice, never strong, appeared increasingly feeble as he attempted to keep pace with public opinion in Smethwick. 'This is a British country with British standards of behaviour. The British must come first,' he announced in the *Smethwick Telephone* at the end of August 1962. He even tried to use immigration as a political weapon against the Conservatives. 'The whole wave of immigration has occurred since 1951 whilst the Conservatives have been in power. It is false and unfair to blame (*sic!*) the Labour Party for immigration.'[1] And all the while he whistled to keep up his courage in the dark. 'Immigration is not the main issue in this election. As we get nearer the election and bigger issues come up, I think the immigrant problem will become less and less prominent.'[2]

It was a stupid and dangerous strategy. Immigration had clearly been made the main election issue for Smethwick, and to suppose differently fooled no one. Above all, the issue was basically one of racism, and as the development of racism elsewhere has time and again displayed, a qualified opposition, that yields the principles and struggles only over the details,

---

[1] *Smethwick Telephone,* March 13th, 1964.   [2] April 9th, 1964.

ensures the success of the single initiative. The original is seldom discarded for the reflection. By accepting the basis of Conservative hostility to the immigrants, by attempting even to employ prejudice in his own cause, the Smethwick Labour candidate helped to dismantle the very barricades against racism which reason and established propriety had raised. Inevitably the Smethwick electors gathered more and more enthusiastically around the real thing.

Peter Griffiths was emboldened to let himself go. His political column in the *Smethwick Telephone* at the end of July was a masterpiece.

> Labour's much-publicised leaflet on immigration looks like being something of a boomerang. For it came at a time when the dreadful deterioration in public morals is self-evident.
>
> The main difficulty produced by immigration would vanish if there were enough houses to go round.' This is clear enough for the Socialists to stand self-condemned. Their policy appears to be 'build more houses and let-'em-all come'.
>
> Surely if more houses can be built they should go to British people first. Our Labour Council left a back-log of thousands waiting for housing. Would Labour house the immigrants before them?
>
> *In any case, would more houses end the nuisance and filth? Would more houses end the knife fights? Would more houses make the streets safe for young women and girls?*
>
> There are 300,000 immigrants in India and Pakistan waiting to come here if restrictions are lifted. Would Labour house all these too?
>
> Labour opposed the Immigration Control Act. A Labour Government would mean a flood of immigrants as soon as the Act was lifted.
>
> Your protests and mine would be stifled by the threatened law to 'outlaw incitement' which could mean just anything its sponsors chose.
>
> *If Labour wishes to fight on the immigration issue, so be it. Rarely have I been so angry as to see this cynical, vote-catching attempt to gloss over the most urgent problem facing our town. I will not be silent.*[1]

National attention increasingly focused on Smethwick. Sir Alec Douglas-Home, now Prime Minister and leader of the Conservative Party, was asked on television to comment on the remark by Griffiths that

[1] Author's italics.

'Smethwick rejects the idea of being a multi-racial society.'[1] He replied: 'We should not indulge in statements of that kind.' When Patrick Gordon Walker then asked him to repudiate Griffiths on the basis of this criticism, Sir Alec answered, 'Alderman Griffiths finds himself in entire agreement with what I said.' The Conservative leadership had clearly no intention of disowning a candidate who seemed, on the evidence of canvass returns and public opinion polls, likely to win a 'safe', working-class Labour seat. Much more than Smethwick was at stake.

Smethwick itself, just before polling day on October 15th, was a community swept by racist fever. Canvassers found that immigration was not merely the most important issue, but for many voters the only one. At a packed election meeting Griffiths discussed pensions and education, while restless members of the audience called 'What about immigration?' At last, in reply to a woman who rose at question time to demand an immediate end to coloured immigration, he addressed himself to the subject. He had heard the view of his questioner on thousands of Smethwick doorsteps – he did not need to explain how it had got there – and he would take to Westminster the view of his constituents. That was the function of a parliamentary member. He was asked whether he personally accepted the idea of a multi-racial society, and remembering the mild reprimand of his leader, blandly responded: 'I am not going to decide. The mass of the people of Smethwick will decide.'

On the eve of voting, despite clear signs of a swing to Labour across the country, the long 'safe' Labour seat of Smethwick seemed all but lost, and the last desperate appeal by Gordon Walker did nothing to retrieve the situation. '*Be fair*. Immigrants only arrived in Smethwick in large numbers during the past ten years – while the Tory Government was in power. You can't blame Labour or Gordon Walker for that. Labour favours continued control of immigration, stricter health checks and deportation of those convicted of criminal offences.'[2] Gordon Walker had held the constituency in the 1959 flood-tide of Conservative popularity by 3,544 votes, polling 20,670 to 17,126 for Peter Griffiths. He now lost the seat by 1,774 votes, polling 14,916 to 16,690 for Griffiths. (The Liberal candidate, David Hugill, who had been disgusted at Gordon Walker's retreat before racism and had fought hard with flimsy resources, polled 3,172 votes.) In 1959 Labour had polled 54·7 per cent of the vote; in 1964 it polled 42·6 per cent. In 1959 the Conservative Party had polled 45·3 per cent; in 1964, it polled 47·6 per cent. The national swing towards Labour in the 1964 election was 3·5 per cent, and in the Midlands just

[1] *Smethwick Telephone*, July 3rd, 1964.   [2] Special election leaflet of the Labour Party.

over 2 per cent. In Smethwick, the swing from Labour to the Conservatives was 7·2 per cent, or a deviation of 10·7 per cent from the national average. Just how many Conservatives voted for Labour or the Liberal Party out of revulsion at Griffiths, can never, of course, be established. What was undeniable – and seen by all political parties as such – was that racism had turned a certain Labour victory, measured by the current mood of the country, into a clear Labour defeat. The Conservative supporters at Smethwick Town Hall who celebrated by jeering at Gordon Walker, 'Where are your Niggers now?' 'Take your Niggers away!' knew this. And Peter Griffiths himself knew it better than anyone else. Speaking to Young Conservatives in London soon afterwards,[1] he announced: 'At least twenty seats in London, the West Midlands and elsewhere can be won if the Conservatives take a firm line on immigration.' Twenty seats were four times the immediate overall Labour majority, and if switched, would give the Conservatives a safe lead in the Commons.

Immigration as an election issue was not limited to Smethwick, though nowhere else did it assume such importance. In Southall, London, the Conservative candidate called for a stop to all immigration – 'with the exception, of course, of top priority people like doctors and nurses' – while a national review was undertaken. But the British National Party, which had achieved considerable success in local elections, fielded its own candidate, and Labour retained the seat. In Birmingham, a few Conservatives made much of the immigration issue – though there were, happily, others who explicitly denounced such tactics – and this probably reduced the Labour swing throughout the area. Certainly it seems to have cost Labour another Midlands seat, in Birmingham (Perry Bar). A third seat was lost on the colour issue at Eton and Slough, near London, where the sitting Labour member, Fenner Brockway, had a wide reputation as a campaigner against racial prejudice and saw his majority of 88 vanish into a minority of 11. As *The Economist* subsequently observed:[2] 'In fairness to Sir Anthony Meyer, the Tory who won Eton and Slough, it should be said that even his Labour opponent acknowledged that he personally made not the slightest concession to white unreason. This, however, makes the outcome even more disquieting than at Smethwick, because it suggests that once an anti-wog bandwaggon is rolling in an area, even liberal and decent candidates cannot stop it.'

The Conservative leadership had been generally cautious during the campaign. Sir Alec Douglas-Home and some of his Cabinet colleagues

[1] November 24th, 1964.   [2] December 25th, 1965.

had made much, in immigrant areas, of their control legislation and the flood which would have developed without their foresight. A Gallup Poll in July 1964 had shown 40 per cent in favour of immigration control by British quotas; 28 per cent in favour of control by quotas fixed after consultation with the Commonwealth countries concerned; 20 per cent in favour of total exclusion; and only 10 per cent in favour of free entry.[1] This had revealed a sharp climb in those favouring controls from the 62 per cent at the end of 1961, during the debate on the Conservative Immigration Bill. But no one could be sure that a party making an election issue of the immigrant would not antagonize more voters than it attracted. Smethwick clearly illustrated the advantages of racism, and Leyton confirmed them. To a by-election there, in January 1965, came Patrick Gordon Walker, dignified by the new title of Foreign Secretary and the old, less tenable one of 'nigger-lover'. Leyton was, like Smethwick, a safe Labour seat, though one threatened by disgruntlement at the austerity measures of the new government. And in a surprise result, the Conservative won by just over 200 votes, with a swing of 8 per cent. At the simultaneous by-election in Nuneaton, a safe Labour seat safely retained, the swing to the Conservatives was 5 per cent, or 3 per cent less. The Conservative Party itself, still vaguely embarrassed by the Smethwick result, had been careful to keep the racial issue out of the Leyton campaign; but there had been intruders from the far right ready enough to exploit it, and besides, Gordon Walker had helplessly brought it with him from Smethwick. In a subsequent public opinion poll, 29 per cent of respondents in the Leyton electorate attributed the Labour defeat to 'race feeling'.

At first the Conservative Party treated the new member from Smethwick uncertainly, while the Labour Party for a short while displayed open contempt. 'A parliamentary leper', Harold Wilson, the Prime Minister, called him, to an outcry from the Conservative benches. But Griffiths himself delivered a maiden speech beaming racial goodwill, and the press accorded him a warmer welcome than it had given to the Prime Minister's scornful description. He was soon in substantial demand by Conservative groups as a speaker, and was so taken to his party's heart that he was given the job of moving all the major Conservative amendments to the government's Race Relations Bill in its committee stage. The killing of the Albatross, after all, had brought back the sun.[2] Griffiths continued to lead the Conservatives on the Smethwick Council, which took powers to buy (colour-owned) houses for sale to whites only, and with charac-

[1] *The Times*, September 17th, 1964.

teristic smoothness, he explained that such steps were necessary to prevent the production of 'black ghettoes'. He failed to announce any plans to promote the purchase of (white-owned) houses for sale to coloureds only, but then the practice of prejudice required less and less explanation.

Both the Labour and Conservative Parties now showed how well they had learnt the lesson of Smethwick. In February 1965 Sir Alec Douglas-Home raised the immigration bid in a speech at Hampstead. All immigrants who entered illegally should be repatriated; the government should assist those who wished to return home; the number of immigrants allowed to enter should be further reduced; and the limit set on immigration should include dependants. On the following day Sir Frank Soskice, the Labour Home Secretary, announced in the Commons that he would seek powers to repatriate all immigrants entering illegally and would tighten up the control regulations. The Conservatives shifted front bench responsibility for Home Affairs from the 'dove', Sir Edward Boyle, to the 'hawk', Peter Thorneycroft, and the clamour for a more severe policy on immigration increased. 'It is not unreasonable', declared Mr Angus Maude, M.P., one of the party's intellectuals, 'for a white people in a white country to want to stay a white country.' When Sir Cyril Osborne produced in early March a motion for sterner control measures, Sir Alec Douglas-Home, Peter Thorneycroft and Edward Heath (soon to be elected Conservative leader) supported him in the division. Three days later, at a meeting of the Central Council of Conservative and Unionist Associations, Patrick Wall, M.P., declared, without rebuke this time, that 'British must for the moment reject the multi-racial State.' There were still Conservatives who openly opposed the racist drift – seven of them voted against the Osborne motion – but like their counterparts in the Labour Party, they were a dying breed.

---

[2]And I had done a hellish thing,
And it would work 'em woe:
For all averred, I had killed the bird
That made the breeze to blow.
Ah wretch! said they, the bird to slay,
That made the breeze to blow.

Nor dim nor red, like God's own head,
The glorious sun uprist.
Then all averred, I had killed the bird
That brought the fog and mist.
'Twas right, said they, such birds to slay,
That bring the fog and mist.

The Rime of the Ancient Mariner, by Samuel Taylor Coleridge, lines 91–102.

In March the Prime Minister, lamenting the evasions of the Immigration Act, announced a high-level mission, not – as previously promised – to negotiate 'a satisfactory agreement ... with the Commonwealth,' but in order to 'examine what can be done to stamp out evasion at source.' The mission report was highly confidential, but responsible rumour suggests that the governments of the coloured Commonwealth countries told Britain that they would not help to dress the nakedness of her racial policy in emigration control. When George Brown, First Secretary of State and one of the very few influential radicals of the Gaitskell type remaining, proclaimed in a public speech that the economy was short of labour and 'it is mad to talk of restricting immigration', the outcry in his own party was overwhelming. The government did, as it had promised, introduce some measures to promote integration, but they were timid and weak. The junior minister appointed to head a government inquiry had negligible powers, as did the Co-ordinating Committees established to nourish better race relations. One by one the teeth in the race discrimination measure, pledged by Labour since the 1958 race riots, were pulled, till little more than the gums of piety were left. At the insistence of the Conservatives, the government replaced criminal sanctions with conciliation in dealing with those who discriminated against coloured and other minorities in public places, and the Race Relations Bill did not apply at all to the crucial areas of housing and employment. It was, in the sharp phrase of the liberal *Guardian*, 'a step sideways'. Meanwhile the immigration auction continued, and in July Selwyn Lloyd, chairman of the Conservative Party's policy group on immigration, proposed a 'one for one' exchange, by which an immigrant would be allowed to enter for every immigrant leaving the country. Conservative M.P. Norman St John Stevas described the new proposal as 'arbitrary, inhuman and unjust'.

At last, in August 1965, the new Labour government published its 'White Paper on Immigration from the Commonwealth'. Since September 1964, vouchers for immigrant entry to Britain had been issued at the rate of some 400 a week or 20,800 a year. Now the rate was to be cut by well over half to 8,500 a year, of which 1,000 vouchers would be reserved for (white) Maltese. The issue of 'C' vouchers, for unskilled labour, would be discontinued immediately, and all future immigrants therefore would either have to possess assured employment (the 'A' voucher) or possess recognized skills in medicine, education, science and technology (the 'B' voucher). Children aged 16 and 17, until now admitted freely to join one or both parents, would generally be prohibited entry, and visits by Commonwealth citizens would be limited – with reasonable extensions – to six months. Immigration officers might require new immigrants to register with the police, and immigrants would normally be expected to produce evidence of medical fitness. The provision that Commonwealth citizens might be deported within five years of residence on the recommendation of a court after conviction of a crime punishable by imprisonment was extended to a general power by which the Home Secretary could repatriate any Commonwealth citizens within five years of residence if he considered it in the public interest to do so.

The effective figure of 7,500 immigrants a year from the coloured Commonwealth countries had been reached – as the debate at the subsequent Labour Party Conference revealed – without rational investigation or regard for the requirements of the British economy, let alone any reference to the proper interests of the Commonwealth; it was simply the lowest figure, short of a total ban, that the government supposed would escape derision. Indeed, it was not unlikely, with the immigrants who returned each year to their original countries for good, that the government might succeed in surpassing the Conservative Party's 'one for one' proposal and produce a gradual decrease in the immigrant population. The exclusion of children aged 16 and 17 from automatic entry to join their parents promised gratuitous suffering – were their numbers so substantial as to menace the whole British way of life? – while the new powers of deportation demanded by the Home Office placed immigrants in a no man's land beyond the law, subjects for five years of the Home Secretary's personal will. Not least, the careful retention of entry for skilled workers came strangely from a party that had devoted so much of its election campaign to the need for developing the Commonwealth. *The Times*, a newspaper with a wide enough throat, one would have thought, found such expediency difficult to swallow.

> It now appears to be taken for granted that Britain is entirely within her rights in poaching skills from countries less well off and thus to absolve herself from making the effort to enlarge her own reserves and to use them more efficiently. Britain gets the best of the bargain in the short term, no doubt. But to governments even shorter of financial and material resources, it is bound to seem rather like sharp practice.[1]

The White Paper studiously avoided the word 'colour', and where

[1] August 3rd, 1965.

separate figures for immigration had to be given, produced the two categories of 'Citizens of Canada, Australia or New Zealand' and 'Commonwealth citizens from other Commonwealth countries and dependent territories'. But inside the parcel of hypocrisy – indeed, irony[1] – and the tissue paper of integration measures (Voluntary Liaison Committees and a National Committee for Commonwealth Immigrants, all without perceptible powers), the collapse to prejudice was plain. In less than four years, the Labour Party had paraded its way, behind the banner of realism, to a policy of racial exclusion. How far – and how near – was the cry of Gaitskell in November 1961: 'The immigrants are healthy, law-abiding, and are at work. They are helping us. Why, then, does the government wish to keep them out? We all know the answer. It is because they are coloured and because in consequence of this there is fear of racial disorder and friction.'

In the event, the general election of March 1966 revealed little impact on the polls from the race issue. The Labour Party returned to power with a much increased majority, and Smethwick returned to its traditional allegiance by 18,440 votes for Andrew Faulds, the Labour candidate (who had himself strongly opposed the racism of the Immigration White Paper), to 14,950 votes for Peter Griffiths and 508 for a candidate of the British National Party. Labour had succeeded – for the while – in reducing the electoral importance of the race issue, but only by showing itself just as ready as its Conservative opponents to pacify prejudice.

Sealed off by their poverty, the shortage of housing, the prejudice of property-owners, and the general timidity of local councils, reluctant to provide slum clearance for coloureds while there were whites in need, the coloured immigrants inhabited black ghettoes in the most squalid, decaying parts of the cities. Sealed off by widespread discrimination, the coloured immigrants continued to inhabit black ghettoes of employment, their skins confining them in the main to the least skilled and poorest

[1] 'Any discussion of immigrants and the health services must begin with a recognition of the valuable contribution made by immigrants towards the staffing of these services. The efficient running of our hospitals, in particular, depends in no small measure on the service given by doctors, nurses, domestics and other staff drawn from all parts of the Commonwealth. The government gratefully acknowledges the essential contribution they make to the well-being of the whole community, and are glad to feel that those who later return home obtain experience here which will be of value to them in their own countries.' para. 52.

'The good name of Britain, our relations with other members of the Commonwealth, and, above all, justice and common humanity, demand that Commonwealth immigrants in this country should be absorbed into our community without friction and with mutual understanding and tolerance. The government believe that the good sense of the British people will prevail and that this will be achieved.' para. 78. Conclusion.

paid jobs. Yet no one who came into frank contact with the immigrants could long doubt that they constituted an uncommonly enterprising, ambitious sector of the population; their very existence as immigrants testified to their initiative and aspiration. Racial prejudice was doubly damaging; it kept Britain from gladly imbuing her culture and economy with new and creative elements, to their and her own obvious benefit; and it distorted the minds of white and black alike with fear, hatred and resentment.

Instead of a productive assimilation, there was a destructive antagonism. Encouraged by their success, racists flung themselves with zeal into new endeavours; immigration control organizations began campaigning for a reduction of coloured numbers by assisted repatriation, and merely local bodies, established to protect white areas from coloured encroachment, multiplied, while small groups of hooligans – like the British Ku Klux Klan, which took to burning crosses and setting fire to the houses of chosen coloured victims – concentrated on intimidation.

An American-type civil rights movement – the Campaign Against Racial Discrimination, or CARD – was founded in late 1964, and soon afterwards came the more militant Racial Adjustment Action Society, whose leader, Michael De Freitas, a former West Indian, had been influenced by Malcolm X and the American Black Muslim movement. Claiming a membership well in excess of 45,000 – with support, significantly, from Asians as well as West Indians – R.A.A.S. spoke in the accents of rejection and defiance.

'Brothers and sisters, you've got to learn how to deal with this white man. You used to turn your cheek when he hit you. You turned and twisted to please him. Stop twisting and hit him back. I tell you, he's afraid ... We are a family. Our last name is Black.'[1] White racial solidarity inevitably produced its coloured counterpart. A strike at a rubber factory in the west of London for six weeks in 1965–6 received wide publicity because the strikers, almost all Indians, were supported by local Indian landlords, who waived rents, and by local Indian shopkeepers, who extended credit.

Inevitably, too, just as international experience had helped to form domestic racial attitudes, so domestic experience now helped to form international attitudes and conduct. The coloured Commonwealth countries themselves were – according to their different expectations – dismayed, angered or justified by Britain's cynicism and racial preoccupations. Many people of the islands, who had long if foolishly looked

[1] A newsletter from De Freitas, quoted in the *Observer*, July 4th, 1965.

to Britain as the motherland, pledged and ready to welcome her colonial children – and her children in a very real sense they were, since no one else had seized them from Africa, to scatter them across the Caribbean – were bitter at their rejection, alarmed at the sudden end to their relief from population pressures, and driven to a deeper racial awareness. Those Africans and Asians who had attached some meaning to the Commonwealth and the British connection were appalled by the ease with which Britain herself unilaterally renounced basic Commonwealth obligations and the long-proclaimed virtues of a multi-racial society. They now went to swell the already considerable numbers of those who believed that the British were first and foremost whites, with the racial arrogance of long dominion, who beckoned the coloured peoples with talk of equality and co-operation while they had something to gain, but turned their backs abruptly as soon as such talk promised to cost them anything.

Britain's own international outlook was no less influenced by the domestic temper. The Labour Prime Minister himself, who had emerged from his party's militant left wing, revealed a patronizing attitude to the coloured Commonwealth which his Conservative predecessors would have regarded as tactless and inept, if not altogether unjustified by the facts of culture and power. Neither Harold Macmillan nor Sir Alec Douglas-Home would have instigated a Commonwealth mission – especially one which depended for any prospect of success on the enthusiastic participation of African and Asian neutralist members – with the exclusive deference for the view of Australia's Sir Robert Menzies that Wilson, in his Vietnam peace initiative, publicly displayed. Some of the African leaders attending the Commonwealth Prime Ministers' Conference of June 1965 subsequently complained that they had been treated like clients, with the Vietnam initiative directed more at the effect on British public opinion polls than at the production of a peace settlement. Wilson's insistence on holding the chairmanship of the Commonwealth mission while maintaining British government support for United States policy in Vietnam was significantly responsible for the refusal by Peking, Hanoi and even Moscow to take the mission seriously, and caused widespread resentment among coloured Commonwealth leaders who believed that their neutralist influence had been exploited and endangered to no purpose. Indeed, the British government's whole Asian policy, with its 'East of Suez' military presence and its submissive commitment to assist the United States in the containment of China, promised to drive Britain still farther, as it was driving the United States, from the coloured world.

It was over Rhodesia, however, Britain's last important African colony, where a white settler minority maintained political and economic dominance, that white and coloured within the Commonwealth immediately and most angrily clashed. At the 1965 Commonwealth Prime Ministers' Conference, the African states led a demand for a constitutional conference – 'at an early date, say within three months' – of all political leaders in Rhodesia, to promote effective progress to independence on the basis of majority rule. If the Rhodesian government refused to attend such a conference and release the nationalist leaders in detention, Britain should suspend the 1961 Constitution, under which the white minority regime legally operated, and appoint an interim administration to repeal all discriminatory laws and prepare the way for free elections. But the British government did little more than take note of such views, reasserting Britain's responsibility for Rhodesia and committing itself only to the ultimate principle of 'one man, one vote'. One Commonwealth state, Tanzania, publicly dissociated herself from the Rhodesian section of the Conference communiqué, since she had failed to get an assurance that negotiations already in progress between the British and Rhodesian governments were aimed at achieving independence on the basis of majority rule.

Tanzania was not alone or mistaken in supposing that these negotiations were concerned more with persuading the white minority regime not to seize independence unilaterally than with promoting any fundamental change in the shape of power. It became increasingly apparent that Britain could exercise her ultimate authority only with the effective threat or use of force, and that despite her repeatedly shown readiness to use force against coloured recalcitrance, she immediately announced her rejection of any such course against whites in Rhodesia.

Assured by the British Government itself that they risked no prospect of military intervention, the white minority leaders persisted in their refusal to accept any constitutional change which might produce majority rule within a measurable period, while threatening to seize independence themselves if it were not soon given to them. Peter Griffiths, the M.P. for Smethwick, spoke for a substantial body of British public opinion in admiring the settler regime of Ian Smith and calling on the British government to 'set Rhodesia free'. This would, of course, lead to such international repercussions that even the Conservative Party leadership had rejected it; but an indefinite pause, during which the white colonial government of Rhodesia could continue, under formal British suzerainty, to practise racial discrimination unmolested, would have commended itself to the bulk of British opinion, whatever the opinion of the coloured Commonwealth and the United Nations.

The Rhodesian whites, however, were not to be deflected by a cynical circumspection, and in November their leadership declared Rhodesia independent. This, as the British government grandiosely proclaimed, was not merely rebellion but treason; yet the traditional remedy for rebellion and treason, the exercise of force to sustain law and the pre- rogatives òf the Crown, was rejected. The Conservative Party, of course, supported the Labour government against the clamour of African states for military intervention – Edward Heath, Leader of the Opposition, went on television to announce that using force would produce burning, looting, murder and rape; in short, another Congo – but also demanded that the economic sanctions imposed should not be punitive. The Organi- zation of African Unity, enraged by Britain's refusal to use against whites the same weapons she had so often used against blacks, called on its member states to break off diplomatic relations with Britain in protest, and several of them, including Ghana[1] and Tanzania from the Common- wealth, did so. It was just one more stage in the developing division between white and non-white inside the Commonwealth and beyond, throughout the world.

*   *   *

If London was for long the capital of white dominion over the coloured world, Moscow was to set itself up as the capital of coloured emancipa- tion. Lenin himself had early seen the advantage no less than the justice in appealing to the racial minorities within the Russian empire, and the success of the Bolshevik cause in 1917 was not unrelated to the promise of national independence for the subject races. The subsequent period of civil war and foreign intervention only confirmed Lenin in his view. The expected rising of the proletariat in Western Europe did not materialize, and the Soviet leaders increasingly directed their attention to the West's coloured empire, as the fragile foundation of capitalist power and wealth.

Marx had supposed that proletarian revolution and so the eventual accomplishment of communism would take place first in the developed and class-strained economies of the West, with their aware and disaffected workers. Lenin, however, coming later in time as he did, proclaimed the ability of capitalism to buy off domestic disaffection by shrewdly dis- tributing a share in the dividends of colonial rule. 'Imperialism, which means the partition of the world ... which means high monopoly profits

[1] Which restored diplomatic relations after the military coup there.

for a handful of very rich countries, creates the economic possibility of corrupting the upper strata of the proletariat.'[1] The working class itself became, at its higher reaches, bourgeois in attitude, and as intent as the banker or textile manufacturer to prevent upheaval. (Lenin was not, of course, to foresee how the prosperity of the Soviet Union might make her leadership fearful of upheaval, too.) Inevitably the imperial powers would compete and wage war against each other for markets and sources of raw material, so weakening their colonial hold; but this was no reason for the Soviet Union to wait on history, and the Soviet leadership set out to hasten the end of Western dominion and so capitalism itself by exciting the coloured peoples of Africa and Asia to revolt. Coloured revolutionaries like the Indian M. N. Roy were welcomed in Moscow, and the K.U.T.V.U. – the University for the Toilers of the East – was founded especially to educate students from the coloured world. The Soviet leadership, of course, gave particular attention to the largest coloured country of all, China; but it did not neglect the rest of Asia, Africa, or the Negro population of the United States.

Stalin sneered at the European socialists for their approval of white supremacy.

> The tens and hundreds of millions of the Asiatic and African peoples suffering from national oppression in its crudest and most brutal form did not as a rule enter the field of vision of the 'socialists'. The latter did not venture to place the white peoples and coloured peoples, the 'uncultured' Negroes and the 'civilized' Irish, the 'backward' Indians and the 'enlightened' Poles on one and the same footing. It was tacitly assumed that although it might be necessary to strive for the emancipation of the European non-sovereign nationalities, it was entirely unbecoming for 'decent socialists' to speak seriously of the emancipation of the colonies, which were 'necessary' for the 'preservation' of 'civilization'.[2]

That Stalin was justified in his scorn on the whole – there were notable exceptions, of course – few who know the record of colonial struggle will easily deny. The same record, however, is far from altogether kind to the communist movement.

The early League for the Liberation of the East, provoked by Stalin

[1] *Imperialism – The Highest Stage of Capitalism*, by V. I. Lenin (Lawrence & Wishart, 1948), p. 126.
[2] *Marxism and the National and Colonial Question*, by Joseph Stalin (Lawrence & Wishart, 1947), p. 111.

to encourage revolution in Asia, had small success, and the Soviet representatives in the Comintern or Communist International promoted the
summoning of a world-wide Anti-Imperialist Conference at Brussels in
1927, to further the struggle of Africans and coloured Americans as well
as Asians. The conference, discreetly organized so as to encompass progressive elements outside the communist movement, assembled moderate
and militant nationalists alike from Asia, the Middle East, Africa and the
Americas – among the delegates was Jawaharlal Nehru, from the Indian
National Congress – and the League Against Imperialism, established as a
result, promised a broad front of colonial struggle. Indeed, the Sixth
Congress of the Comintern, meeting at Moscow in 1928, severely
reprimanded the Communist Parties in the metropolitan countries for
their indifference to the mass movements in the colonies, and commanded
them 'to afford energetic support both in the imperialist centres and in the
colonies themselves to these movements[1].' The Comintern instructed its
affiliates in Western Europe to establish local Leagues Against Imperialism, and though the Communist Parties generally lacked the enthusiasm
to promote their new objectives adequately, the Leagues themselves
excited interest in colonial problems far beyond the confines of the
communist commitment.

With the rising menace of fascism in Europe, however, the Soviet
Union resolved to reach an accommodation with Britain and France,
signalling the change in her policy by joining the League of Nations in
1934. Any accommodation with Britain and France, the foremost of the
imperial powers, demanded, of course, a muffling of effort for colonial
insurrection, and the Seventh Congress of the Comintern in 1935 confirmed the decision to sacrifice the struggle against imperialism to the
needs of the struggle against fascism. And as though to underline the
suzerainty of Soviet interests, at any cost to the liberation – or surviving
liberty – of the coloured peoples, Stalin sold oil to Mussolini during the
Italian invasion of Abyssinia in 1935. Many Africans, Asians, West
Indians, and American Negroes abandoned their communist connections
in disgust, and the League Against Imperialism disintegrated in the ardour
of the Popular Front.

In Britain the search for allies led the Communist Party to talk much
less of the need for colonial revolution, and even enthusiasm for the
Indian cause, long a mark of communist endeavour, gave place to the
demands of European struggle. In France the Communist Party joined

[1] Quoted in *Pan-Africanism or Communism?*, by George Padmore (Dennis Dobson, 1956),
p. 327.

forces with the Socialists and Radicals, and the resultant Popular Front won a huge majority in the elections of April 1936. The movements of resistance in the French colonies, however, were soon to be disappointed in their hopes of a government that contained crucial communist representation. The new France ordered the release of Bourguiba and other leaders of the nationalist Neo-Destour in Tunisia, but she did not withdraw the ban on the Neo-Destour itself, since, no less than the old, she categorically refused even to consider the retreat of her rule. Increasingly distrustful of French communist intentions, the Tunisian nationalists – in an initiative to be subsequently followed elsewhere in French Africa – broke away from the Confédération Générale des Travailleurs, the French communist trade union federation, and formed their own organization of workers. The experience of Algerian nationalism was no less bitter. At first the Popular Front government showed itself less intransigent than its predecessors had been, lifting the ban on the nationalist movement and allowing its leader, Messali Hadj, to campaign in Algeria. Messali Hadj, indeed, had long worked closely with the Communists, Socialists and others of the Left, had attended the Anti-Imperialist Congress in Brussels, and looked for tolerance, if not encouragement, from his former colleagues. But under pressure from the white settlers in Algeria, the government banned the nationalist movement again and forced its leadership underground. 'Experience and time were to prove', commented Messali Hadj, 'that French leaders, whether belonging to the extreme left or extreme right of the government, have one and the same colonial policy.'

By 1939 the anti-fascist front had been disrupted by the Hitler-Stalin pact, and the war with Germany was being denounced by the communist movement as an imperialist one. Then Hitler attacked the Soviet Union, and the imperialist war became a world-wide struggle against fascism. Once again the emphasis was lifted from colonial revolution, to be placed securely now on achieving the widest support in the West for the war effort of the Soviet Union. In South Africa the Communist Party called on the non-whites to join the armed forces, where they were restricted to duties that did not involve the bearing of arms, and those who opposed the call, claiming that the war was a white one and so an opportunity for political and economic struggle, were attacked by the very colleagues who had made that claim themselves shortly before. In India, where Congress refused to support the war or even desist from civil disobedience without the pledge of independence and an immediate earnest in the form of Cabinet rule, the Communists abandoned the nationalist front for collaboration with the British.

The alliance between the Soviet Union and the West did not end suddenly with the ending of the war, and Stalin avoided any support of revolution that might provoke Western antagonism and so impede his European purposes. Even in China, where the communist armies of Mao Tse-tung looked to Moscow for a proper encouragement, the Soviet ambassador clung to the status quo, attending the decay of the Kuomin-tang and negotiating agreements with the Chiang Kai-shek regime until the last. In France the Communist Party showed yet again how shallow was its commitment to the cause of colonial enfranchisement. During the war itself, the National Liberation Committee, which encompassed all the major resistance groups in France, had released Communists and Socialists from their Vichy detention, but had left in confinement nation-alist leaders like Messali Hadj, without recorded protest from any repre-sentatives of the left-wing parties. Then, in September 1944, two weeks after the liberation of Paris, General de Gaulle established the Government of National Unanimity, with two prominent Communists among its members. The French Communist Party was delighted at the prospect of using its participation in power to influence domestic reform and foreign policy; in return it acquiesced not only in the dissolution of the resistance groups that it controlled and in a limitation on working-class demands, but – without apparent unease – in the traditional policy of colonial repression.[1] In Algeria, the armistice riots were followed by a military pacification that left many thousands of Muslim dead in its wake. In Tunisia, the hostility of the French authorities led Bourguiba to flee in March 1945 and continue his nationalist campaign from Cairo and other centres of support in the Arab world.

The election of a Constituent Assembly in France revealed the Com-munist Party as the largest single organized force, with over five million votes and 158 seats, compared with the next contender, the Christian Democratic M.R.P., which took four and a half million votes and 152 seats. But the Communists were not bent on revolution, in France or anywhere else, and accepted de Gaulle's offer of five posts – none of them crucial – in his Cabinet of twenty-two. Then two months afterwards, in January 1946, de Gaulle himself retired, in disgust at the whole party system, and the coalition government of Communists, Socialists and M.R.P. continued under a succession of compromise premiers. It made no significant difference to colonial policy. The French attempted to re-establish control of Indo-China, where Ho Chi Minh, the head of the revolutionary Viet Minh, had proclaimed the Democratic Republic of

[1] See *De Gaulle*, by Alexander Werth (Penguin Books, 1965), pp. 170–203.

Vietnam in September 1945. Violence spread, and in November 1946 a French cruiser went into action against the port of Haiphong, killing some 6,000 civilians. The Viet Minh replied with a massive attack on French forces in December, and the war which was to last till 1954 and cost so many lives had begun. The communist representatives in the French government approved on March 23rd, 1947, the required military credits and dispatch of troops. Six days later rebellion broke out in Madagascar, and once again the French government moved to ruthless pacification; it would take till the end of 1948, and cost the lives of 80,000 islanders alongside 1,000 French soldiers before all resistance was crushed.[1]

But the Communists were not to watch the career of French force from the government window. The demands of the cold war and the mounting differences between the Communist Party and its parliamentary allies over the handling of industrial disputes led to the expulsion of the Communist members from the coalition in May 1947. Now in opposition, the Communists passionately opposed the Indo-China war. But their loyalty to imperial power was not at an end. After Mollet, the Socialist Premier, had surrendered to the rioting whites of Algiers in February 1956, his government appealed to the National Assembly for 'exceptional powers' to crush the nationalist rebellion. His Socialist Resident-Minister in Algeria addressed the deputies with all the fervour of an outraged patriotism. 'The time for promises is over; the time for action has come. France's presence in Algeria will be maintained ... No French government will ever abandon Algeria.' At the end of the debate Raymond Guyot, on behalf of the Communists, announced that his party would give the Mollet government a chance to pursue a democratic policy and bring peace to Algeria. The plenary powers were granted by 455 votes to 76, with only the extreme right – opposed to even so congenial a repression as this, when under Socialist command – voting against the government.[2]

The Communist Party of the United States was subordinated to Soviet views and interests with peculiarly corrupting effects. Indeed, the conduct of the Soviet government itself widely alienated Negro support. In the early 'thirties the cinema industry in the Soviet Union engaged a group of Negroes from the United States to help in making a film on racial discrimination in the Deep South; but the protests of Southern white engineers who were directing the construction of an important Soviet

1 *Madagascar*, by Olivier Hatzfeld (Presses Universitaires de France, 1960), pp. 93–4.
2 *The Strange History of Pierre Mendès-France and the Great Conflict over French North Africa*, by Alexander Werth (Barrie Books, 1957), pp. 291–300.

hydro-electric project led Stalin to command that the film be immediately abandoned, and the Negroes were sent home after a little soothing entertainment. News of this, followed by reports of Soviet oil sales to Italy during Mussolini's invasion of Abyssinia, did little to recommend Soviet motives to the leading Negro intellectuals.

It was the cynical manoeuvres of the communist leadership within the United States, however, and their generally obvious genesis abroad, that produced the deepest distrust of communism as an answer to the Negro problem. Established in 1920, the party set out to stretch its influence among Negroes by infiltrating the powerful Garvey movement. But Garvey himself, a self-proclaimed 'race man', deeply distrusted white radicals, encouraged his disciples to break up communist street meetings in Harlem, and assailed Negro Communists as 'Red Uncle Toms', whose revolutionary success would 'put their majority race or group still in power, not only as Communists but as white men'.[1] The Communist Party then, instead of merely propagating its policy in contrast, with stress on the racial emancipation which its own doctrine of world revolution entailed, responded by openly attempting to disrupt Garvey's organization. It was a costly mistake. Even those Negroes who found Garvey's methods crude and his personal posturings absurd were antagonized by this assault on a movement which was, after all, making colour and the African relationship a source of Negro self-assurance and militancy.

What followed, however, was worse. After the arrest, trial and deportation of Garvey, and the collapse of his movement, the Comintern slowly swung to an appreciation of why Garveyism had been so successful, and in an attempt to capitalize its appeal, launched a campaign in the 'thirties for the establishment of a Negro national home in the 'black belt' of the Deep South. It was the snap Stalinist solution for a 'national minority', and it was political suicide. The establishment of an independent Negro republic in the United States was not just wildly impractical; it represented the ultimate in racial segregation. But the Comintern was undeterred by argument, and those Communists – most of the influential Negroes in the party – who rejected the new programme were expelled as 'right-wing deviationists'. The Negro leaders outside the communist movement united in a strident derision. *Crisis*, official organ of the National Association for the Advancement of Coloured People (N.A.A.C.P.), declared: ' … in advancing this theory of separation, the Communists are hand in hand with the southern ruling class which they so delight to lambast. But since the Moscow masters are opportunists in

[2] Quoted in G. Padmore, op. cit., pp. 303–4.

the matter of war profit,[1] who would dare to criticize the American followers for opportunism in a little thing like race segregation? Who, indeed, except the segregated American Negro?'[2] No less havoc was caused by the Comintern policy towards South Africa, where the 'black republic' thesis, imposed on the local Communist Party, led to mass expulsions and defections.

Made inescapably aware that the 'national home' thesis was a fiasco, the Communist Party of the United States received permission to discard it and concentrated on the creation of a Popular Front. Ceasing its attacks on the middle-class Negro leadership of existing protest organizations like the N.A.A.C.P., it helped to form the National Negro Congress, with A. Philip Randolph, the socialist trade union leader, as Chairman. But again Soviet interest required a switch in policy, and with the Hitler-Stalin pact of 1939 the Communists in the Congress promoted opposition to any American help for the Western Allies against Germany. Randolph immediately resigned, along with other influential non-Communists, and issued a statement which reflected a racial as well as political disenchantment with the communist movement.

Negroes do not reject the Communist Party because it is revolutionary or radical or because of its alleged extremism. They reject the Communist Party because it is controlled and dominated by a foreign state whose policy may, or may not, be in the interests of the United States or the Negro people. American Negroes will not follow any organization which accepts dictation and control from the Communist Party. American Negroes will not follow any organization which accepts dictation and control from any white organizations.[3]

With Hitler's assault on the Soviet Union in June 1941, the Communist Party in the United States, as elsewhere, abruptly changed its attitude to the war. From attacking the Negro leaders for collaborating with the power structure, it now attacked them for refusing to collaborate, and for agitating, at the expense of the war effort, against discrimination in civilian employment and pay, or segregation in the armed forces. The Communists even openly opposed the March on Washington, organized by Negro leaders under Randolph's chairmanship to protest against the

---

[1] A reference to the Soviet oil sales to Mussolini.
[2] *Crisis*, October 1935.
[3] Quoted in G. Padmore, op. cit., p. 310.

refusal of war plants to hire Negroes, and were all the more derided when
President Roosevelt responded to the March by banning discrimination
on grounds of race, colour or creed in any industry concerned with war
work. It was such political acrobatics that made Negroes in the United
States see the Communist Party as a white movement, dedicated to
advancing the cause of a white foreign state, and not as a movement of all
races dedicated to advancing the cause of oppressed races everywhere.
Moreover, the communist failure within the United States had repercussions far beyond the Negro community there. Like Britain, the United
States attracted as students the very Africans who would return home to
lead movements of colonial rebellion – Azikiwe of Nigeria stayed in the
country during the late 'twenties and early 'thirties; Nkrumah of the
Gold Coast, during the late 'thirties and early 'forties – and the conduct of
the Communist Party there, with its effect on Negro opinion, could
scarcely have failed to impress them. Not the least important reason for
the seeming inability of the communist movement to make substantial
headway in Africa during the days of colonial insurrection was the disappointment with communist policy experienced by Africans visiting
the West.

As the Cold War increased in intensity and the Soviet Union concerned
herself more with the coloured colonial world, Soviet and communist
prestige unquestionably increased. Her very existence as an implied,
occasionally explicit, restraint on Western actions; the opportunities that
her power presented to the newly independent states and still struggling
nationalist movements for putting pressure on the West and attaining
greater freedom of manoeuvre; her vigorous use of the United Nations
for propaganda, all enabled the Soviet Union to put a little shine on her
revolutionary image. But a competitor for communist and revolutionary
influence – the two were not necessarily the same – now existed in China,
and China had the inescapable advantage of colour. A few months before
the Bandung Conference of April 1955, the *Times of India* proclaimed:

> Much will depend on whether Peking considers itself more Asian
> than Communist or *vice versa*. If the Asian-African Conference
> accomplishes nothing more than reveal to what extent the Com-
> munist is willing to co-operate with its Asian neighbours and Arab
> States, it will be a worthy attempt on behalf of Asian solidarity.
> Peking will then be given an opportunity to establish its *bona fides*
> and if possible to confound those sceptics who feel that, by the fact of
> being Communist, China is nearer to its fellow Communist States

in Europe than to its Asian neighbours with which it has racial and cultural ties.[1]

The Bandung Conference was an event of spectacular importance for several reasons. First, it excluded the Soviet Union, despite her long claim to be an Asian as well as a European state, and to be leading the struggle of the coloured colonial peoples to emancipation. The Soviet Union was, for the overwhelming mass of the participants, white and rich and powerful: not necessarily an oppressor or menace, though there were countries represented whose governments unhesitatingly thought so, but a member none the less of the race that had for so long dominated, and dominated still – if not politically, then economically; if not directly, then by the mere fact of its superior wealth and power – the coloured world. Next, the twenty-nine participants conformed to no ideology. They included such allies of the United States as Pakistan, the Philippines and Thailand on the right, to the People's Republic of China on the left, with spokesmen of non-alignment like India and Indonesia in between. They shared only their colour and their consciousness of what this had meant and continued to mean. Significantly one of the most scathing attacks on white racism came from Carlos P. Romulo, head of the Philippine delegation, who had been preceded by a reputation as one of the chief coloured spokesmen for the West. Thirdly, China won general acceptance – sometimes easy, sometimes grudging – as a coloured state rather than a communist one, a state rightfully in place among the gathered representatives of Africa and Asia. For this the chief Chinese delegate, Chou En-lai, was with his careful moderation, his ready reduction of all issues to the common factor of the Conference, substantially responsible. The Soviet Union was assailed time and again in closed sessions, and China did not defend her. China herself had been widely expected to ask Afro-Asian support for her claim to Formosa, but she expressly refused to do so 'because our Conference would be dragged into disputes about all these problems without any solution'. Instead, without mentioning race, she established herself in the racial context of Bandung through its ultimate meaning.

The overwhelming majority of the Asian and African countries and peoples have suffered and still are suffering from the calamities under colonialism. This is acknowledged by all of us. If we seek common ground in doing away with the sufferings and calamities under

[1] December 28th, 1954.

colonialism, it will be very easy for us to have mutual understanding
and respect, mutual sympathy and support, instead of mutual
suspicion and fear, mutual exclusion and antagonism ... We Asian
and African countries, China included, are all backward economically and culturally.[1]

In the ten years that followed, much was to change. The number of
independent coloured states would be swollen, by more than the total
present at Bandung, with the imperial retreat from Africa. China and
India, the major coloured nations, whose temporary understanding had
made the success of Bandung possible, would go to war with one another.
China and the Soviet Union would quarrel with such bitterness that their
rivalry would distract the non-aligned as well as the communist world.
Indeed, the mounting desire of the Soviet Union to attend any future
Bandung-type conference, and the mounting desire of China to have the
Soviet Union excluded once again, were to be materially responsible for
the indefinite postponement of an Afro-Asian meeting at Algiers in 1965.
But the experience of Bandung, however concealed by subsequent events,
remained. There, in 1955, the coloured countries had assembled and seen
not only their needs together and their weakness, but also their strength.
The full results may take a long time yet to ripen, but ripen they must,
  The harsher grew the quarrel between China and the Soviet Union.
and the more important to each of them the support, or at least formal
friendship, of the Afro-Asian states, the more urgently the Soviet Union
canvassed her claim to recognition as a partly Asian state, with a vested
interest, racially no less than ideologically, in the liberation of coloured
peoples from their political and economic subordination. But the demands
of a massive defence budget and a laggard agriculture, with the impatient
appetite of a population in Eastern Europe as well as at home for some of
tomorrow's jam, apparently prevented the provision of much money for
the struggle of the coloured world against economic backwardness.
Soviet aid could be dramatically abundant, as that to Nasser for the
building of the Aswan Dam, but very seldom; Soviet barter agreements
were useful, of course, but scarcely lavish; Soviet grants were small; and
Soviet loans carried a more than nominal, if less than ruling, rate of
interest. Furthermore, the conduct of the communist bloc at the United
Nations, as in the crisis over the 'troika' Secretariat, increasingly reflected
a closer concern with great-power interests than with fortifying an in-

[1] Quoted in *The Colour Curtain*, by Richard Wright. A Report, by the Negro radical and
novelist, on the Bandung Conference (Dennis Dobson, 1956), pp. 135–6.

dependent authority which the coloured states, by the pressure of their numbers, might gradually direct to their benefit. Certainly, it did not need the shrill accusations of China to reveal that the commandments of peaceful co-existence with the West in the nuclear shadow were promoting caution in the Soviet encouragement of revolution. Still, the Soviet Union was willing to supply scholarships as well as sermons, and students from the coloured world might live in the most powerful socialist society on earth, learning its skills and techniques, without encountering the racial prejudice that so marked the capitalist West.

Suddenly, on December 18th, 1963, hundreds of African students, finally provoked, it seems, by the discovery of a dead Ghanaian medical student a few days before in the snow some miles from Moscow, marched to the Kremlin with such slogans as 'Stop killing Africans' and 'Moscow a second Alabama'. Leaders of the demonstration complained that Africans often met with racial hostility from Russians, that those who were seen with white women were sometimes assaulted and that the police frequently took the part of the white assailants. The dead Ghanaian student had been hoping to marry a Russian woman, whose family had made clear their resentment at the association.

Less than a year and a half later, Kenyan students at Baku, in Azerbaijan on the Caspian Sea, went on strike and camped out at the railway station in protest at their treatment and the death of a Ghanaian student. Their spokesmen claimed that Russians had shown themselves contemptuous of Africans, that in restaurants waiters had refused to serve them, that they had been forbidden to dance with white women in the town, and that several of them had been ambushed and attacked by Russian gangs with sticks and clubs. Of the reported eighty-two Kenyans at Baku University, twenty-nine were flown back to Nairobi on their refusal to stay any longer.

Few incidents could have proved more embarrassing than these to the Soviet government, since they appeared to confirm reports, long circulating in the non-aligned world and eagerly seized upon by the West, that colour prejudice was common in the homeland of socialism. Yet the categorical denials of any racial discrimination in the Soviet Union which squeezed through the tight lips of officialdom after such incidents merely heightened suspicion that much was being carefully concealed.

A denunciation of attacks on the Soviet Union for racism, in a letter to *The African Communist*[1] from 'an African Student in the Soviet Union', revealed a great deal in the very listing of explanations. Not without

[1] No. 17, April-June 1964, pp. 55-9.

justice, the correspondent claimed that some of the more than 2,000 African students in the Soviet Union came with preconceptions that it was no business of the Soviet authorities to confirm. 'Sons of chiefs, sheiks and other feudal rulers, relations of middle-class cabinet ministers' found 'the socialist approach to higher education uncongenial'. A few were disappointed in their expectation of 'a gay and carefree life' abroad. Attempts at discipline by the authorities were too easily attributed to a racial prejudice. And the mask of language led to 'misunderstandings and mistaken resentments'. (It is only too probable that African students from privileged, or indeed unprivileged, homes, anticipating so much from a visit to the bright rich world of white power, are often disappointed with the drab isolation of a provincial Soviet town or the less drab, but no less careful, isolation of hostel and language in the capital.) But all this, even for the apologist, was obviously inadequate.

In all the socialist countries, no doubt, there still exist a few anti-social leftovers who suffer from the disease of race prejudice ... It must be said, also, that sufficient effort is not always made from the other side to integrate our students and make them feel more at home. Some elements among the local students resent the fact that the foreign students receive higher stipends than they do themselves, and show this resentment. Instead of understanding that these people are not typical of the socialist society, a few African students generalize their errors to encompass the whole society ... The African student in the Soviet Union is treated as an equal and, apart from minor un-typical incidents (which are energetically dealt with by the authorities) the student body as a whole has no doubts about the absence of racial discrimination in the socialist system.

It is not altogether persuasive. The record of incidents, not only in the Soviet Union but in Bulgaria, Czechoslovakia, Poland, Romania – seldom leading to anything as dramatic as the Moscow riot or the Baku strike, but producing an accumulated African bitterness none the less – is too bulky for parcelling away in irresponsible resentment. To find Western satisfaction at the existence of racial prejudice in the Soviet Union and Eastern Europe disgusting – as even those Africans most bitter at their experiences in the world of white communism do – is not to deny or diminish the existence or effects of the prejudice. Unhappily, a distrust of strangers is a not unnatural response of humanity, and the particular disparagement of colour is a not unnatural response of European history. The ordinary citizens of Sofia and Prague, Warsaw and Moscow are white Europeans before they are – even when they think of themselves as being – Communists. The Soviet leadership, especially after the exposure of Stalinism, lays no serious claim to having inaugurated the millennium. Alexi, the Soviet student in Jan Carew's novel, *Moscow is not my Mecca*,[1] offers one view:

> Many Muscovites are peasants who have just shuffled their way into the city ... you will hear them talking about their fellow peasants as 'dirty brutes', 'uncultured animals', but this is just a reflection of their closeness to the very people they are denouncing. And when they shout 'black monkey' at you on the streets, this is just their coarse and uninhibited way of showing their bewilderment at seeing something new. Strangers are new to all of us – black strangers and white ones ... and now, all of a sudden we have young people from the four corners of the earth amongst us – Arabs, Africans, Indonesians, Guianese, Latin Americans, Indians – you must try and understand our confusion at having these strange people in our midst. Another factor is that we are your hosts; we have been told again and again that your people are hungry and illiterate, victims of imperialist greed and oppression ... we were never told that some of you had travelled to New York, Rome, London, Paris, and that we would envy you your clothes, your way of talking freely about things we don't dare to mention ...

The Africans, and other students from the coloured world, do not behave as their hosts would like them to behave; they object to the segregation from Soviet life that official care and private reserve seek to impose; they want to go where they please and probe; they want to meet women, take them dancing, make love to them, marry them; they compete with white men for white women and there is glamour, too, in the strange; they sometimes criticize what they see or hear or are taught; they do not conform to custom; and they are not apparently as grateful as Soviet generosity expects. Perhaps they see the attitude of the officials with whom they come into contact as more patronizing than it really is. Yet it would be singular indeed if some officials, short enough with their own nationals, could altogether disguise their pride of power in dealing with dark-skinned foreigners; the effort of adjustment must give away much more than it hides. Perhaps the coloured students see more

[1] Secker & Warburg, 1964, p. 90.

specifically racial antagonism than really exists. But it would be silly to suppose that Africans would demonstrate in Moscow and strike in Baku – activities unwelcome to their own governments and by no means automatically productive of richer scholarships elsewhere – on the provocation of an isolated incident and a trivial discontent.

The truth is that the Soviet Union, despite her own insistence that she is just as much an Asian as a European state, seems to care far more about Europe than about Asia. Over 20 per cent of her population is 'non-white', but she regards herself – and is generally regarded – as white. When, therefore, she gives the impression of concerning herself less with the requirements of world revolution than with the further development of her already advanced economy; when she argues for time to establish the superiority of socialism and against running unnecessary risk of war with the West in a nuclear age, there are critics ready to cry that she is fundamentally racist, a rich white state as afraid of coloured insurrection as is any of her formal capitalist adversaries. For such critics, the treatment of coloured students in the Soviet Union, as reflected in the response of the coloured students themselves, is nothing more than what ought reasonably to be expected.

In such a context, the course of the Sino-Soviet dispute has dangerous turnings. Khrushchev, in his last two years of power, had pursued the doctrinal quarrel with a personal vehemence that had not excluded occasional reports in the Soviet press of China's territorial appetites, and the repugnant conduct of Chinese citizens in the Soviet Union. With his fall, the climate had seemed to clear a little. Then, on March 4th, 1965, Afro-Asian students, mainly it seems from China and North Vietnam, demonstrated outside the United States embassy in Moscow against American policy in Vietnam, and clashed with Soviet police. The Chinese press made much of the event, claiming that the police had been brutal and that the Soviet authorities had subsequently conducted 'political persecution of seriously wounded students in the hospitals'.[1] The principal cause of complaint was obvious: 'It is unprecedented in history that the government of a socialist country should have gone so far as to use force in broad daylight to suppress the just struggle of the masses against U.S. imperialism ... ' But the incident was, by the nature of the participants and the issues over which they were engaged, racial as well as political. There had already been – and would be again – reports in the Chinese press of racial discrimination by Soviet against Chinese citizens. And

[1] *People's Daily*, March 15th, 1965.

where the racial aspect was muted in public comment, it was less circum-spectly treated in private talk.

In the novel *Moscow is not my Mecca* written by the first student from British Guiana to visit the Soviet Union on a scholarship, one of the characters, Malcolm, declares himself at a meeting of Guianese students in Moscow on the Sino-Soviet dispute.

If the thousands of Chinese who studied here were treated the way we are being treated by our Russian hosts, then I can understand very well why there is a rift between the two countries. Comrade Hardyal's case is indeed a strong one, he says that we are the victims of Russian generosity and should be grateful, but if Karl Marx had reasoned that the British were his hosts, that they allowed him the freedom of the British Museum, and that he was duty bound to write *Das Kapital* as a work in support of British Capitalism and not one aimed at destroying it, then communism would never have existed ... China is, like Guiana, an under-developed country and a country of coloured peoples and in this respect we are closer to China than we are to Russia. But the Chinese are new converts to communism and we are not. What the dispute is laying bare to us, and we must take heed and ponder over this question, is the arrogance of the senior white partners in the communist bloc to a junior coloured partner. The language of the Russian leaders, when they speak of the Chinese, is sounding more like that of a Southern racialist talking about Negroes, and this, plus my own experiences of racial discrimination here, makes me somewhat suspicious of the Russian claims, even though we are all being bombarded with propaganda to support the sane and logical Russian case for coexistence with the West against the irrational, overzealous and intransigent Chinese.[1]

Whether exaggerated, finally unfair, or not, such a sentiment is as much a fact now of international life as poverty and colour.

[1] Pp. 81–3.

6

The Yellow World of China

When that scout of a still dark and largely feudal Europe, Marco Polo, visited China in the thirteenth century, he found a country which had climbed out of feudalism some fifteen hundred years before and which he considered, by his European standards, to be the most powerful, stable and efficiently ruled in the world. His wonder was not unique. Since the rise of Rome at least and until the nineteenth century, the flow of commodities was overwhelmingly from East to West. Europe sought silks and spices, and paid China in silver and gold. Moreover, though the West now takes peculiar pride in its technological achievements, the transmission of major new techniques was, until the mere yesterday of the industrial revolution, no less overwhelmingly from East to West. From the West, China took the screw, the force-pump for liquids, the crankshaft and clockwork. But China knew the rotary fan some fourteen centuries, and porcelain some twelve centuries, before the West; paper, the wheelbarrow, magnetic compass, suspension bridge and deep drill, with cast iron and water power, some ten centuries; gunpowder and printing, some six centuries; and the draw-loom, some four.[1]

China seemed indeed a country of infinite promise, where merchants might make money, and priests, converts, with exuberant ease. But the Chinese empire was self-sufficient and satisfied, it welcomed neither Western manufactures nor religion; and it displayed a cultural arrogance which the expansionist West regarded as its own monopoly. Repeated Christian missions to China had little success and diplomatic overtures even less. The Chinese government dealt with tributaries, not equals, and insisted on a *kowtow* before the imperial presence which Western envoys considered humiliating. But if China wanted nothing from the West, the West wanted a great deal from China – silk, porcelain, lacquer and, above all, tea. At first the Western merchants paid in silver; but then they discovered in opium a commodity cheap to produce and, once consumers had been nourished to need it, costly to buy, so that silver was

---

[1] These items are a selection from the twenty-six cited by Dr Joseph Needham in his *Science and Civilization in China* (Cambridge University Press, 1961), Vol. I, pp. 240–43.

soon streaming back into their pockets. The Chinese government made agitated efforts to restrict the trade while the British merchants and manufacturers urged their government not only to protect it, but to force a passage for other commodities. In 1839 the Opium War broke out between China and Britain; the British, with their mass-produced armaments and naval superiority, proved successful; and the Treaty of Nanking (1842), with subsequent agreements, prised China open to Western enterprise. China was forced to pay a huge indemnity to Britain for the cost of fighting the war; a tariff on all imported goods – low enough to discourage domestic industrialization but high enough to produce the necessary tribute – was imposed; and the Western nations secured not only the right to trade at a number of ports, where autonomous foreign settlements were established, but also jurisdiction over their respective nationals. Moreover, Britain, confident in her industrial supremacy and consequent allegiance to free trade, forced from China the concession that all foreign countries could enjoy the privileges that any one of them obtained. China became an international colony, prey to any state with the merchant ships and guns to satisfy its appetite.

The humiliation for a country that had so long considered itself the centre of the world was for the time stupefying. Traditional tributaries were snatched away: Burma by Britain; Indo-China, by France. Western missionaries multiplied, many of them openly contemptuous of Chinese culture, yet protected from reprisal by the support of their governments. The Manchu dynasty, already in decay and with its prestige shattered by the Opium War, was held in place by the European powers, who naturally preferred a corrupt and manageable regime to an efficient, popular and self-confident one. The Taiping Rebellion, a part peasant, part nationalist rising against Manchu rule, broke out at the end of the eighteen forties, lasted seventeen years, and cost some twenty million lives; its eventual suppression was made possible only by military assistance, in officers and material, from the Western powers. The real rulers of China were no longer in the palace, to be displaced by traditional methods when they had outlived their value; they were beyond the seas, and their hunger had not yet been appeased.

While Russia advanced her frontier from the north, Britain and France acted in concert from the south. Lord Elgin was sent from London as Envoy Extraordinary to pursue a more vigorous policy, and marched north with French and British forces to acquire new Treaty Ports and other trading privileges. He was frank at least in his diary, where he described his commission as 'resorting to the most violent measures of

coercion and repression on the slenderest provocation'.[1] War inevitably
followed, the Europeans captured Peking, and as a salutary lesson in
civilized conduct, sacked the Summer Palace. They then took ten new
Treaty Ports, some of them far inland; established embassies in Peking;
imposed another huge indemnity to meet the cost of their exertions, and
took control of the customs service to ensure payment; grabbed Kowloon,
a stretch of territory opposite Hong Kong, for British rule; legalized the
importing of opium by the imposition of a tax; and enforced formal
agreement to the activities of Christian missionaries and converts throughout the country. The United States, suddenly awakened to the opportunities in the Far East, demanded and received the same privileges as the
European states had secured. The Russians, as a reward for helping to
negotiate a settlement with the Western assailants, acquired not only the
commercial and diplomatic rights forced out of China by Britain and
France, but a substantial stretch of territory, which extended her southern
frontier to the border of Korea and provided her with the site for the
town of Vladivostok.

Japan had since the seventeenth century pursued a seclusion policy,
and as she apparently possessed no noticeably desirable commodities,
like China's silk or tea, she was left alone by the European maritime
powers. With her expansion to the Pacific, however, the United States
grew interested in Japan, especially as a station on the way to Shanghai,
and in 1853 threatened force if the country was not opened to her. Japan
was not so secluded as to be unaware of what China had suffered from
Western ships and guns; she gave a little. But it was enough; the United
States, joined now by Britain, Russia and France, demanded more. She
attempted resistance and was immediately defeated. Reformers, drawn
from the military caste, took power in the name of the emperor and
applied themselves to making their country respected by the means
which the West had used to such profitable effect. With industrialization
and massive armament, Japan soon felt herself strong enough to seek
control of neighbouring territories, both as an outer defence and a step
towards further expansion. In 1894 she clashed with China over Korea.
The Manchu Court had been living in a state of luxuriant lethargy, consuming much of the money raised by special taxes to strengthen and
modernize the armed forces. China was again humiliated, forced to
acknowledge the independence of Korea, cede Formosa to Japan, and pay
a huge indemnity into the bargain.

[1] Quoted in *The Invasion of China by the Western World*, by E. R. Hughes (Adam and Charles
Black, 1937), p. 26.

The European powers were seriously disturbed at this arrival of a new-comer – and a coloured one at that – to share in their exploitation of China, and they hastened to extend the regions of their individual con-trol; Russia, Britain, France and Germany acquired 'leases', or colonies in all but name, and railway concessions that offered economic bridgeheads to yet further advance. The process of foreign expansion seemed likely to end only in the total dismemberment of China, and nationalist resent-ment gave rise to a multitude of secret societies, aimed at overthrowing the Manchu dynasty and expelling the 'foreign devils' from the country. In 1894 Sun Yat-sen, a young doctor who had studied in the West, began collecting arms for a revolt in the south, but the plot was discovered and Sun forced to flee into exile. Disaffection steadily mounted, and in the last years of the century one secret society, known to the West as the Boxers,[1] achieved a massive following in the north. The Manchu Court, capable now of nothing more than intrigue, sought desperately to deflect the threat to its own survival by associating itself with the movement against the foreigners; in the Boxer Rebellion of 1900, some two hundred European missionaries were murdered, and the European diplomatic settlement in Peking besieged. An international force arrived, took the capital and looted it, imposed one more huge indemnity, and prohibited the importation of arms and ammunition for two years. Yet the Manchu dynasty was permitted to remain, a lacquered ventriloquist's doll of the main foreign powers. China was ready for partition on the African model, but the United States in 1899 had proclaimed an 'Open Door' policy, by which any imperial encroachment was to be shared with American trade and enterprise. The United States had two objectives: to secure her proper portion of the plunder, and to prevent foreign rivalries from flaring into war; but if she succeeded lavishly in the first, she failed in the second.

Inevitably the principal powers feared each other's appetite. Japan was already seeing herself as the dominating force and beneficiary of a move-ment to sweep the whites out of Asia, and in 1904 she went to war with Russia for possession of Manchuria. Her victory reverberated through the world; for the first time in centuries a non-white people had defeated in war one of the foremost white powers. Racial sentiment was rising; in 1904 China responded to American bars against Chinese immigration with a nation-wide boycott of American trade. Thousands of Chinese students now went to Japan where Sun Yat-sen was in exile and planning the foundation of a republic. Revolutionary ideas coursed through China,

[1] Because its members were trained in a special form of boxing.

with resistance to the Manchus increasingly assuming the shape of demands for provincial autonomy. At last an imperial edict taking centralized control of the main railway system sparked off rebellion; one province after the other declared its independence, and in February 1912 the Manchu empire came to an end.

The West was less than enthusiastic; any successful experiment with democracy would have a most unsettling effect on colonial peoples. Japan herself was a divine empire and could not reasonably be expected to relish the prospect of a republic so near by, eager and one day strong enough to take back all that a weak imperial China had lost. The foreign powers circled, but did not have to swoop. The parliament elected in 1912 was scarcely less corrupt and ineffectual than the Manchu Court had been; votes were openly sold, and the successful candidates directed themselves to the urgent task of appropriating large salaries. Yuan Shih-kai, the only leader in possession of a modern army, was elected first President; proved his moderation by confirming all the privileges that the foreigners had snatched by the 'unequal treaties'; and secured an enormous loan from the European powers without consulting parliament, so placing himself beyond the tedious restraints of the constitution. The militant nationalists under Sun Yat-sen turned violently against him, and in 1916, after failing in an attempt to establish a new imperial dynasty, Yuan died.

The new republic was being torn apart. Seizing the opportunity offered by the First World War, Japan swallowed the German interests in Shantung and presented 'Twenty-One Demands', whose acceptance would have turned China into a virtual vassal. Western intervention prevented any such submission, but China was none the less compelled to grant several important Japanese 'leaseholds' and control over two major railway lines. With the collapse of all real central authority, she fell a helpless prey to war-lords, each trying to capture Peking and so recognition of the right to the customs revenues which the foreign representatives were collecting. The European powers busily adopted different contenders, hoping to find one able to govern China on behalf of his backer and meanwhile profitably disposing of the arms that the end of their own war had left so heavy on their hands. Japan herself carefully supported several war-lords at the same time, to prevent an effective dictatorship and keep China distracted enough for further conquest. Over a prostrated peasantry, the generals fought each other for money, selling official posts, promoting the opium trade, taxing the people for years in advance and finally retiring to the safety of the foreign concessions, while the civil service, the great irrigation works, communications and commerce fell into decay. In the south, at Canton, Sun Yat-sen established a republican regime, but he was no less dependent than the central government at Peking on the whims of the war-lords, who used his popular following to hoist themselves to power and then discarded him. Only the Chinese communities abroad, in the United States and the European colonies, turning from the discrimination that they everywhere encountered to the promise of a once more powerful and proud China, supplied him with encouragement and resources.

The gaze of the Chinese revolution had been westwards to begin with, an adoption of the democratic standards that seemed to have made Britain, France and the United States such formidable forces. But democracy was showing itself unable to cope with either internal militarists or external aggressors, while the principal democracies themselves fed on Chinese chaos. Desperately Sun Yat-sen appealed to Britain and the United States to recognize his regime and help in the overthrow of the war-lords; he was refused. The Russian Revolution had stirred only a few intellectuals at first, but in 1920, when the Soviet government at last gained control of all its territory, it offered to renounce its imperial privileges in China. This gesture was all the more effective by contrast with the rigorous assertion of their rights by the Western democracies, and in 1921 Sun Yat-sen met Adolph Joffe, Soviet emissary, in Shanghai. In the name of his Kuomintang, or Nationalist Party, Sun accepted the aid of the Soviet Union and the collaboration of the still infant Chinese Communist Party, for a nationalist programme aimed at expelling foreign privileges and power; Chiang Kai-shek and other Kuomintang militants went to Moscow for military training, and Soviet advisers attached themselves to the Kuomintang forces. By 1925, when Sun Yat-sen himself died, peasants, merchants and intellectuals were united in demanding an end to warrior rule and foreign intrusions. For them, the white Westerner especially, with his overweening power and wealth, was to blame for the sorrows of China; once he was driven out, his privileges abolished and his concessions seized, the country could stride towards unity, modernization and respect.

On May 30th police of the International Settlement in Shanghai fired on a crowd of demonstrating students, and all China seemed to rise in rage. Early in 1926, on a crest of popular enthusiasm, the armed forces of the Kuomintang under Chiang Kai-shek moved north from Canton, sweeping away the half-hearted resistance of the war-lords. And outstripping their speedy advance came social revolution, as Communists scattered through the countryside, organizing the peasantry against the landlords, or excited the workers of Shanghai to rebellion.

The Western governments grew alarmed, and as the army of the Kuomintang approached Shanghai, Britain rushed a strong force of troops there to garrison the International Settlement, while warships anchored off the ports where foreign concessions existed. The workers of Shanghai under communist leadership seized control of the Chinese city from the local war-lord, and when the Kuomintang army arrived a few days later, the revolution and the forces of the foreign powers faced each other across a stretch of barbed wire. War with the West seemed inevitable, if the nationalist coalition did not split, and the Russians had instructed the Chinese Communists to maintain the coalition at all costs. Then suddenly in April 1927 Chiang Kai-shek struck, killing those communist leaders he could catch, proscribing the Communist Party itself, and sending the Russian advisers back to Moscow. The Western governments were delighted, and when Kuomintang forces captured Peking in the following year and moved the capital from there to Nanking, the Chiang Kai-shek regime was formally recognized as the rightful government of China.

The Communists were quite unprepared for separate revolutionary action. China was not an industrial society and possessed only a small urban proletariat, so that the Russians had advised – indeed commanded – their Chinese colleagues to promote first a 'bourgeois nationalist' revolution through the Kuomintang. Now that Chiang Kai-shek had made such collaboration impossible, the Russians produced a disastrous directive: since the peasants were, by Marxist teaching and Russian experience, not a revolutionary force, the Chinese Communist Party would have to make do with the proletariat there was and try to seize the cities. The Communists were obedient, and massacred. The remnants fled to the mountain fastness of Chingkangshan, and there found in Mao Tse-tung a military leader of genius.

Mao and Chu Teh, who had brought a portion of the Fourth Army under the red flag, established a communist regime based on the peasantry, with land reform as its policy and guerilla warfare its defence. Moving to southern Kiangsi in early 1929, they set up a base area which was to become the Chinese Soviet Republic, and to all commands from Moscow through the Central Committee of the Chinese Communist Party that he should concentrate his forces on organizing the workers in the cities, Mao replied by accepting the validity of such advice and doing meanwhile what he believed to be more profitable. Mao himself found his military guidance not in Russian tracts or instructions, but in the maxims of Sun Tzu, the Chinese sage of the fifth century B.C.

By discovering the enemy's dispositions and remaining invisible ourselves, we can keep our forces concentrated while the enemy must be divided ... Hence there will be a whole pitted against separate parts of the whole, which means that we shall be many in collected mass to the enemy's separate few.

All warfare is based upon deception. Hence, when able to attack, we must seem unable; when using our forces, we must seem inactive; when we are near, we must make the enemy believe that we are far away; when far away, we must make him believe we are near. Hold out baits to entice the enemy. Feign disorder and crush him. If he is secure at all points, be prepared for him. If he is superior in strength, evade him.[1]

On such classic principles, Mao Tse-Tung was to develop a strategy that would not only hold off the vastly superior forces sent repeatedly against him by Chiang Kai-shek, but in the end win all China for the Communists.

'We use', he declared, 'the few to defeat the many – this we say to the rulers of China as a whole. We use the many to defeat the few – this we say to the enemy on the battlefield. That is no longer a secret, and in general the enemy is by now well acquainted with our method. But he can neither prevent our victories nor avoid his own losses, because he does not know when and where we shall act.'[2]

On the Chingkangshan, the Communists invented a slogan that reflected Mao's flexible strategy.

'The enemy advances, we retreat;
The enemy camps, we harass;
The enemy tires, we attack;
The enemy retreats, we pursue.'

Chiang Kai-shek himself meanwhile satisfied neither the appetite for social reform nor the nationalist demands for the expulsion of the foreigner. The countryside with its depressed peasantry and its rapacious

[1] Quoted in the biography of Mao Tse-tung by Dr Stuart Schram, to be published by Penguin Books.
[2] Ibid.

landlords remained virtually unchanged, and the Kuomintang offered
no promise but a distant democratic constitution. The foreigners renounced a few of their concessions, but kept the important ones together
with all their privileges. Above all, the Japanese pursued their policy of
expansion with little effective check from Nanking. Already in control
of Manchuria, they were to annex it in the wrapping paper of the Manchu dynasty, wrest North China from Kuomintang command, and at
last openly invade the whole country. But while the people, led by the
still loyal intellectuals, clamoured against the abandonment of province
after province to the aggressor, Chiang Kai-shek squandered his forces in
costly campaigns against the Communists in the south. The policy of
'internal pacification before resistance to external attack' encouraged
Japanese expansionism without crushing internal revolt.

Chiang Kai-shek's first vast encirclement campaign of December 1930
to January 1931, which pitted 100,000 Kuomintang soldiers against the
40,000 in the Red Army, ended in total failure and heavy casualties. The
second campaign, of April to June 1931, sent 200,000 men against the
Red Army's 30,000; but by dividing the forces ranged against him, Mao
repeatedly defeated them, and in addition captured a huge quantity of
needed arms. Thoroughly aroused, Chiang went south himself at the head
of 300,000 troops for the third campaign; but after a series of delaying
actions and then sudden victorious attacks by the Red Army, the Kuomintang forces were withdrawn in September, on news of fresh Japanese
aggressions. From April to October 1933 the fourth encirclement campaign took place with 250,000 Kuomintang troops, to end in the destruction of three Kuomintang divisions and the capture by the Communists
of several thousand rifles. Meanwhile, however, within the Kiangsi
Soviet itself, Mao's policy and influence were coming under increasing
attack from a number of Moscow-trained and -directed students, who
had arrived in Kiangsi as guardians of orthodox communism. With the
support of colleagues like Chou En-lai, who had master-minded the
Shanghai workers' uprising in February 1927, they claimed that Mao's
strategy no longer suited a Red Army that had grown to a strength of
several hundred thousand soldiers, and they promoted instead a policy
of offence, signalled in the new slogans 'Attack on all fronts' and 'Seize
key cities'. It was the old Moscow obsession with the proletariat, and it
was to cost the Communists dear once again. The fifth and greatest
encirclement campaign in 1934, involving 400,000 Kuomintang troops,
was conducted by Chiang Kai-shek himself under the guidance of German
military advisers, with the construction of concrete block-houses in a ring

round the whole Soviet area in Kiangsi. Mao may still have been able to counter this positional warfare by tactics of his own, but he was no longer in command, and the Moscow line required costly engagements which finally led, in Mao's own words, to 'complete passivity'. By the summer, it became clear that the Communists would have to break through the siege and withdraw from Kiangsi if they were to survive. The Chinese Soviet Republic had already declared separate war on Japan in April 1932, and it now announced its retreat from Kiangsi as the march of an 'anti-Japanese vanguard' northwards to fight the invaders.

The Long March, as it is known to history,[1] nearly ended in disaster at the outset, through the advice of the Comintern's German emissary, who had advocated the costly positional defence of the fifth encirclement campaign and now proposed taking a direct route to the North, even though this meant a head-on collision with far stronger Kuomintang forces. After one serious defeat, however, Mao was at the beginning of 1935 confirmed again in complete control, and his circuitous tactics, with the heroism of his following, saved the communist army from annihilation. The endeavour was stupendous, as were the costs. Some 100,000 set out – 85,000 soldiers and 15,000 political cadres; less than 20,000 entered northern Shensi, just below the Great Wall, in October 1935, a year after the departure from Kiangsi. The journey covered over 6,000 miles, and was made on foot across some of the most turbulent terrain in all Asia, with frequent battles and forced marches along the way; the forces of Mao, ill-equipped and overstrained, had to break through the enveloping armies of ten provincial war-lords, as well as defeat or evade the troops of the Kuomintang sent against them.

Yet the very effort was immensely productive. The Communists passed through twelve provinces with more than 200 million people in them, and wherever they went, in the intervals between fighting, they held huge mass meetings; gave theatrical performances; confiscated the property of officials, landlords and tax-collectors, and distributed it among the poorer peasants; preached and practised the revolution which the Chinese countryside craved. In their wake they left new perceptions and demands, together with arms for peasant rebellion and political advisers to train a multitude of eager partisans. And at the end, in the north-west of China, they were facing the Japanese, in a struggle which the Kuomintang had shirked and to which they now themselves brought the nationalist aspirations of the whole country.

Above all, what the Chinese Communists had done, they had done on

[1] Eloquently described by Edgar Snow in *Red Star Over China* (Victor Gollancz, 1937).

their own. While the Western powers, democratic and fascist alike, had sent aeroplanes, tanks, guns, ammunition and military experts to Chiang Kai-shek for his wars against the Communists – the American Army had released officers to train the Kuomintang air force, and Nazi Germany had provided one of its most able generals, von Seeckt, with a large supporting mission – the Soviet Union had given the Communists in return little more than dangerous directives. There had been no foreign adviser with the Red Army during the first five years of its existence, and the one who finally arrived in 1933 would have done a good deal better to stay in Moscow. Financial aid from the Soviet Union had amounted at most to a few thousand dollars a month, while the West had poured millions into the coffers of the Kuomintang; one American Wheat Loan to Nanking in 1933, worth $50 million, had been of crucial value to Chiang Kai-shek in his campaigns against the Kiangsi Soviet.

Despite this foreign help, however, the Kuomintang was steadily losing ground. Drafts for a democratic constitution snapped at each other's heels, with none producing a popular assembly and every new version offering still more power to the executive than its predecessor had done. While Chiang Kai-shek played off one faction of the Kuomintang against the other, imprisoning, banishing or killing his more serious rivals, the countryside sank further into misery and disaffection. In December 1936 he launched an 'extermination drive' against the new communist regime in Shensi, but a portion of his forces – eager to fight the Japanese rather than the Red Army – mutinied and arrested him. The Communists demanded a peace pact with the Kuomintang and a united front against Japan, offering in return to place their army at the disposal of the central government and formally recognize its authority. Chiang Kai-shek had no alternative but murder at the hands of the mutineers, and agreed. To all China, especially the educated class which had by and large abandoned the Kuomintang, the Communists now appeared patriotic rural reformers, ready to sacrifice power for the good of China, responsible for ending the civil war and compelling the government to resist Japan. To the Yenan university of the Communists in the Shensi hills, students streamed from all over China, seeking and finding the promise of an escape from twenty-five years of corruption, confusion and incompetence.

When Japan had invaded Manchuria in 1931, the Western powers had stood by, reassuring themselves that Japanese expansionism would be ultimately directed against the Soviet Union and that meanwhile it was prudent to let Japan shoulder the main responsibility for law and order in China. The League of Nations had decided with great dignity to do nothing – a source of subsequent encouragement to Italy and Germany – while private investors in Western Europe and the United States, with the acquiescence of their governments, had greedily joined the Japanese in exploiting the new Chinese conquests. Then, in July 1937, Japan manufactured an 'incident' at a bridge outside Peking and set out on a full-scale invasion of China. Again the Western powers, now fearful of embroilment in a general war, took no steps to halt Japan, and the United States, seeing no reason to turn her back on the enhanced possibilities for profit in the Far East, continued for four years more to supply the Japanese with two-thirds of the war materials that they required for their war of aggression against China.[1] At first the Kuomintang forces fought fiercely, yielding the whole of North China under irresistible pressure but defending Shanghai for three months. The outside world admired such courage and endurance, but provided nothing to sustain it, and by the end of the year the Kuomintang government was driven from its capital at Nanking. As the Japanese absorbed more and more of the country, with the richest and most populous of the provinces, the Kuomintang lost heart. Canton was taken by the Japanese with such ease that only betrayal or a paralysing despair seemed to offer an adequate explanation. From the end of 1939 the Kuomintang regime sat in Chungking, its war capital, making small effort to recapture any of the lost territory and waiting for the course of the world war to sweep the Japanese away.

The Communists, on the other hand, sent guerilla bands into the occupied areas, organizing partisan warfare, installing effective government wherever Japanese control did not reach, collecting taxes and promoting land reform. The Japanese burnt villages and massacred peasants in reprisal, but could never get to grips with the partisan forces. Alarmed by this communist arming of the peasantry, the Kuomintang sent no material aid for the guerilla effort, and continued to pursue its policy of 'selling space for time'. Moscow, of course, still enveloped in visions of the slow measured progress required by a proletarian revolution, approved of the united front with Chiang Kai-shek, but was reluctant to offend Japan. Stalin himself remained unimpressed by the methods and potential of the Chinese Communist Party, and had not forgiven its leaders for their persistent disobedience. As late as 1945 he would tell the United States that he did not regard the Chinese Communists as a serious force and recognized Chiang Kai-shek's regime as the only proper government of China.[2] So once again, the Chinese Communists were on

[1] *The New Cambridge Modern History*, Volume XII (C.U.P., 1964), p. 235.
[2] *Revolution in China*, by C. P. FitzGerald (The Cresset Press, 1952), p. 17.

their own, receiving help neither from their new ally in the national united front nor from their old one in the citadel of world communism.

At last in December 1941 Japan attacked the American fleet at Pearl Harbour, and Chiang Kai-shek had the time for which he had sold so much space. But the West, far from helping to take China now by force, fell back from one possession after the other in the Far East before Japanese attack, and such prestige as the white West still enjoyed crumbled under the salvos of its weakness. The Kuomintang army, short of food and munitions, with its troops steadily losing their morale and its officers devoting themselves to personal profit, even to the extent of covertly trading with the enemy, seemed sunk in stupor. Only the success of the communist guerillas roused Chiang Kai-shek to bouts of frantic energy, and when the New Fourth Army, as the communist formation was now called, crossed the Yangtze to carry resistance into the south, it was attacked by Kuomintang troops. The government forces in Shensi even blockaded the communist base area of Yenan, cutting it off not merely from munitions but from medical supplies contributed by sympathizers in the West. The united front was in ruins, and only the Japanese presence prevented the flaring of full-scale civil war.

The dropping of atomic bombs on Hiroshima and Nagasaki in August 1945 – an act which would in time be assailed as illustrating the peculiar disregard of the white West for yellow Asian lives – brought immediate Japanese surrender, and the West hastened to take command of China, though not before the Soviet Union had marched into Manchuria and occupied Japan's one-time puppet empire of Manchukuo. An immediate challenge faced the Western Allies – effectively now the dominant United States – in the Japanese-held cities. The Americans did not hesitate. It was perfectly clear to them, President Truman was later to write, that if they told the Japanese to lay down their arms immediately and march to the seaboard, the entire country would be taken over by the Communists. And so the Japanese were instructed to hold their places and maintain order. In due course Chinese troops under Chiang Kai-shek would appear. The Japanese would surrender to them, march into the seaports, and then be sent by the Americans back to Japan.[1]

This was serious enough, when applied to South China, where the communist guerilla forces were weak; when applied to Peking and the other great cities of the North, where the Communists controlled the countryside and the Kuomintang had not been a significant presence for eight years, it invited civil war. Many Chinese hoped now for a coalition

[1] Years of Trial and Hope 1946–1953, by Harry S. Truman (Hodder & Stoughton, 1956), p. 66.

government of the two rivals which would restrain the revolutionary
fervour of the one and excite the reaction of the other into needed reforms; but the spectacle of Japanese formations holding their posts under
American orders until American aeroplanes could reach them with
Kuomintang troops turned even moderate Chinese opinion against
Chiang Kai-shek. Was American power in Kuomintang clothes to
replace the Japanese? The Communists retaliated by cutting all railway
communication between North and South, so that the Kuomintang garrisons in the northern cities could be reached only by air. The American
government, aware of Kuomintang weakness but aware too that American public opinion would not support, so soon after the ending of war
with Japan, further large-scale military involvement in Asia, attempted a
reconciliation between the Communists and the Kuomintang. Truman
sent General Marshall as his personal emissary to mediate, but it soon
became clear that the contenders were too far apart. The Communists
wanted sufficient control of the government to promote radical land
reform, while the Kuomintang wished to retain power precisely in order
to prevent this. Moreover, the Americans were hardly disinterested
mediators, since they continued to organize, train and equip Kuomintang
forces throughout the period of negotiations.

None the less, Marshall found the communist representatives initially
more 'tractable'[1] than the Kuomintang, confident that they could win
their battle on political grounds, while Chiang Kai-shek appeared to be
determined to pursue a policy of force. It soon became clear that Chiang
was appealing, through the 'China lobby', over the head of the President
to the Congress of the United States. In clear disregard of American
wishes for a democratic façade to his regime, he arrested, exiled or assassinated liberal intellectuals who criticized his rule. President Truman
severely reprimanded him and threatened to cut off aid. He wrote expressing the continued hope of the United States that a strong and democratic
China could yet be achieved under Chiang Kai-shek's leadership, but
asserting that he would be less than honest if he did not point out the conclusion, forced upon him by recent developments, that the selfish interests
of extremist elements, equally in the Kuomintang as in the Communist
Party, were hindering the aspirations of the Chinese people. He admitted
to a growing conviction that an attempt was being made to settle major
social issues by resort to force, military or secret police, rather then by
democratic processes.[2]

Yet the United States government continued to support a regime which

[1] H. Truman, op. cit., p. 79.   [2] H. Truman, op. cit., pp. 87–8.

it knew to be corrupt, increasingly unpopular and ineffectual. Stalinist
Russia, which might have been expected now to help the Communists, if
only as a counter-weight to the American presence behind the Kuomintang, continued to recognize the Chiang Kai-shek regime and carefully
handed back the cities of Manchuria to its troops, after systematically
stripping the industrial plants of their equipment and reducing China's
most developed region to little more than a shell. There can be small
doubt now, if there was room for any larger doubt then, that had she
surrendered Manchuria intact to the Communists, who already after all
controlled the countryside, she would have swung the struggle in China
immediately and decisively in their favour. Was it sheer near-sighted
greed that dictated her conduct? Did she still doubt that the peasants in
the Chinese Communist Party were capable of winning a civil war? Or
was that precisely what she now no longer doubted, and so wished to
keep from a communist state on her doorstep a powerful enough industrial base to permit independence and even rivalry? Whatever the
reason, her plunder of Manchuria at such a time did nothing to nourish
the gratitude of Chinese Communists for her help in the past, and much
to excite their distrust of her intentions in the future.

Chiang Kai-shek set out to conquer the North, against the firm advice
of General Marshall and other American military advisers. Despite huge
American help he failed, walling up his crack troops in cities while the
Communists surrounded and starved them. When the communist
counter-offensive to the South began in the summer of 1947, Kuomintang
resistance steadily crumbled. And if the military situation was bad, the
economic one was worse. Inflation had swallowed the national currency,
while the leaders of the Kuomintang engaged in a frantic race for personal
enrichment by appropriating property, manipulating controls and
auctioning offices. If American military advisers, at least, were left to
sustain the troops, it was because they could not be pocketed like money
or sold like arms. The alienated intellectuals were guarded by the 'Te
Wu', the special secret police, who swooped on anyone expressing the
slightest dissent. The middle class was reduced to a terror and impoverishment which allowed hope only from a communist revolution.

The Communists themselves were aware of the disintegration both at
the Kuomintang front and behind the lines; their supporters were in
every Kuomintang centre, organizing the disaffection and supplying
intelligence. Yet to a communist conference held in July 1948 to discuss
the tactics of the coming autumn campaign, Stalin sent a message, urging
continued guerilla warfare without pushing the struggle to a conclusion,

so as to waste American strength in useless aid to the Kuomintang. The Chinese communist leaders rejected the advice.[1] The Kuomintang in Manchuria collapsed at the end of October, and by the end of the year the Communists were at the Yangtze, close to Nanking. In January 1949 Peking itself fell; in April the Communists crossed the Yangtze; and at the end of September the People's Republic of China was formally inaugurated. The Soviet press heralded the triumph of Chinese communism – Stalin had reopened Soviet consulates in communist territory during the summer – and Chiang Kai-shek, with the rump of the Kuomintang, glowered from across the sea on the island of Formosa (Taiwan).

The new communist state that emerged in China was accordingly an independent power, victorious by the efforts and resolution of its leaders and people; owing nothing to Soviet assistance, indeed resentful of the role that the Soviet leadership had played; and – since large territorial bites from imperial China by Tsarist Russia had not been returned – with occasion for serious dispute still outstanding between Moscow and Peking. As far back as 1946, in an interview given by one of their leaders, Liu Shao-ch'i, the Chinese Communists were claiming in their own revolution a model for colonial societies to follow, and if the need for Soviet economic aid now muted their claims to an independent ideology, they increasingly saw Mao rather than Stalin as their prophet. Above all, the Soviet Union was a European power, with her primary interests in Europe; China was an Asian one, with her main concerns in Asia and, it would subsequently appear, a proclaimed solidarity with the whole non-white world. To believe that a country with the size, population and potential, the long history, cultural pride and recent experience of China would ever willingly be a satellite of the Soviet Union was stupidity or culpable ignorance.

The Second World War had advanced the cause of nationalist rebellion all over Asia; but though the British at last withdrew from the Indian sub-continent in 1947, the French in Indo-China decided to stay and fight it out. Vietnam nationalism, with a strong communist presence under the guidance of Ho Chi-minh, had already taken to terrorism in the 'twenties, and the collaboration between the 'Vichy French' and the Japanese in the Second World War had not crushed resistance. Now after a series of largely meaningless constitutional arrangements had failed in persuading the Vietminh nationalist movement to accept the return of French rule, France bombarded the northern port of Haiphong in November 1946, and eight years of bitter warfare followed.

[1] C. P. FitzGerald, op. cit., pp. 102–5.

The next neighbour and historical tributary of China to erupt was Korea, which had been divided after the war along the 38th Parallel into a northern region under Soviet, and a southern region under American, occupation. Claiming that all attempts to negotiate a unification of the country had failed, the Americans in 1948 supervised the election of a National Assembly in the South, and ended military government with the inauguration of a republic under the presidency of Syngman Rhee; the Soviet authorities in the North then inaugurated a republic there also and announced the withdrawal of all Soviet forces. If the North, under Stalinist suzerainty, did not present the spectacle of a flourishing democracy, the South, under American protection, was scarcely alluring. President Truman himself seems to have had few illusions. In his memoirs he subsequently described President Syngman Rhee as a man of strong convictions, having little patience with those who differed with him. From the moment of his return to Korea in 1945, Rhee had attracted to himself men of extreme right-wing attitudes; he had disagreed sharply with the political leaders of more moderate views, and the withdrawal of military government had removed restraints preventing arbitrary actions against his opponents. Truman recorded that he had himself not cared for the methods used by Rhee's police to break up political meetings and control political enemies, and that he had been deeply concerned over the Rhee government's lack of concern about the serious inflation sweeping the country. Yet the Americans, Truman declared, had had no choice but to support Rhee.[1] In January 1950 the American government signed a defence agreement with the Rhee regime.

Whatever the immediate cause of the crossing into South Korea of North Korean forces in June 1950, there seems little doubt now that the Chinese were not initially involved. No less respectable a Western research source than the Rand Corporation, commissioned by the United States Air Force to examine why China entered the Korean War, reported that the Chinese government had not participated in planning the move across the frontier and had not intervened until General Douglas MacArthur, Commander of the United Nations forces, appeared to threaten the crossing of the Yalu River into China.[2]

If the Soviet Union herself had been a party – and it is difficult to believe that the North Koreans would have made so important a move entirely on their own – the state of Chinese military preparations on the

[1] H. Truman, op. cit., pp. 347–8.
[2] Toronto *Globe and Mail*, February 22nd, 1961, quoted in *The Wall Has Two Sides*, by Felix Greene (Jonathan Cape, 1962), pp. 282–3.

mainland suggested either the gross incompetence of the new Chinese rulers (which the long revolutionary war made improbable) or a faulty line between Moscow and Peking. 'The initiation of hostilities in Korea in 1950 can be rather confidently taken as a Russian move, if only because it made sense in terms of Russia's resources and situation ... and did not make sense in Chinese terms.'[1] Yet the United States government treated China from the outset as a satellite of the Soviet Union and a virtual belligerent. It dispatched the Seventh Fleet to the Formosa Straits, to prevent any attempt by China to seize the remaining part of her own territory from the Kuomintang, and gave increased aid to the French forces in Indo-China. Claiming such action as necessary to prevent any widening of the conflict,[2] the United States was effectively on her own now directly intervening in the Chinese civil war and the Indo-Chinese nationalist struggle. The United Nations Security Council itself (then being boycotted by the Soviet Union and with China excluded from her rightful place as a permanent member), in sanctioning military intervention in the Korean War without ordering an end to unilateral American action against China, displayed a strange interpretation of its peace-keeping functions.

Though several member states of the United Nations, notably Britain, contributed forces to the collective support of South Korea, the vast bulk of military intervention rested on American shoulders, and it soon became clear that the American and United Nations Commander in the Far East, General MacArthur, was not reluctant – seemed even eager – to provoke a war with China. His publicized visits to Chiang Kai-shek, with his known views on the need for an aggressive posture towards the Chinese Communists, led to agitated representations from America's allies and careful admonitions from President Truman. The U.N. troops in Korea were driving the Northern forces out of the South, and the National Security Council of the United States recommended in September that MacArthur cross the 38th Parallel only if there was no indication or threat of intervention by Soviet or Chinese forces. At the beginning of October, South Korean forces crossed the Parallel, and Chou En-lai, then the Chinese Foreign Minister, summoned the Indian Ambassador and informed him that China would intervene if U.N. forces entered North Korea. MacArthur dismissed such a threat as flimsy – he assured President Truman that 60,000 men would be the ceiling on Chinese involvement –

---

[1] 'China in the Postwar World', by A. M. Halpern, in *The China Quarterly*, No. 21, Jan.–March 1965.
[2] H. Truman, op. cit., p. 352.

and received permission to advance. On October 19th Pyongyang, the capital of North Korea, fell to the U.N. forces, who then raced north-wards, with American units in front despite a clear instruction to the contrary from the Joint Chiefs of Staff. The American State Department advised MacArthur to issue a statement that he intended no interference with Chinese power plant operations on the Yalu River, but MacArthur felt 'that he did not wish his hands tied in such a manner, and the state-ment was therefore not issued'.[1]

What could the new rulers of China reasonably have supposed Ameri-can intentions to be? On August 25th, the U.S. Secretary of the Navy, Francis Mathews, had spoken in Boston of the need for a 'preventive war'. Was it to this that the U.N. advance towards Manchuria was being directed? In the middle of October the first Chinese troops moved across the Yalu River; at the end of the month they were in the battle area; and in early November the supplies of men and material entering North Korea became a flood. The other U.N. member states with forces in Korea opposed any extension of the fighting to China, and President Truman himself saw such a possibility as 'a gigantic booby trap',[2] which might well provoke war with the Soviet Union. MacArthur was refused permission to bomb bases in Manchuria, and U.N. forces were driven relentlessly southwards under Chinese pressure. On December 4th, alarmed by a press conference at which Truman had allowed the possi-bility of using the atomic bomb should the military situation require it, Clement Attlee, the British Prime Minister, flew into Washington. The British believed that China was not a Soviet satellite – Attlee even suggested that she was 'ripe for Titoism' – and that she should be brought into the United Nations. The Americans were principally concerned to see their presence in the Philippines and Japan protected, saw Formosa as a western flank that had to be secured, and opposed Chinese entry into the U.N. as a major concession which would only increase Soviet power. One short exchange, recorded by Truman himself, lit the world of fantasy into which American policy had slipped.

The nation that the Americans had hoped to establish – China – Truman complained, had not only fallen into unfriendly hands, but was now viciously hostile to the United States . . . The Americans could not open their whole flank now by giving up Formosa to that country. They just could not agree with that. In the long run, he thought, the Chinese would realize that their real friends were not in Moscow and Siberia; they were in London and in Washington.

[1] H. Truman, op. cit., pp. 394–5.   [2] H. Truman, op. cit., p. 400.

The British Prime Minister replied – without smiling, Truman records – that the Americans would not bring the Chinese to that realization if they kept fighting them.[1]

Well, perhaps not altogether fantasy. The friendship between Peking and Moscow was not to last much longer. But for the time being the Soviet Union was unequivocally committed to the defence of China. A senior Soviet diplomat at Peking in the middle of November had promised that if Manchurian airfields were bombed by United Nations planes, the Soviet Air Force would strike back in force. It was a widely reported promise, which immediately agitated America's allies and could scarcely have left America herself unmoved. Possibly when the Chinese leaders were later to denounce the de-Stalinization campaign of Khrushchev, it was the promise of November 1950 that they remembered. They certainly knew much of Stalin's fallibility themselves, but if he had failed them frequently, he had supported them crucially once, with a commitment which his successor seemed rather less willing to risk.

MacArthur's continued demand for an extension of the war to China and his open criticism of official American policy, led in April 1951 to his replacement as Commander of the U.N. forces and his recall home. The fighting fluctuated round the 38th Parallel, and in July armistice negotiations began, to take two years before producing a formal peace. Yet if the Korean hostilities in the end left the frontier between North and South where they had found it, they did not treat the rest of the Far East or the relationship between China and the West in the same way. Under American pressure and against the votes of the non-aligned like India, the United Nations had branded China an aggressor – an act which rankles still with the Chinese leadership – and so provided an excuse for keeping her from her place as a crucial member state. The picture of a United States in military alliance with Portugal, on excellent diplomatic terms with South Africa, and helping France fight a brutal colonial war in Indo-China, while raging self-righteously against China's disregard for the liberty and independence of other peoples was scarcely edifying, whatever the facts of the Korean conflict. The picture of Chiang Kai-shek's rump regime on Formosa speaking for a quarter of the world's population as a permanent member of the United Nations Security Council was merely ridiculous. The exclusion of China herself from the organized international community was mad. It weakened the United Nations and America's own standing without weakening China. It made American dominance of the United Nations blatant and correspondingly repugnant.

[1] H. Truman, op. cit., p. 433.

It did not stunt but nourished the Chinese search for leadership, directing it outside the orthodox plains of international diplomacy into the very forests of revolutionary struggle where the West was most vulnerable. Above all, it openly pitted the greatest white power against the greatest non-white one in a world where the non-white peoples were increasingly resentful of white ascendancy. The warfare of ideas was relentlessly changing into a warfare of race.

The Korean War produced, too, new American defence commitments in Asia. By taking Formosa and the Chinese offshore islands under the protection of the Seventh Fleet, the United States had shackled her policy and prestige to the protection of Chiang Kai-shek, in violation not only of previous undertakings but of political common sense. That Formosa was an integral part of Chinese territory had been proclaimed no less clearly by the American government than by 1,300 years of Chinese history. In the Cairo Declaration of 1943 Britain and the United States had promised that 'all territories Japan has stolen from the Chinese such as Manchuria, Formosa and the Pescadores shall be restored to the Republic of China', and the Potsdam Declaration of 1945 had confirmed the pledge. In January 1950 President Truman himself had declared:

> The United States had no predatory designs on Formosa or any other Chinese territory. The United States has no desire to obtain special rights or privileges or to establish military bases on Formosa ... The United States Government will not pursue a course which will lead to involvement in the civil conflict in China. Similarly, the United States will not provide military aid and advice to the Chinese forces on Formosa.[1]

Yet involvement in the Chinese civil conflict was precisely what the United States had now chosen, and on the side of a force so relatively small that her own presence was massively obvious. It was not even possible persuasively to claim that the millions of native Formosans looked to the discredited Kuomintang as the guardian of their liberties. At the Japanese surrender a horde of Chiang Kai-shek's officials had descended on the island, bearing with them little more than their appetite for enrichment and their talent for corruption. The islanders had risen in disgust, and only the most ruthless repression had preserved Kuomintang control.[2]

[1] F. Greene, op. cit., p. 274.
[2] *Flood-tide in China*, by C. P. FitzGerald (The Cresset Press, 1958), p. 228.

No one in Asia could reasonably doubt that the Chiang Kai-shek regime survived at American pleasure, and the struggle for possession of Formosa and the Chinese offshore islands accordingly appeared as less one between two non-white Asian peoples than between a non-white Asian people and a white American one. Moreover, the United States had allied herself not only with the wrong side – in law and whatever passed for morality among most members of mankind – but with the losing one. Sooner or later, when the Kuomintang finally fell apart or its leaders made their peace with Peking – for they were, all of them, Chinese, and could hardly be expected to abandon China for ever – the Americans would have to accept the surrender of the islands or take control of them in an act of crude and anachronistic colonialism. In the summer of 1957 an attempt to shield an American serviceman from local jurisdiction provoked a mob in Taipeh, the island's capital, to sack the American embassy offices, while police stood by without attempting to interfere. It was a warning of how close to the surface ran an affronted nationalism, contained only by the ageing hope of a war that could return the mainland to Kuomintang control. Yet would the United States go to war for Chiang Kai-shek?

When the Chinese bombarded the offshore islands of Matsu and Quemoy in 1954, Republican leaders in the United States Congress and several of the military chiefs pressed for 'an all-out showdown' with Peking,[1] but President Eisenhower, nudged by Britain and France, shirked such a solution, and even when the Chinese seized the Tachens, islands two hundred miles north of Formosa, contented himself with threatening war over the Pescadores or Formosa.

With each step taken, each statement made on China by the American government since, the room for American manoeuvre has been reduced, not least by the American public attitude to China that official belligerence has promoted. There may well have been a time, immediately after the Second World War and even after the communist victory on the mainland, when an American government could, with relative ease, have accommodated public opinion to living reasonably in the same world alongside a communist China; by its own muddle, mistakes and inflexibility, it has produced a clamour that prudence and self-interest may one day wish, but find it difficult, to silence.

The Korean War also brought the United States firmly to the aid of French imperial policy in Indo-China. Just as the failure to see that the Chinese Communists were not Russian minions had excited the mistakes

[1] *First Hand Report*, by Sherman Adams (Hutchinson, 1962), p. 108.

of the late 'forties and early 'fifties, so the failure to see the struggle in Indo-China for what it was – a nationalism with communist elements, naturally congenial to China but indigenously sustained – would excite the subsequent mistakes of American policy. With Laos and Cambodia as well as Vietnam in popular revolt, the French stood little chance even with massive material support from the United States. At Diem Bien Phu in May 1954 a huge French force surrendered to the Vietminh, and since France was unable to send sufficient reinforcements in time, her whole power in the region collapsed. There seems little doubt that the Vietminh could have occupied all of Vietnam,[1] but they decided to compromise, and the subsequent Geneva Conference of Western and communist states accepted a temporary division of Vietnam along the 17th Parallel, with general elections to decide the future of the whole country in July 1956. The United States now increasingly committed herself to securing South Vietnam as an Asian ally.

American power was replacing French in Indo-China, as a fence against any communist expansion in South-east Asia. Yet inevitably this brought the United States less into immediate conflict with China, the Soviet Union or even North Vietnam, than with the nationalists of Laos, Cambodia and South Vietnam themselves, who found foreign intervention, whether Chinese or American, repugnant. Indeed, if intervention was unavoidable, the Chinese were likely to be the more warmly welcomed, since they would come as Asian revolutionaries, while the Americans, white as the French yet recognizing open white rule as undesirable, were already present as protectors of right-wing regimes, the old dependable coalitions of landlords, militarists and profiteers.

This new American involvement, dangerously aligned as it was against indigenous nationalism and the natural demands for radical reform, was no mere assumption of the imperial mantle that Europe had been forced to drop, though Asians who thought so could scarcely be considered irrational. American policy was based on two major premises, all the more passionately propounded for being suspected as myths – that Chinese expansionism into South-east Asia and Formosa threatened the Philippines, Japan and so the security of America's own western seaboard; and that a China, isolated and 'contained', might in time cast off communism under the stress of military threat and international rejection.

In January 1954, the Assistant Secretary of State for Far Eastern Affairs, Walter S. Robertson, appearing before a House of Representatives Committee, agreed that American policy was directed at keeping alive a

[1] See *The Revolution in Southeast Asia*, by Victor Purcell (Thames & Hudson, 1962), p. 153.

constant threat of military action against China, in the hope of internal breakdown, though this would mean for an indefinite number of years 'American dominance in the Far East'.[1] Certainly, from 1950 onwards the American Central Intelligence Agency, acting first under the name of 'Western Enterprises, Inc.' and then as the 'Department of the Navy', helped to train, equip and finance Kuomintang commando raids on the Chinese mainland, from the offshore islands of Matsu and Quemoy. In 1963 the Chiang Kai-shek regime announced that frogmen and commando teams had been most active in Kwangtung Province, facing Formosa, and that 873 guerilla agents had infiltrated the mainland between March and December 1962.[2]

Despite protests to the contrary, therefore, the United States has been at war with China since 1949, and it has been China whom the United States has considered herself to be fighting in South-east Asia, whenever her protégés have been faced by indigenous rebellion. Just as she saw the Soviet Union behind the communist struggle in China, so now she sees China behind the struggle – communist only in part – of South-east Asian nationalism. And because she does not have the manpower to defeat China on land, she relies on nuclear warfare as the ultimate 'containment'. Repeatedly she has threatened China with the atomic bomb,[3] and though the political effects of using such a weapon have grown steadily more dissuasive, the military need has only increased. For neither China nor the revolutionary peasant nationalism on her borders will be defeated on the ground. The immediate neighbourhood of China has already slipped from Western control – in North Vietnam, despite French power, in Cambodia and Northern Laos despite first French and then American power.

'In the final analysis U.S. policy has been based upon nuclear bluff, and it has become apparent to everyone that it *is* bluff. The wall of containment has been made of fissionable material, in two senses.'[4]

Whether revolutionary war, against regimes under American protection, should be encouraged even at the risk of humiliatingly calling the American nuclear bluff and so perhaps making it real, was soon to become a major element in the dispute between the two great communist powers themselves, the Soviet Union and China.

At the Bandung Conference of 1955 in Indonesia, China – with her

[1] Exchange quoted in F. Greene, op. cit., p. 276.
[2] *The Invisible Government*, by David Wise and Thomas B. Ross (Jonathan Cape, 1965), pp. 109–10.
[3] See, for instance, S. Adams, op. cit., on the Korean truce negotiations.
[4] *Asia in the Balance*, by Michael Edwardes (Penguin Books, 1962), p. 121.

prestige much enhanced by the performance of her forces in the Korean War, and her reputation for flexibility promoted by Chou En-lai's sweet reasonableness at Geneva – dominated the proceedings. The Soviet Union was not present, and in the company of the non-white Afro-Asian states represented, China was the foremost power. It could not have escaped her attention that the non-white world was seething with discontent, and that race could be made a ready recruit to revolutionary leadership.

China herself proclaimed solidarity with the neutralist governments and five principles of international conduct: the recognition of national independence; of national sovereignty; of equality among nations; of no interference in internal affairs; and of self-determination. She did everything to remove causes of quarrel in her relations with other Asian states, even advising overseas Chinese to assume the citizenship of the countries in which they were living, offered trade and, despite the backwardness of her own economy, dispensed aid. She called publicly for talks with the American government, and her diplomatic representatives met American ones at Geneva and then Warsaw. A far-sighted American government might have used this sudden warm weather to retrieve the mistakes of the past and set out on an altogether different course. But the rigid John Foster Dulles was American Secretary of State. The United States showed herself concerned only to extract from China a pledge not to use force over Formosa, and refused Chinese requests for a political conference of foreign ministers from both countries to discuss all outstanding issues. For China this was a formal rebuff to the five principles of international conduct, for continued United States protection of the Kuomintang on Formosa defied them all. It was a rebuff that would sour the whole new Bandung mood of negotiation, and stress instead the need for a revolutionary alternative.

Lenin had firmly believed in the inevitability of war as long as capitalism existed anywhere on earth, because capitalist societies were driven by the economic pressures inherent in their systems to fight for markets. Communism itself came through violent revolution, as Russia herself had shown, and social reform merely confused the issues, braking the momentum of change. From war itself, which weakened the capitalist states, and violent revolution in societies ready for it, therefore, world communism could at last be accomplished. After Stalin's death in 1953, Malenkov, who inherited power as Prime Minister, suggested that nuclear war might destroy communism as well as capitalism; but Khrushchev, First Secretary of the Communist Party, denied any such apocalyptic possibility, and held that though the communist states would be seriously damaged, it was only the capitalist ones that would be destroyed. The argument was of more than academic interest to the Chinese, for they were at virtual war with the United States, the citadel of the capitalist world, and the United States possessed the nuclear bomb. She had not used it yet against the Chinese at least in part because China's principal ally possessed the nuclear bomb as well. But what if the Soviet Union now, in denouncing the inevitability of war, was merely offering an excuse for contracting out of her obligation to defend China, even at nuclear cost? Mao Tse-tung may well have flung his influence and prestige against Malenkov, and helped Khrushchev to control of the Kremlin.[1]

Yet when Khrushchev, now in possession of power, came to address the twentieth Congress of the Soviet Communist Party in February 1956, it was not only the character and cult of Stalin that he denounced. (That in itself angered the Chinese, since they had not been consulted over the declaration of this policy, which marked so great a rupture with the past that it was bound to affect the whole communist world.) The 'Socialist camp', he declared, was now so strong that no one dared attack it; war was no longer 'fatally inevitable'; and with the inspiration of the Soviet Union, 'certain countries' might reach communism through evolutionary, even parliamentary means. The new Soviet leadership was clearly aware that nuclear war would devastate the homeland itself, and since violent revolution might move relentlessly from local to wider and, perhaps inevitably then, nuclear war, violent revolution itself was – except where the risks seemed small – to be abjured. Where, the Chinese must have wondered, did this leave them? Was Formosa to reach them by parliamentary means? Or United States threats to be deflected by evolution?

There was, however, no immediate rift between the Soviet Union and China. Perhaps Khrushchev reassured Mao about his intentions, explaining that his remarks were necessary for domestic consumption; perhaps China, still in the Bandung mood and soon, in early 1957, to undertake the short-lived liberal experiment of the 'hundred flowers', saw some possibility of a negotiated settlement with the West. She certainly made no public objection to Khrushchev's sudden wooing of Titoist Yugoslavia in 1956, though this would soon become a major issue of dispute between Moscow and Peking. It was, in any event, a time when China was apparently expanding her own influence within the communist world, even to the point of intervening in European affairs. For in response to Khrushchev's campaign against Stalinism, first Poland and then Hungary

[1] See *The New Cold War*, by Edward Crankshaw (Penguin Books, 1963), pp. 22–3.

rose in revolt for greater freedom from Soviet control. Against Poland
the Soviet Union stood ready to use troops, but there is some evidence
that Chou En-lai intervened, pressed the Russians not to use force, and
offered the Gomulka regime in Warsaw Chinese support. Then, in the
Hungarian revolt that followed, Khrushchev offered to withdraw Soviet
troops but was, it seems, pressed by China to march on Budapest and
suppress the uprising by force. The difference was shrewd. Poland
was surrounded by communist territory, and the revolt there was a
communist one; concessions would avoid a civil war without opening a
passage for the West. Hungary, however, bordered on Austria and Yugoslavia; the army there had turned against the Communist Party, and the
revolt was aimed at establishing a parliamentary democracy, with a
neutral posture between East and West. But the two reputed Chinese
interventions were also crucial beyond their immediate effects, for they
laid claim to an equal place with the Soviet Union herself in the leadership of the communist world. Khrushchev had travelled through Asia in
1955, offering aid and dispensing compliments to the neutralist regimes on
China's borders. Now China was travelling in Europe, offering guidance
and dispensing advice to the Soviet Union about regimes under her
control.

In 1957 the Chinese outlook hardened. The Suez adventure of Britain
and France in late October and early November of the previous year had
displayed a nostalgia for gun-boat diplomacy that contradicted Khrushchev's confidence in Western discretion; when the West had blocked
Egyptian foreign exchange during the crisis, China had shown her concern by giving Egypt $5 million in Swiss francs. Despite Chinese readi-
ness for high-level negotiations with the United States, the American
government remained inflexible over Formosa, and despite Chinese
wooing of neutralist sentiment in Asia, American military bases and
hostile American-backed regimes remained to menace her. Within
China, the 'hundred flowers' of experiment and criticism had bloomed so
rankly in the early summer of 1957 that the government felt it necessary
to pick them before they smothered the revolution itself. Enormous
economic strides had been taken since 1949, but now Soviet aid to China
was being reduced, not only because Khrushchev was putting a billion
dollars into Eastern Europe to counter satellite discontent, but because
Soviet credits were flowing to neutralist states. That the most populous
communist state on earth should want, while there were countries in
Africa and Asia taking from East and West alike, was scarcely an eloquent
advertisement for revolution. Soviet economic aid to China had, in any

event, never been all that large,[1] totalling supplies and pledges of equipment for key industrial projects, worth little over $2,000 million.[2] And such aid had to be repaid in commercial – mainly agricultural – exports to the Soviet Union. Actual loans amounted to $300 million in 1950, and $130 million in 1954, a total well below those extended by the Soviet Union to an equivalent population of neutralists. India alone received nearly $700 million, and Indonesia $370 million during the 'fifties. That Soviet technical assistance was valuable, cannot be denied; but for the crucial five-year period from 1952 to 1957, as much as 97 per cent of the investment for basic development came from the Chinese people themselves.[3] In May 1957 Li Fu-chun, Chairman of the State Planning Commission, declared that the Chinese would have to rely on their own strength as much as possible, and one month later Po Yi-po, Chairman of the State Economic Commission, proclaimed that China would have to decrease her 'reliance on foreign countries'. Yet relations between China and the Soviet Union were still so close that in October the two countries signed an agreement under which the Soviet government would supply the Chinese with new information on defence technology; the Chinese today[4] claim that a sample atomic bomb and technical information on its manufacture were included. Then, in the same month, the Russians launched the first *sputnik* and confirmed their possession of ballistic rockets. But while China thought that this would mean a more aggressive attitude to the West, a new application of pressure from strength, Khrushchev talked instead of the deterrent value that such weapons possessed.

To the Moscow Conference of Communist Parties in November 1957, therefore, China came as a great power demanding a say no softer than the Soviet Union's in the government of the communist world, less dependent than at any time since the revolution on Soviet economic aid, and concerned to secure united support for the promotion of her own security. The Soviet Union herself was not prepared to provoke conflict with the West, but after the Polish and Hungarian revolts was in no mood for an open clash with China. Mao Tse-tung attended the Conference and called Western imperialism a 'paper tiger', however nuclear its teeth. He also proclaimed his now celebrated slogan 'The East Wind

[1] For a fuller account of the economic relations between the two states, see Chapter VII, 'The Colour of Want'.
[2] *China and Her Shadow*, by Tibor Mende (Thames & Hudson, 1961), pp. 338–9.
[3] 'Economic Development', by Choh-ming Li, in *China Quarterly*, No. 1, Jan.–March 1960, p. 39.
[4] *Peking Review*, No. 33, 1963, p. 14.

prevails over the West Wind', though its implication then was the triumph of the communist world over the capitalist one, and not, as subsequently, the triumph of China over the Soviet Union within the communist movement, or of the revolutionary non-whites led by China over the reactionary whites, led by the United States and the Soviet Union together. In the end the Soviet Union and China jointly sponsored a Declaration which stood midway between their attitudes. War was still not 'fatally inevitable', but there were no conciliating references to the possibilities of educating the West. Communism was still possible by evolution, but now seemingly just for states in an advanced economic condition. In the backward world of Asia, Africa and Latin America, it was implied, violent revolution remained the only effective route to real change. National liberation movements were, accordingly, to be encouraged and assisted.

The Moscow Declaration was clearly open, as any such compromise, to conflicting interpretations, and the conflict was not long in appearing. On July 14th, 1958, revolution broke out in Iraq, to topple the throne which was one of the West's principal supports in the Middle East. On the following day President Eisenhower sent American marines to the Lebanon, to prop up the shaky Chamoun government there, while Britain airlifted troops to Jordan. The military preparations were such as to suggest the possibility of intervention in Iraq, and China immediately demanded a show of strength. 'There cannot be the slightest indulgence towards American imperialism's act of aggression,' the *People's Daily* of July 16th proclaimed. 'Therefore let the people of the whole world take emergency action.' Khrushchev, however, less willing to run the risk of nuclear war, wrote on July 18th to Eisenhower, 'not from a position of intimidation but from a position of reason'. He clearly meant to do all he could to avert a head-on collision with the United States, and appealed for a summit meeting – of the four Western powers and India. Five days later he accepted Eisenhower's counter-proposal for a meeting within the framework of the Security Council – a meeting from which China would not merely be excluded but her seat occupied by the Formosan pretenders.

The Chinese leadership must have made powerful representations, for five days later again, on July 28th, Khrushchev withdrew his agreement, declaring that he had wanted a 'special five-power meeting, not a regular session of the Security Council'. But China was not reassured. If the Soviet Union had conducted herself with such circumspection over the Middle East, how could she reasonably be depended upon to respond vigorously when China was threatened? In 1958, the Soviet and Chinese governments began clashing over economic policy as well. In the spring Mao Tse-tung had launched the 'Great Leap Forward', with its emphasis on huge agricultural communes and its objective of laying in consequence the foundations of communism immediately. Khrushchev, only too aware of Soviet difficulties in promoting collectivization, derided both the new policy and its ambitious claims – even, in December, to Senator (now Vice-President) Humphrey of the United States. Such disloyalty to a principal ally before a principal enemy was hurtful, not least because the 'Great Leap Forward' was already showing signs of failure under peasant resistance.

American approaches on a 'two-China policy', by which Chiang Kai-shek's possessions would be internationally recognized as a sovereign entity and guaranteed against invasion, while both China and Formosa would be admitted to the United Nations, were soundly rebuffed. Such a solution would support Chiang Kai-shek's claim to represent China and demonstrate to the world that the United States could impose her will on the Chinese leadership. The diplomatic meetings between China and the United States were broken off; the United States rushed missiles to Formosa; and Chiang Kai-shek fortified his garrisons on the offshore islands. On August 23rd the Chinese began shelling Quemoy, and air battles followed. Again nuclear war seemed near. Then on September 8th Khrushchev notified the American government that he supported the Chinese action, and eleven days later declared that a nuclear attack on China would produce a nuclear reply by the Soviet Union. At the end of the month, under pressure from public opinion on both sides of the Atlantic, the American government announced a reduction of forces on the offshore islands and a pledge that Chiang Kai-shek would abandon his plans to reconquer China in exchange for a cease-fire.[1] The immediate crisis was over, but China believed that she had succeeded in four major objectives: she had extracted a public pledge from the United States that an American-backed invasion of the mainland from Formosa would not take place; in doing so, she had shown how threadbare was the whole American policy towards China; she had forced Khrushchev to commit himself to the nuclear defence of China; and she had shown the communist world, by confronting American pressure and compelling it to retreat, that an assertion of communist strength could yield dividends. Khrushchev, however, must have been less invigorated by the success of this essay in brinkmanship, especially since it had been none of his own

[1] T. Mende, op. cit., pp. 293–4.

making. Next time, the United States might, rightly or wrongly, refuse
to retreat. In the summer of 1959, the Soviet government, according to
subsequent Chinese statements,[1] unilaterally tore up the 1957 agreement
to provide defence technology.

At the same time, Khrushchev twice referred to the need for an understanding with the United States, in phrases that the Chinese must have
found menacing, and even insulting. 'Our country and the United States
are the two most mighty powers in the world. If other countries fight
among themselves, they can be separated; but if war breaks out between
America and our country, no one will be able to stop it. It will be a
catastrophe on a colossal scale.'[2] This seemed a blatant sacrifice of ideology
to nationalism. The Soviet Union was addressing herself to the future
not as a leader of the communist bloc, but as a nation state all but exclusively concerned with its own prosperity and safety, ready to police the
world alongside the United States in their joint interests – while the world
revolution could go hang or, if it proved recalcitrant, be hanged by the
new custodians of international order. How, without the threat or outbreak of war, was China ever to win back her lost territory? Why, with
the Soviet Union and the United States together policing the peace,
should the United States feel herself compelled to withdraw from Asia?
If the Soviet Union, her sights trained on providing her population with
washing machines and television sets, wanted, like the United States, to
enjoy now her economic success and secure her political power, China
and – as China could scarcely be unaware – the teeming nations of Asia,
Africa and Latin America had no such success to enjoy and in varying
degrees little but political vulnerability to secure. The peaceful road to
steel mills and socialism that the new complacent Soviet Union advised,
offered hundreds of millions of peasants under one or other form of
repressive oligarchy less a long thoroughfare to a different future than a
short cul-de-sac. Of what relevance was Khrushchev's sudden faith in a
market economy to backward, largely subsistence societies without the
prospect of acquiring or, as matters stood, engendering sufficient capital
for investment in industry? The Soviet Union had had her revolution.
Was she now to deny its need and benefit to others? What, indeed, did
the Soviet rulers know of revolution any longer? They were professional
bureaucrats, the parvenu heirs to an achievement for which their

[1] *Peking Review*, No. 33, 1963, p. 14, and No. 37, 1963, p. 12.
[2] On July 28th at Dnepropetrovsk. A similar statement had been made to a group of American
state governors touring the Soviet Union a short while before. Quoted in E. Crankshaw,
op. cit., p. 85.

predecessors had laboured. The rulers of China were revolutionaries all, who had fought for forty years and were still fighting for the fruits of socialist endeavour. If the Soviet Union would not – could not – lead the world revolution, why should China not take her place? China, like most of the world, was a peasant society, and her solutions, like her problems, were far more relevant to the poor of Colombia or the Congo than were the sophisticated economies of the Soviet Union and the United States. Furthermore, China, like most of the world, was non-white, while the Soviet Union, like the traditional imperialists of the West, was white. Could it reasonably escape general attention that all the rich states (with the exception of American-backed Japan) were white, and all the poor ones were non-white? Was the world revolution not, inevitably, a revolution of race? But how much of the non-white world was yet aware of its revolutionary goals? And what role were existing non-aligned governments in it to play as the confrontation approached?

Tibet had for countless centuries – and persistently – been recognized as Chinese. Britain herself had acknowledged Chinese suzerainty in 1792, and during Chiang Kai-shek's period of power the United States had refused to admit a Tibetan trade delegation without visas from the Kuomintang authorities. But communist success in China changed the Western attitude. In 1949 an American mission under Lowell Thomas visited Lhasa, and a 'top-secret' military briefing on Tibet for American troops was subsequently circulated with the undoubted knowledge of the Chinese.[1] Tibet, a medieval theocracy with a non-Chinese population, appeared a likely lever for Western intervention, and the Chinese government set out to secure its hold. In August 1950 a Chinese declaration promised the entry of the People's Army into Tibet 'with the object of wiping out British and American influence there', and when two months later the process of 'liberation' had begun, the Indian ambassador in Peking lodged a strong protest from his government. The Chinese responded by accusing India of imperialist influence, but though their army entered Chamdo they went no further. Then, in July 1951, Takster Rimpoche, brother of the Dalai Lama and himself prominent in Tibetan politics, escaped to the United States, and 'the possibility of American intervention may well have seemed imminent'.[2] In September the Chinese army marched on Lhasa, and though the new administration initiated a series of reforms, redistributing land, abolishing the practice of mutilation,

[1] 'China and Tibet', by George N. Patterson, in *The China Quarterly*, No. 1, Jan.–March 1960, p. 93.
[2] G. N. Patterson, ibid.

and building roads, schools and hospitals, its professed revolution
was greeted with increasing resistance. The priests and landlords were
outraged by changes which threatened their religious no less than their
secular hold, and tribesmen rebelled against a massive Chinese presence
that promised ultimate absorption. Resistance provoked repression: and
repression, resistance.

The Sino-Indian Trade Agreement of 1954 recognized Tibet firmly as
a 'region of China', but by 1958 increasing unrest in Tibet sharpened
Chinese suspicions of India, already centred round the claims of both
countries to territory in the vague border area between them, both in the
west where Tibet and Sinkiang touched Indian-held Kashmir, and in the
east between Tibet and India's North-east Frontier Agency. The precise
frontiers of India and China were so clouded by historical and contemporary expert dispute that a disinterested observer soon lost himself in the
details. Certainly the area of hottest quarrel, in the west, was so remote
and abandoned by Indian administration that a multitude of Chinese were
able to build a road across a corner of Ladakh, to connect Sinkiang with
Tibet, and the Indian government seems to have discovered its existence
only when its completion was celebrated in Peking. Incidents along the
border in 1958 embittered relations between the two countries, and then
in March 1959 armed revolt flared across Tibet, and the Dalai Lama fled
with several thousand refugees to India. There he gave press conferences,
received ambassadors, and appealed for foreign intervention to liberate
Tibet, while Nehru visited him in Mussoorie and expressed his sympathy
for Tibetan aspirations in the Indian parliament. Articulate Indian public
opinion, in the newspapers, opposition political parties, and Congress
itself clamoured against Chinese armed intervention in Tibet, and
frontier incidents in Ladakh, more than ordinarily a symbol of national
dignity and power for being part of Indian-held Kashmir, produced a
fury of affronted patriotism.

That China believed her own case in the quarrel to be just, there is little
doubt.[1] But other motives may well have nourished her resolution. If she
had a contender at all for leadership of the non-white world, it was India,

[1] 'Perhaps the Chinese Government is the more intransigent because it knows that it has a
better case for frontier revision than the world has realized. The quarrel with India is about
frontiers which were fixed by the British imperial power. Britain having conquered India,
pushed out her frontiers as far as they could be carried without a major war. In doing this,
Britain occupied a border area much of which was inhabited by non-Indian peoples. The
frontier of China, where demarcated at all, was fixed arbitrarily and surreptitiously, or by
treaties which Peking now denies were correctly negotiated with the Chinese Central
Government of the time.' Guy Wint in the Observer, November 22nd, 1959.

and India with her 'bourgeois democracy' – a dangerous distraction from revolutionary principles – was being courted by the Soviet Union as well as by the West. If the Soviet Union continued to back India, even when China and India were in border conflict, her allegiance to communism could the more easily be discredited and her real objectives arraigned before revolutionary forces everywhere. If the Soviet Union broke with India and came, however belatedly, to China's aid, then the Chinese view of an aggressive posture towards the West would have won a nuclear armoury. In the event, when the border conflict detonated briefly in the summer, the Soviet government remained studiously neutral. TASS, the Soviet news agency, issued an official statement on September 9th advising both the Chinese and Indian governments to resolve this 'misunderstanding', despite a formal request from the Chinese leaders, to whom the statement had been shown only a few hours before, not to do so. The Chinese government not unreasonably regarded it as a betrayal of the most basic communist principles for the Soviet Union to treat her socialist ally and a 'bourgeois' state like India in the same way; both Chinese and Soviet spokesmen seem to date their open conflict from this moment.

In September Khrushchev, following his appeal for a joint patrolling of world peace by the two great powers, visited the United States himself, while the Soviet press rejoiced in the prospect of a 'turning point'. At Camp David the Soviet and American leaders talked, and Khrushchev flew back to Moscow bouncing with hope and praise of Eisenhower as a man of peace. The Chinese must have found it difficult to believe their ears, and when Khrushchev visited Peking for the tenth anniversary celebrations of the Chinese revolution, he was doubtless asked to explain Formosa and South Vietnam to his hosts. The explanation seems to have given small satisfaction, for the attention paid by officialdom and the press to the Soviet leader might well have affronted a minor ambassador. Khrushchev returned to tour the Soviet Union and exult in her prosperity. While China was suffering from calamitous weather and the economic dislocations of the 'Great Leap Forward', Khrushchev offered no new massive aid but engaged in public day-dreaming about the four-hour working day on the technological Soviet horizon.

The Kremlin began criticizing the Chinese attitude and explaining its own with mounting asperity. In a speech to the Supreme Soviet on October 30th, Khrushchev attacked those who would test the power of imperialism by force, stressed Soviet neutrality in the Sino-Indian border dispute, and supported de Gaulle's proposals for ending the Algerian war (while China herself continued encouraging the F.L.N.). In February

1960, at a meeting of leaders from the Warsaw Pact states in Moscow, Khrushchev delivered a blunt attack on Chinese policies, while Marshal Konev made it plain that the Soviet Union had no intention of giving nuclear arms to China. On April 16th, in the fortnightly *Red Flag*, the Chinese Communist Party replied, in a 15,000-word article entitled 'Long Live Leninism', which accused the Soviet leadership of having betrayed communism. Doctrinally the Chinese were in a powerful position. The texts from Marx and Lenin that they cited were the scriptures of classic communist belief, and Khrushchev (in the person of Tito) could be persuasively displayed, under the arc-lights of long sacrosanct theories, as the arch 'revisionist'. But the merely doctrinal quarrel, however signifi- cant for pious Communists, was of secondary importance. The claim for orthodoxy was nothing less than the claim for leadership of the revolu- tionary world.

The Chinese began[1] by affirming the Marxist doctrine that the working class had to use revolutionary means to seize power and dismantle the machinery of bourgeois rule. They then affirmed the Leninist gloss: that imperialists not only exploited the masses in their own countries, but sought to plunder the rest of the world; that 'so long as capitalist imperial- ism exists in the world, the sources and possibility of war will remain'; and that 'the emancipation of the proletariat can only be reached by the road of revolution, and certainly not by the road of reformism.' Since the days of Lenin, the Chinese now added, the power of imperialism had shrunk, and would shrink inexorably further. 'The struggle naturally has its twists and turns, but on the whole the storm of the national liberation movement is sweeping over Asia, Africa and Latin America on a daily increasing scale.' The United States, in her 'self-appointed role of world gendarme for suppressing the revolution in various countries', established military bases and seized 'the intermediate areas', but everywhere aroused instead 'a new upsurge of the people's revolutionary struggle'. Yet Tito had declared in December 1959: 'Today the world has entered an epoch in which nations can relax and tranquilly devote themselves to their internal construction tasks.' The Chinese poured scorn on such 'modern revisionists'. Could the colonial and semi-colonial peoples 'relax'? Had armed intervention by the imperialists in Asia, Africa and Latin America become 'tranquil'? Was there 'tranquillity' in the Formosan Straits, when the U.S. still occupied 'our country's Taiwan'? Was there 'tranquillity' in Africa, when the Algerians and others were 'subjected to armed

[1] For the full text, see *The Sino-Soviet Dispute* published by *The China Quarterly*, London, 1961.

repressions by the French, British and other imperialists'? Was there any 'tranquillity' in Latin America, 'when the U.S. imperialists are trying to wreck the people's revolution in Cuba ... '?

The Chinese assailed Khrushchev's own assault on the inevitability of war at its weakest points – Leninist doctrine and the realities of recent history. 'Is the question of war and peace no longer an issue? Is it that imperialism no longer exists, the system of exploitation no longer exists, and therefore the question of war no longer exists? Or is it that there can be no question of war even if imperialism and the system of exploitation are allowed to survive for ever? The fact is that since the Second World War there has been continuous and unbroken warfare. Do not the imperialist wars to suppress national liberation movements and the imperialist wars of armed intervention against revolutions in various countries count as wars? Even though these wars have not developed into world wars, still do not these local wars count as wars? Even though these wars were not fought with nuclear weapons, still do not wars using so-called conventional weapons count as wars?'

The Chinese firmly grasped the nuclear nettle. Imperialism was using the atom bomb to blackmail the world, and the 'Tito clique' helped by spreading terror of atomic warfare among the masses. Yet, as Marxist-Leninist doctrine taught, it was man, not technique, that determined the fate of mankind. Had not the Chinese themselves proved this in their war against the technologically superior Japan? Then, too, there had been a 'weapons-mean-everything theory'. Had the Chinese and Korean peoples not triumphed over the United States, despite her command of far superior weapons, in the Korean war? 'An awakened people will always find new ways to counteract a reactionary superiority in arms and win victory for themselves. This was so in past history, it is so at present, and it will still be so in the future.' The imperialists no longer had a monopoly of nuclear weapons, and if they launched atomic warfare, 'the result will be the very speedy destruction of these monsters encircled by the peoples of the world, and the result will certainly not be the annihilation of mankind.' Indeed, 'on the debris of a dead imperialism, the victorious people would create very swiftly a civilization thousands of times higher than the capitalist system and a truly beautiful future for themselves.'

A peaceful transition to socialism might, in exceptional circumstances, be possible. But in general, as Lenin wrote, 'no ruling class in the world ever gave way without a struggle', and 'not a single great revolution in history has ever been carried out without a civil war.' Parliamentary democracies (read 'India') might permit temporary room for manoeuvre by revolutionaries, but the ruling bourgeoisie would in the end always use the system to divide and deflect the revolutionary forces. Empty talk of peaceful transition to socialism sought to paralyse the revolutionary will. For the modern revisionists, 'the peace movement is everything, the aim is nothing.' The Chinese Communists were themselves struggling in defence of world peace. 'At the same time we support the revolutionary wars of the oppressed nations against imperialism. We support the revolutionary wars of the oppressed people for their own liberation and social progress because all these revolutionary wars are just wars.'

Shortly after the publication of 'Long Live Leninism', an American U2 was shot down over Soviet territory, and the Chinese scorn at Khrushchev's courtship of Eisenhower was given timely material. Khrushchev himself must have been furious, and he sabotaged the summit meeting in Paris with a display that was at least in part directed at the communist gallery. But he did not change his ultimate views, and when communist leaders met at Bucharest in June for the Third Congress of the Romanian Communist Party, the Soviet representatives distributed a circular which outlined their case against the Chinese. The present epoch, the letter proclaimed, was marked by the disintegration of imperialism, the transition to Socialism, and the consolidation of the socialist world system. There were such strong forces working for peace that these might be sufficient in themselves to prevent the imperialists from resorting to war. It was talk of war's inevitability that paralysed the revolutionary struggle by dismaying the masses. Peaceful co-existence did not rule out armed struggle in the movement for national liberation; it simply involved 'gaining time' for the consolidation of the socialist system, while the imperialist bloc further disintegrated under its own stresses. The argument of *Red Flag* that war was not to be feared because the ultimate victory would be a socialist one was utterly unacceptable. 'The Communist Parties cannot permit society to be thrown back hundreds of years.' Soviet economic aid to neutralist governments (like India) promoted the cause of peace and weakened imperialism, while the disarmament campaign was aimed at eliminating overseas U.S. bases. The Chinese attitude could lead only to a continuation of the cold war and the arms race.

When Khrushchev himself spoke, he attacked Mao Tse-tung by name, as 'oblivious of any interests other than his own, spinning theories detached from the realities of the modern world'.[1] The Chinese simply did not understand the meaning of modern war. The dispute with India was pure nationalism and set back the socialization of India. His speech was bitter

[1] E. Crankshaw, op. cit., p. 107.

and transferred the dispute from the ideological plane to the openly national and personal one. Peng Chen, Mayor of Peking and the Chinese delegate, replied in kind. Mao was far more closely in touch with the modern world than was Khrushchev, who compromised the whole struggle of the masses by being now aggressive, now conciliatory, towards the imperialist powers. Soviet actions spoke more loudly than words. The Chinese themselves had shown in Korea, as in the struggle against Japan, that they had more experience of modern war than any other people in the world.

The Soviet Union set out to show the Chinese that she had more than mere words in her armoury and wrote announcing that all Soviet technicians would be withdrawn from China in August. The Chinese protested, complaining that such action violated the Sino-Soviet treaty, tearing up 'hundreds of agreements and contracts', that it would weaken China's industrial programme and comfort only the imperialists. But the technicians were withdrawn, taking their blueprints home with them. When communist leaders gathered in Moscow towards the end of September to prepare the ground for a conference of all Communist Parties, Teng Hsiao-ping, Secretary-General of the Chinese Communist Party, made the bitterness of his government clear, not only at the withdrawal of technicians but at Khrushchev's stubborn refusal to give China nuclear weapons.

From November 11th to 25th there was held in Moscow the conference that was to try and settle the dispute between the two major communist states. Teng Hsaio-ping, for the Chinese Party, was adamant. The struggle for peaceful co-existence, he proclaimed, was only a tactical manoeuvre, a means of morally disarming the peoples and materially disarming the governments of the capitalist world. True disarmament and peaceful co-existence could come only when there were only socialist governments on earth. He was especially bitter about Khrushchev, whose flattery of imperialist leaders he denounced: 'No considerations of protocol can explain away Khrushchev's tactless eulogy of Eisenhower.' He attacked Soviet 'state relations' (the withdrawal of technicians and aid) and criticized the low level of Soviet assistance to China, which had not exceeded China's own aid to other parties and was in any event a duty that 'gives no grounds for presumption or bragging'. The Indian bourgeoisie had placed itself squarely in opposition to the struggle for socialism at the time of the 1959 'counter-revolution' in Tibet, and the Soviet Union had supported it. The Soviet party was the leading one (for the moment?); but in the world communist movement, the minority was not bound by the will of the majority. Lenin himself, by splitting the Social Democratic Party into Bolsheviks and Mensheviks, had formed a minority movement to win in the end a majority.[1]

This was a warning of all-out ideological war. On China's side were ranged only the Burmese, Malayan, Australian and Albanian parties (Albania had by now openly broken away from the Soviet Union and was being economically sustained by China), with support on important issues from the Japanese, North Koreans, Indonesians and Vietnamese as well; but as Latin American delegates stressed, Chinese activity was fast producing fissures in their own various movements. The Chinese, indeed, placing themselves in the leadership of the former colonial – and coloured – world, persistently upheld at the Conference the need for recognizing national dignity, and denounced any hint of superiority by the European Communists. But it was not yet time for an open split, and the Moscow Declaration to which the delegates in the end subscribed was so ambiguous on all the major issues that the Belgian Politburo later declared that 'it was possible to quote from it to support the statement, the defence, and the application of political views diametrically opposed, and often outrageously divergent.'[2]

In July 1961 the Soviet Communist Party produced its new programme, the third in its history. There was little in it on the difficulties of other poorer socialist states, still less on the needs of the Chinese revolution; instead there was much on the material progress of the Soviet Union, her promise of being even more prosperous than the United States within twenty years, and the early prospect of free bread and a host of social benefits for her own citizens. Yet what of the world communism mission? Were the citizens of the Soviet Union to comprise a privileged class within the socialist societies, while peasants in their hundreds of millions, prodded awake by the prophets of revolution, went on struggling for any bread at all from a safe distance? 'The new Party programme could be summed up as the White Man's hymn of praise to himself. About the White Man's burden there was nothing.'[3]

The rancour steadily rose through the summer of 1962; the Soviet Union promised to supply India with jet fighters, and the air was thick with rumours of a possible agreement between the Soviet Union and the United States to limit the spread of nuclear weapons. Then both the

---

[1] Source mainly 'The November 1960 Moscow Meeting: A Preliminary Reconstruction' by William E. Griffith, in *The China Quarterly*, No 11, July–September 1962.
[2] *Le Drapeau Rouge*, February 22nd, 1962.
[3] E. Crankshaw, op. cit., p. 140.

Soviet Union and China became embroiled in power collisions. Khrushchev's humiliation at Kennedy's hands in the Cuban crisis of October was
a star witness for the Chinese case. What was more irresponsible and
adventurous than to have placed nuclear rockets on Cuba? And what was
more dangerous than, once having done so, to withdraw them under
American menaces? The Chinese conducted themselves differently. In
retaliation for Indian military infiltration of the border area, which they
themselves had infiltrated with such unnoticed ease previously, the
Chinese now launched massive attacks, obliterating the Indian frontier
posts, and overwhelming the Indian Army in the east with a four-week
campaign that brought them to the edge of the Assam plains. Then,
without any proclaimed threat of Western intervention, they withdrew
to all but the absorbed border area, leaving the debris of Indian policy and
prestige scattered behind them. By requesting substantial military aid from
Britain and the United States, the Indian government seemed seriously to
have compromised its allegiance to non-alignment, while a large proportion of India's sparse resources for economic development had been –
and would now increasingly be – diverted to military purposes. The
raj-polished image of the Indian Army as an efficient weapon of war had
been thickly tarnished; Indian government officials in the threatened areas
had behaved with rather more circumspection than valour; and China
herself had emerged as indisputably the greatest non-white power in the
world, with her prestige in Asia, Africa and Latin America commensurately heightened. Though all the communist states in Europe except Albania
rebuked China in words or by their assiduous silence, India herself received little support from the influential non-aligned, who might reasonably have been expected to rally round her in common protest. It was
clear that India's recent indifference to anti-colonial struggle had combined with Chinese trade and aid initiatives to erode her standing in the
third world. But the flexed military muscles of China were a factor as
well. Anyone who had frank exchanges with African leaders, both in
government and opposition, at the time can scarcely have failed to note
the new respect with which they viewed China. The West – and perhaps
the Soviet Union – might have been distressed but should not have been
surprised that the display of power seemed to excite such regard. Such
an assumption was basic to Western and Soviet policies in the 'sixties,
as it had been basic to the policies of states for decades and centuries
before.

   At the Congress of the Italian Communist Party in December 1962, its
leader, Palmiro Togliatti, publicly proclaimed the new outlook that his

colleague, Longo, had already introduced to the world communist movement at the time of the 1960 Moscow meeting. Communists in Italy
would devote themselves to the peaceful transition from capitalism to
socialism, concentrating on the achievement of reforms which were
calculated to produce more political power and higher material standards
for the workers. And this domestic movement of reform might be
mirrored in a new international order, by which productive forces and
democracy in the undeveloped world could be promoted, and widespread
starvation eliminated, through negotiations rather than war. Capitalist
and socialist states alike could jointly intervene to stimulate and supervise
progress, in a peaceful co-existence that was dynamic rather than negative.

The Chinese were quick to reply. The *People's Daily* of December 31st
rightly pointed out that this approach was a long way from Leninism and
traditional communist doctrine. And it declared: 'In the last analysis, the
stand taken by Togliatti ... boils down to this – the people of the capitalist
countries should not make revolutions, the oppressed nations should not
wage struggles to win liberation, and the people of the world should not
fight against imperialism.' But the principle of peaceful co-existence
applied only to relations between countries with different social systems,
'not to relations between oppressed and oppressor nations, nor to relations
between oppressed and oppressor classes'.

Khrushchev was himself expanding the doctrinal dispute into a national
and even racial one. He allowed, if he did not provoke, the Soviet press
to report accounts of misbehaviour by Chinese citizens in the Soviet
Union; accused the Chinese of harbouring designs on Soviet territory (as
well they might – or on that part of it, at least, which had not so long
ago been theirs); and 'did not scruple to exploit the most basic Russian fears
about the "yellow peril".'[1] His personal vendetta, with his resolve to call
an international communist conference that would excommunicate the
Chinese, seemed more and more distasteful and dangerous to influential
Communists outside and within the Soviet Union, and contributed no
small part to his overthrow in October 1964.

At the beginning of March 1963, the Chinese themselves issued a formal
declaration of doctrinal war.[2] The gospel of the communist movement,
the Manifesto of 1848, had begun with the words: 'A spectre is haunting
Europe – the spectre of Communism.' The Chinese now launched their
own onslaught in cruel imitation, castigating not the powers of old
Europe but the new holy alliance of Khrushchev and Togliatti and all the

[1] A biography of Khrushchev by Mark Frankland, to be published by Penguin Books.
[2] The *People's Daily* of March 1st; *Red Flag* of March 3rd.

apostles of accommodation with power in the West. 'A spectre is haunting the world – the spectre of genuine Marxist-Leninism, and it threatens you. You have no faith in the people, and the people have no faith in you. You are divorced from the masses. That is why you fear the truth.' The reference to masses was pointed. The socialist states of Europe, with the communist parties of the still capitalist West, were rooted in industrial society, and an industrial society moreover which provided most of its citizens with a standard of living far higher than that enjoyed by any but the rich in the rest of the world. They might well believe that they had much to gain by tranquillity and much to lose by turbulence. The masses of mankind, however, were poor and sunk in a peasant society that had changed scarcely at all over the centuries. They had nothing to lose and everything to gain by a redistribution of the world's wealth, little to risk and much to acquire by conflict. A freezing of ideological frontiers where they now were might well suit the workers of Milan. But where would it leave, for instance, the peasants of South Vietnam?

The Geneva Conference of 1954 – in which representatives of China, Britain, the United States and the Soviet Union participated as well as those of France and the Vietminh forces – recognized the 17th Parallel as an armistice line between the northern zone of Vietnam, under firm communist control, and the southern, still largely in French hands. But the Final Declaration of the Conference proclaimed that 'the military demarcation line is provisional and should not in any way be interpreted as constituting a political or territorial boundary' (paragraph 6). The Conference provided instead for free general elections over the whole country, under international supervision, in July 1956 (paragraph 7), and prohibited meanwhile 'the introduction into Vietnam of foreign troops and military personnel as well as of all kinds of arms and munitions' (paragraph 4).

The United States reserved her position, but having noted the terms of the Final Declaration, announced that she would 'refrain from the threat or the use of force to disturb them'. Whatever the United States found it prudent for the moment to proclaim, however, she was clearly determined to prevent the spread of communist power across the 17th Parallel. The armistice line was to be perpetuated as the new frontier of the free world. While the Democratic Republic of Vietnam in the north took its stand on the terms of the Geneva Agreement, therefore, confidently expecting the reunification of the country under communist control with the promised popular elections, the regime in the south concentrated on perpetuating partition and establishing a separate sovereignty. The government of Ngo Dinh Diem, a Catholic who had withdrawn from public life rather than collaborate with the French, and whom the Americans had now propelled to power[1] as a nationalist alternative to Ho Chi Minh, denounced the Geneva Agreement, while profiting from the cessation of Vietminh pressure which the Agreement had produced; refused to discuss the scheduled general elections with the regime in the North; and imprisoned those in the South who demonstrated in favour of elections and reunification. Though the North offered the fullest facilities for ensuring free voting to the International Control Commission, the American Secretary of State, John Foster Dulles, announced at a Washington news conference on August 13th, 1955, that free elections were not possible for the time being.

American economic and military aid, with 685 soldiers to train its forces, rushed to the nourishment of the Diem regime, which confirmed itself in power by increasing intimidation and fraud. The referendum of 1955 offered a choice for first President of the Republic between only Diem himself and Bao Dai, discredited as first a Japanese and then a French puppet; 'the final results surpassed even the most sanguine expectations, as the votes cast in some cases exceeded the number of votes on the electoral roll.'[2] The election of a national assembly in 1959 produced no more than the façade of choice. Opposition candidates were disqualified on the flimsiest of excuses or threatened with prosecution as Communists before military courts if they did not withdraw their nomination papers.[3] The only successful opposition candidate was Dr Phan Quang Dan, an anti-Communist loathed by the Diem regime for seeming capable of providing an alternative nationalist leadership, and he was not allowed to take his seat in the Assembly. The whole government of South Vietnam was in the close clutch of Diem and his family, with one brother, Ngo Dinh Nhu, in charge of internal security; a second, Ngo Dinh Can, effective governor of Central Vietnam; a third, Ngo Dinh Thuc, Archbishop of Hue and Dean of the Catholic episcopacy; a fourth, Ngo Dinh Luyen, ambassador to Britain, while other relatives were scattered through the Cabinet and diplomatic corps. Anxious to eliminate all disaffection, the Diem regime by ruthless repression only nourished it. Thousands were arrested and detained in 'political re-education camps'; 'dissidents', supposedly communist but involving all those – democrats, Socialists, liberals as well as Communists – who criticized the government, were hunted down with increasing brutality; at the word of informers,

[1] 'An American nominee selected by the Central Intelligence Agency' – The Times, December 15th, 1965.
[2] The Emancipation of French Indo-China, by D. Lancaster (O.U.P., 1961), p. 399.
[3] The Last Confucian, by D. Warner (Penguin Books, 1964), pp. 111–12.

villages were encircled, searched and plundered, their inhabitants questioned, and many of them – frequently innocent of all political activity – tortured and deported. Even the captive National Assembly in Saigon echoed the mounting popular unrest at police repression, and the government-loyal newspaper *Tu Do* cried (March 4th, 1958): 'We must have done with arbitrary arrests and imprisonment. The citizens of a free and independent country have the right to be protected in accordance with the spirit of the Constitution.'

From 1958 onwards, the Vietminh Communists inside South Vietnam began fighting back, seeking out and shooting informers, village chiefs who collaborated with the regime in its repression, and members of the militia. The police and the army, their sources of information drying up, attempted to sink new wells by further terrorism, but only drove the peasantry into taking up arms against them.[1] The opponents of the regime, with a mounting subsidy of deserters, found it increasingly easy to find hide-outs in the countryside, to fortify villages and transform them into bases for military operations. In the course of 1959 the struggle spread from scattered attacks to partisan warfare. Yet far from exciting or materially assisting the resistance in the South, the government of North Vietnam did no more than protest in diplomatic notes against the Diem terror. Hanoi, following in all essentials the Soviet, not the Chinese, line on peaceful co-existence, seemed reluctant to provoke yet further American intervention, despite reports of bitterness among Vietminh cadres at its lack of support.

It was in such a climate of feeling that, in 1959, responsible elements of the Communist Resistance in Indo-China came to the conclusion that they had to act, whether Hanoi wanted them to or no. They could no longer continue to stand by while their supporters were arrested, thrown into prison and tortured, without attempting to do anything about it as an organisation, without giving some lead to the people in the struggle in which it was to be involved. Hanoi preferred diplomatic notes, but it was to find that its hand had been forced ... It was thus by its *home* policy that the government of the South finally destroyed the confidence of the population.[2]

[1] 'The International Commission and other independent sources have shown that Diem's ruthless suppression of assumed sympathizers with the Vietminh sowed the seeds of the present war.' Report in *The Times*, December 15th, 1965, on the British government Blue Book Cmnd. 2834 on 'Documents relating to British Involvement in the Indo-China conflict, 1945–1965'.
[2] 'The Struggle for the Unification of Vietnam', by Philippe Devillers, in *The China Quarterly*, London, No. 9, January–March 1962, pp. 15–16.

The non-communist and even anti-communist opposition to Diem recognized that it would have to associate itself with popular resistance if this was not to be monopolized by the Vietminh. In a manifesto of April 26th, 1960, eighteen prominent figures of varying political affiliation warned of revolution if the Diem regime did not cease its repression. At the beginning of November, an influential nationalist journal declared: 'In a country where the most elementary rights of the people are ignored ... the will of the people can only make itself felt by means of force, that is to say, by means of a revolution and the taking over of the government ... We nationalists, all of us, know that there is a race against the clock taking place between the Vietminh and ourselves.'[1] An attempt by disaffected army officers to unseat Diem in the same month failed and led to a frantic purge which further antagonized nationalist opinion.

Meanwhile the regime in the North was in a crisis of doubt. Its agents sent into the South to test peasant opinion were received coldly and denounced as cowards,[2] while at the Third Congress of the governing Lao Dong or Workers' (Communist) Party held in Hanoi during September 1960, the issue of support for Southern resistance brought Soviet and Chinese delegates into the fray. The leading Soviet delegate, Mr Mukhitdinov, is reported to have counselled prudence, declaring that 'peaceful co-existence was the only line ... in complete accord with the ultimate aim of communism', while the leading Chinese delegate denounced revisionists who betrayed the teachings of Leninism.[3] Though Ho Chi Minh proclaimed the need for greater efforts to achieve unification, and Le Duan, a former guerilla leader in the South, was elected Party Secretary, it seems that the Soviet approach was adopted, and certainly the official communiqué subsequently issued after talks between the Soviet and North Vietnamese governments announced a 'complete identity of the points of view'.

It is therefore doubtful that the Northern regime had much to do with the establishment of the South Vietnam National Liberation Front in December 1960. The contention of most governments in the West, and especially the government of the United States, that the fighting in South Vietnam was from the outset a subversive campaign provoked and conducted directly by Hanoi, corresponds neither to the course of the developing conflict nor to the policies apparently pursued by the governments of the Soviet Union and North Vietnam at the time. Just so

[1] *Pour le Viêt-Nam*, Paris, No. 2, November 1960.
[2] Jean Lacouture in *Le Monde*, Paris, April 15th, 1965.
[3] Philippe Devillers, *The China Quarterly*, p. 17.

mistakenly had the long course of the Chinese revolution years before been attributed to the master-minding of Moscow.

The Front itself may well have been dominated from its founding by Communists. For the Communists constituted the most experienced and disciplined of the partisan fighters. But the Front remained none the less an alliance of resistance groups, and the allotment of principal offices to known non-Communists (the Secretary-General was a representative of the Democratic Party, while only one of the five Vice-Presidents was a Communist) implied far more than a façade of nationalist coalescence. A real popular unity of resistance had come into being, and if it centred round the Communists, it was because the Communists provided effective leadership and training. Just so had the Communist Party of China succeeded in placing itself at the centre of popular revolt, while the nationalists in the Kuomintang concerned themselves with the profits of corruption and the crushing of dissent. If the National Liberation Front of South Vietnam was to fall increasingly under communist control, it was because the Front was treated – by the Diem regime and the Americans alike – as a communist conspiracy to seize power for its own sake.

Certainly the Southern Communists showed no willingness merely to echo Northern policy. The Front leadership campaigned increasingly for 'independence', not 'reunification', and when in July 1962 it published 'four proposals for national salvation', the fourth was the creation of a neutral zone to include South Vietnam, Laos and Cambodia, with each state retaining its 'sovereign rights'. The issue of reunification with North Vietnam was not even raised.

As one political commentator in France has judged it: 'All that is happening seems to show that the guerillas in the South have decided to create a hierarchy, a mythology, and a political programme which are fundamentally Southern.'[1]

By the end of 1961 popular support for the Front was such that some 80 per cent of the countryside was under its ultimate control, while the partisan forces themselves had increased from an estimated 3,000 in 1959 to 15,000. For following the example of the Chinese Communists, the front was promoting a more equitable distribution of land. The working peasantry, some 80 per cent of the total population, had owned only 20 per cent of the arable land, and from 40 to 60 per cent of a peasant's produce would commonly go in rent to the few landlords who owned the bulk of the rest. By 1965, some five million acres belonging to

[1] Jean Lacouture, ibid.

'traitors and collaborators' would have been confiscated and redistributed to poor peasants, while a rent ceiling of 25 per cent was fixed for all 'liberated areas'. This amounted to a vast rural upheaval; and, as in China, peasants would now fight not merely to complete the revolution but to secure that part of it already achieved.[1]

Yet the United States continued to act as though the steadily mounting resistance of the peasantry was contrived by North Vietnam as an agent of naked Chinese expansionism. American economic – as distinct from military – aid rose year after year, till by 1958 it was accounting for 62 per cent of total public expenditure in South Vietnam, while the American military commitment rose from 785 advisers in 1960 to 2,000 in 1961; 11,000 in 1962; 15,500 in 1963; and 23,000 in 1964. But the policy of increasing involvement was inevitably self-defeating. The more dependent that the Saigon regime seemed to be on American money and guns, the more alien it appeared, and the less likely it was to secure popular acquiescence, let alone support. The government increased its military forces, but the more soldiers it conscripted from a hostile peasantry, the more deserters there were and the greater grew the guerilla appeal. By the end of 1964 official American estimates ranged from 34,000 regular troops and 80,000 guerilla irregulars, to 50,000 regulars and 100,000 guerillas at the disposal of the Front. The Saigon regime, on American advice, promoted a programme of 'strategic hamlets', fortified villages supposedly safe from guerilla terrorism and so subversion. But the enforced removal of peasants in their hundreds of thousands from their traditional lands only sharpened popular resentment. The guerillas carefully attacked not the mass of inhabitants in the hamlets but the symbols of the regime – the hamlet chief, the military, the official youth leaders – and the armoured outposts of Saigon rule succoured rebellion at night. The peasants began abandoning the hamlets. In September 1963, the government claimed that 200,000 people lived in 219 strategic hamlets; in January 1964, a correspondent of the New York Times estimated that 20 or fewer hamlets were functioning under government control day and night.[2]

While the Front tightened its hold on the peasantry, the regime rotted in Saigon. Diem's increasing favouritism towards the Catholic minority and the popular opposition to the war led to Buddhist demonstrations in 1963, and at the beginning of November troops attacked the presidential palace. Diem and his brother Nhu were reported to have committed

[1] A *Pravda* report republished in *The Times*, July 7th, 1965.
[2] Hendrick Smith, *New York Times*, January 12th, 1964.

'accidental suicide', and a Revolutionary Committee under General Duong Van Minh took power. The new regime lasted only three months, however, and was succeeded by a series of coups in which senior military officers displaced each other or dismantled hastily constructed civilian façades. Public demonstrations in Saigon and other cities against military dictatorship and the war increased in frequency and force, but the American government, correspondingly embarrassed, saw in the armed forces the only alternative to victory by the National Liberation Front. It therefore connived at the coups or even incited them when it hoped helplessly for a spurt in popularity and efficiency by change; but its room for manoeuvre steadily diminished as popular disaffection in the cities as well as the countryside spread; it needed the armed forces, and whoever seemed able to control them, as much as they needed it. And inevitably the heads of the armed forces had a vested interest in perpetuating the war. In June 1965 the 'Young Turks' under Nguyen Cao Ky, head of the air force, seized power, with a policy that discounted altogether the need for a popular base and concentrated on the ruthless prosecution of military victory.

The only escape for the Americans seemed to lie in a massive and direct military commitment, to try and turn at last the fortunes of the fighting, and so produce negotiations from strength or stalemate, not from weakness. The American government announced its intention to send up to 125,000 American troops into the battle by the end of 1965 – in the event, there would be almost 200,000 – and in February ordered the bombing of strategic and industrial areas in North Vietnam, as well as accelerated air and land activity against the guerilla forces in the South. In a speech on April 7th, President Johnson proclaimed the purpose of the policy.

> We do this in order to slow down aggression. We do this to increase the confidence of the brave people of South Vietnam who have bravely borne this brutal battle for so many years and with so many casualties. And we do this to convince the leaders of North Vietnam – and all who seek to share their conquest – of a simple fact. We will not be defeated. We will not grow tired. We will not withdraw, either openly or under the cloak of a meaningless agreement.[1]

The extension of the war to North Vietnam was based on the assumption – commanding respect merely for its age – that the war had been

---

[1] Quoted in *Vietnam*, No. 1 in the Read-In series (Eyre & Spottiswoode, 1965), p. 134.

launched by North Vietnam in the first place and could be brought to an immediate halt by North Vietnam command. Yet the White Paper entitled 'Aggression from the North' published by the American government on February 17th, 1965, offered only the flimsiest evidence of a flow, in men and materials, from North to South. It cited the capture of 15,100 weapons from the guerillas in the period 1962–4, but the State Department subsequently admitted that the guerillas had captured 27,400 weapons from government forces in the same three years.[1] The White Paper claimed the massive infiltration of men from the North, but produced the names of only six North Vietnamese, after five years of wide-scale warfare. An American commentator observed tartly:

> There is reason to wonder whether the count of infiltrees may be as bloated as the count of Viet Cong dead: in both cases the numbers used are estimates rather than actual bodies ... None of this is discussed frankly in the White Paper. To do so would be to bring the war into focus as a rebellion in the South, which may owe some men and material to the North but is largely dependent on popular indigenous support for its manpower, as it is on captured U.S. weapons for its supply.[2]

Undoubtedly the North was helping the struggle in the South, but only – the overwhelming weight of evidence suggests – after partisan warfare had begun, the Liberation Front had been formed, and further inaction by Hanoi would have severed all relationship with popular leadership in the South. The North Vietnam government had to intervene, if only to protect itself by securing some small measure of influence over the partisan command. But the proportion of Northern involvement in the total struggle – estimated by the French newspaper Le Monde in April 1965 at between 15 per cent and 20 per cent – was 'not enough to condition its course or change its character'.[3]

Whether American policy was moral or consistent with long hallowed pretensions, however, was of less moment to the American government itself, or any other interested government for that matter, than whether such a policy promised to be successful. The prognosis was dismal. The bombing of the North was directed at forcing the government there to withhold all support for the struggle in the South and negotiate an

[1] I. F. Stone's Weekly, March 8th, 1965.
[2] Ibid.
[3] Le Monde, April 15th, 1965.

armistice. But for North Vietnam to cease supplying the Southern partisans would not only constitute a humiliating surrender to arbitrary force but admit the validity of American claims that the whole war in the South was a Northern contrivance. Above all, how could the North negotiate an armistice on behalf of the Southern partisans without their express approval? And why should the Southern partisans be driven to an armistice by bombardment of the North? Since the North was therefore helpless to stop the fighting in the South, it might reasonably react to American attacks not by diminishing, but by increasing its material support for the Southern struggle. What more could it risk by further involvement, since it was being bombarded already? The Americans might then extend their assaults to Hanoi and other vital industrial centres. But any such extension might well draw China into the conflict, and the Americans would be forced to fight a major war.

American policy in Asia was essentially directed at containing the power and influence of China. Such at least had been the periodic official excuse for taking the war in South Vietnam so seriously. Yet American policy was, in its effect, spreading the power and influence of China all the time. North Vietnam, which had aligned herself in the main with the Soviet Union in the early stages of the Sino-Soviet dispute, drew closer to Peking as her ultimate dependence on Chinese help in the event of war with the United States became increasingly apparent, and by 1965 was openly committed to the Chinese line. Moreover, the steadily spreading war in Vietnam, with the mounting American involvement, fortified China's whole contention. It demonstrated that American troops would be used to suppress national revolution, even to the extent of pushing the conflict beyond its natural borders, and that the Soviet policy of peaceful co-existence meant an effective surrender to American suzerainty over the whole third world. If the Soviet Union was to retain the allegiance of Communist Parties in Africa, Latin America and Asia, where popular discontent required revolutionary change, she would have to help North Vietnam and postpone any accommodation with the United States. All progress towards conciliating the Soviet Union and widening her breach with China, therefore, an objective to which American policy was increasingly directed, could only be hampered by the 'escalation' of the war in Vietnam.

The effect of the expanded American commitment within South Vietnam itself was likely to prove no more profitable. The war could never be won unless the peasants were induced to help the government against the guerillas; but the increasing reliance of the government forces on bombing raids, artillery and the use of terror weapons like napalm, could only confirm peasant hostility. The predicament was obvious. Since the peasants were overwhelmingly behind the guerillas, the careful isolation of insurgents for attack was impossible. Yet the more indiscriminate the force used, the more united the peasants and the partisans became. What was the purpose of political neutrality, if the neutral and committed were blown to pieces together from the air? The *Washington Post* of July 18th, 1965, commented on the bombardment of villages by artillery. 'Since there can be no realistic prospect that an artillery shell, lobbed into a village from a safely bunkered soldier miles away, will actually hit a Communist guerilla, this tactic amounts to nothing more than raw, random terror. Is there a swifter or more effective way to lose the war in Vietnam?'

Furthermore, the firmer the hold of the Front on the countryside became, the more alien did the regime in the capital appear. By 1965, the Front had developed a stable administrative structure at every level across the country, awaiting only a final political shift at the top to surface and exercise control in the open. Some 10,000 political administrators governed the areas in guerilla hands – many of them once-loyal government civil servants – collecting taxes in cash and kind, encouraging local administration, and redistributing the land of absentee owners to promote the long-needed rural reform.[1] The regime in Saigon, meanwhile, stripped of indigenous support, survived and was seen to survive only by increasing American involvement. Instead, therefore, of posing an indigenous revolutionary alternative to the Front, the United States government was more and more manifestly assuming the sovereignty of South Vietnam and the responsibility of official administration. With every day, the conflict in the country seemed less like a civil war than a colonial one.

In this lay the ultimate suicide of American policy. For the natural consequence of massive American involvement in the Vietnam war was to make the conflict racial as well as political and economic. The provision of American military and financial aid to the Saigon regime sufficiently damaged its standing as a nationalist force. The participation of substantial American forces in the fighting gave the war a dangerously new character. For no amount of propaganda could disguise the fact that white soldiers were shooting and white pilots were bombing coloured peasants. The presence of a Negro minority within the American forces scarcely changed their overwhelming complexion. If the war continued to seem in the white world a free and fundamentally coloured struggle against

[1] Peter Grose in the *New York Times*, January 24th, 1965.

communist expansionism, in the coloured world it increasingly assumed the appearance of an arrogant white intervention in the protection of racial dominance. Even in Japan, where American motives were in the main generously treated outside of the organized left, moderate newspapers and political groups stirred in public discomfort at this confrontation of colours.[1]

Why is the United States fighting in Asia at all? One can discount, surely, the power of a democratic commitment. A country that can support the current Saigon regime, the military despotism in Thailand and Taiwan, is concerned less with positive values than negative ones. The United States is waging war not for democracy but against communism. The conventional communist explanation is the economic profit to be made by capitalism out of virtual colonies. Yet does the United States really require tied markets and sources of raw materials? There are private American companies which certainly profit from exploiting the American sphere of influence or the military engagement of American forces across the world. But the American economy is surely strong enough to survive in a free and peaceful market, and if it isn't, the sooner it changes its character, so that it can, the better for both the Americans and the rest of mankind. A society that needs the suffering of so many peasant peoples to survive is a cruel and corrupt one. Yet the technological strength of the United States, a strength that a shift in emphasis from military to peaceful productivity ought only to advance, should enable her to prosper and increase her prosperity by assisting economies all over the world to develop.

The evidence suggests that American policy in Asia is conditioned far more by fear than by greed. Every territorial advance of communism seems to menace the security of the United States herself, on the assumption that it strengthens China, whose ambitions must mount with her influence, till all Asia is within her grasp and the Pacific frontier of the United States appears as the next easy victim. But this is a fear without foundation in the past or reasonable provocation in the present. China historically has concerned herself less with colonies than have the democracies of the West. She alone of all the traditional great powers deliberately neglected naval resources because she did not want an overseas empire. Her very arrogance, her assumption that she was complete in

[1] George Kennan, former American diplomat and one of those principally responsible for the policy of 'containment' against the Soviet Union, stressed this aspect of the war in his testimony before the U.S. Senate Foreign Relations Committee on February 10th, 1966. The conflict in Vietnam had done considerable damage in Japan, the good disposition of which was the greatest American asset in east Asia, he declared.

herself, persuaded her to seek only the protection of nominal tributaries
on her borders. Can the United States complain, with her own long-
proclaimed Monroe doctrine of preserving Latin America as a sphere of
influence, that China should want a friendly or neutral ring around her?
Far from containing China by placing American power along her
frontiers, the United States merely excites her to seek security through
expanding her influence. When President Johnson proclaims that 'China
wants all of Asia', the reply is that, on the evidence, the United States
appears a more eager candidate for continental domination. U Thant
himself, Secretary-General of the United Nations, has examined Chinese
policy towards Burma.

> The Burmese Communist Party is still underground after seven-
> teen years and still illegal. But ... there has not been a single instance
> of outside help to the Burmese Communists ... Burma has over
> 1,000 miles of land frontier with mainland China. If only the
> Burmese government had decided at some stage to seek outside
> military assistance ... then I am sure that Burma would have
> experienced one of the two alternatives: either the country would
> be divided in two parts or the whole country would have become
> communist long ago.[1]

The truth is that the United States has rejected two crucial realities of
the contemporary world: the indefinite survival of communist power in
China; and the inevitability of revolution to transform those societies
now aligned only with poverty and despair. The indictment written in
1958 by an Australian academic is scarcely less valid today than it was then.

> No mention of China is regarded as full or complete unless it con-
> tains the suggestion that the Peking regime is tottering to its fall, has
> no public support, and represents the worst of all possible govern-
> ments for China. No attempt is made to acquaint the public with the
> very real material development which has taken place under this
> government ... Nationalist (Kuomintang) propaganda stories are
> endorsed as if they were proven truths, objective reporting is con-
> demned as Communist propaganda. Vague but menacing language
> is used suggesting the ultimate use of force against China in favour
> of the Nationalist regime.[2]

[1] *China and the Cold War*, by John Gittings, to be published. Quoted in *Vietnam* Read-In,
p. 166.
[2] *Flood-tide in China*, by C. P. FitzGerald, p. 239.

It is this attitude which denies China any sense of security,[1] by protecting a hostile force on her own territory, excluding her from the organized international community, and attempting to contain her power meanwhile by surrounding her with American client states. This is stupid and dangerous, for China is there, her communist regime confirming its popular hold with every year it survives, and growing stronger all the time. Since she is denied the ultimate security of a full international acceptance, she must try to profit from insecurity, by weakening her enemies everywhere. She is not allowed to concern herself peacefully with her own development, to assume herself unmenaced from outside. Her encouragement of hostility to the United States in the rest of Asia, in Africa and Latin America, is the natural consequence of American policy towards her.

It is mistake piled on mistake, injury on injury. Senator Fulbright, Chairman of the U.S. Foreign Relations Committee, recognized no less during a television interview at the beginning of February 1966. The treatment of China in the past by the Western nations, he declared, had been 'the most disgraceful period maybe that I can think of in our history', and the Chinese had every reason to hate the West. 'What we should be doing is to try to find ways to rectify the terrible wrongs that we and nearly all the other Western nations inflicted on China.'[2] Yet the essence of America's policy towards China is not to rectify the wrongs she has helped to inflict or inflicted on her own, but to secure herself from the need to do so, from the need even to admit the need, by new wrongs which seem somehow to hide for her the old ones.

And that is not all. The United States sees popular revolution itself as an extension of Chinese power, so that the containment of China becomes the containment of revolution. Indeed, just as the United States rejects the reality of a communist China, so she rejects the reality of revolution as a

[1] The *New York Daily News* may not be America's best or most influential newspaper, but it has the largest circulation in the country. How are the Chinese expected to respond to such expressions of its view as this? 'Red China now has the beginnings of a nuclear weapons setup. Advices from Hong Kong have Red China echoing with talk of a coming war with the United States.

'Probably Peking is peddling the talk just now to take their slaves' minds off their real troubles. But you can bet that the Peking fanatics or their successors will attack us or our descendants as soon as they feel strong enough nuclearwise to wreck us.

'So why shouldn't the current commander in chief, while he is about this Far East war waging, move to rectify the Truman error by ordering our bombers and/or missiles to take out Red China's nuclear facilities? And why shouldn't he at the same time give Chiang Kai-shek the green light for his long-planned attack to retake the mainland via a counter-revolution there?' Quoted in the *New York Herald Tribune*, January 29th–30th, 1966.

[2] The *Guardian*, February 2nd, 1966.

mass response to the traditional, but now unendurable, inequalities existing throughout much of the world. That is why the war in South Vietnam is projected as a war to contain Chinese expansionism, though no
evidence is ever produced that China fired peasant insurrection in 1958,
formed or now dominates the National Liberation Front, or has sustained
the struggle with men and materials. Yet revolution must take place, and
can only be advanced by an American intervention that subsidizes it with
all the force of an outraged nationalism.

Such revolution does not have to be communist, though communism
may well be the most suitable ideology for poor peasant societies seeking
a rapid transformation. Certainly it will be communist, if it is invariably
treated as such by an alien power that misunderstands its objectives and
attempts by force to suppress it. But whether communist or not, it need
expand the power and influence of China only if the conduct of United
States policy makes an assertive independence impossible. If ever a nation
was historically determined to preserve its independence from a giant
neighbour, Vietnam was; if ever a nation was compelled to rely more and
more on the ultimate protection of a giant neighbour to secure any
possibility of independence, it has been Vietnam. The United States has
been proved spectacularly wrong in its long assumption that China was
no more than a satellite of the Soviet Union's. Would an independent
Vietnam not soon enough prove her refusal to be a mere satellite of
China's? Chinese influence would doubtless be paramount in the area, as
is the Soviet Union's in Eastern Europe. But even the United States
government has woken up at last to the independence that a Poland or a
Romania can display, within a broad alliance. And communist Albania
has broken with the Soviet Union altogether.

Yet the United States sees only the advantage of China in revolution
and would harness the whole West to a containment of change. To the
North Atlantic Treaty Organization, United States representatives come,
with apocalyptic warnings of mounting Chinese power, while Britain
bobs obediently to help preserve the Western presence east of Suez. It
is – as the Chinese themselves are not slow to proclaim – the white world
hastening to secure the political and economic subordination of the
coloured one. Is Asia to be denied all revolutionary change as a challenge
to the ideology and power of the West? And is all attempt to escape the
long past of poverty and despotism, therefore, to require the confrontation of race?

The United States and those of her Western allies that she can drag with
her in her policy of containment may be thinking of the future; Asia – like

Africa and Latin America – is thinking also of the past. The presence of white forces in Asia sustaining unpopular regimes – in the name of what? – is not only a denial of the promise that revolution offers to the otherwise hopeless, but a reminder of the arrogance and cruelty of conquest, the racial mastery that is supposed to have gone. Why is the white man, then, still there? He talks, when he talks at all so that one can understand him, of freedom and independence. But when did he ever bring either? And what does he bring now, but old fire from the gun and new fire from the skies, and a guard for the landlord, the moneylender, and the general? He shouts about the Chinese. But where are the Chinese? And why should he care at all if there is not something that he wishes to take for himself?

As Chou En-lai remarked to a Western visitor, 'China exists, and China can wait.'[1] The momentum of revolution in that part of the world where the bulk of humanity exists can only increase, as it is fed by precedent and despair. What can the United States do? She can attempt to contain the power of the Chinese by bombing their nuclear installations and, if the Chinese respond by using their enormous land forces in Asia, using nuclear bombs to devastate their cities. But such a policy, if public opinion in the United States and the rest of the West could be persuaded to sanction it, would almost certainly incite the intervention of the Soviet Union and the last holocaust. Nor is there much time in which to take the risk of Soviet neutrality. For it cannot be long before China possesses a delivery system able to reach Soviet, if not yet American, cities with nuclear warheads, and so ensure the certainty of Soviet intervention. And if the nuclear option is lost, what is left? South Vietnam is swallowing enough American men and money. How many South Vietnams can the United States sustain?

There are those, of course, who dream of a new alliance, an accommodation of the whole West with the Soviet bloc to contain the revolutionary world. The Soviet Union, runs the argument, is primarily concerned with Europe and would give a great deal in return for a suitable European settlement, especially since she is not herself without alarm at China's potential. There are still, after all, territories historically Chinese which a Tsarist Russia seized and a communist Russia retains. It seems inconceivable that such an alignment could come about. Yet no less inconceivable alignments have come about before. It would not help. Revolution can be contained no more than can poverty; while the bulk of mankind is in want, the bulk of mankind will revolt. If history has consistently taught one lesson, it is the power of human rejection.

[1] *Return to China*, by James Bertram (Heinemann, 1957), p. 89.

But history has taught another lesson – the power of race. And it is this power which the circumstances of want in the world threaten to provoke beyond the most terrible experiences of the past. By attempting to contain revolution, the white world – because it is white and rich and strong and still in control – is driving the two powers together, in an alliance of unparalleled fury, which may well howl itself away only in the ruins of humanity. For if revolution is rational, race is not.

The answer is that revolution cannot be contained. It must be released, allowed to change and create; helped to achieve its objectives. For what in the objectives of an end to poverty and to hunger, to ignorance and to disease, to weakness and to subjection, is repugnant? The world is in danger of destroying itself from fear of the very things that it claims continually to want. And if in fact it does not want such things, then its destruction is a questionable loss.

7

The Colour of Want

British politicians, when occasion requires them to praise the Commonwealth, are given to describing it as a family of nations which represents, in its variety of races and cultures, an image of the world. Leaving aside the 'family' platitude, which has no application to the past of most members and little enough to the present, the surviving claim has some validity; the Commonwealth resembles the world, and in the variety not only of its races and cultures but also of its economic circumstances. In the scale of *per capita* annual income, Canada exists at one end, with £570, and Malawi at the other with £12½, or just over 2 per cent of that amount. The Commonwealth, like the world, is less a single home than a street, with the rich residing behind high windows and the poor struggling for life in the gutters below.

If a *per capita* annual income of £170 is the frontier of wealth,[1] only five Commonwealth countries – Canada (£570), Australia (£544), New Zealand (£452), Britain (£448) and Cyprus (£193) – have crossed it, and they encompass only 88 million people, or some 11 per cent of the 790 million in the whole association. India, with 471 million people, has a *per capita* income of £24; Pakistan, with 106 million, one of £25; and Nigeria, with 55 million, one of £35. The overwhelming mass of the people in the Commonwealth – some 89 per cent – are poor, and so poor as to find mere survival the proper object of hope. Moreover, wealth and want have different skins. The five countries that have crossed the economic frontier are all 'white', while with the tiny exception of Malta (324,000 people and a *per capita* income of £140), all those still behind it are 'coloured'.[2]

It is this correspondence of colour and poverty that gives the Commonwealth its fundamental meaning. For the whole world is similarly divided into the rich who are nearly all white, and the poor who are coloured, with the poor and the coloured in a massive majority. The regions of relative wealth – North America, Europe and the Soviet Union,

[1] *The Rich Nations and the Poor Nations*, by Barbara Ward (Hamish Hamilton, 1962), p. 35.
[2] Figures in the *Guardian*, June 17th, 1965.

Australasia and Japan – contain some 1,000 million people, with only Japan and her 100 millions providing a significant exception to the rule of income and race. Across the remaining map of mankind, some 2,250 million people or 70 per cent of the total, almost all of them coloured, live in general want.

Figures for *per capita* annual income are, of course, in themselves commonly misleading. They emerge only through a corridor of distorting mirrors – currency exchange rates; the guesswork of economists on the value of subsistence agriculture; the necessary reduction to averages. The existence of vast discrepancies in income between members of the same society makes the condition of the poor even worse than the *per capita* figures may suggest. A relatively few merchants, managers and professional men – not infrequently involved in the operations of expatriate companies – produce by their contributions a level of average income which, however low, is still above, sometimes far above, that attained by the mass of society.

The available figures for *per capita* national income are useful as no more than crude guides to the enormous differences in standard of living between the rich countries and the poor ones. It says something about the world that the average Australian has an income more than twenty-two times as large as that of the average Indian. And the difference is not one of a capacity to purchase luxuries. It is a difference of no less than the capacity to survive. The poverty of the world's poor is hunger, malnourishment, illiteracy, needless disease and early death. At least 500 million people go hungry every day of their lives, at least another 1,000 million are seriously undernourished, and the numbers increase every moment. More meaningful for a measure of the distance between the rich white peoples and the poor coloured ones than any figures for cash income can be, are the statistics for infant mortality and life-expectancy.

What is finally terrifying is not so much that the gap between the rich and the poor is so wide already but that it is widening yet farther all the time. Possessed of the capital and skills necessary to increase the yields of agriculture and industry, the rich societies steadily grow richer, saving more than their generally low birth-rate adds to their consumption, and so enabled to invest more in the production of capital and skills. Like the rich man who spends steadily less than his income and so swells his capital and the income from it by merely standing still, the rich nation prospers on the very momentum of money. The poor, by the same rule, grow poorer as they stand still. Without the capital and skills necessary to develop their economies, and with a generally high birth-rate adding constantly to the pressure on their resources, they have less and less to spend, until their very survival is threatened.

Country	Population 1964 Estimates	Infant Mortality (per 1,000)	Life Expectancy Male	Female
Sweden	7,661,000	13·6	71·32	75·39
Australia	11,136,000	19·5	67·14	72·75
Japan	96,906,000	20·4	67·21	72·34
Czechoslovakia	14,058,000	22	67·21	72·83
France	48,440,000	23·4	67·2	74·1
United States	192,119,000	25·2	66·6	73·4
U.S.S.R.	(1963) 224,764,000	30·9	65	73
Spain	31,339,000	37·9	67·32	71·9
Mexico	39,643,000	67·7	55·14	57·93
Colombia	15,434,000	88·2	44·18	45·95
Senegal	3,400,000	92·9	— 37 —	
India	471,627,000	139	41·89	40·55
Morocco	12,959,000	149	— 49·6 —	
Brazil	78,809,000	170	39·3	45·5
Haiti	4,551,000	171·6	— 32·61 —	
Tanganyika	9,990,000	190	— 35 to 40 —	
Burma	24,229,000	193–300	40·8	43·8
Zambia	3,600,000	259	— 40 —	

Source: *United Nations Demographic Yearbook, 1964*

While the population of the world increased by 2 per cent in the year 1963–4, food production in the poor, hungry countries increased at a generally lower rate or not at all The important gains were made in those very areas – like North America (4 per cent) and Australasia (3 per cent) – where food surpluses already existed. (Indeed, in several areas of the world, *per capita* food production today is less than it was thirty years ago, during the depression of the 'thirties.) Yet how can the poor afford to buy food from the rich? India herself, with a seventh of all humanity inside her borders, has escaped widespread famine during the past few years by importing food from the United States, on terms made easy by political – and so demonstrably undependable – considerations.

The hunger of the poor is, however, only the most obvious attribute of their poverty. They are weakened, when not killed, by diseases which more or better food, sanitation and medical services would prevent or cure; they can seldom read or write; those who escape the stagnation of the countryside live in burgeoning city slums, sometimes not even in shanties but on streets in the shelter of a wall; millions have no work at all, and many more, much less work than their time and surviving energies could accommodate. Such poverty is self-defeating. The sick, the ignorant, the idle do not need any the less to be fed and clothed and housed, but they give correspondingly little to help the society sustain them. Like children they are potentially productive, but meanwhile more obviously mouths than hands.

The pat explanation for the persisting poverty of the poor is their high birth-rate. If only, like the rich, they would have less children, they could save more of their income for investment in their future, instead of having to spend all that they earn on keeping alive their enlarging families. Certainly, despite the much higher death-rate among the poor, the accomplishments of modern medicine have enabled them to increase their numbers much faster than the rich apparently choose to do.

	Rate of Population Increase (%)		
Area	1958–63	1960–63	
World	1·8	1·9	
Europe	0·9	0·9	
U.S.S.R.	1·6	1·6	
North America	1·6	1·6	
Asia	1·8	1·9	Source: *United Nations*
Africa	2·3	2·5	*Demographic Yearbook,*
Latin America	2·7	2·8	*1964*

By the middle of 1965, the population of the world had reached 3,308 million, and the U.S. Population Reference Bureau reported in early 1966 that if the present growth rate continues, the world's population will top 7,000 million by the year 2000. In 1965 there were 125 million births and 60 million deaths, and not one of the 'developing' or poor countries, the Bureau declared, had yet achieved an effective reduction in traditionally high fertility.

A cheap and easy contraceptive is the cry of the rich to the murmuring of the poor. It is altogether too glib. The rich themselves do not commonly limit their families in dedication to the economic advance of their societies, or because amenable forms of contraception are more available to them than to the poor. In France, where the annual population increase is only 1·1 per cent, the government has long encouraged larger families by financial benefits, periodic exhortation, and the pious outlawing of contraceptives widely used in near-by countries. In India, where the population increase is twice as high, government encouragement of birth-control meets steady resistance from those who see in many sons (and daughters, after all, arrive despite the most fervent prayers) help in the labour of the fields, support in old age, and the consolation of ritual at and after death. How can the state discourage the production of sons when it offers no alternative means of social security? How can the state contradict the commandments of tradition by the mere distribution of pills, loops and advice? The hard truth is that societies seem to reduce their fertility less with the advance of contraceptive methods than with the rise in general income and education. The dilemma is complete: the poor are likely to become rich by limiting their numbers, and only likely to limit their numbers by becoming rich.

The rich could, of course, help the poor by providing them with the huge amount of capital necessary for dynamic development. But they are far more concerned in promoting a yet higher rate of economic growth for themselves; in, sometimes, attempting to eradicate the islands of poverty and human waste in their midst; in protecting the strength of their national currencies; and, perhaps above all, in ensuring their military power. The defence budget of the United States alone is now almost $60,000 million a year, while the total expenditure on defence by all the rich societies is well over twice that figure, or enough to reshape the future for hundreds of millions of the poor. Indeed, in the estimate of Senator Fulbright, Chairman of the United States Senate Foreign Relations Committee, the single war in Vietnam cost the United States in 1965 some $15,800 million,[1] or more than three times the foreign economic aid given to India in the twelve years from August 1949 to December 1961.

The total net flow of capital from the rich to the poor is about $6,000 million a year, or something like the sum spent each year just by Britain on defence. And this sum of $6,000 million – which represents no more than 0·6 per cent of the collective gross product achieved by the industrial countries – is itself far from a donation. Much of it is made up by private investment for dividend return, and much of it by loans bearing a high annual interest. George Woods, President of the World Bank, recently claimed[2] that the service on debts incurred by the underdeveloped countries now stands at more than a tenth of foreign exchange earnings, and that when amortization, interest and dividends are considered together, the poor are losing half of what they gain each year from the rich in new capital.

The aid given by the communist rich, while often more efficient, more productive, and when in the form of loans, more generous than that provided by the capitalist rich – the Communists charge on the whole half the interest rate required by many Western sources – is, in its extent, scarcely impressive. In the period 1954–64 annual aid from the communist

[1] *The Times*, February 5th, 1966.   [2] *The Times*, December 17th, 1965.

countries – mainly, of course, the Soviet Union – to the 'third world' of
the poor ran at $665 million, a tiny fraction of the aid provided by the
West and of the Soviet Union's individual national income. And when,
in 1964, communist aid rose sharply to $1,700 million, it was largely the
result of intervention by China – competing for influence against the
Soviet Union – which provided a quarter of the total, while the Eastern
European states were responsible for another quarter, and the Soviet
Union for half. It says little for the seriousness with which the Soviet
Union regards her obligation to help promote the economic progress
and political independence of the poor that she should be providing, under
the provocation of the Sino-Soviet dispute, only twice the aid that China,
so much poorer and herself in need of aid, seems ready to supply.

The fact is that public opinion in the rich countries is even less enthusiastic than officialdom about devoting resources to alleviate the anguish
of the alien poor. After the harsh years of the Stalinist era, the people
of the Soviet Union want some of the so-long-promised recompense for
their suffering, and Stalin's successors, their command of power less
secure, are more concerned with securing popular approval than Stalin
felt it necessary to be. Furthermore, the unrest that culminated in the
Hungarian revolt of 1956 revealed the dangers of allowing popular disaffection in Eastern Europe to develop beyond apathy, and such sub-
ventions from Soviet wealth as the Soviet leadership has considered it
possible to spare have, since then, increasingly been devoted to nourishing
support within the European bloc.

In the West itself, where individual enrichment and conspicuous
consumption are the objects of common endeavour, the needs of the
poor have recommended themselves to attention, when at all, only as
increasingly irritating threats of communist advance, and military intervention where necessary has appeared a more effective method of containing communism than has economic aid. The de Gaulle government
in France, provoked less by compassion for the poor than by an anachronistic dedication to national grandeur, has devoted a higher proportion of
national income to economic aid than has the government of any other
Western state, and has come under mounting public criticism for such
extravagance. Indeed, whether reflecting the moral indifference of British
prosperity after the austere years of the war and its immediate aftermath,
or the moral materialism of the Yankee which sees poverty as the natural
desert of idleness or stupidity, Western public opinion has acknowledged
no real obligation or interest in helping the poor of the world to escape
their condition. And its indifference or opposition has been fed by the

apparent inability of the poor to practise those same virtues of voluntary individual sacrifice for the common good, the eradication of personal privilege, and the emphasis on human rather than on national advantage which the rich themselves have for so long so cheerfully ignored. Costly clashes among the needy, like the war between India and Pakistan in 1965, are proclaimed as proving the pointlessness and even damage of economic aid, although the rich have themselves promoted the purchase of military equipment – by offering far easier terms of payment for aeroplanes and tanks than for combine harvesters and trucks – and it is the impossibility of getting anywhere near sufficient aid for significant economic advance that has encouraged many of the poor to seek distraction in nationalist adventures.

Indeed, the value of aid has, far from merely failing to increase, been actually diminishing. The flow of funds from the rich world as a whole remained virtually unchanged from 1961 to 1965, though inflation steadily eroded its purchasing power, and the largest donor of all, the United States, has recently made substantial cuts in foreign aid. The 1965 American programme was the lowest since 1948 and worth less than half the programmes of 1951, 1952 and 1953.[1] And the programme for 1966 promises yet further cuts. The total of $2,469 million requested by the President for economic aid was $235 million lower than his 1965 request, and represented less than 0·4 per cent of the country's gross national product. The largest single item in the programme – $550 million – was for South Vietnam, as part of the war effort there; aid for all Latin America, under the much advertised Alliance for Progress, was to be $543 million (from $580 million in 1965); and an amount of $665 million was recommended for development loans to countries – mainly India, Pakistan, Nigeria, Turkey and Korea – with a total population of over 700 million. Moreover, the President made no effort to conceal the strings attached. Aid was to go to countries which not only gave 'solid evidence that they are determined to help themselves', but which were 'not hostile to us' (a criterion subject to wide differences of interpretation).

The condition of the poor is even more desperate, however, than their too rapidly increasing numbers, capital hunger and accumulated indebtedness suggest. It has for several years been a buyer's market in the very commodities that the poor produce for sale to the rich. The price of natural products like cocoa, sugar, rubber, cotton, coffee, tea, and of most

[1] 'A New Look at Trade and Aid', by Susan Strange, in *International Affairs*, Vol. 42, No. 1, January 1966.

important base metals has fallen, so that the most strenuous efforts at increasing yields have led to little or no rise, sometimes even a drop, in overall income. By heavy capital investment in disease and pest control, new acreage and plants, Ghana and Nigeria enormously increased their production of cocoa within a decade.

Country	Year	Cocoa Crop	Approximate Earnings
Ghana	1954–55	210,000 long tons	£85,500,000
	1964–65	590,000	£77,000,000
Nigeria	1954–55	89,000 long tons	£39,250,000
	1964–65	310,000	£40,000,000[1]

Together Ghana and Nigeria, therefore, tripled their production of a commodity crucial to their economies and saw their earnings from the sale of it abroad fall from a combined £125 million to £117 million. In the looking-glass world of the poor, one must run very fast to stand still.

Britain's National Institute of Economic and Social Research has revealed a major decline since 1947 in the export prices received by primary producers.

Year		Total Index Figure	Food	Non-Food
1957		100	100	100
1958		90·4	95	83·1
1959		90·7	90·8	90·6
1960		91·2	88·8	95·2
1961		84·7	84·2	85·7
1962		82·7	82·9	82·2
1963	I	87·7	88·6	86·2
	II	95·1	99·9	87·3
	III	92·3	96·4	85·8
	IV	99·9	105·8	90·4
1964	I	101·9	108·2	92
	II	98·6	104·4	89·3
	III	94·9	99·5	87·6
	IV	91·9	96·4	84·8
1965	I	89·7	94·3	82·5
	II	90·2	94·4	83·4[2]

Such price declines have eaten away at, and even altogether swallowed the effects of aid for economic development; the supply of United States aid to Latin America, for instance, has long been offset by the overall fall in the price of major Latin American commodities. Moreover, the very

[1] Neo-Colonialism, by Kwame Nkrumah (Nelson, 1965), p. 10. The figures for 1964–5 are estimates.
[2] The Times Supplement on the Food and Agriculture Organization, October 16th, 1965.

instability of prices makes it impossible for the poor societies properly to plan economic development, and put their available resources to the most productive use.

While the products of the poor have fallen in price, however, the products of the rich have risen, steadily widening the gap between what the poor must pay and what they manage to earn. The average price of machinery and transport equipment exported by the West to the poor societies, products necessary for the economic progress of the poor, has increased year by year, rising over 45 per cent in little more than a decade. With an index figure of 100 in 1958, prices stood at 73 in 1950, and rose to 80 in 1951; 85 in 1952; 88 in 1953 and 1954; 89 in 1955; 91 in 1956; 96 in 1957; 101 in 1959; 103 in 1960; 105 in 1961; and 106 in 1962.[1]

Nor is the profit appetite a concern only of the capitalist West. The Cuban government, selling sugar to the Soviet Union in exchange for manufactured goods, found the price of such manufactures frequently higher than that ruling on the world market, and only after repeated representations achieved an agreement by which Soviet prices would be cut wherever it could be shown that similar goods from other industrial countries cost less. Between the buyer's market for natural products and the seller's market for manufactures, the trading position of the poor persistently deteriorates. Overall, average unit prices of commodity exports from poor countries were 12 per cent lower in 1962 than they had been in 1955, while average unit prices of imports from the rich countries to the poor rose over the same period by 16 per cent.[2]

Even the ultimate consolation of the poor, that their products are necessary to the industrial economies of the rich, has diminishing validity with the development of manufactured substitutes for agricultural commodities. Synthetic fibres increasingly compete with cotton, wool, jute and sisal, while synthetic rubber is displacing not only natural rubber but even leather. In the period 1959–61 world exports of such synthetics – almost entirely from the rich industrial nations, of course – totalled in value some 24 per cent of world agricultural trade. Indeed, the extent to which the growth in the production of synthetic raw materials is outstripping the growth in the production of natural ones threatens the poor societies with the loss of one market after the other.

How may the poor hope to compete except by industrializing themselves? And how can they industrialize when the cost of industrialization constantly rises? Year by year the price of effective technology increases,

[1] *United Nations Statistical Yearbook*, 1964, p. 499.   [2] S. Strange, ibid.

PRODUCTION INDICES OF NATURAL AND SYNTHETIC RAW MATERIALS

| | Natural Fibres | | Synthetic Fibres | | | | |
Year	Cotton	Wool	Rayon	Non-Cellulosics	Total	Natural Rubber	Synthetic Rubber
1952	100	100	100	100	100	100	100
1953	104	101	118	123	118	97	106
1954	103	103	126	151	128	101	82
1955	109	109	142	204	147	107	124
1956	106	116	149	237	155	105	138
1957	104	113	154	314	166	106	144
1958	112	120	142	323	156	108	142
1959	118	126	157	446	179	114	186
1960	118	126	162	549	191	111	214
1961	119	128	168	648	204	117	225
1962	125	127	179	835	228	118	255

Source: Report of the U.N. Food and Agriculture Organization, quoted in *The Times*, October 5th, 1964.

capital requirements are higher, and the established producers, by accumulating skills and resources, make commercial competition from others all the more difficult and unlikely. Having achieved their lead in history – not without the assistance of conquest, subjugation and pillage – the rich are not merely maintaining but persistently increasing it. According to George Woods, President of the World Bank,[1] *per capita* income in the poor world may rise, if present trends continue, from $120 (£43) today to $170 (£61) by the year 2000. In the United States *per capita* income will increase from $3,000 (£1,270) today to $7,500 (£2,685) in the same period. Such predictions, however, suggest that the rate of growth both among the rich and among the poor will stay as it is. But whereas the rich will probably increase their rate of growth, with their command of skills and capital, the poor show every sign of having their already low rate yet further reduced. In 1950–54, the rate of increase in gross national product among the poor as a whole was around 5 per cent. In 1955–60, this rate dropped to 4½ per cent, and in 1960–64 to 4 per cent. With the population increasing too, with mounting loan charges and debt repayment, this meant for many poor countries no rise in *per capita* income at all, or even a fall.

Since the rich show no sign of effectively helping the poor – indeed, their own problems of liquidity, with the weakness of crucial trade currencies, make further reductions in foreign aid more likely than any increases – the poor must depend on their own efforts to secure economic progress and even the reasonable prospect of survival. From their very

[1] Reported in *The Times*, December 17th, 1965.

want they must squeeze capital, for investment in machines, power, transport, education; if they consume little, they must learn to consume less, and if they are already saving much, they must learn to save more. The demands of change are high. 'Economists fix a level of about twelve to fifteen per cent of national income as the range needed to cover all possible increases in population, some increase in consumption, and a high expanding level of investment.'[1] When national income is already inadequate for the proper sustenance of life, the saving of something like an eighth is more than exceptional effort; it becomes organized suffering.

India, the largest 'free' society in the world of the poor, with a government at least formally dedicated to socialist planning, has been saving at a rate of less than 10 per cent, and only substantial foreign aid, from East as well as West, has pushed the figure over 13 per cent. But the widespread corruption in business and administration, leading to an even more widespread cynicism about official policy or competence; the traditional addiction of private profit to seek security in such sterile investment as gold and precious stones; the conspicuous ability of the rich to get richer while enormous numbers of the poor experience little or no alleviation; the squandering of scarce capital, materials and foreign exchange on armaments and unproductive consumer goods; the surviving listlessness of the masses, so bent beneath the weight of religious teaching and tradition that they see what is under and behind them, not in front, all combine to convey more alarm and despair than self-assurance and a persuasive prospect of change. The multiplying millions of unemployed, the ever increasing multitude of those without shelter even in the slums, the constant presence of hunger saved from periodic famine only by emergency supplies of food from the West, provide no model for the restless masses of the poor in the rest of the world.

The success story of free enterprise in the coloured world, Japan, has about as much relevance for the contemporary poor as has the United States. It was a century ago that Japan, made agonizingly aware of her weakness with the forced opening of her ports by the main trading powers of the West, set out to transform herself in the image of a Western industrial state. The ruling class ruthlessly reformed agriculture, accumulated capital for investment by enforced popular saving, established industries, dispatched men to acquire skills abroad, promoted mass literacy, and pursuing the Western model still further, employed her new strength to seize an exploitable empire. Vastly enriched by her own technological advances and her exploitation of Chinese resources, she set

[1] B. Ward, op. cit., p. 46.

out to dominate Asia, extending her Chinese conquests to costly levels
and at last colliding not only with the older colonial powers of Europe
but with the United States in the climax of the Second World War. The
devastation of her human and material resources was enormous; but much
of her industrial plant survived, alongside her accumulated skills and
modern technological outlook. When the United States, seeking a
bastion of capitalism in Asia after the war, provided massive aid to restore
the Japanese economy, she added essential investment to an existing
industrial mentality and to a tradition of organized effort fortified by the
demands of national recovery. For Germany and Japan alike, indeed,
devastation was not without advantage; new and more efficient industrial
equipment replaced the worn and obsolete which in countries like Britain
the war had spared and peace then merely preserved. The stupendous
economic development of post-war Japan, therefore, must appear largely
meaningless to coloured countries which have yet to produce that revolution in popular outlook and that base of industrial equipment and skills
developed by the Japanese long ago, when the costs of competitive industrialization were so much less than they are today. Like the very low
rate of population increase, an annual 0·9 per cent, the bustling economy
of Japan is less the cause than the consequence of the escape from rural
stagnation, mass ignorance, uncoordinated effort, and the whole vicious
circle of poverty. The example of Japan, like that of Britain and the
United States, mirrors more the circumstances of the past than the
possibilities of the present.

To the poor unpersuaded of the likelihood that they can now, successfully and speedily, mimic the success of the long industrialized states,
communism offers a cruel but efficient remedy. Since significant economic
growth can only be procured by the massive saving and investment of
capital, with the proper deployment of human and material resources,
the state, under the control of a dedicated élite, must itself take complete
command of the struggle, enforcing co-ordinated effort and sacrifice in
the cause of an ultimately general prosperity. Capitalism, after all – the
Communists argue – requires effort and sacrifice as well, but does so for
the profit of a few, with a distortion of values and resources that only
foreign exploitation can prevent from producing serious stress. The poor
are, indeed, poor largely because they are the victims of such foreign
exploitation, if no longer commonly through overt political control, then
covertly through the operations of mining, industrial, commercial and
financial companies. Capitalism by its very nature demands the exploitation of others, and how are the poor to make themselves rich by exploit-

ing themselves? Of course capitalism coats its character with the varnish of individual freedom, but how free are the workless and hungry, the ignorant and diseased? Even if capitalism could prove capable of generating national wealth without plundering the poverty of other peoples, how satisfactory would it be to substitute a domestic plundering for a foreign one?

Such arguments meet a ready response in the experience and predicament of the poor. The Soviet Union points to the success of her Five Year Plans, which pushed domestic saving relentlessly to 25 per cent and even 30 per cent of national income. If terrible hardships were involved, and not a little capricious cruelty, the echoes are drowned in the bleepings of space satellites and the pulsations of Soviet industry. Moreover, this ascent to the status of a super power, rivalled for the moment in resources only by the United States, has taken less than half a century and so been watched by many still alive. (It is true that admirers of the Soviet accomplishment belittle or ignore the importance of the industrial base already constructed in pre-revolutionary Russia, but it is also true that they are generally unaware of the vast damage done to the Soviet economy – and not partly repaired afterwards with American aid – by the Second World War.) The influence of the Soviet experiment has spread far, even among national leaderships like the Indian Congress which passionately eschew communism itself. Most poor societies emerging from foreign capitalist rule adopt the panoply of plans, the centralized state authority, the encouragement of collective agriculture (in however mild a form), and the concentration of investment in the development of industry (rather than the promotion of more profitable agriculture) that were pioneered by the Soviet revolution, even when the strong sense of purpose and the ruthless discipline are absent.

Yet if the Soviet Union appears to possess more relevance for the poor than does the United States or any of the older imperial powers in Europe, her appeal has none the less to shine through a series of slats. She is a white state, however significant she would wish to make her coloured minority. She has not suffered the crude disparagement of her race and culture. And the very extent of her success intimidates pursuit. African, Asian and Latin American visitors are more stunned than spurred by the sophistication of the Soviet economy. It is China, in the very process of finding escape, who represents far more the predicament and the promise of the poor. Like other coloured societies long stricken and scorned, she seeks in revolution a path not from poverty alone but from weakness and historical humiliation. And through the jungle of hunger and disease, ignorance and superstition, helplessness and despair, she uses humanity itself to hack a way, proclaiming the clear supremacy of man over his past. If China is not burdened by people, ceaselessly pressing on her resources and consuming her effort, what country is? And if China can use her people as the very material of endeavour and advance, what country cannot? The progress of China in fifteen years from a poor, distracted and weak country to one disbursing rather than entreating aid, united in national effort and pride, even arrogance, and powerful enough to make the peace of the world dependent upon her acquiescence, has not been lost on revolutionary opinion among the poor, distracted and weak everywhere. The emergence to such international influence of a coloured people long held in ultimate subjection by the white powers of the West cannot but impress coloured peoples till recently themselves openly subjected and still ultimately under Western supervision.

The extent of Chinese economic progress and present strength is, of course, the subject of considerable dispute. The regimented derangement of the Great Leap Forward in 1958, with the three years of natural and man-made distress that followed, has not escaped recognition. Official Chinese claims no longer receive the easy acceptance that they once so widely did. But there are achievements which, for the coloured world, the most hostile propaganda cannot defeat. In the Korean War the Chinese army withstood the greatest military power on earth, and the Chinese government displayed a popular command that made all talk of widespread discontent and ready rebellion absurd. If the ultimate sanction of Soviet nuclear power prevented the United States from employing the full measure of her might, it was Chinese strength which effectively met in the field a force far superior in armaments; and if Chinese strength was able effectively to meet such a force, it was because the Chinese people were overwhelmingly united behind their revolutionary government. The Great Leap Forward a few years later may well have produced substantial economic disruption and gratuitous suffering, but the very crisis of error confirmed the most vaunted claim of the regime – the egalitarianism of the revolution. A strict and fair rationing system, which reduced living standards impartially, prevented vast areas of famine around privilege and surplus. (Unfriendly critics of communist China, in their very assault on the authoritarian distemper of the 'Great Leap Forward', stress that only the rigorous rationing conducted by the regime prevented widespread starvation.) Among the refugees who poured into Hong Kong, representative of many different localities and occupations, there was a general similarity of undernourishment, but no marks of famine.

Nor did refugee comment, scarcely a sympathetic source, commonly suggest any cruel discrepancies in the distribution and consumption of food. In a continent where government has long been synonymous with corruption, this was no small – or lightly marked – accomplishment.

The savings squeezed from the Chinese people for investment, increasingly for the development of heavy industry, were enormous, constituting a collective sacrifice without precedent in the poor coloured world. By 1952, China was investing at the same rate that Japan had achieved between 1887 and the start of the First WorldWar; by 1957, she had reached the rate achieved by Japan during the imperial and wartime expansion of the 1930s.[1]

The effect on the development of modern industry was inevitably impressive.

The tables overleaf reflect more than China's considerable growth rate, both in itself and in relation to the economic progress of other important poor coloured states. They reveal the vast gap existing between a rich country like France or Japan – let alone a great power like the Soviet Union or the United States – and a populous poor one like Indonesia or Brazil. If China is far from even approaching entry to the race of the rich, she is, in the race of the poor, an evident front runner. And her achievement is all the more remarkable – and remarked – for having been accompanied by relatively little outside aid.

India, treated with scant enough generosity by the rich world – her income per head from foreign aid has been amongst the lowest in the league of the 'uncommitted' poor – none the less received, between August 1949 and December 1961, a total of some £1,860 million ($5,208 million),[2] excluding important food subventions from the United States under P.L. 480. And of this, some £210 million ($588 million) were in outright grants. From East and West alike came grants and loans for steel mills, oil refineries, fertilizer plants, machinery. By the middle 'sixties, aid to India from the West alone was running at a rate of £375 million (over $1,000 million) a year.

China was far less favoured. The course of her revolution, the nature of her leadership and the inflexible hostility of the United States, cut her off from India's major source of foreign aid, the West, and forced her to rely on the communist bloc or, effectively, the Soviet Union alone. The

[1] 'Capital Formation in Communist China', by William W. Hollister, in *The China Quarterly*, No. 17, January–March 1964, pp. 39–55.
[2] The precise figure is 28,409 million rupees. *The Times of India Directory and Yearbook 1962–63*, pp. 152–7.

GROSS FIXED INVESTMENT 1950–59

	1950	1951	1952	1953	1954	1955	1956	1957	1958	1959
% of Gross National Product	5·5	6·4	9·1	12·4	13·9	13·8	17·9	15·9	23·9	25·7

DIRECTION OF GROSS FIXED INVESTMENT 1950–59

	1950	1951	1952	1953	1954	1955	1956	1957	1958	1959
% for Modern Sectors	48·8	54·4	56·5	54·5	55·4	57·5	59·3	61·1	64·3	65·7
(% on heavy industry alone)	(11·6)	(12·6)	(23·4)	(24·5)	(27·6)	(31·9)	(33·9)	(36·9)	(45·1)	(44·3)
% for Traditional Sectors	51·2	45·6	43·5	45·5	44·6	42·5	40·7	38·9	35·7	34·3
(% on agriculture)	(45·2)	(38·7)	(34·6)	(26·2)	(26·6)	(28·3)	(24·4)	(25·2)	(26·4)	(26·6)

PRODUCTION OF ELECTRIC ENERGY (in million Kwh.)

	1948	1953	1954	1955	1956	1957	1958	1959	1960	1961	1962
China	4,308*	9,195	11,001	12,278	16,593	19,340	27,530	41,500	58,500	—	—
India	5,725	8,681	9,669	10,877	11,972	13,757	15,415	17,794	20,123	22,957	26,227
Indonesia	362	718	796	863	894	983	1,005	1,081	1,161	1,220	1,335
Japan	35,579	55,698	60,076	65,193	73,580	81,272	85,411	99,101	115,472	132,022	140,383
Brazil	6,797	10,341	11,871	13,655	15,447	16,963	19,766	21,108	22,865	24,405	27,158
Nigeria	108	179	214	243	285	331	353	430	562	662	786
France	28,851	41,462	45,570	49,627	53,829	57,433	61,599	64,507	72,118	76,489	83,093
U.S.S.R.	66,341	134,325	150,695	170,225	191,653	209,688	235,350	265,112	292,274	327,611	369,275
U.S.A.	336,808	514,169	544,645	629,010	684,804	716,356	724,752	797,567	844,188	881,495	946,527

* 1949
Source: *United Nations Statistical Yearbooks, 1962 and 1964*

PRODUCTION OF CRUDE STEEL (in 1,000 metric tons)

	1948	1954	1955	1956	1957	1958	1959	1960	1961	1962	1963
China	—	2,225	2,853	4,465	5,350	11,080	13,350	18,450	9,500†	10,000†	12,000†
India	1,277	1,712	1,732	1,766	1,742	1,842	2,473	3,287	4,084	5,149	5,971
Indonesia	—	—	—	—	—	—	—	—	—	—	—
Japan	1,715	7,750	9,408	11,106	12,570	12,118	16,629	22,138	28,268	27,546	31,501
Brazil	483	1,148	1,162	1,375	1,299	1,362	1,608	1,843	1,995	2,088	2,812
Nigeria	—	—	—	—	—	—	—	—	—	—	—
France	7,236	10,627	12,592	13,398	14,096	14,616	15,218	17,281	17,570	17,240	17,557
U.S.S.R.	18,639	41,434	45,271	48,698	51,176	54,920	59,971	65,293	70,755	76,306	80,198
U.S.A.	80,413	80,115	106,173	104,522	102,253	77,342	84,773	90,067	88,917	89,202	99,120

Source: *United Nations Statistical Yearbooks, 1962 and 1964*

† Estimates of U.S. Bureau of Mines.

PRODUCTION OF CEMENT (in 1,000 metric tons)

	1948	1953	1954	1955	1956	1957	1958	1959	1960	1961	1962
China	660*	3,877	4,600	4,503	6,393	6,860	9,300	12,270	13,500†	8,000†	8,000†
India	1,578	3,841	4,468	4,559	5,008	5,691	6,186	6,936	7,845	8,246	8,586
Indonesia	38†	149	147	149	145	267	299	413	387	445	505
Japan	1,859	8,768	10,675	10,563	13,024	15,176	14,985	17,270	22,537	24,632	28,787
Brazil	1,265	1,655	1,683	2,771	3,275	3,393	3,790	3,841	4,474	4,711	4,971
Nigeria	—	—	—	—	—	—	113†	121	168	303	483
France	5,830	9,227	9,557	10,770	11,388	12,710	13,629	14,184	14,349	15,685	16,852
U.S.S.R.	6,455	15,961	18,992	22,484	24,858	28,896	33,308	38,781	45,520	50,864	57,328
U.S.A.	35,210	45,001	46,433	52,993	56,152	52,573	54,830	59,763	56,063	56,718	58,937

* 1949   † Estimates of U.S. Bureau of Mines.   Source: *United Nations Statistical Yearbooks, 1962 and 1964*

POPULATION ESTIMATES, MID 1963

China	over 725,000,000	(1957: 646,530,000 – official Chinese statistics
		1958: 670–680,000,000 – semi-official estimates
		1960: 686,400,000 – International Labour Organ-
		ization estimate.
		Annual increase of 2% would be some 14,000,000
		people.)
India	460,490,000	
Indonesia	100,045,000	
Japan	95,899,000	
Brazil	76,409,000	
Nigeria	55,670,000	
France	47,853,000	
U.S.S.R.	224,764,000	Source: *United Nations Demographic Yearbook,*
U.S.A.	189,417,000	*1964.*

importance of Soviet aid to Chinese economic development in the decade after the revolution ought not to be belittled. Made up in the overwhelming main of 'aid projects' which supplied machinery – often entire industrial plants – technical aid and training facilities, this foreign contribution, while a tiny part of China's total investment in economic growth,[1] provided the framework for the massive attempt at industrialization. Soviet blueprints for factories and machines were of immeasurable value, as were the 10,800 Soviet and 1,500 East European technicians working in China, or the 14,000 Chinese students and 38,000 industrial apprentices being trained in the Soviet Union, during the years to the end of 1959.

To declare this, however, is not to deny the very low ceiling of Soviet generosity and China's help from abroad. As far as is known from Soviet as well as Chinese sources, the Soviet Union gave China no single outright grant of equipment or money. The 'aid projects', amounting in value to some $2,025 million, were to be repaid, and since only two low-interest cash loans, totalling $530 million, are on record as having been provided, the burden of repayment fell mainly on the export of commodities – however urgently needed by China herself – to the Soviet Union. (A further agreement, for projects entailing supplies worth $1,250 million, was signed by the Soviet Union for the years 1959–67: but in July 1960, with the Sino-Soviet dispute reaching a new plateau of

[1] Ping-Chia Kuo in *China: New Age and New Outlook* (Penguin Books, 1960, p. 148) calculates that total capital investment under the First Five-Year Plan (1953–7) amounted to some $30,000 million, of which Soviet credits represented in value some $2,000 million or 7½ per cent.

rancour, 'the Soviet authorities ... suddenly and unilaterally decided on a complete withdrawal of the 1,390 experts who were in China ... tore up 343 contracts for experts and the supplements to these contracts and abolished 257 items for scientific and technical co-operation, and since then they have reduced in large numbers the supplies of complete sets of equipment and key sections of various other equipment.'[1] Furthermore, China appears to have paid, with commodity exports to the Soviet Union, even for the technical assistance she received from Soviet specialists.[2]

In the middle of 1957 the Chinese government announced that it had received the equivalent of some $2,240 million in 'loans and credits' from the Soviet Union, and it seems clear that this did not include the value of the 'aid projects'. Since only a sum of $430 million seems to have consisted in loans for economic purposes, the remaining $1,810 million must in large measure represent the value of military equipment supplied during the Korean War and afterwards. Certainly the Chinese authorities have complained, repeatedly and with mounting bitterness, that China had to bear the full burden of the Korean War, including the cost of Soviet-supplied arms. Then, in 1955, the Soviet Union finally transferred her shares in various Sino-Soviet joint stock companies, a legacy of Chinese dismemberment before the revolution, for payment through long-term debts.[3]

Soviet aid to China, therefore, and so – since East European aid must have constituted no more than a relatively trivial amount – virtually all foreign aid, from the revolution to the early 'sixties, totalled some $4,265 million, or almost $1,000 million less than the amount supplied to India, a country only two-thirds the size and starting with a much stronger industrial base. If the cost of Soviet supplied military equipment and imperially pillaged assets are excluded from the Chinese total – and neither cost appears a notable feature of the listed foreign aid programme to India – economic assistance to China must be accounted hardly half the Indian total.

Moreover, while India groans under a huge foreign debt and its necessary servicing, China has all but paid off her foreign debts by running a constant surplus in her trade with the Soviet Union, even during the years of economic depression in 1961–2.

[1] *People's Daily*, December 4th, 1963.
[2] *Essays in Economic Relations of the U.S.S.R. with China*, by M. I. Sladkovskii (Foreign Trade Publishing House, Moscow, 1957), p. 333.
[3] *China and Her Shadow*, by Tibor Mende (Thames & Hudson, 1960), pp. 176–7.

SINO-SOVIET TRADE, 1958–62 (in million roubles)					
	1958	1959	1960	1961	1962
China's imports from the U.S.S.R.	571	860	735	331	210
China's exports to the U.S.S.R.	792	991	763	496	465
China's export balance	221	131	28	165	255

Source: 'China's Industrial Development, 1958–63' by Choh-ming Li, in *The China Quarterly*, No. 17, January–March 1964, p. 33.

Between 1958 and 1962 alone, therefore, China paid back to the Soviet Union 800 million roubles or almost $900 million. In an official communiqué issued at the end of the National People's Congress in December 1963, the Chinese government announced that all debts to the Soviet Union, including interest, would be repaid by 1965.

Finally, where India, like almost all poor countries, has considered her own situation far too desperate to allow for the disbursal of any significant aid to others, China has given large and increasing amounts in loans and grants. Starting with a $200 million grant in 1953, she had, by the end of 1961, pledged over $1,500 million to North Korea, almost two-thirds of which had been spent. From 1956, with a grant of $22 million to Cambodia, she began giving aid to the non-aligned, and by late 1964 had pledged more than $500 million, with $150 million of this amount to countries in Africa.[1] China claims that she has already given as much to deserving countries as she has received from the Soviet Union in economic aid, and the available evidence is persuasive.

Yet her economic progress has been far from free of setbacks, some of them self-inflicted. There is a limit to the discipline and effort that a government, however popular, can command from a people, and that limit was reached with the 'Great Leap Forward' of 1958–60. The rise in domestic investment to over 25 per cent, the frantic endeavour at rapid and intensive collectivism in the 'communes' – heralded as the step from socialism to communism – the crescendo of appeals to greater and still greater sacrifice, combined to produce a state of hysteria. Huge bottlenecks developed in industry, with transport unable to shift accumulating materials; millions of peasants loyal to the regime but opposed to the new demands of the 'communes' resisted without rebelling; and a series of natural distresses, floods and droughts, cut yet further the agricultural crops. The economic depression which ensued was certainly serious, but it would have been immeasurably more so had the regime been less

[1] 'China in the Postwar World', by A. M. Halpern, in *The China Quarterly*, No. 21, January–March 1965, p. 34.

flexible and popular. Industrial targets were reduced, and the flow of agricultural labour to industrial construction not only stemmed but reversed. The 'commune' was kept as 'the basic social organization',[1] but some of the heat was taken off the peasantry, and the cultivation of tiny private plots, with the private rearing of animals, more easily permitted. Since 1961 open markets for agricultural products, the *chi-shih*, have been allowed to develop alongside the monolith of the state system, and though few suppose this to be anything but a temporary measure, it has helped to reconstitute popular confidence and provoke further effort, as has the production of more consumer goods to raise – however slightly – general living standards. Above all, the regime has recognized the paramount importance of agriculture to the whole economy, increased the share of domestic investment given to it, and redirected the function of industry. 'In the earlier period heavy industry was developed for the sole purpose of serving heavy industry, while now it is developed for the sake of serving agriculture.'[2]

This reflected a profound change in the official Chinese attitude. Gone was much of the euphoria that characterized the 'Great Leap Forward', the supreme confidence of an industrial millennium within reach. The new recognition, echoed in countless official statements, was of China's terrible poverty, which decades and not years of work and sacrifice alone would surmount and which drew China, in her problems and endeavours, close to all the poor and resolute of the world. It was a mood far more amenable to the other poor than that of an exultant communism, claiming to have leapt over obstacles which less vigorous and enlightened peoples feared even to climb. With the apparent renunciation of their infallibility, the Chinese themselves seemed more accessible, more appropriate guides through the achievements and inevitable mistakes of determined authority and organized sacrifice. Their increasing emphasis on the doctrine that the function of aid is to reduce the recipient's dependence on others – a doctrine remarkable mainly for the disregard it has enjoyed among traditional donors – has been suitably appreciated by those it has served. There are few of the rebellious poor who do not recognize the relevance of the Chinese contention that self-reliance is essential to real national independence. Certainly, the preaching would have small effect if it were not manifestly wrapped up in practice. But the

[1] 'Collectivisation of Agriculture in China', by Liao Lu-yen, *Peking Review*, No. 44, November 1st, 1963.
[2] 'On the Problem of Accumulation and Consumption', by Yang Po, *Red Flag*, No. 21, November 1st, 1962.

experience of several African states testifies to the deliberate self-efface-
ment of Chinese assistance, its haste to make itself no longer necessary.
'China's aid has been comparatively efficient in operation and has been
administered with considerable political and psychological sensitivity.'[1]

Chinese confidence in the need for self-reliance was passionately confirmed by the experience of 1960, when Soviet aid was withdrawn at a
time of economic crisis, inflicting 'incalculable difficulties and losses on
China's economy, national defence, and scientific research'.[2] Yet the
Chinese economy not only survived Soviet abandonment in the very
midst of its other setbacks, it managed to pay off several hundred million
dollars' worth of debt and to purchase with scarce foreign exchange some
16 million tons of food, mainly from Canada and Australia, in the period
1960-63. The contrast with India, increasingly dependent on foreign aid
and the virtual gift of massive food shipments by the United States, is
notable and scornfully noted by the Chinese themselves. (United
States food exports to India, with the threat of famine after the failure
of the monsoon, are expected to total some 10 million tons in 1966
alone.)

Since the autumn of 1962, when the depression appears to have been
successfully surmounted, the Chinese economy has again raced ahead,
though with more balanced and circumspect an effort. China is not only
purchasing with hard cash from export earnings whole industrial plants
from the West, but even intervening in the London gold market to
exchange her surplus holdings of foreign currency. Oil production, long
regarded in the West as the weakest link in China's economy and the one
making her ultimately dependent on Soviet good-will, leapt, with the
exploitation of the new oilfield at Taching, from 966,000 metric tons in
1955 to 5,500,000 in 1960 and, by 'the best informed estimates', to somewhere between 8,000,000 and 9,000,000 tons in 1965.[3] (Indian production,
at 347,000 tons in 1955, had reached 1,653,000 in 1963.) The Taching
oilfield, with its modern plant completed despite the 1960 withdrawal
of Soviet technicians, 'seems to put China into the top rank of the world's
technologically advanced countries',[4] while the figure for current
domestic production supports China's claim to be now virtually self-
reliant in petroleum. The message of Chinese endeavour is more and
more relevant to the poor.

[1] A. M. Halpern, ibid.
[2] 'All-Round Improvement in China's Economy', by Fan Chung, in *Peking Review*, No. 34,
August 23rd, 1963.
[3] *The Times*, January 13th, 1966.
[4] Ibid.

PRODUCTION OF NITROGENOUS FERTILIZERS (*in 1,000 metric tons*)

	1949	1955	1956	1957	1958	1959	1960	1961	1962	1963
China	27	332	523	751	1,118	1,333	1,500	1,085	1,628	2,187

	1948/49–1952/53	1955/56	1956/57	1957/58	1958/59	1959/60	1960/61	1961/62	1962/63	1963/64
India	23·6	81·7	80·8	80·8	80·8	87·3	110·2	151·3	193·2	220·9
Japan	407·2	704·4	780·5	882·8	986·3	921·7	1,029·9	1,088·6	1,151·4	1,279·3
France	252	408·2	450·7	510·0	538·5	573·6	670·8	772·6	753·3	—

PRODUCTION OF SUPERPHOSPHATES (*in 1,000 metric tons*)

	% P_2O_5	1948	1955	1956	1957	1958	1959	1960	1961	1962	1963
China	17	—	21	100	120	344	444	500	362	542	729
India	16	22	75	82	144	170	252	318	372	448	580
Japan*	16	993	1,795	2,058	1,864	1,758	1,852	2,150	1,879	1,809	1,663
France	17	1,643	1,115	1,078	1,211	1,220	1,136	1,261	1,374	1,475	1,549

* Excludes a small quantity of the concentrated form (36%), totalling 24 thousand tons in 1963.
Sources: For Chinese figures, Fertiliser Application in Communist China', by Jung-chao Liu in *The Chinese Quarterly*, No. 24, October–December 1965, p. 32. Other figures from the *U.N. Statistical Yearbooks*, 1962 and 1964.

Such economic growth – the concentration of savings on the establishment of heavy industry; the employment of heavy industry in the
efficient exploitation of the poor country's fundamental asset, agriculture;
and the creation of an agricultural surplus for yet more heavy industry
and the manufacture of consumer goods – offers the escape way from
perpetual want or, at best, perpetual dependence on the favours of the
rich. It is a process likely to recommend itself more and more, if not to
the present rulers of the poor, then to others asserting leadership of the
hungry, the unsheltered and unschooled, in a revolution of rejection and
affronted pride.

It is scarcely surprising that among those in the Western democracies
who know anything at all of the Chinese revolution and its economic
conquests, so few find the precedent of China very congenial. Leaving
aside those whose concern is nakedly with Western interests, and who see
Chinese strength as a threat to Western security, influence and wealth,
there are some, manifestly humanist, who are repelled by Chinese regimentation, the apparently absolute power of the Communist Party
leadership, and the short shrift given to any expression of dissent. Reports
that Chinese schoolchildren are taught to mouth dogmatic slogans, and
official Chinese suggestions that the thought of Mao Tse-tung is necessary
even to the proper playing of ping-pong, stir a dismay that no triumphant
array of economic statistics can subdue. Of what advantage to humanity
can a revolution be if its obvious victim is free individual development?

That such dismay is the product of a largely rich and open society does
not make it any less just, or any less irrelevant to the situation that exists
rather than the situation that should exist in most of the world. What
room is there for free individual development in the streets of Calcutta
or the dust tracks of Uttar Pradesh? The regular election of an Indian
parliament by free vote is surely desirable; but might it not be equally
desirable – conceivably, even more desirable – to the voters themselves
that they should be fed? It may be true that most people in the rich and
open part of the West would rather starve than surrender their right to
vote – few of those who claim this have, happily, themselves had to choose
– but is this true for most people in the closed world of the poor? The Westerner must ask himself not whether he would rather live in India than
in China, but, if he were a peasant, which form of society he would prefer.

To speak of China today as though she has hurtled from a long past of
individual liberty into the sudden tunnel of communist repression is
patently absurd. For the vast mass of the Chinese, personal freedom – in
the expression of personal opinion, a share in the control of resources and

institutions – has never existed. What does exist now, that never existed before, is an assurance against starvation, if not yet hunger; a steadily increasing access to better shelter and health and education; an end to the extravagant disparity between rich and poor; above all, the hope of a general advance from want, to an abundance of long-incredible opportunities. Is all this not, fundamentally, an increase in individual liberty? And with the back of poverty broken, is greater liberty of the mind not likely to follow? The riches of the Soviet Union afford a degree of dissent that poverty ruthlessly denied.

Where else in the poor world does individual liberty exist? In a few states across the expanse of Asia, Africa and Latin America the formal rights proclaimed by the democratic West may exist, though – as in India – alongside a common want that merely mocks them. But for most of the states there exist neither such rights nor the economic assurances of China. Complacently, or desperately, the West may include them in its definition of 'the free world'; but this bears about as much relation to reality as does the condition of the Mississippi Negro share-cropper to Madison Avenue. The present leaders of most poor states may well scorn the Chinese experiment and proclaim the virtue, indeed sanctity of anti-communism; but it is not reasonably to be supposed that their view will perpetually prevail over the restless deprivations of their subjects.

This does not mean, of course, that the Chinese precedent will, mistakes and all, be mirrored by other societies attempting to escape the deep human humiliation of their circumstances. Still less does it mean that peoples in Africa, Latin America and Asia will welcome a Chinese suzerainty to replace the Western one which has for so long afflicted them. What it does assuredly mean is that they will not be deflected from attempting to imitate the economic success of the Chinese revolution by the terrible warnings of the West that they will be sacrificing a multitude of traditional liberties in the process. And what it does probably mean is that many societies will, in varying degrees, adopt communist forms of political organization, without proclaiming a communist allegiance, and without surrendering their individuality or independence.

Julius Nyerere, President of Tanzania, is the antithesis of that wild-eyed extremist so many Westerners expect to see at the head of a radical African regime. Genial in manner and circumspect in judgment, he led a struggle by Tanganyika against British rule that was marked by scarcely any violence and by rapid success. His clear hostility to racism was generally interpreted in the West as a sign of his moderation – or, to the more cynical, of his manageability – and for a short while he had no rival as the black favourite of the white world. But he was clearly hostile as well to the economic degradation of his country, one of the poorest in Africa, and to the efforts of the West to secure its interests by sustaining white settler rule elsewhere on the continent and attempting to discipline African independence. His government increasingly displayed a socialist commitment, with a strongly centralized programme of popular econo-mic endeavour, a militant Pan-Africanism and a policy of international non-alignment. Then, in early 1964, a rising in near-by Zanzibar, led in part by young men under the influence of the Cuban and Chinese revolu-tions, tumbled from power the regime of Arab planters, and set up a revolutionary government which immediately directed itself to radical land reform. The island's new leadership gradually moved to an accom-modation with the Nyerere government on the mainland opposite, and Tanzania was established as a union of the two countries.

Julius Nyerere is no longer regarded as moderate or admirable in the West. Chinese technicians and aid are welcomed by the Tanzanian government, whose policy of strict non-alignment does not preclude a warm relationship with Chinese Communists. And Nyerere has repeatedly proclaimed the relevance of China's economic efforts to a poor, all but entirely rural society like Tanzania. 'This, too,' he has said, reporting on a Chinese multitude of makeshift factories, with leaking roofs and the earth for floors, but with an enthusiastic and efficient output of simple manufactures, 'we can do.' Tanzania itself is a one-party state, with mass peasant effort mobilized by the party for collective agriculture and public works, with the trade unions under rigorous government control and with a few recalcitrant political opponents – mainly trade unionists – in detention.

Yet no one who knows Tanzania and Africa as a whole would call the Nyerere government despotic, and Tanzanian society communist. Un-impeded attempts by an opposition party to attract popular support during the early days of Tanganyika's independence failed appallingly, and today elections for members of parliament within the one-party system are conducted with a freedom that challenges many Western pretensions. The 1965 general election dismissed so many sitting members and Cabinet Ministers that it was a political landslide, while in one con-stituency an Asian Minister and in another a white one were returned against African opponents by an overwhelmingly African electorate. (It is not impertinent to ask whether the effective choice of party rather than representative in Britain bestows a much greater degree of political freedom on the individual voter, especially when the parties represented in parliament differ scarcely at all on major issues and compete against each other for the allegiance of the 'floating' vote. Nor is it impertinent to wonder why members of proportionately small racial minorities are elected to parliament by general suffrage in Tanzania, while no single member of the proportionately larger coloured minority in Britain sits in the Commons.)

The truth is that if Tanzania has taken from communist societies, it has sieved it through African political experience. The one-party system in Tanzania is closer to the tradition of tribal consensus than is the system of party conflict in Britain. The habits of the past combine with the needs of the present to produce a new social form. There is the puritanism of communist society in Tanzania's economic endeavour, but there is, too, an astonishing lack of blind submission to dogma, an eagerness to experiment and a sensitivity to public response. What has happened so far can scarcely be termed a revolution – so little has changed – but change has begun, and must in its necessary course produce yet new experiences and new forms.

Nothing is more certain than that revolution will sweep the societies of the poor, and nothing is less true than that such revolutions will all be carbon copies of a communist original. Where, in any event, is the original? The Soviet, the Chinese and the Cuban revolutions, within the communist definition, differ significantly from one another, each reflecting the character and circumstances of the people involved. Because China is the most populous state on earth, and because, despite the striking success of her revolution, she still shares with the poor of the earth poverty, an overwhelmingly agricultural economy, and the long historical dominance of her colour by the white rich, she exercises a special influence. But it is the influence of her revolution, not of herself.

When the West applauds an apparent diplomatic defeat of China in the coloured world, it is applauding an irrelevancy. China does not need a large array of friends to become a great power. If her own vast resources cannot provide her with the means, the sympathy of half a hundred poor and weak states will not do so; if they can, the hostility of half a hundred poor and weak states will not matter. What China does seek, as a way of assailing Western – especially American – and increasingly now also Soviet power is revolution, and such diplomatic defeats as she has suffered do little, if any, damage to this aim.

Indeed, some defeats are victories. The furious hostility of a Dr Banda in Malawi to Peking imperialism would carry much more weight if Dr Banda himself was not at the same time firmly attached to a British

alliance, on excellent terms with the Portuguese, opposed to economic
pressure on white South Africa, contemptuous of militant Pan-Africanism,
and contentedly presiding over a capitalist regime and primitive economy
dominated by expatriate firms. With most of his major colleagues in the
independence struggle and early government now in open rebellion, his
views are not unopposed inside Malawi itself and are generally opposed
in the rest of independent Africa.

Recent military coups in the Central African Republic and Dahomey
have been immediately followed by the expulsion of a Chinese presence,
with attacks on Chinese meddling in internal matters. Since neither coup,
however, appears to have been provoked by the desire for fundamental
economic and social change, radical opinion in Africa may reasonably
wonder whether the attack on China was not for Western consumption
or, if the Chinese were really meddling, whether their meddling was
altogether without justification.

South Africa has long used communism as a tag for all those who
oppose white supremacy, and has only succeeded as a result in making
communism attractive to the non-white intellectuals. This does not mean,
of course, that African, coloured and Indian leaders in South Africa have
rushed to take out membership of the local party, let alone that they are
conspiring to provide China or the Soviet Union with a satellite. It merely
means that they are provoked, in substantial measure by government
tirades against communism and persecution of opponents as communist,
to investigate the source of so much alluring hostility and fear. Similarly
Chinese meddling is becoming the tag for all opposition in independent
Africa to official corruption, privileged élites, the power of expatriate capital, and surviving Western dominance. It is an identification that will not
produce Chinese satellites in Africa but will excite an increasing number
of the disaffected to find out what, after all, the Chinese revolution was,
and is, about. It is a search unlikely to leave African society undisturbed.

Cries by the West and African regimes of Western alignment that
China is trying for an empire in Africa are not taken seriously by the
radical opinion to which it is directed. The prospect of Chinese colonies,
snatched suddenly by direct assault or trained agents, seems extravagantly
improbable, while the existence of Western influence and even intervention is too apparent for doubt. In short, African revolution will
address itself to fighting what is, not what may be, and attempts to
frighten it by posing invisible menaces can only draw attention to the
precedents of change.

This is, of course, no less true of Latin America. Cuba's recent open breach with China may have an impact on the attitude of particular communist parties and even non-communist revolutionaries towards the Chinese state (though it may also have the effect of casting suspicion on the policy of the Soviet state and the purposes of its protection); but it can scarcely damage the Chinese call for revolution. Castro himself and *Fidelismo* as a doctrine are committed to encouraging armed revolutionary struggle, and any reversal of such a commitment would strip both of their continental influence. Paradoxically, too, the Soviet Union, in her very efforts to counter the influence of the Chinese state, is spreading the influence of Chinese policy. For if she is not to discard the allegiance of revolutionaries altogether in an ultimate accommodation with the West, she must confirm her own militancy. And at Havana in the Tri-Continental Conference of December 1965 and January 1966, this is just what she attempted to do. Under pressure from China and Cuba, she subscribed to the thesis that the United States is the ultimate opponent, that small countries should not be left to confront United States power alone or unaided, and that designated areas in Latin America (Colombia and Venezuela in particular) are ripe for assisted guerilla warfare. Accommodation with the West would doubtless put a stop to this militancy, but would then also increase the direct influence of China.

In Asia itself, where Chinese power can more reasonably be displayed as a threat to national independence, Chinese economic progress by its very example stirs the impoverished peasantry to revolt against rich and not uncommonly corrupt governing elites. And to China's claim that she has eradicated privilege and promoted, however relentlessly, a national endeavour for general economic advance, the traditional alliance of landlord, merchant and civil or military administrator provides an unpersuasive reply, especially when it seems to require Western protection. Revolutionary imitation can itself, of course, go hand in hand with hostility to China and fear of her territorial ambitions. It may be remembered that Japan, in a revolution conducted by traditional authority, set out a century ago to borrow from Western society for the transformation of her economic structure, and not so that she might succumb to Western power, but so that she might be able to withstand it. Similarly in Asia today, there are nationalists who would borrow from Chinese society so that their countries, too, from being poor, distracted and weak, may escape into a dynamic independence.

Such nationalists are aware that they cannot unite the peasant masses in enthusiasm for a system which allows the existence of huge private landholdings alongside millions of the landless; which channels so much of peasant effort, through high rents, to the support of city leisure; which cannot prevent, in the midst of hunger, the manipulation of food supplies by merchants for personal enrichment; which surrounds government with middlemen trading in taxes, contracts, licences, jobs, and – where necessary – votes. The peasantry needs a radical redistribution of land, an end to commercial and administrative corruption, the confiscation of accumulated wealth, and an investment of national resources in rapid economic development. It is at this point that the nationalist and Communist meet, in a common desire for revolution that will sweep away the old rotting society and put in its place a new and vigorous one. And it is at this point that the West sees a threat to its interests and security.

The West – ultimately, the government of the United States – can scarcely fail to recognize the need for reform and a popular base to the regimes with which it is aligned. But it will not, of course, allow the rise of the revolutionaries to power, for revolution will destroy the economic system in which it itself believes and command a degree of independence in international affairs inevitably damaging to Western influence and strategy. Furthermore, revolution with communist participants can easily become a communist revolution, adding directly to the power of the communist world and even – worst of all – the power of China. Revolution must be avoided at all costs: if it is communist, because it is; and if it is not, because it may become so. Since reform remains necessary, however, if revolution is to be kept from attracting the mass of the population, the existing regimes must promote it, with resources, advice and encouragement provided by the West. Yet reform is so necessary precisely because the existing regimes are so corrupt and devoted to the interests of the traditionally rich and powerful. Measures of land reform, pledged under Western pressure, accordingly never leave the desks on which they are drafted, and economic aid, ear-marked for a multitude of public projects, disappears into private pockets, leaving its trace in an inflation which makes food and other essentials still scarcer and more expensive for the poor. Peasant discontent rises, and the repressions of the established regime drive it into open struggle. The West is now faced with the very revolution that it fears, and commits itself with an increasing involvement of prestige as well as resources to a direct confrontation. But warfare only heightens the economic problem, producing new scarcities, ruinous inflation, and an administrative dependence on foreign power which nourishes corruption, while the presence of Western soldiers in the field alienates the mass of the population further from what is now seen as a puppet despotism. The regime in the capital changes its personnel, in desperate search of someone able to command greater public support, but does not change its nature and so drifts into ever greater isolation. Then, as the revolution spreads, to involve most of the rural areas, the Western military presence becomes both more blatant and destructive, killing and maiming unarmed peasants and their families, devastating crops and homes, in pursuit of the armed guerillas, and so increasing the appeal and recruitment of revolution. It is a self-defeating policy, but an inevitable one if Western power is to feel itself having any significant impact. For the superiority of the West in war lies not in men but in weapons, and the more effective the weapons, the less discriminate they are likely to be in the object of their destruction. And so, soon, by the mounting strength of the revolutionary forces and the mounting weakness of the native regime opposed to them, Western military involvement rises to a point where the war seems less a civil than a foreign one, with a white power engaged against coloured people for control of their country.

This escalation from peasant discontent to the appearance and ultimate reality of race war is no figment of an idiosyncratic alarmism. It provides a not unreasonable record of steps towards the present state of conflict in South Vietnam. Of course, the Vietnam revolution has its peculiar elements: the long struggle against the French, the temporary partition of the country into North and South by the Geneva compromise of 1954; the rivalry of the South between the majority Buddhists and the minority Roman Catholics. Revolutions are no less peculiar than the peoples and circumstances that produce them. But they display, none the less, like the peoples and circumstances themselves, a fundamental similarity.

'Show me a society that is overwhelmingly agricultural and poor, with the vast bulk of its peasantry landless or in virtual servitude to rent; a society in which a tiny elite owns enormous tracts of land, controls commerce and such industry as exists, and commands political power; a society in which mass illiteracy, undernourishment and hunger, disease and early death exist alongside luxury and corruption; a society of coloured people ruled in the past by whites and still dominated by the economic or strategic interests of a white state; and I will show you revolution.' One may suitably say no less of almost every revolution that has taken place in recent years or is taking place now. One may reasonably predict no less from the condition in which dozens of countries and hundreds of millions of people are today placed. 'Show me a revolution, and in almost every instance I will show you a Western attempt to crush or control it.'

But the West, in the long run, must fail. The Chinese see the struggle as a protracted guerilla one, a war of attrition which will drain the West of its resources, especially its manpower, till it is forced to cry 'enough'. They claim that the West is psychologically unprepared for indefinite campaigns in several parts of the world, with the ever mounting loss of Western life they will entail and with no dramatic victories to compensate. The war of the peasant is a hard one for the drafted undergraduate or salesman to fight. Western society is spoilt for the struggle by its very wealth and comfort and increasing sense of individual security. And it is spoilt, too – though the Chinese lay no emphasis on this – by the power of public opinion in a democracy. It was public opinion in France that called a halt to the Vietnam war in 1954; it would not have acquiesced in yet more bleeding. The British government may bob obediently in support of United States action in South Vietnam, but the British electorate would not take kindly to the sort of casualties that a direct British involvement would entail. And public opinion in the United States is growing more disturbed by the war in Vietnam as American casualties mount. For all the bombast of official declarations, the prospect of not one but several guerilla wars engaging American troops, whether for the defence of 'the free world' or not, in the paddy-fields and mountains and jungles of three continents, does not appeal to the American electorate.

The cost of containing revolution is prohibitive, for it is nothing less, in the present state of Western policy, than an attempt to perpetuate poverty and privilege, hunger and corruption. And because want has a uniform colour, just as abundance, it involves a spreading confrontation of race. Such a determination is certain of defeat, for it must rot humanity itself, and Western man most of all. It is idle to suppose that the white world can attempt to hold down the coloured one in a commitment by both to unremitting violence, without destroying every value of a free and rational society. One need only consider the corruption of white South Africa to see, in the world of the moment, the cumulative consequences of fear (for the loss of privilege and security) and hatred (for whoever may be suspected of menacing either) hideously magnified under the glass of race. Yet many of those in the West who recoil in disgust from the character of white South Africa and their view of how it must still further decay do not recognize the possibilities of a similar corruption, for similar reasons, of their own society. The war in South Vietnam is cruel to all who participate in it, but inevitably less cruel to those who are fighting for food and land and the promise of an escape from the old degradations than to those who are fighting to preserve the world as it is.

The Chinese, paradoxically, by their conduct and beliefs, imply a fundamental trust in American humanity. Guerilla warfare will force American dominance to its knees, without stripping it of all civilized inhibitions. The nuclear tiger is a paper one, because the United States will not use it effectively even if assured of Soviet neutrality (and such a possibility must more and more exercise Chinese calculations) and of China's inability (for some years yet) formidably to respond. But if she does use it, surely she will destroy herself. Is it not reasonable to see in such Chinese calculations something more than the likely strategic consequences of nuclear warfare? The predictions of who may survive, and how a whole coloured world may rise in a fury of revulsion? Is there not also the confidence that a society which would kill, as it would have to do if its nuclear intimidation was to succeed, people by the hundreds of millions, must meet the self-destruction of the insane?

If the Chinese do, indeed, entertain such trust, there are those who do not. I remember an evening in Kingston, Jamaica, with an urbane West Indian novelist and his white English wife. It was a few weeks after China had exploded her first nuclear device, and I was telling him of the reactions I had encountered among American Negroes. 'You do not think, surely,' he said with sudden anger, 'that the whites will ever allow a coloured people to get too powerful? They've ruled us all so long, they wouldn't know how to stop. They'll bomb China to hell, you'll see, and any other coloured country that becomes big enough to frighten them.' I could hear myself shouting against such ideas, when he broke in again. 'They'll find an excuse, somehow, that most whites will swallow. If it works, it won't seem so bad, afterwards.' 'And in the end?' I demanded. 'Ah, in the end … ' he sighed, and we went in to dinner.

Is it really, then, a choice for the West of defeat at a terrible loss or some desperate disaster, a sort of derangement of humanity? Is it conceivable that the whites who have ruled so long will at last see rule itself, and the survival of poverty anywhere, as a violence done to life? Is it impossible that they should provoke revolution, rather than set out to prevent or crush it; surrender much of their wealth in the perception that riches and want should not and will not long survive together; allow and protect the opportunity of men to sort out their future through sacrifice and error and discovery? Have freedom and knowledge and peace any meaning beyond the men who make and use them? And if the mass of men cannot be trusted in the end to find, in their own way, all three, what is the point of them?

Index